The "Pope" Of Sailing

by

Paul Franklin Henderson

Known as the "Pope of Sailing", Paul Henderson is a devoted sailor who dedicated many of his later years to running ISAF, the International body that governs our sport. ISAF represents all yachting nations from around the world and it requires strong leadership to balance the various interests and expectations. He is certainly a leader who is not afraid to make a tough or unpopular decision when issues need to be resolved.

Whilst I haven't always agreed with Paul's views, when he was President of ISAF I've always respected him for standing up for what he believed was right for the sport – even if that meant treading on a few toes! He passionately defended the racing rules on propulsion, when those "pumping and rocking" techniques were becoming more prevalent and were being debated at all levels of the sport.

He has always defended fair racing and upheld the integrity of the sport and has never compromised those values. Even when under pressure from Olympic Games officials, Paul stuck to his simple principle that above all else, the racing has to remain fair.

Paul has also been sensitive to protecting the interests of "grass roots" sailing and did not allow the sport become dominated by commercial interests. Over the years, he has fought hard to keep the sport representative of the majority of sailors rather than the few at the top.

Any time Paul is around sailors, especially Finn sailors, his passion is obvious and his enthusiasm infectious. When you are engaged with him in a conversation about sailing you will hear all kinds of fantastic stories involving many of the great sailors such as Melges and Elvstrom.

Russell Coutts - Olympic Gold Medalist,
3x Winning America's Cup Helmsman

Paul's "gospel" – what more could you ask? At last, he tells all and, as usual, pulls no punches. It leaves very few 'what ifs?' to be answered – in sailing the "Pope" has been at the centre of the action and lived to tell the tale. Perspicacious and amusing – just like the man himself.

– Bob Fisher, "Renowned English Yachting Journalist"

If there's anyone alive today who knows the sport of yacht racing from every aspect its Paul Henderson. He has a lifetime of stories to tell about sailboat racing at the highest level, as a frequent winner in the International 14 class and as an Olympic competitor in the Flying Dutchman and Finn. As his involvement in the sport deepened he found himself elected to positions of responsibility and influence and capped a distinguished and often controversial career by leading the International Sailing Federation through the difficult years from 1994 to 2004. His feistiness on the racecourse won him silverware, and this same strength and resolve won him the respect, sometimes grudgingly, throughout the vast and varied world of international sailing.

– Bruce Kirby, Yacht Designer

Paul Henderson is a man of strong words. He does what he says and gets it done.

Love him or hate him, you always know where he stands. He is an honest and caring human being. He has been an incredible promoter and supporter of sailing and other sports in Canada and worldwide. When he was the president for ISAF he traveled to many World Championships to congratulate not only the winners but all participants. He just cares about sailors, people, his friends and of course, and most of all his family.

I am very lucky to be his friend.

– Hans Fogh, Olympic Medallist and World Champion

"To all those who took interest in a kid from Toronto Island and pushed him to heights beyond which he would not have achieved but especially to Mary, Sandra, John and Martha who were always there through all the storms."

The "Pope" of Sailing
ISBN 978-0-9865520-0-7
© Paul F. Henderson, 2010

Published in 2010 by: Paul F. Henderson
                        paulhenderson141@rogers.com

Design by Huziak Graphic Design Studio
Printed and bound in Canada by Positive TIPS Inc.
Tel. 416-429-6500   Email: imaging@positivetips.ca

Table of Contents

Introduction

I am a sailor and sailing has no reverse gear. Sailors get nowhere until we untie our boats from the dock. I seem to be constantly trying to unravel tangled ropes and, when they are untied, trying to get the boat to move forward. It was easy when I started because the bowline knot usually worked in all cases, but the tangles are much more complicated now—or so they appear.

It has been an interesting exercise to recount what has been 73 years of a voyage which I hope still has many chapters left. It seemed appropriate to give some account of the people who have shared them with me or whom I have had the privilege to meet. It is really surprising to me how many influences have come to bear on my life that I had very little to do with, and how many just happened by chance.

I trust it is interesting for others to see that the paths I followed were different from those of most of my friends, especially those who went into the corporate world and were employed by others. My view is that those who are self-employed, entrepreneurial businessmen, and who have to meet a daily payroll using their own resources, look at the world differently. I feel that most self-employed people with a social conscience have learned to look at where money comes from differently from those who distribute money that is not theirs.

I am troubled by the expense and lack of leadership that has crept into many projects in Toronto, and indeed in all of Canada these days. Often left-wing academics in control of most debates have instituted seemingly endless forums attended by various "stakeholders"—whatever that euphemism means. I make no apology for my distrust of what is often an expensive and delaying process.

I have always tried to get directly to the issues without worrying about being politically correct. Being in the maintenance plumbing business means that I have many times been required to make decisions and then get on with the job. When you get a call from the police at midnight regarding a broken pipe on the eighth floor of the Medical Arts Building with water surging down the staircases and out the front door onto St. George Street, you can't just say, "Put an aspirin in it and call for an appointment a week Thursday." You had bloody well better be there immediately, put your thumb in the hole and get it fixed.

I inherited the family plumbing business on the death of my brother when I was 20, and sold it in 2000 in the firm belief that if it were to survive after more than a century, then a new generation must take it over. Since there was no Henderson who wanted to do that, R. G. Henderson and Son Ltd. was sold and is in fact doing quite well without me, perhaps even better. My trust in the next generation can be traced to the fact that I was given so much support when I was young and given my head to proceed, whether in business or in sport. The support I was given by my elders left me with a great respect for experience and the advice it often brings.

It may seem strange to notice how things in my life fit into four-year cycles although that should not be so difficult to understand, as almost everything I did revolved around the Olympic Games, which have been so important to me. It becomes very intense in the fourth year and then with the extinguishing of the Olympic Flame there is an abrupt end to that Olympiad. The four-year cycle then begins again. During the first two years of the cycle life is pretty normal, and that is when I focused on family and business. Then like the "Olde Fire Horse," as the Games came closer, I reared up and charged ahead again. It was a cycle I followed for over 50 years. I competed in every Canadian Olympic Trials from 1952 to 1984. It is always confusing to me whether to call the world governing body for sailing the International Yacht Racing Union (IYRU) or the International Sailing Federation (ISAF). In 1994 the last thing the previous administration did before I took over as President was to change the name. This I opposed, but I had to live with it. So I use IYRU up until 1994 and then switch, but even then I sometimes still call it the IYRU. There is now a term limit at ISAF and a President must retire after eight years, although in my case, due to a change in election dates, I stayed 10 years.

Although older members are grandfathered, the current policy of the International Olympic Committee (IOC) is that new members must retire at age 70. In my case, I reached the end of my 10-year term as President of ISAF in the same week that I turned 70 in November, 2004. Retirement has afforded me the luxury of being even more outspoken and direct than I was previously, if that is possible.

In 1994, after becoming ISAF President, I encouraged members of the sailing fraternity to use email and the Internet, which can lead to even more direct communication lacking in political correctness than either fax or formal letters. Almost everyone accuses me of being blunt, direct and irreverent—someone even labeled my emails "NastyGrams." In my own defence I usually reply, *"Did you ever have to read my directives twice?"*

At one of the first IYRU meetings I attended, President Beppe Croce asked the Council, *"What do you think the grass-roots sailors want on this subject?"* The brilliant Polish naval engineer, C.A. Marchaj, author of the famous sailing book, *Aerodynamics of Yacht Racing*, put up his hand and said, *"With all due respect Mr. President, the majority is usually wrong!"* I have always stated my position up front and let others debate it. I trust I am mature enough to see when I am wrong, change my position if necessary, and move ahead.

Another policy I have explained to other sailors is really bravado, but my oft-quoted response when people ask how I got away with continually buying racing boats is this: *"The secret to keeping sailing is to own many boats, so when your wife tells you to sell one, you still have lots of boats left."*

I have always been an independent person marching to the beat of my own drummer, and I have always been quite happy to be alone, especially in my sailboat and dreaming. I attribute this to both the influence of Toronto Island and the fact that I never really worked for anyone except myself. Having been born early in the morning, I am a morning person and since sailors always look for the next shift, not dwelling on the last one, I have always gone to bed early in order to be ready for what the morning might bring. I haven't changed and I doubt I ever will.

The title of this book is based on the nickname I acquired when I became President of the International Sailing Association. It has been fun remembering all the stories and putting them down on paper. I hope that readers will be at least quietly amused, and in some cases gain new insight through my eyes. My undying thanks go to my ever supportive Mary, the only woman who could ever put up with me. For a kid from Toronto Island, it has been a great ride!

Paul Henderson

Here is the simple summary I supply when people ask what I've done in my life. I hope it provides some context for the accounts that follow:

Paul Franklin Henderson, B.A.Sc, P. Eng.

Education:
Graduate Engineering and Business: University of Toronto
Master Plumber, Master Heating Installer, Master Gas Fitter.

Business:
Owner and CEO: R.G. Henderson and Son Ltd. Mechanical Contractors

International Sport Positions:

President, International Sailing Federation 1994 -2004

Vice President, General Assembly of International Sport Federations 2000 - 2007

Executive Member, Association Summer Olympic Sport Federations 2000 - 2004

International Olympic Positions:

Member, IOC 2000 -2004

Member, IOC 2012 Olympic Bids Evaluation Commission

Member, IOC Sport and Environment Committee

Member, IOC Women in Sport Committee

Member, Board of Directors, Vancouver 2010

Inductee, Canadian Olympic Sport Hall of Fame 2001

President/CEO, Toronto 1996 Olympic Bid

Sailing Career:

Member, Canadian Olympic Team 1964, 1968, 1972, 1980,

Competitor in every Canadian Olympic Sailing Trials 1952-1984

Canadian National Champion seven times

USA National Champion four times

Bermuda, Dutch, North American Champion

World Champion

Other Positions:

President, Toronto Racquet Club

Director, Harbourfront Disabled Sailing Association

Honorary Commodore, Royal Canadian Yacht Club

Chairman, Italian +39 America's Cup Challenge

Chairman and Co-Founder, Toronto International Dragon Boat World Championship 2006

Member, Board of Directors, Metro Toronto Convention Centre

Member, Board of Directors, Ontario Place

Member, Board or Directors, Toronto Visitor and Convention Bureau

Chapter 1:
Early Life and Toronto Island

I always say I was born on Toronto Island, specifically Ward's Island, because it is what I remember most about growing up. I believe it was a major factor behind most of my adult behavior. It is not quite the truth, however; my mother carried me on the Island, but I was born at the Toronto General Hospital on an auspicious Saturday in November, 1934. It was the day Santa Claus came to town. As I was born in the early hours of that day, my mother held me to the window to see Santa arrive—or so she told me. For years we celebrated my birthday on the day of the Santa Claus Parade.

Henderson's Arriving in Canada

My great-great-grandfather started the Henderson family exodus to Canada by a practice which may have been acceptable in those days, but is very strange in today's world. The family lived in Edinburgh, Scotland at a very bleak time. My great-grandmother had recently died in an epidemic, leaving her three young sons in the dubious care of their alcoholic father. The three boys were put in an orphanage and 1880 put on a boat to Canada with 120 other waifs and 5 adults. Robert Grant Henderson was 9 years old.

They were met at the docks in Quebec City by local volunteer Scottish ladies and sent to the frontier of Canada, which in 1880 was Ontario. My grandfather ended up apprenticed to a "tinker" in Berkley near Owen Sound with an old man who must have liked him. When "Grandpa Bob" was 15, the farmer apprenticed him to a plumber in Toronto. He walked some 150 km down Yonge Street to the outskirts of the big City of Toronto, which was then just south of St. Clair Avenue. (The City now sprawls much farther north.) He had little formal education but was well read and educated himself by never missing a Wednesday afternoon matinee at the Royal Alexandra Theatre. He also read every non-fiction book available at the Public Library in Yorkville.

My grandfather became an accomplished sheet metal worker and in 1896 founded the plumbing company bearing his name R.G. Henderson. He added "and Son" after my father went into the business with him in 1910. He was interested only in his weekly salary and never had more than one employee. Like most of his descendants, he had several interests outside business.

He died in 1944 when I was 10 years old. He must have been quite a guy. I remember that he liked ripe black bananas and brown sugar on his well buttered toast, to say nothing about the love of Scottish shortbread which he passed on to all of us. He had been on the first payroll of the 48th Highlanders, the most prestigious highland regiment in Canada, becoming Company Sergeant Major and going off to World War I. Dad would take us down to University Avenue during World War II and watch grandfather march in his kilt to St. Andrew's Church, the 48th bagpipes in full throat. He was buried with his kilt on.

Although there are many Hendersons in the Toronto phone book, very few are my relatives that I know of. The only one with whom I have ever kept in touch is Jean McLean Morrow, who has been quite supportive over the years and whom my sister Sandra sees often.

My mother's father, Sammy McGinnis, came from Northern Ireland and was a small fastidious man, always well dressed in his bowler hat, vest and tie. His wife Emma was a large upright woman and a joy. She was the person we all went to when we were in trouble or needed a good meal. She sang in the choir at St. Timothy's Anglican Church and spent endless hours at quilting bees. She lived well into her 90s.

My father was a tall, elegant man and—I am sure—much admired by the ladies. Living on McPherson Avenue, Dad went to Jesse Ketchum Public School with the "Big Train," Lionel Conacher. They were both good athletes, with Lionel becoming arguably the greatest Canadian Athlete of the Twentieth Century. In Grade 8, the two were fooling around (so Dad told the story) when Lionel threw a brick at him. He ducked and the brick went through the front window of the school. Dad was expelled and never went back. He soon entered into the plumbing business. His full name was Albert John Grant Henderson, but everyone called him "Ab." Our Jewish customers called him "Abe."

Lionel Conacher went on to become a Member of Parliament. Fittingly, both are now buried three metres apart at St. John's York Mills Cemetery. If you find bricks around their graves, they must be up to their old tricks.

My mother, Edythe Mary McGinnis, was born in 1899 and was a typical Victorian Lady—at least she tried to be, considering the family she bore. She was the one who kept the finances in order and forced Dad to buy the family residences, first at 56 Snowdon Avenue, which they built mostly by themselves. Later they traded up to 249 Golfdale Avenue. My mother was a little woman, but very determined. Like all mothers, she was an excellent cook. Her Scottish Shortbread was the best ever, as was her Maple Cream Icing Cake. Too bad we had to eat the cake—we kids would have preferred just to peel off the maple cream icing.

The Fairlawn Theatre was at the corner of Snowdon Avenue and Yonge Street. Dad and Mom went for a walk one night in 1954 past a place where the Kiwanis Club was holding a raffle for a new Plymouth car. Mother bought a ticket but Dad didn't. At midnight the phone rang. There was a scream from the bedroom and we all rushed in. Mom had won the new Plymouth. We were all really good for about a week, hoping that the kids would get the car since Mom did not drive and we did not think she would learn at age 55. Then, one evening at dinner, she announced that she had enrolled in a driving school. The car was hers and she was going to keep it for herself. Over the years she replaced the Plymouth with new cars as the need arose, and drove till she was 88 when her eyes failed. She lived well into her 90s, as did all my forebears who did not smoke.

Siblings

Ab and Edythe had three children. John, born in 1930, was a big, strong, handsome man like my dad and almost five years my senior. He hated school and quit at age 16, going into the plumbing business with Dad. They were very close. His real name was Albert John Henderson Jr. but he was called John. He believed this was ridiculous. Nobody could find him in the telephone book because nobody would look under Albert. So from the time he entered kindergarten he always signed his name John A. Henderson. Junior was not a name for him.

Sandra was the last of our tribe coming less than four years after me. She had everything going for her. She was beautiful, tall and lanky like Dad and John, and bright. She eventually became Assistant Professor of Speech Pathology in the School of Medicine at the University of Toronto. We are and always have been great friends, and she gets along with my family extremely well.

I was the middle kid. I was a free spirit and since I found school easy, especially math, chemistry and physics, life was a joy. I was round and short and did not look like either of my siblings, who resembled Dad. He loved to say I looked like the milkman. Really I looked like Mom but acted like none of the others. It was really John who brought me up, and he made sure I was included in everything he did. If I stepped out of line too far—and I did occasionally—he really let me have it. Although he smoked when he was 12 and started to drink at 14, he threatened me that if he ever caught me smoking or drinking he would beat the hell out of me. For self-preservation I never smoked and didn't even touch alcohol until I was past 40.

Tragedy Strikes

One Friday night in January 1955, my island sailing friends Gerry Pangman and Billy Wilson were to play handball with John at the Central YMCA at six o'clock as we often did. At seven o'clock John still had not arrived so I phoned home to see where he was. An unfamiliar voice answered. It was our minister, who told me I had better get home quickly. John had had a very serious accident. When I arrived the atmosphere in the house was terrible and the minister took me aside to tell me that John had been killed installing a pump in the basement of the Coleman Lamp Company on Queen Street. The electrician had made a mistake and wired it incorrectly. The tradesmen could not solve the problem and John, in his usual aggressive manner, went down to help them out. The floor was wet; he put his hand on the motor of the pump and, due to the faulty wiring, was electrocuted and died instantly. He was only 25 years old. They say time heals. No it does not completely. The pain may become less acute, but you never heal. I had lost my mentor and best friend.

I now became the first son with all the responsibilities of that role. I was in my third year in Engineering at the University of Toronto at the time. After a few months of mulling over my future, I decided to follow the family tradition and become a plumber. I do not know to this day why I did it, but it was the right decision and I became my own boss.

I often wonder what would have been my fate had John not died.

Toronto Island and Schools

Ward's Island, where I spent my formative years, was a unique place to grow up. Toronto Island was the original cottage community for the beautiful people of Toronto before they discovered Muskoka and Georgian Bay. There were magnificent cottages, some with more than 20 rooms, along the Lakeshore and Boardwalk, which stretched almost from the "Main Drag" at Centre Island to the Wards' cottages at the east end. The homes at Hanlan's point to the west were equally impressive. The Lake Ontario winds provided the natural air-conditioning that made Toronto summers bearable (see map).

Every year we moved to the Island from Snowdon Avenue in North Toronto on May 24, Victoria Day, and came back to the City in mid-September, which meant we missed many days of school. If we did attend, it was a great trip. We took the T.J. Clarke ferry and then the "Red Rocket" streetcars up Yonge

Street to Bedford Park Public School. Some days Dad picked me up from school at 3:30 and drove me to the Island Ferry. One day when I was 12, he forgot. As usual, I had no money or street car tickets. I stood outside Errington's candy store at Yonge and Ranleigh till 4:30 and realized Dad had forgotten. So I started to walk down Yonge Street to the ferry docks, which is about a 10 kilometre hike. I expected my dad to come up Yonge Street as the plumbing shop was at Yonge and Scollard. I had a great time strolling down Toronto's main street but was quite hungry. Dad never came and I kept walking and was just on time for the 8:30 p.m. ferry.

The ferrymen knew all the Island kids so they let me on for free. When I got off the ferry, Mom and Dad were there. My dad had forgotten because he had to umpire a softball game that night between the Osoezes and the Otazels. (The other Ward's teams were the Brownies and the Dingbats, and these names explain the mentality prevalent in the Toronto Island community.)

Dad was active in the Ward's Island Association (WIA), becoming President in 1938 when he built the WIA clubhouse which you can still see today as you leave the ferry docks. The Islanders presented him with an Owen Staples painting of the view from the back of our cottage. The painting now hangs proudly in my living room. No cars are permitted on the Island save for the doctor, police and fire. In my day the only possession any Island kid had was an "Island bicycle," strong but usually rusted with bent wire baskets attached to the handle bars. It did not matter what economic bracket your family had in the City—you all had these strange bikes. We seldom had our bikes stolen by the city slickers who came to the Island. They were not worth much and, if anyone tried, the Island ferry boatmen would ensure they were returned.

Island life was idyllic. Everybody knew everyone else, as happens in a small town. The rule for kids was that you had to be home by the time the street lights came on, which in June and July was after 9:00 p.m. If you were out after that, you would be sent home by any parent who saw you. Eaton's and Simpson's department stores delivered to the cottages. The brothers Lamantia had a fruit cart they dragged through the streets selling fresh produce. Bill Ward and his assistant, Ken Lye, delivered large blocks of Lake Simcoe ice, which they also dragged through the streets. Poyntz, Pikes and Hopmans delivered fresh meat from their Toronto stores. What a life it was!

World War II

I was four years old in 1939 when World War II broke out, and several memories are still vivid to this day. Toronto Island Airport became "Little Norway" where the Norwegian Air Force trained. Beside the airport at Hanlan's Point, a former tuberculosis sanatorium was converted into a rehabilitation hospital for injured Norwegian fliers.

Twice a week my mother would bake cakes and cookies which, together with cigarettes that she bought, filled our wire handlebar baskets, and we would set out on our little bikes with little legs pumping to ride five kilometres to Hanlan's Point to deliver the goodies to the aviators. It was necessary to pedal very quickly past the Gibraltar Point Lighthouse because it was haunted. When we arrived at the fence that separated the Norwegians from the Islanders due to wartime regulations, we threw our mother's cooking and cigarettes over the fence. In return, the Norwegians would give us matchboxes that they had kept for us. The trip took most of the day so, being five years old, it meant we always slept well. We would go along the Boardwalk where it was forbidden to ride bicycles—but we were Islanders and it was our Boardwalk. We would arrive at the Centre Island "Main Drag," the main street with several hotels and souvenir shops, a drug store, and food market. In those days there was also a bowling alley and cinema. We usually stopped at Borden's for an ice cream cone, and at Trusty's bicycle shop to get our tires pumped up.

One day when we were all on the Wards' beach, playing in the sand and swimming in the lake, and the Norwegian trainers were flying overhead as usual, two of them touched wings and crashed off the end of the Eastern Gap, killing all four fliers.

Two doors down from us on Snowdon Avenue in the City, lived the Stewarts whose one boy, Sonny, was a bomber pilot. Mr. Stewart and my father were great friends. I remember Dad and me standing in the driveway when Mr. Stewart came with the letter from Ottawa saying Sonny had been shot down and killed. On VE Day, I was in Grade Five at Bedford Park School when the teacher came in and announced the war was over. Everyone cheered except Billy Robins, who cried because his brother had been killed at Dieppe. I have never fired a gun in my life. Every time I watch a war movie and see the dead lying there, no matter which side they're from, I have the feeling that they had no idea why they were there. And I wonder if they wouldn't rather be sailing off Ward's Island.

Summers on the Island

Our cottage at 21 Third Street backed onto the east end of Toronto Bay overlooking the Eastern Gap and Cherry Street. When I was young, there were large coal piles on the Cherry Street docks. At night they glowed with small fires of spontaneous combustion. Near the coal piles were oil tanks and storage tanks for manufactured gas. The coal piles disappeared several years later when the great gas pipeline arrived from Alberta, and Toronto converted to natural gas for heating. At that time, environmentalists tried to stop the pipeline, but it proved to be a boon for Toronto. With the opening of the St. Lawrence Seaway in 1959, the area became docks. There were so many ocean freighters they had to anchor in the Bay. This lasted for about 10 years, until the introduction of containers changed shipping and Toronto Harbour became almost completely recreational. The Portlands became a wasteland and political football. During election campaigns, politicians at every level promise how the future of this area will be a priority, but they never seem to deliver on their promises.

Schools

I went to only three schools; Bedford Park Public School, Lawrence Park Collegiate Institute, both walking distance from

Snowdon Avenue, and then the University of Toronto. I looked upon school as filling in time before returning to Toronto Island to sail. I could have been described as a loner, not really involved with the usual peer groups or associations that kids tended to gravitate to. The truth is I was a dreamer, a true Islander with an idyllic life style. If I wasn't sailing, my attention span was less than adequate. As I have grown older it has become worse.

Bedford Park Public School

I must have been one of the few kids who failed Grade 1. I still remember my teacher, Miss White. I guess she did have a case, since I was not there very much and had a problem with writing. As usual, I did not show up until halfway through September, a few weeks after school had started. Then I seldom went to school in June, having the "Ward's Island Itch." On top of all this I had the measles three times after Christmas—German measles twice and red measles once, or maybe it was the other way around. That contributed another six weeks to my delinquency.

The final straw came when I cut my chin for 20 stitches. Our garage was made out of tin, as befitted a plumber. One Sunday morning in January, the ice was blocking the door so we had to free it before we could get the car out to drive to church. I went out to help my dad, manned with my trusty little hatchet. I was chopping away when I slipped and ripped my chin open against a piece of tin that was sticking out of the garage. Fortunately Dr. Kitchen lived just three doors down. Dad whisked me off to be sewn up. The only problem is that he left a raised stitch hole, which I have continually shaved off because it still sticks up. Dr. Kitchen told my mother that the scar would go away, but it has not. I have concocted many stories over the years attributing it to a hockey fight, duel and so on, but the truth is it was a piece of tin on our garage that did it. Miss White told my mother that I could not attend class because the bandage was not nice for the other children to see. That was fine by me, as I could skate all day on the rink my dad had flooded in our back yard, shooting pucks at the back porch.

Miss White recommended that I spend another year in Grade 1. Mother, as usual, did not accept this and convinced the Principal, Mr. McAdam, to let me go to Grade 2 on trial provided I show up for the whole school year. I passed Grade 3 and 4 with little difficulty. In Grade 5 in those days, the focus came on mathematics and as dumb as I was with languages, I was good at math. We also took Canadian history that year. Most kids who have an aptitude for math and sciences also enjoy history with all its dates and intrigue. My marks shot up and from then on I stood near the top of the class, which allowed the family to stay on Ward's Island, arriving late and leaving early before the end of each school year without much hassle.

Even in those days, achieving good marks was something of a liability in the schoolyard. There arrived at Bedford Park Public School a tough kid recently landed from the United States. Buddy Vercher was 13 and I was 11. He smoked and hated school, and all he could talk about was quitting school as soon as possible and joining the United States Navy. He wore a U.S. Navy hat all the time and it made him look like Popeye. Buddy considered me the class "suck", which I guess I was. He would wait in the schoolyard after class with his little group of friends and challenge me to fight. I was not much of a fighter but I was fast, and since he smoked I could outrun him. About the third day of this bullying, he cornered me and we tussled. I survived.

When I got home Mom noticed I was quite ruffled and anxious. She asked, and I told her what was happening, which upset her very much. Her solution was to go immediately to the principal, whom she knew quite well by this time. Mom waited for Dad to come home for dinner, and he had a different solution. One of Dad's old friends from Jesse Ketchum Public School (the only school he ever attended) had become a good professional boxer and had a gym in his basement in Toronto's Junction area where he taught boxing. For three weeks Dad would meet me at 3:30 in front of the school and take me to his friend's gym. I would run out the girls' entrance, avoiding the confrontation with Buddy Vercher and his entourage.

Dad's friend taught me how to punch and not hurt my hand. I practised on a punching bag on which he had painted a large face dominated by a nose. When he thought I had that under control, he taught me how to sucker my adversary into thinking I was scared and then bop him directly on the nose. He announced I was ready.

It seems like only yesterday that I walked out the boys' entrance looking sheepish, and there was Vercher ready to beat me up again. I did exactly what I had been taught: "Look scared. Turn sideways. Raise your left shoulder. Hide your right hand." When he lunged at my left shoulder, I pivoted and planted my right fist squarely into his nose. He fell to the ground grabbing his face, bleeding profusely from both nostrils.

Dad was right, and thanks to his friend I was never bothered again. As "One-Punch" Henderson I left my boxing career behind, although for other reasons I attended many professional fights as a guest of famous announcer Tommy McClure, who was also a sailor and a fellow Islander.

Lawrence Park Collegiate

I entered Lawrence Park Collegiate Institute (LPCI) a year ahead of schedule with great anticipation. John had gone there, and being a large man he had played football. Although he was into that part of high school, he left in Grade 11 at 16 to become a plumber. I was small and quick, so I played on the Basketball Team where, being short, I was always running into the tall players' elbows, especially the ones from North Toronto Collegiate Institute and Northern Secondary School, which rearranged my nose—that and the several times I did not duck the boom while sailing.

LPCI was a great experience because Principal, "Frosty John" McKellar and Vice-Principal Mr. Baker were math teachers, and so understood students like me. Within two weeks of the start of Grade 9, Frosty John knew every student by his or her first name. In those days the curriculum included French and Latin, both of which I was utterly incapable of comprehending.

About November, I got a summons to come to Mr. McKellar's office. Boy was I scared!

He sat me down and read my future according to his wonderful outlook. He informed me that along with 10 other male math students, I was never going to graduate from high school—but he had a plan. I would drop Latin and enroll in music appreciation with Mr. Paul Sweetman as teacher. This would provide the credit I needed to get through Grade 12, and then if I made it that far he would orchestrate my passage through Grade 13.

He then explained that there were commitments the 10 of us had to fulfill. We had to sing in the choir and perform in the annual Gilbert and Sullivan Operetta. What a stroke of genius that was. In the choir were about 40 girls and 15 guys, ten of whom were the "Math Mafia." We were exposed to all forms of classical music and Mr. Sweetman lived his name. The Gilbert and Sullivan operettas *HMS. Pinafore, The Pirates of Penzance, The Mikado* and *Trial by Jury* have made me an aficionado to this day, and I look forward to the performances at Ontario's Stratford Festival each year with great anticipation. The Stratford interpretation of *The Mikado* was in a class by itself.

Vice-Principal Baker also took great interest in us. He sat all of the Math Mafia at the back of the math class to save us from learning at the level of the lowest common, boring denominator. He had a quiver of math problems that he would challenge the Math Mafia to solve while he taught the not-so-swift students at the front of the class. We all got through Grade 12 and then Messrs. McKellar and Baker kicked in their Grade 13 plan. In those days, every student in the Province of Ontario wrote the same exams prepared by the Ministry of Education, and these also served as university entrance exams.

We were called into the principal's office and explained reality. Mr. Baker would be the point teacher and we would complete the math and sciences Grade 13 courses by November. This we could all do without any trouble. We would then leave those subjects behind. Frosty John pointed out the obvious and announced that we were all incompetent in French and English. These subjects would be our only focus for the rest of the year, and we took two periods of each every day, accompanied by copious quantities of homework. The hope was that we would sneak through with a passing grade and make it to University.

We were given the most compassionate and sensitive English teacher, Miss Waugh, a spinster who loved her male math students. She would cry at the front of the class when we were too stupid to understand her directions. We all loved her and were discouraged when we upset her with our stupidity. One day she announced that every fours years or so the provincial English exam was prepared like a math exam with multiple choice questions, the object being to determine whether students read all the books and remembered the detail. The other three years it required mostly essays and esoteric answers which, frankly, would be a challenge to the Math Mafia. She insisted we read all the books, not just the required minimum number. By the luck of the draw it was the fourth year and because the exam was not geared to the true English students, LPCI achieved the lowest number of First Class Honours in its history, with only seven in the entire Grade 13 class—I and one other of the Math Mafia being among them. I hope Miss Waugh was proud of her boys.

My marks finally came in July and I had passed with a bare 50 per cent in French grammar, which I believe they gave me, as it was I who usually owed the teacher marks.

I had no idea what I wanted to do, as I was only 17 and a year under the usual university entrance age. The LPCI guidance counselor said I was best suited for commerce and finance. My mother demanded that I go to the Church of England faculty, Trinity College. I enrolled and received a nice letter saying I had won the Elliott Grasset Memorial Scholarship with the highest marks in mathematics entering Trinity that year. My mother was ecstatic and looked forward to the LPCI commencement exercises with my name being enshrined on the wall. I really think she wanted to invite Miss White, My Grade 1 teacher, but that was most likely Dad's devious mind at work. She was not happy when I gave up the scholarship.

U of T Engineering

Sailing again intervened in directing my life. John always went to the International 14-foot Dinghy Regatta at the Essex Yacht Club in Fenwick, Connecticut, during the first week of September. I went with him as crew. We won the prestigious Connecticut Cup, arriving back in Toronto two weeks after university had started. This was normal for me so I wasn't worried, but Trinity College was not amused.

I went to my first class in the history of economics and was bored out of my mind. God, was I depressed, and since in Liberal Arts you only go to class about 15 hours a week, I was at a loose end. On my third day at the University of Toronto I decided to walk through the campus. In the middle of the central campus I ran into James Mylrea, an old friend from Toronto Island. I told him of my depression over Trinity College and economics and accounting, especially the 500 students in each class. Jim went into a sales pitch for mechanical engineering, especially the Engineering and Business program, which was geared to those with an aptitude for engineering who wanted to go into the business management world.

I kept walking south to the Mining Building which then housed the Faculty of Engineering offices. I went to the reception desk and announced that I wanted to be an engineer. The woman behind the desk was very friendly and gave me an application form. She said she hoped to see me next year, as all courses for the current year were overbooked. Only the top students were accepted, she said, so I must study hard. I tried to explain that I wanted to enter that year.

My life more often than not has been changed by dramatic occurrences, over most of which I have had no control—they just seem to happen. Call it the "Henderson Horseshoes"; just at that moment a tall, grey-haired, distinguished man walked by and enquired as to the nature of my problem. *"I want to be an Engineer and they say I must wait to next year."*

"*Step into my office and let's discuss it,*" he said. It was Dean Tupper, the university's dean of Engineering. I explained my dilemma and that I had no idea what I wanted to be, but I liked mathematics and sciences, and that I did not fit in Liberal Arts, where I was enrolled. He then gave me the advice that I give to all young people today: "*It is wrong for educators to think that teenagers should know what they want to be at 18. Students should take the university subjects they like and are interested in and hopefully at the end of their university undergraduate experience they will be sane and have more insight into what they want to do with their life.*" What a profound man!

He explained how full all the engineering courses were and that his staff was right. He then turned to me and asked if I had the transcript of my Grade 13 marks, which by luck I did. Dean Tupper looked at them and immediately turned around and dialed the university registrar. "*I have a student here named Henderson. He must be in class in 15 minutes.*" So started my four wonderful years at "Skule," the descriptive name we all called the Faculty of Engineering in the Engineering and Business program.

In several classes, with true engineering logic we were seated in alphabetically order. Under "S" was a Sutherland from New Brunswick, whose father was a doctor. They would let him come to the University of Toronto only if he pursued a profession: dentistry, medicine or engineering. He chose engineering, although that was not the profession he wanted to enter. He was a big, rawboned man but rather strange. He wore sandals with no socks even walking through the snow in the dead of winter. One of the drafting lecturers took pity on him, taking up a collection to buy him several pairs of socks. In "Skule Night", our annual review, Sutherland was a riotous performer. He completed two years of engineering and then took off for Victoria College to study the arts. I lost track of Sutherland for a few years until I got a call from Cam Ferguson, a close friend in Ottawa, asking if I had seen *The Dirty Dozen*. I went to see it, and there was Sutherland on the big screen in that memorable scene where, as the private, he mocks his superiors. Everyone lauded this great acting performance, but I said he was not acting because that is exactly what Donald Sutherland was like in engineering class. One of the finest actors Canada has ever produced, he married Tommy Douglas' daughter Shirley, and they produced another fine actor, Kiefer Sutherland.

Toronto Racquet Club

In 1956, when I was still a student at the University of Toronto, the ever present Royal Canadian Yacht Club (RCYC) Commodore R.D. Grant said I should take up squash racquets, so I joined the Toronto Racquet Club (TRC), which is a unique organization. It has never strayed from its original objectives formulated in 1905 when it was established as a men's club for squash "to provide some game which will give a moderate amount of exercise at not too extravagant a price." The oldest such club in North America, it has not succumbed to the usual pressures to become a multi-activity club. World champion Jonathan Powers played out of the TRC.

In 1956, the annual fee was $60, and an excellent "Leo's Special Sandwich" cost 50 cents. Every member had a key, which meant you could play whenever you wanted to. The refrigerator was well stocked with beer and soda pop, which was available on the honour system. Shortly after joining the club, I learned of a great bonus of membership. We all got to know the chef at the exclusive York Club next door. He was very friendly and after a late game, we could walk over to the back door for the finest roast beef dinner in Toronto provided at no charge, which made it extremely attractive!

In 1959, construction began on the Bloor-Danforth subway line. This meant that the TRC coach house was to be demolished. Any property in the vicinity of the University of Toronto was too expensive. I was playing at the TRC with my old sailing friend Eddie Ballon when the subject of continuing the club was discussed. He said that if we moved to a less expensive area of town maybe we could stay independent. I had several suggestions because our company did the plumbing all over downtown. We drove to the area around the Wellesley Hospital which, although it was only about 10 minutes from the TRC, was in a much less expensive area than the university district. We drove down Bleeker Street and there was a For Sale sign on a reasonably sized lot. Eddie thought this was a great location because, if a member got cut by a racquet or snapped an Achilles tendon, it would disrupt play for only a few minutes while the injured player was carted off to the Wellesley Hospital.

I phoned TRC President and well known Toronto lawyer Doug Jennings, and the TRC bought the land for $25,000. The whole club was built for $115,000 with two singles courts (now three) and a doubles court. In my opinion, doubles squash is the finest and most enjoyable racquet sport of them all, and one of my most cherished sport accomplishments was winning the 1966 TRC doubles championship with my great friend Ron Bertram.

The club's design was worked out by Doug Jennings with several unique features. For one thing, the layout had the courts facing each other, with a lounge in between at the upper level, which had never been tried before. Second, the court walls were fiberglass, which costs less than wood and is easier to maintain. Doug and his squash friends were active doubles players and he liked to use a high lob serve. Being in the construction business, I would drop by Bleeker Street on my regular tours and check on the club's progress. One day I just happened to be there when the concrete blocks were being laid at the top of the doubles court. Jennings instructed the bricklayer to put in three extra rows of block and paid him to do so. As a result, the TRC doubles court is considered to be one of the best, and most courts are now built according to the height requested by Doug Jennings.

One of the club's traditions going back to 1924 when the TRC moved to the coach house of the York Club, was that squash balls were provided free of charge. Club wags say that any visitor who pockets our free balls loses theirs.

During the TRC's initial difficult years on Bleeker

Street, there arrived annually a cheque from R.A. (Bobby) Laidlaw covering the operational shortfall to the cent. Laidlaw, a philanthropist, was a true gentleman and a very successful businessman in the lumber industry. His chauffeur would drive him to the annual general meeting (AGM) every year until he died at close to 90. He would sit, impeccably dressed, renewing old acquaintances. In 1972, I became President and each year at the AGM I would give the same speech: *"I would like to announce to the membership of the TRC that this year I did absolutely nothing."* The cheers were deafening. Peter Rae, one of the Queen's Owns Rifles and a retired bank executive, was engaged as manager and treasurer. Peter put in much needed controls and pushed every nickel through a strainer, with the result that the TRC made a profit of $532.76 during the first year of my tenure. It had absolutely nothing to do with me.

I decided that I should go and see Bobby Laidlaw with the annual report. He was well into his 80s by this time and it was difficult to get through to him, because every not-for-profit agency was after him. Fortunately, Commodore R.D. Grant knew him well and set up the meeting. I went to his home on Jackes Avenue and we had a wonderful discussion. I handed him the financial statement showing the first TRC profit in club history. He smiled his lovely smile and immediately responded, *"You do not need to send me the cheque for the surplus. All my old friends, years ago, told me not to support the Toronto Racquet Club, but it has been a joy to do so. By the way I have a number of charities which are in trouble. Would you and Peter Rae like to run them?"*

The 75th anniversary of the Toronto Racquet Club was held in 1980 at the York Club. In true TRC style it was a black tie affair and many of the old members attended. Roast Beef was served, but we had to pay. The meeting chairman was David Mills of the Queen's Own Rifles, and there were many speeches. At the end of the evening he became quite maudlin and, almost weeping, thanked Bobby Laidlaw for his years of support. He announced to the gathered throng that Mr. Laidlaw had underwritten a large part of the evening. He then turned to Bobby and said, *"Sir, thank you very much, and I trust all of us will be here for the 100ᵗʰ anniversary of the Toronto Racquet Club. Would you kindly say a few words to end the evening?"* Mr. Laidlaw slowly got to his feet, and with his unique smile said, *"I won't be here then but send me the bill anyway."* and sat down.

Now that I have returned home from many travels around the world, I have lots of time to play squash again. Going back to the TRC every week to play is wonderful. Many of my old friends are still there and the atmosphere has not changed. The TRC has never been healthier than it is today. The 100ᵗʰ anniversary was held a few years ago at the York Club with the usual roast beef dinner, and with more than 200 members in attendance. I am sure Bobby Laidlaw was there somewhere, smiling.

Eddie Ballon gave his usual delightful speech. Back in his 75ᵗʰ anniversary speech he had clearly explained the camaraderie which continues to this day at the Toronto Racquet Club:

> *We salute our founding members—*
> *They're still very much alive;*
> *We merely carry on today*
> *Their start in nineteen five.*

Chapter 2:
R.G. Henderson and Son Ltd.

❧❧❧

My grandfather, Robert Grant Henderson, founded R.G. Henderson and Son, Ltd. (RGH) in 1896. The son was my father Albert (Ab) John Grant Henderson, who started in 1910 when he was 14. My brother John worked there from 1946 until he died in 1956. I came onto the scene after my 1957 graduation from the University of Toronto in engineering.

Toronto from the Perspective of a Plumber

On the death of my brother, I immediately apprenticed as a plumber. During my fourth year at the University of Toronto, I would go to RGH at 7:30 a.m., then show up at school for a few engineering classes, and then go back to close down the business. At night I went to Central Technical School, a union requirement for the plumbing trade. One of the skills a journeyman had to master and which was taught at the trade school was the wiping of a lead joint. You had to buy a wiping cloth and saturate it with lard so the molten lead would not stick. The lead pipe was laid horizontally and the molten lead poured on it, dripping down onto the lard cloth. The apprentice would then wipe it around, making a nice silver joint. The problem is that a new cloth always sticks, and you end up inadvertently pouring molten lead directly into the palm of your hand. The instructors apparently got great joy watching the rookies jump around in pain, and would invariably comment, *"The lead gets extremely heavy, doesn't it?"*

RGH was a small operation with only four employees. Its gross sales were less then $75,000 a year. During the second year of my involvement we lost money. My salary was $50 a week, and I am sure Dad thought he was grossly overpaying me. Mom made him change the signs on the trucks from "Plumbers" to "Sanitary Engineers."

A few months later, the Ontario Society of Professional

Engineers phoned Dad and pointed out that he did not have the right to use the word "Engineer." He took great pride in telling them that his son was a graduate engineer and RGH had the right to use that designation. The real problem was that a number of our customers, seeing the new signs on our trucks, thought we had gone out of the plumbing business! I believed that "Plumbers" was a more accurate term, and changed the signs back.

Because of my engineering background, the authorities allowed me to write for my master plumber's license after eight years instead of the usual 10. I had to sign an affidavit committing never to work with the tools. The hardest exam I ever wrote in my life was the master plumber's exam, which I passed in 1965. This ended the formal education phase of my life. Dad died four years later.

Patronizing Plumbers

I got some great reactions whenever I announced that I was a plumber. The International Yacht Racing Union had their 1979 mid-year meeting in Sydney, Australia. At the end of the meeting, there was a reception and dinner held for the delegates at the prestigious Royal Sydney Yacht Squadron. I had gone to see the recently completed Sydney Opera House, as I knew my wife Mary would want to know what was like, and as a result I was about half an hour late for the reception. As I walked in the front door of the Squadron a society matron sashayed up to me and gushed, *"I have met His Majesty King Constantine, and the vice-president from the Soviet Union, and the distinguished President Beppe Croce from Italy and the Commodore of the New York Yacht Club and all the other visitors. Where are you from?"*

"Taranta," I replied.

"Where is that?" she asked.

"Toronto, Canada," I stated more clearly.

"What do you do there?" she enquired.

"I'm a plumber." It was my stock answer.

She immediately turned around and went back to her

other new found friends. About 15 minutes later, I was circulating through the crowd when I bumped into her again.

"*I know,*" she said. "*All you doctors say you are plumbers.*" She could not bring herself to accept that a member of the world sailing hierarchy could really be a plumber.

Customers

When I first arrived at RGH after university, my father did not know what to do with me. Sometimes he would send me to collect unpaid accounts. He said there was a tough Jewish real estate owner who owed us a lot of money. I was to go down to the corner of Wellington Street and Bay Street, which is now in the heart of Toronto's financial district. This customer owned the land where the Royal Bank tower now stands. Back then it was a three-storey red brick building. I went in through the side door and up the staircase to the second floor, trembling at the thought of what lay in store for me there. All over the stairways and on the office walls was an incredible collection of modern art. I sat down and waited. Finally out came a very short man: "*Are you Abe's son?*"

"*Yes sir,*" I nervously replied.

"*Come into my office,*" he said warmly.

I went in and sat down. He explained why he did not pay in the usual manner. In the early 1930's, when he had immigrated to Canada from Russia, life was difficult for a Jewish businessman with a heavy accent speaking little English. He had acquired a small four-plex apartment in the west end of Toronto. The Toronto tradesmen treated him very badly. Someone suggested he use "Abe" Henderson as his plumber. My father treated him with respect, introducing him to the honest plasterers, drain men, electricians and other tradesmen. He had great respect for Dad. As he became a bigger and bigger landowner, he delegated the day-to-day management of his properties to his employees. The only way he could renew acquaintances was to pay his bills only when his old friend "Abe" Henderson came to pick up the cheque. Dad had set me up.

I finally asked him about his rather unusual collection of modern art. He ushered me into another room, which measured about 10metres by 10metres with a four-metre ceiling, and was stacked with paintings. He said it was his wife's collection adding, *"When you buy art by the gross, you have to be right some of the time."*

I enjoy telling this story to my wife Mary's volunteer friends at the Art Gallery of Ontario (AGO). This intriguing man was Samuel Zack who, along with his wife, donated a major gallery and art collection to the AGO.

Speaking of our Jewish customers, we had a "Sheeney" who came around to buy our scrap lead pipe. "Sheeney" is a derogatory term, but that is what we called them in those days. He had a long, white, flowing beard, and always wore a fedora, white shirt, braces and tie. He dragged a large pull cart, which he loaded with our scrap. Dad and he would negotiate the payment in cash. He used to make his own dandelion wine, and once gave Dad a bottle, which Dad put in his roll-top desk and promptly forgot about. That summer was very hot and the office was not air-conditioned. This potent mixture kept fermenting and exploded like a Molotov cocktail, blowing a large hole in Dad's desk and almost destroying the office. Fortunately, it happened over a weekend so no one was injured. When this man's only daughter got married, they invited Dad and I to the synagogue for the wedding. It was the most sumptuous and elegant wedding I ever attended.

We also did a lot of work for the Mafia in Toronto. They paid well, but also only if you went to pick up the money. Dad sent me down to their office, which was above a pub in the west end of Toronto. I did not listen carefully to his instructions about which door I should enter. I went in the wrong door and was immediately thrown down the stairs by two burly bouncers. Picking myself up, I remembered my dad's instructions and went in the right door. There, sitting on a table in three brown paper bags packed with $5 and $10 bills, was $10,000—a lot of money in 1958. When *The Valachi Papers* was published, there was a chapter on the Toronto Mafia. I must have known two or three people on each page.

Between Christmas and New Year's Day, Toronto usually experiences a deep cold snap. Since Dad was the expert on hot water and steam heating, we were invariably busy responding to panicked calls during that period. Dad had often taken me with him when I was 13 or 14. We once got a call that one of the downtown customer's heating had stopped working. It was in a taxi company office. As we there at about 11:00 p.m., he told me not to look around or remember who was there. Down in the basement, there was a well appointed room which housed the most high-stakes crap game in Toronto, with rollers from among the business, judicial and political elites of Toronto.

Another year we were called to service a heating problem in the city's most exclusive residential area. Dad instructed me not to look around and to forget what I saw, since it was none of our business. We went into the basement and I was shocked. The walls were lined with velour drapes with a throne raised up at one end of this seven metre by seven metre room. The walls were adorned with photographs of nude young men and boys. There was a full photo and development room off to one side. At my tender age, I did not realize that this was a meeting place for pedophiles from all over North America. Knowing what I know today about this deviant and illegal behavior, I would call in the police if I found myself in such a situation again. Back then, we just did the job we were called to do and left.

We also did all the work for the doctors in the art deco Medical Arts Building. The top floors are tiered, so there are flat roofs outside some of the offices. Flat roofs have drains that sometimes get plugged up. My brother John once went to clear a roof drain and had to climb through the window of an otolaryngologist's office to get to it. When he got out onto the roof, the doctor closed and locked the window, pulling down the shade because he was with a patient. This left John marooned on the roof, so he simply put his foot through the window, reached inside, and unlocked and raised the window. As he walked past the doctor he said, *"Sorry sir but my next customer is waiting and your drain is now running fine."*

Mr. Sydney Hermant owned and ran the Queen's Club in a true-to-tennis tradition. He was the owner of Imperial Optical and played tennis in long white trousers and always played with traditional white balls. The showers were terrible. When I applied for membership, I offered to refurbish the showers with new showerheads to ensure proper water pressure in lieu of an entry fee. This would have been a good deal for the Queen's Club. In true Hermant style, he shot back, *"How will that improve your tennis game?"* I paid the fee and the showers are still bad all these years later.

Every time I drive down Sherbourne Street past an area which used to house an old manufacturing plant, I laugh at the story my dad used to tell. He got a call to go down and repair a large generator motor which had stuck. Arriving at the plant, Dad studied the generator and gave it a big kick. The motor immediately started up and the plant was back in business. The owner was appreciative and asked to settle the account. Dad gave him a bill for $248.53. He always believed you never gave a bill in round figures. The owner then said, *"That is a lot of money for kicking a motor. I want an itemized account."*

Dad rewrote the bill as follows:
$ 55.21 for kicking the motor.
$193.42 for knowing where to kick the motor.
Total = $248.53

We also did most of the work for members of the judiciary who lived in Toronto, and this led to an incident that proves that sometimes it is important who you know. I had just acquired my wonderful mahogany Flying Dutchman sloop, which Skip Lennox and I later sailed in the Tokyo Olympic Games and which was like a piece of fine furniture. One Sunday afternoon, we went to train in Lake Ontario. This meant we had to sail in and out of the Eastern Gap. On a warm day in July the Eastern Gap is as busy as any eight-lane highway and really a challenge to navigate. We were returning at about 5:00 p.m. when the Harbour Police boat went screaming out to the lake at top speed, throwing up a great wave. I knew they were not on a safety mission, but merely going out to pick up the lifeguards who were through their shift patrolling the Island beaches. I was aware that the traditional, well schooled boatmen, who had served Toronto Harbour so well for decades, had been replaced. Their replacements were rookies from the Metropolitan Toronto Police who had no idea what they were doing on the water.

As they went by I shouted, *"Slow down you stupid SOB's!"* They stopped and came back, demanding that I submit to a safety check in the middle of the Eastern Gap on a Sunday afternoon no less, when the weekend traffic is at its peak. I told them it was an unseamanlike request and we would sail directly over to the dinghy docks at the Royal Canadian Yacht Club. They could do a thorough inspection there and I would even buy them a beer, which on such a hot day I was sure they would welcome. *"Do you refuse to lower your sails and submit to our inspection?"* they yelled. *"Yes!"* I forcefully responded, and kept sailing. They demanded my name and address, which I gave them. They responded that they were charging me with the felony of resisting arrest.

First thing Monday morning, I phoned Chief Reagan of the Harbour Police, whom we all knew quite well and with whom I had given good boating lectures at several clubs on a number of occasions. I explained the situation. He was very apologetic, but said that under the new political structure he could do nothing and that the charges had already been laid. A few weeks later I was summoned to appear in Court. I did not know the judge, but he knew my Dad and was familiar with my abilities as a sailor.

The charges were read and two officers related accurately what had happened and how I had refused to submit to an inspection in the Eastern Gap. The Judge asked the officers directly, *"How long have you been assigned to the Harbour Police Marine Unit?"* *"One month,"* they both replied. *"It is obvious that Mr. Henderson knows more about safety in sailboats than you officers do. Case dismissed!"* lectured the judge. This was wonderful but I was taken aback as I had worked hours on my rebuttal, but was never given an opportunity to deliver it.

Glenn Gould

The Park Lane Apartments was an upscale apartment building on St. Clair Avenue west of Yonge Street. The efficient superintendents, Mr. and Mrs. Appleyard, were the parents of the well known jazz musician, Peter Appleyard. They were so proud of their son that every time I went there they told me all about Peter's latest accomplishments. In the penthouse lived the eccentric genius Glenn Gould, considered by many to be the most accomplished interpreter of J.S. Bach. The building was steam-heated and Mr. Gould was always cold. He would often call us in the middle of summer to jack up the heat. Dad and I would arrive and there he was, in 80 degree temperature (27 degrees Celsius), wearing a heavy sweater, large scarf, and gloves. He was a kind and gentle person, and would play for us as we adjusted the heat. He would invariably ask us to have tea with him, then give us tickets to one of his performances at Massey Hall. In a similar vein, Tommy McLure would give us tickets to major boxing matches, and these two gracious celebrities increased my enjoyment of Toronto considerably.

Opportunity Knocks

In the 1950s and 1960s, there were only a few restaurants and bars in Toronto. Dining out was reserved largely for the wealthy who belonged to exclusive private clubs, and R.G. Henderson provided much of the maintenance service in these clubs. We received a call from the Royal Military Institute on University Avenue to repair a large commercial steam cooker made by the Market Forge Company of Everett, Massachusetts. Dad sent me to look at it, considering that my engineering background might be helpful in diagnosing the problem.

It seemed straightforward to me, but then most things

do. Life, however, is never as simple as I believe it is. There was a sticker on it from the manufacturer's agent who sold the equipment, a G.G. Brown and Company on Yonge Street. Mr. Brown said his major problem was that he could not find a reputable firm to act as service agent for these units, which were installed in the city's major hotels, hospitals and clubs. I picked up the necessary parts from Mr. Brown and went back and fixed the unit at the club. I told Dad I thought this was a good business to get into, but it meant that I would have to go to the Market Forge Company in Boston for training. I drove my Volkswagen Beetle all the way there, towing my dinghy behind to race in Cape Cod. While at Market Forge I signed up RGH as the authorized parts, service and warranty company for all their products.

What a stroke of luck this was! Shortly afterward, I convinced Russ Prowse and his financial officer George Attridge of Garland Commercial Ranges to use RGH as their authorized parts, service and warranty company in Ontario. This was the start of a new era for our business. In reality, we were never again plumbers because these new opportunities expanded our business dramatically.

There are now more than 15,000 restaurants, schools, hospitals, hotels and other catering establishments in southern Ontario. If my father took my mother out to Murray's Restaurant once a year in the 1950s, he was a hero. Today, if we do not take our wives out at least twice a week, we are bums. RGH got into this expanding marketplace on the ground floor and effectively had an unwritten monopoly on the parts, service and warranty business for most of the commercial cooking equipment in Ontario because we had the only trained technicians and had invested over $1 million in parts.

A story that best explains this business began when Nelson Mandela came to town. A formal dinner for some 5,000 guests was scheduled in the various banquet halls of the Royal York Hotel. At 5:00 p.m. we got a panicked call from the hotel because their enormous dishwasher, about the size of a garbage truck, had broken down and had to be fixed by 7:00 p.m. We mobilized five of our best technicians and got it back in operation in time for the big Mandela soiree. After we submitted our bill, the hotel's chief engineer phoned, protesting the exorbitant invoice.

"*Why do you use us?*" I retorted.

He said, "*You are the only ones who know what you are doing and who stock the parts.*"

"*That is expensive,*" I pointed out.

I ran the business using lessons I learned from my father. Even in the depression, Dad paid the staff before himself. We always paid our employees more than the competition and had the best dental, medical, insurance and pension programs. It is always more expensive to train new employees than it is to pay your existing staff a little more so they stay.

We always had new, clean trucks and smart uniforms because we wanted the employees to be proud of their company. RGH was based on the old guild system, in which I am a strong believer. I feel it is wrong to keep teenagers in school when they would rather be working with their hands in a trade. Falling asleep in high school, or dropping out and hanging around the local mall, or joining gangs leads to a waste of a good citizen. We would take on apprentices and start their learning from our trained technicians, then send them to the major appliance manufacturers for factory training.

The trained technicians became the father figures many of the apprentices did not have. A number of our trained technicians left over the years to set up small businesses of their own, and we always supplied them with parts and technical manuals because they could serve the smaller market segments that did not require our more sophisticated business structure. Some also moved to smaller communities across Canada and became our agents. Thus they became members of our expanded service network, not our competitors.

Dad's Health

Shortly after I joined the company, my dad had a massive ulcer attack and had to have most of his stomach removed. This meant he was away from the company for several months, and marked the end of his day-to-day business life. This left me, still wet behind the ears, to make all the business decisions, strategic and otherwise. I remember going into his hospital room, the third night after his operation, with my childhood friend Gerry Pangman. Dad had a tube inserted down his nose and taped to his forehead to pump out his stomach. As Gerry and I walked in, Dad got that engaging, mischievous smile on his face and, being a Scot, recited:

> *"Me name is Robbie Burns.*
> *I stand on the pier at Leith.*
> *I've lost the key to my asshole.*
> *I'm shitting through my teeth."*

I knew Dad was on the way back.

Thirty years later my telephone rang and a voice recited the Robbie Burns poem.

> *"Me name is Robbie Burns.*
> *I stand on the pier at Leith.*
> *I've lost the key to my asshole.*
> *I'm shitting through my teeth."*

Gerry had had the same operation as Dad had years before, and he remembered the poem. Unfortunately Gerry died five years later, much too young, from a massive heart attack.

Arrival of Bill Blum

We landed a big plumbing job to install the washrooms at the Junior Club of the Royal Canadian Yacht Club, and our journeyman plumber needed a helper. By chance there showed up at our door a very clean-cut fellow about my age, 25 at the time. who needed a job. His name was Bill Blum and he had recently been laid off by another plumbing company near the end of his five-year apprenticeship. (Many plumbing companies lay off their apprentices in the fifth year if business is tight because apprentices have to spend a lot of time at school that year and get paid almost as much as a journeyman.) Bill had two young children and no income. He was from Cologne and had done everything he could to get rid of his German accent. His father had died in World War II and his mother had immigrated to Canada with Bill and his older brother to start a new life.

I don't know why, but I took a shine to him and hired him. Bill had to go to George Brown College to complete his apprenticeship and we had to pay him for going to school. On his own volition he would come in and work on weekends cleaning up the building. Dad came down one Sunday and found Bill in the basement painting the walls because he wanted to work for his pay. Dad took an immediate shine to Bill and they became great friends.

Bill's first son Rick, a dedicated and direct man, worked with us in the summers. He became a Chartered Accountant, training at Ernst and Young and then becoming financial officer at a company that made gas fireplaces. I kept in touch with Rick and several times I suggested he would be the person who would one day take over R.G. Henderson and Son Ltd. In the end, his firm got swallowed up and Rick was given a golden handshake. Thanks to David Yule, who had trained Rick at Ernst and Young, we eventually worked out the sale of the company to Rick Blum.

People ask if it was difficult to turn the business over to someone else when it had been in the Henderson family for over 100 years and was the only job I had ever known. The answer is emphatically No!

It was time to leave the company to the next generation if it was to keep growing successfully. I knew I had sold it to the right person when I asked him, *"Rick, when do you want to take over?"*

"Monday," he replied.

"When do you want me to leave?"

"Sunday," was his immediate reaction.

I did and he did. Our son John still works at RGH and is very happy with the arrangement.

Chapter 3:
Clapp's Cove and Junior Sailing

There is a small cove, nestled between the north end of the Eastern Gap and Ward's Island in Toronto Bay and our cottage backed onto it. The Clapp Family lived just around the corner on Channel Avenue and the small area at the back of our cottages was called "Clapp's Cove." Jackson Clapp owned the Clapp Shoe Store on Yonge Street just north of Wellesley Street. He had two sons, Don and Doug. Don was my brother's age and Doug was a year older than I was. Each day, Jackson Clapp would row his lapstrake boat across the Eastern Gap to Winslow's lighthouse on the city side in order to avoid paying the ferry fare and parking charges.

On Sunday we always had dinner in a small room at the back of the cottage. It had a large picture window overlooking the Bay. One Sunday in 1941, Dad noticed that Don was rowing his father's rowboat into the wind. He would stow the oars, raise two canvas deck chairs, and then go downwind.

"What is Donnie doing?" Dad wondered. *"Let's go to the shore and ask."* We went down and when Don landed, Dad asked him what he was up to. *"I'm sailing!"* responded 11-year old Don Clapp.

I did not realize how this would dramatically change my life. Being only six years old, I didn't really care.

Sabots: (see picture)

Jackson Clapp was a five-year enthusiast. He would take on hobbies for five years, dedicating all his energies to the project, until he took up another interest. That winter, while reading *Popular Mechanics* magazine, he saw a little eight-foot sailboat, called a Sabot, that could be made out of two four-by-eight foot sheets of plywood. Mr. Clapp decided that this would be a great boat for Don and Doug.

He found a master carpenter named Leadbetter to build them

for him. Next he convinced his neighbours around Clapp's Cove—Dad and Ted Lye among them—to purchase a Sabot for $50 complete. This seems a small sum today, but to my dad in those days, it was a substantial expenditure. The first summer of the Cove Fleet, I was considered too young to own a boat. John was the one who was allocated the Sabot, but I was allowed to sail it. By the time I was nine, I got my own boat. I was enthralled and sailed every day all summer long, dreaming that I was sailing across the oceans of the world. John was a big gangly 14-year old who hated light winds, and he really did not fit into the cramped Sabot.

I was usually accompanied by Doug Clapp on my voyages around Toronto Bay. I knew the captains of all the large cruise boats, such as the *Cayuga, Kingston, Port Dalhousie,* and *Northumberland,* plus all the Toronto Island ferries. The captain of the *Cayuga* was great; he always blew his loud whistle as we sailed along in our little boats. We had great fun cruising the three kilometers to Mugg's Island, which is where the Island Yacht Club now stands. Our mothers would pack a lunch for us and off we would sail, taking some two hours to get there. We would have lunch with old Mr. Lye, who had squatter's rights on Mugg's Island as long as he lived, and he would tell us stories of Toronto Bay.

It would take us most of the afternoon to sail back home. The greatest fun we had was sailing up the Cherry Street ship channel in the Portlands. Cherry Street has a lift bridge that spans the ship channel. Doug and I would sail up the channel and even though our masts were so low we could sail under the bridge, the operator would sound the alarms, lower the gates, raise the bridge and stop all the traffic as we sailed with great arrogance down the waterway. About 30 minutes later we would sail back and the same charade was played out. If you were stopped on Cherry Street in those days, seeing no reason to be held up, it was because Doug and Paul from Ward's Island and Clapp's Cove were out sailing the channel.

Mr. Clapp was a great promoter and enlisted the help of fellow Islanders, Tommy McLure and his sidekick Ted Lye.

McLure was a unique man. He had sailed all his life, but professionally he was a barker for just about any event going, including the water show at the Canadian National Exhibition (CNE), the Hell Drivers, with whom he traveled all over Canada, and most boxing matches held in Toronto. Tommy would give us free tickets to all the heavyweight bouts in Toronto. He always had a cigar clenched in his teeth even when he was out sailing his Sabot. The spray would make the juice drip down his cheek but he didn't care. With his connections at the CNE, the Cove Fleet would race inside the seawall with McLure announcing the races. We wore specially printed Cove Fleet shirts because Mr. Clapp said we needed uniforms. Such apparel is commonplace today but was unique then. We grandstanded for the CNE audience, putting on a fine show.

I had very light skin and thin hair, even when I was a kid. My mother would always make me wear a broad brimmed hat when sailing and that was almost 70 years ago. Most of my sailing friends now have skin cancer but I have not yet had any trouble. Thanks Mom!

Junior Competitions

The first regatta I remember was held by the Lake Yacht Racing Association. The largest regatta on Lake Ontario, it was held that year at the Queen City Yacht Club with hundreds of racing boats competing. I was nine at the time. The wind was blowing the shingles off the roof. Our course was through the big yachts moored in Toronto Bay off Algonquin Island, over to the front dock of the RCYC and back.

Sailing like a fly on the side of a soup bowl and full of water, I went past an elegant yawl flying a large Stars and Stripes from its aft stanchion. They had finished the day's racing on the Lake. The crew was sharing a little rum when they peered over the side and saw me struggling to get up wind. *"Come alongside!"* one of them yelled. They picked up my eight-foot Sabot with me still inside, and put it on the deck. I jumped out and the distinguished skipper gave me a Coca Cola. They dumped the water out, put my boat back in the lake, and sent me off to continue the race. The skipper was Rooney Castle, who founded the Castle Dental Centers with offices across the United States. His family was renowned on the lake and his son Jerry is a great sailor. They were from the Rochester Yacht Club. I sailed in Rochester many times and Mr. Castle would always come out as my mother ship, serving me sandwiches and Coke. He said if I won the regatta he would give me his stylish Brooks Brothers sailing hat. With Skip Lennox, my outstanding crew, I always sailed well whenever we raced in Rochester, and I always looked forward to getting a new hat.

Out to the Lake

Sunday dinner on the Island was a command performance, with the entire family expected to be present. After dinner we would stroll, as was the custom for all Island Families, out to the lake and either go west along the Boardwalk or east out to the end of the Eastern Gap, where we would watch the yachts returning from their weekend cruise. When I was nine, I begged my parents all summer long to allow me to sail my eight-foot boat out the Eastern Gap to the lake beyond. In late August, after I had begged all summer, Dad convinced Mother to give in and allowed me to sail out of the Gap. I could not believe the picture I saw in the lake as these sailing yachts appeared like model boats on the horizon, getting bigger and bigger as they approached. I could see this magnificent gaff rigged, black 60-foot yacht bearing down on me. It was the famous "P" class yacht *Patricia* with its renowned skipper, Commodore T.K. Wade at the helm. He was originally a dinghy sailor and always steering with a tiller—never a wheel. He was standing with the tiller at his back, puffing on his ever present pipe. *Patricia* had a quarter wave larger than my little eight-foot boat. Commodore Wade sailed to leeward of me and as he passed he leaned over and said, *"Mister! You are taking my wind!"* and sailed on. This was the start of a long friendship with Commodore Wade, the great-uncle of my good friends Peter and Gerry Pangman.

My mother was deathly scared of the water and high winds, and did not swim. Like all good sailors, John and I loved strong winds. Mom would come down to the dinghy launching ramps when the wind was strong and tell us not to go sailing. This inaugurated her oft heard retort, *"One word from me and you do as you want!"*

Much later, when I was sailing in St. Petersburg, Florida, at the United States Olympic Classes Regatta, Mother was wintering on the other coast in Fort Lauderdale. Hearing that a storm was forecast to hit Florida, she phoned my sister, Sandra, back in Toronto, urging her to phone me in St. Petersburg with a warning not to go out that day as it would be very rough. I was 40 at the time and had been on three Olympic teams.

Aphrodite Cup

Doug Clapp and I were sent off to the Junior Club of the RCYC following in my brother's footsteps. Because my parents were not members, I was proposed to the Club by two lawn bowlers from the Island, Read Davis and John Whitton. By this time Doug was 11 and I was 10, and we had sailed hundreds of races at Clapp's Cove many more than any other junior sailor, most of whom were just starting to sail.

RCYC Commodore R.B.F Barr, who owned the yacht *Aphrodite,* started a Canadian junior championship for sailors 16 and under, inviting competitors from Montreal and the Great Lakes, including clubs in the United States. Jackson Clapp talked the Queen City Yacht Club into entering the young sailors from Clapp's Cove and giving us one dollar memberships. The first regatta was held at the Royal Hamilton Yacht Club. Being a rambunctious lad, I was running around the club and slipped, slamming my knee into a brick wall and cutting it for five stitches. Even with my stiff leg we did quite well, finishing second behind the team from the RCYC. The next year the regatta was held at the RCYC in our bay. Doug Clapp and I sailed the *Brutal Beast* (see photo), the RCYC junior trainer. Doug was brilliant and we won. Doug Hall and Don See made up the second team from the Cove Fleet. The regatta was held the next year again at the RCYC, and we again won for the Queen City Yacht Club.

RCYC Junior Club

By this time the Cove Fleet had being going for over five years and Jackson Clapp was moving on. Many of the young sailors were moving up to the senior club, sailing 14–foot dinghies. (see photo) During that winter, RCYC Commodore T. K. Wade approached my father at the Masonic Lodge and convinced him that Gerry Pangman and I should sail for the RCYC, because the junior championship was to be held at the competitive Royal St. Lawrence Yacht Club in Montreal. Dad came home and announced that I was going to sail for the RCYC in the summer of 1948. I had no input and at that age did not care as long as I was sailing competitively. As usual I caused a problem, but it was really Billy Cox, in his unique way, who orchestrated it.

Billy was always organizing something, and he eventually became the best Olympic team manager we ever had. When I was 14 and Billy 15, we had boat inspection once a week, when we pulled the indestructible *Brutal Beasts* a shore to wash them and do any necessary repairs, including splicing and whipping the ropes. At the start of the summer each skipper was given half a bar of soap. After about three weeks of the six-week Junior Club, the soap was either used up or lost. One wash day it was sunny and hot, and the three instructors, Bud Whittaker, Ralph Sorsoleil and John Strebig, noticed some young ladies swimming in the club pool and went to survey the pulchritude, leaving Billy Cox in charge. Big mistake!

Cox believed he had been appointed senior official and could do what he thought right. He immediately occupied the instructors' office where the soap was stored. Anyone else would have stolen one bar of soap for himself and the instructors would never have noticed, but not Cox! In true Cox fashion, he marched out onto the front porch of the Junior Club, conscripting me to carry 25 bars of soap. He called a skippers' meeting and handed out a bar of soap to each of the junior club fleet. Bud Whittaker, with whom I play squash with to this day and who was one of my brother John's best friends, returned and immediately expelled Cox from the

Junior Club. I announced that I had aided and abetted Cox, and I was thrown out, too. Cox was in deep trouble because he lived in the city and was driven down to the docks by his father. Billy was afraid to tell him, so he sat on the waterfront during his expulsion. I lived on the Island so I went to Ward's Beach and went swimming. What Bud Whittaker had forgotten was that, since I had been expelled, I would not be able to sail for the RCYC in Montreal the next weekend.

My brother came home that night, and he thought the whole episode was rather funny. My mother was very upset, especially since she had convinced Dad to take one of his few holidays to drive the team to Montreal that weekend. I told the family not to worry as I had already started to put together a Cove Fleet Team with plans to sail for the Queen City Yacht Club. John was committed to the RCYC and announced that he would act as arbitrator to find a solution. He orchestrated a compromise: I would be reinstated and could sail for the RCYC, but Cox was gone. At 14, I replied, *"No Goddam way! They only want my sailing talent and to hang Cox. Either we both get reinstated or I am going to sail for the Queen City Yacht Club."*

John agreed, as did my dad, and he went back to the Junior Club committee. They backed down and we were both reinstated. This was not the last time Cox and I pulled off something like this and I still talk to him every week. As we left for Montreal, the instructors informed me that if the RCYC did not win, we were not to come back.

We had a great team. Gerry Pangman was one of the finest natural sailing talents and I was a thorough preparer of my equipment and won many races, because my boats held together or because I knew what the sailing rules were. Gerry's crew was Paul Smith and mine was Harry Bruce, who later moved to Nova Scotia and became a famous journalist and author. We won, and when we returned to the RCYC, the soap incident was forgotten.

There was a rule in the Aphrodite Cup that instructors could not compete. Gerry and I had one year of eligibility left, but a number of clubs, mostly from the United States, asked that we be made Junior Club instructors. Thus we were retired early, our junior competitions at an end.

Another friend from the Junior Club, who also was a very keen sailor, was John Roberts who, later in life served as Minister of Justice in the Trudeau government. Olympic rowing shells and canoe equipment were imported into Canada free of duty, but Olympic sailboats had long been subject to excessive tariffs. In 1980, John was able to get our Olympic boats included with the rowing shells and canoes, thus saving our Olympic sailors a lot of money.

Noronic

One Friday night in the middle of September 1949, at about 3:00 a.m., there came an insistent rapping on my bedroom window. It was Doug Clapp. *"Paully, get up!"* he whispered. *"The City is on fire."* I jumped up and sneaked out, and saw that the whole Bay was alight. There was a very strong wind blowing but that had never stopped us before. We rigged our eight-foot Sabots, sailing over as close as the police boats would allow us, and watched the *Noronic* cruise ship burning. We could see hands sticking out the portholes and bodies floating in the water. It was the worst marine disaster in Toronto's history and left a lasting impression on me.

Life at the RCYC

After graduating from the Junior Club in 1959, I was hired on as an instructor. I could again spend my summers on the Island. I taught many of the Junior Clubbers, to sail, and I count some of them among my close friends to this day.

Instructor's Challenge

Commodore T.K. Wade, well into his 70s, would serve us tea and regale us with stories of his youth at the RCYC. He was a dignified gentleman with a great sense of tradition coupled with a love of life. An executive with Lipton Tea, T.K. was known affectionately among his friends as "Tea Kettle."

At 18 I became head instructor at the RCYC Junior

Club, where we had a few difficult children and teenagers — to say nothing of their parents. One unruly boy who was always getting into trouble did something that was not right and it came to the attention of the Junior Club board, who insisted that I expel him from the Junior Club.

That night, I got a call from Commodore Wade. He said he had pacified the board and asked me to agree not to expel the boy. T.K. held me to strict confidence and told me the story. T.K. attended Jarvis Street Baptist Church, which is on the edge of a rather poor neighborhood. For years he had sponsored as members of the Junior Club a number of young church members who came from difficult homes, the latest being this unruly boy. Society today is quite aware of the problem of less fortunate children, but in 1950 T.K. Wade was certainly ahead of his time — as was the RCYC. It has always been RCYC policy to have at least 25 per cent of the Junior Club comprised of the children of non-members. I myself was one of them, as my father became a member only after John and I had joined.

I had no trouble reinstating the boy. In fact, I quite liked him. He went on to serve as a member of the RCYC for some 40 years. He seemed always to be pushing the rules, and this was not the only time I had to get him out of trouble. Later in life he was stricken with pancreatic cancer and I made a point of visiting him in the hospital to say good bye. About three weeks later I ran into him at the club.

"*What happened to you?*" I asked.

"*Good pint of blood,*" was his reply. It seems his cancer had gone into remission, and he lived with it for another five years.

RCYC Annex

On Labour Day in 1939, the day after World War II was declared, the RCYC teenagers gathered on the upper veranda of the RCYC Annex and all got quietly drunk. The next day they enlisted and went off to war. R.D. Grant, who was later to become Commodore of the club, was none too happy when he was refused by the Canadian Navy due to his colour-blindness. He ended up as a tank commander with the Fort Garry Horse and was in the first wave of Canadian tanks ashore in France on D-Day. It was very rough in the English Channel and the tanks were launched into the water a few hundred yards offshore. Most of the tank drivers were from the Prairies and had no idea how to maneuver in the waves. The tanks were unstable and many were disabled. With his sailing expertise, Grant knew how to use the waves and made it ashore and off the beach. Unfortunately, the tanks arrived 10 minutes late. The infantry of Toronto Queen's Own Rifles landed first and suffered major casualties. Grant would hang his head as he lamented, *"If we had only arrived 10 minutes earlier, so many lives would have been saved."*

In the 1950s there emerged at the RCYC a group of some 25 dinghy sailors who had banded together as a rather strange fraternity. Most of them decided to live in the Annex, a house with about 15 rooms that provided basic accommodation and served as bachelor quarters. At a cost of $100 for the summer, two to a room, it became the centre of activity for a great group of energetic and sometimes uncontrollable young sailors. Billy Wilson and I shared a room.

Billy built the bunk beds and he took the lower. He constructed the upper three feet from the ceiling. He also demanded that I, being a plumber, should install a bar and sink with running water. In a midnight exercise we managed to get the job done. Tapping into the water lines was easy but the drain pipe was a challenge. By a stroke of luck my father's clothes locker was directly below our room. We drilled through the floor and ran the drain pipe right through the middle of Dad's locker. It worked perfectly and, fortunately for us, Dad found it rather amusing.

As the RCYC is on an island, the only way to get reach it is by boat. The club has two classic yachts: the *Hiawatha,* the world's oldest vessel in continuous service in Lloyd's registry, and *Kwasind.* The names come from *The Song of Hiawatha* by Henry Wadsworth Longfellow.

Up to the 1980s there was a sign which decreed, "Ladies are Requested Not to Use the Forward Deck." One race night, with all the sailors on board the *Kwasind,* one of our well known Eight Metre sailors showed up with two rather provocative women whom we referred to as "Jarvis Street Debutantes," Jarvis Street being in the heart of Toronto's red light district. They were dressed in pant suits and the quartermaster refused to allow them to board ostensibly because that was a violation of the dress code. They asked, *"Are mini-skirts allowed?" "Yes,"* came the answer. So the two of them buttoned up their jackets, took off their pants, and with great dignity walked aboard to the cheers of all the sailors present.

RCYC Sail Past

Every year yacht clubs have a sail past during which the commodore stands on his yacht and salutes the fleet as they sail past him. With more than 400 boats, the RCYC sail past is invariably an impressive parade. Because it is held on the last Saturday in May, the weather can be extremely unpredictable—it even snowed one year.

During one sail past during Commodore Grant's tenure, it was cold and "blowing the shingles off the roof" from the north. I was sailing the single handed Olympic Finn dinghy then and had to honour him by sailing past. Being on the leeward shore, the club was receiving the full force of the gale. Commodore Grant decided to delay and perhaps even cancel the sail past. My boat was on the city side, which meant that I was on the windward shore protected from the wind, so it was a planing reach to the club. From that shore the conditions looked good to me and as I was rather confident of my ability, I launched and screamed across Toronto Bay on a full plane. Arriving at the dinghy docks I spun around, jumped out, and pulled my boat up. Witnessing this grandstand performance, Commodore Grant said, *"If that little bugger can do that, the sail past will commence at 3:00 p.m."*

In those days we had a large and accomplished group of Finn sailors. The Finn is the toughest dinghy ever to sail, and if you can sail it, it means you're good. Six of us set out to sail past the Commodore. The Finn Fleet was programmed to sail to weather of the other boats and at the appropriate time, like a flock of Canada Geese, we were to scream by the Commodore. Just as the Finn sailors were about to start this performance, a vicious squall hit. I took off on the ultimate grandstand, not looking behind as my total focus was on keeping upright. After giving the royal salute I looked aft and nobody was there. All the others had capsized.

A bit later, during the early 1960s, one of the sail pasts was held during a particular weather condition that occurs quite often on Lake Ontario. The wind blowing out of the northwest for a few days blows all the warmer water off the top. While it is never truly warm at the end of May, the temperature can drop to as low as 40 degrees Fahrenheit (10 degrees Celsius). If a wind then blows in from the southwest, it can get very warm and humid. Sailors refer to this phenomenon as "the Mississippi Suck." The warmer wind hits the cold water and creates a dense fog, a metaphorical pea soup. When it happened that year, it was impossible to see more than a few yards, even though it was warm and sunny on shore. The sail past had to be cancelled.

By this time the gang was resident in the Annex, which we had come to refer to as the "Royal Annex Yacht Club." We decided that we would have our sail past as scheduled with Commodore "Tea Kettle" Wade taking the salute from the upper veranda of the Annex. It meant that only dinghies and canoes could perform because it is shallow close to shore. Signs were posted around the club announcing that "the Royal Annex Yacht Club First Annual Now Famous Sail past will Commence at 3:00 p.m. as Recently Scheduled."

Imperial Poona Yacht Club

The next week, a number of RCYC members, who believed they were the keepers of the Royal decorum, complained that we were being disrespectful by appropriating the word "Royal" and we were censured by the Committee of Management. Bill Gooderham, who was at that time Canada's best known sailor and whose family had a room in the Annex, came to the rescue. Bill had won the prestigious Seewanka Cup on Long Island Sound a few years earlier and had run into the English team and Sir Reginald Bennett, who had founded the anti-traditional Imperial Poona Yacht Club (IPYC). Bill, with great ceremony, had been inducted into the Canadian Outpost.

If you read the history or regulations of the IPYC, you would think everyone was mad. They are—but the membership is impressive. Poona is a hilly outstation in India where the English elite would go to get away from the heat of the summers. It is 2000 kilometres from any water. In the early 1950s when young Reginald was at university, he needed permission to enter a regatta, but couldn't because he belonged to no club. Being a great spinner of blarney, he thought up the name "Imperial Poona Yacht Club." He convinced the organizers that it was a legitimate club and they let him race. Bennett was as unusual a character as ever I met. He once decided to run for the United Kingdom parliament from his home town of Bristol, where a considerable portion of the electorate takes the ferry across Bristol Harbour every day at rush hour. He campaigned on the ferry, lobbying the captive crowd and was elected.

The IPYC has some unique rules, written in true Gilbert and Sullivan prose:
- You can be exiled from the IPYC for not thinking imperially, but you cannot be thrown out for not thinking.
- Annual Meetings, called "Tiffins," are always held on All Fools Day, the only item on the agenda being the scheduling of the next Tiffin.
- IPYC will be non-political whenever politic, one of it founding principles being that it will have no principles. Every member will be capable of speech.
- Membership will be temporarily suspended on death.

All Poona members go by fanciful names. The most senior official, HRH Prince Philip, is known as the Maharajah of Coochparwani, (which in reality means nothing at all), and is regularly reported in the British tabloids as attending Tiffins.

The IPYC has several outposts. The Hong Kong outpost is called "the Middle Kingdom Mandarins"; the American outpost operating out of the New York Yacht Club is known as "the Revolting Colonist Outpost"; and the Canadian outpost was named "the Repulsive Non-Revolting Colonist Outpost". No more than 25 members are permitted per outpost.

All this fitted our required change of name, and the group was led by John Langton, Billy Wilson and Bill Cox.

The burgee of the IPYC is bright yellow with three red balls, and our uniform was a blue RCYC blazer with brass buttons, yellow Bermuda shorts, red knee socks and a white pith helmet. In full dress we always wore our Poona ties, which were silver emblazoned with red pith helmets (see photos). The salutation from one Poona Sahib to another is "Chotah Hazri". (In 1981 HRH Prince Philip laid the cornerstone of the new RCYC City Club before going over to the Island Club where he noticed Johnny Langton standing off to one side wearing his Poona tie. HRH left the assembled dignitaries and without hesitation hailed Langton with, *"Chotah Hazri!"* much to our delight). Bill Gooderham was installed as the Celestial Commode and I was called the Intolerable Bhoi and given a medal that I had to wear at all functions. My role was to win races, so it was decreed that during all regattas I must be in bed by 11:00 p.m. and not drink. This posed no problem as I was a morning person and didn't drink anyway, but the ceremony that evolved was truly over the top.

Cox and Wilson decided that the Poona needed a band and that they would march, lining up on the RCYC bowling green in their uniforms. Marching through the club, they would pick me up and escort me back to the Annex and tuck me in. This happened most Saturday nights. Some members waited for the performance and others were disgusted at the disruption of the activities of their Royal Club, but it continued for about four years until marriage broke up "that old gang of mine."

The band had only one tune, *The Colonel Bogey March*. Only three out of 25 could play any instrument—

Pangman the penny whistle, Jimmy Dingle the trombone, and Cox a pump organ carried by young wannabees or "memsahibs." I had acquired the pump organ in a trade for a plumbing repair with Paul Hahn Pianos on Yonge Street. The rest beat drums or cymbals and I blew the tuba.

We always enjoyed sailing at the Rochester Yacht Club, where we had many friends—and we usually won. One year during the Poona's heyday, we were housed in the Coast Guard station, all in one room, sleeping on cots. On the Saturday night, the Poona Band decided to march. We went down the street to Tiny's Bengal Inn, a dive where the locals were lined up to get in. The Poona Band was making a terrible racket when the Monroe County Police cruiser arrived. The officer rolled down his window and said sternly, *"If you Canucks cannot play* The Star Spangled Banner, *get a move on."* Gerry Pangman without hesitation, played the whole anthem on his penny whistle. The police listened, hands over their hearts, then rolled up the window and drove away. That caper having lost its focus, we went across the Genesee River to the amusement park. It had a beautiful, antique merry-go-round. Don Sutherland was the first person I ever knew who got thrown off a merry-go-round for drunk driving when he tried to pull the ears off the donkey he was riding.

Returning to the Coast Guard station, Davey Angus noticed a stuffed moose head mounted on the wall and, liberating it from captivity there, hoisted it up to the top of the Coast Guard flagpole—no mean feat, as it must have weighed 25 pounds. Early Sunday morning, the militia arrived for their exercises and did not look up when they raised the Stars and Stripes. When they unfastened the halyard, the moose head came plummeting down, just missing a poor cadet and scaring the hell out of him. Had it hit him he would have been awarded a Purple Heart, but we were lucky and the moose head just bounced off the pavement and was relatively unscathed.

There were many pranks we played on warm nights at the RCYC, ably assisted by the ever present memsahibs. We would put an old mast across the swimming pool, greasing it with liquid soap. To the encouragement of wildly cheering spectators, a pair of jousters would shinny across with pillows. We also learned that four strong guys running and pulling on a rope could get the lighter weight memsahibs to water ski in the pool. I think this started the still popular, though now much more provocative, wet T-shirt fad. On another occasion, it seemed a good idea to steal a donkey from the petting zoo on Centre Island, and with military precision, transfer it to the RCYC tennis courts. Colonel Ovens, the club manager, was not amused.

Royal Yacht *Britannia*

With some reservation, we accepted a new boy, Roger Wilson, who was 18 at the time. He is still around on "Poona Probation" 60 years later. Roger rented a cheap cottage that was about to be torn down on Hanlan's Point. To get into our good books, he decided to host a party and invited all the Poona along with their memsahibs. Being the head Junior Club instructor and not imbibing, I was allowed to drive the *Victor,* a long, low, open, elegant launch. (The *Victor* was usually driven by Max and Don Croucher, originally from Port Carling in the Muskoka Lake region who were employees of the club and ran the races. They watched over the dinghy sailors and rescued us when we capsized.)

The Poona decided that we would use the *Victor* to transport the party goers to Hanlan's Point, which was a trip of about four kilometres through the back lagoons. The *Victor,* although having a shallow draft, had a propeller which hung down quite low. There were about 40 of us on board, with about half on the bow like *The African Queen,* when we took off for Hanlan's Point. We returned home with no problem until we got to the back dock at the RCYC. I miscalculated the depth of the boat in the water and cleaned out the *Victor's* starboard running lights on the dock.

Early Sunday morning, Cox and I decided to face the music and went to see Colonel Ovens at 8:30. We waited outside for half an hour until Max Croucher came out. He smiled and walked quickly away. Cox and I were called, and as we faced

Commodore R.D. Grant and the Colonel, we were shaking. The Colonel immediately started the process: *"Max has just been here and said he wiped out the starboard running lights of the Victor."*

We breathed a sigh of relief thinking, *"Good old Max!"*

The Colonel continued, *"Max and Don have a family reunion in Port Carling this week and will not be available for duty. You two thugs will be on call all week from 5:00 p.m. till midnight. The Royal Yacht Britannia is in Toronto and its officers have all been invited to use the RCYC. There are several receptions scheduled and I do not want to hire a boat operator when I have you two."* What a man the Colonel was! As we were leaving he added another challenge: *"The Club is very quiet the third week of August. The Poona thinks they can run a party. I bet you cannot get 200 of your tribe to come to an open air event that weekend."*

What a week Cox, Billy Wilson and I had running the *Victor* from the RCYC to the *Britannia* and back. When we would get near the Royal Yacht, the RCMP would blow their horns and sirens, and check our credentials. We went through security and picked up the officers. They asked us aboard and took us on a guided tour of this magnificent yacht. I could not believe the paint job on the hull—it was better than the finish on our dining room table.

The next challenge was to get 200 people to a party. The Poona swung into action and one or another of us met every ferry boat, handing out pamphlets announcing the spaghetti and Chianti party on the dry sailing area. More than 600 showed up and ate every scrap of food that the RCYC had, including roast beef and steak. It was one helluva bash. The Colonel had met his budget for August.

Sneaking In

During our formative years between 18 and 25, the triumvirate of Billy Wilson, Gerry Pangman and I had no money, so we would often sneak into major events in Toronto. Sneaking into the Grey Cup football game or a Toronto Maple Leafs hockey game was as easy as slipping unnoticed into the cinema, which we did with increasing frequency as we got older. We would dress well and either find a sloppy ticket taker or use the players' entrance or stage door, and just walk in as if we owned the place. On one memorable occasion, we snuck into Massey Hall and sat in the box seats to hear Gracie Fields sing *The White Cliffs of Dover.* Emboldened by this success, we crashed the gate at Maple Leaf Gardens and sat in the gold seats to see Elvis Presley. But we couldn't hear a note he sang—the screaming and yelling of thousands of manic rock and roll fans completely drowned him out.

Marriage and the Poona

The memsahibs started to decimate the Poona with the rite of marriage. It should be noted that we never let our boys marry anyone we did not like. It is a credit to our insight that not one of the group has been divorced, even now after 40 years. When I tell that to young people today, they are awestruck and ask how that happened. Some of us have been successful in business and others not so. Although we did some stupid things, we all had great respect for one another and the traditions and values with which we were raised.

After several engagements that did not culminate in a trip to the altar, Billy Wilson decided to marry Mary Manore from Norwich in Southwest Ontario. She was a great friend of my Mary and I was asked to be Billy's best man. They wanted to be married around the cenotaph on the RCYC front lawn. As usual, Billy never did anything without some strange twist. He refused to be married by someone he did not know. I had to find a clergyman with whom he shared some acquaintance. This was not easy as he wasn't a religious person. The only candidate I could think of was Father Tommy Day, with whom we had grown up on Toronto Island. He had become a Roman Catholic Priest, and I had been invited as the token heathen to his induction into the priesthood at St. Michaels Cathedral.

I had kept in touch with him as he moved from parish to parish, usually when there was a plumbing problem. I phoned and asked him to officiate. He was quite open to the idea, but since neither of the couple was Roman Catholic he had to check with the Bishop. Father Tom phoned back in about two weeks, saying that the Bishop had not been faced with this situation before and would I answer several questions:

"*Is either Roman Catholic?*"

"*No.*"

"*Has either ever been Roman Catholic?*"

"*No.*"

"*Would either become Roman Catholic?*"

"*No.*"

"*Has either been married before?*"

"*No.*"

"*Is she pregnant?*"

"*Not to my knowledge.*"

Father Tom went back to the Bishop and relayed my answers. He phoned back a week later.

"*Well, I spoke to the Bishop and he said this is a rather strange request, but after studying the case, he said it is just like a civil wedding. Roman Catholic priests can officiate at civil ceremonies, so no problem.*"

It was a magnificent, sunny September afternoon and the guests gathered around the cenotaph. Cox played the *Wedding March* and Father Day officiated at the ceremony. It was one of the most beautiful weddings ever, but I had lost my roommate. I had been trying to get rid of my roomy for years, but to no avail. He was best man at my wedding as I was at his. We recently celebrated our seventieth birthdays together.

The Poona still get together after 40 years at the annual Tiffin called "Poona Sunday" on the Saturday before Christmas. We all wear our uniforms and decorate the street with flags and racing pennants. It is customary to put beer mugs on the mantelpiece to remember the Poonas who are under temporary suspension due to death. It is sad to say that the number of mugs are growing.

International 14-Foot Dinghy Sailing

When I was growing up, the International 14-foot Dinghy (I14) was the most popular racing sailboat in Canada, the United Kingdom, New Zealand and the USA. In Toronto we had about 80 active racers, with 40 of them at the RCYC. The rest came from other clubs in the area and the rivalry was fierce. If a sailor could win on Lake Ontario, he or she was at world-class level.

Late in August 1947, the best sailors from around the world came to compete in an international team race at the RCYC. The U.K. team had arrived with the most beautiful mahogany hulls ever. It was a beautiful, warm, sunny Saturday with a strong westerly breeze blowing across the lake. I sat on the dinghy docks dressed in my usual shorts and sailing hat watching the spectacle. A member of the U.K. team walked by, looking like a real Adonis. He asked me if I wanted to go planing across the bay in the beautiful breeze. It was the first time I ever really planed in a dinghy. The man who asked me to go with him was Keith Shackleton, son of famous Antarctic explorer Ernest Shackleton. Keith later became a well known wildlife and marine artist.

My brother John was a very good sailor, especially in heavy weather. I crewed with him when his regular crew did not show up, but I liked to steer (which is a magnificent grasp of the obvious). The Int. 14 is what is called a development class and new boats are constantly being built. John had a mahogany boat built by Greavette in the Muskoka region, but it had been out-designed. Up to World War II, boats were designed to be fast into the wind and were not especially well designed for downwind speed.

In a major design breakthrough after the war, some upwind ability was traded off for speed downwind. John's Greavette *Sunflower KC41* was at a disadvantage, so John decided to get the RCYC's talented designer Charles W. Bourke to design a boat that would be slanted toward heavy wind and his big tough size.

Charlie Bourke was an Irishman with a great and abiding love of life. His innovative creations kept Canada's dinghy sailors very competitive. Proprietor of a tool and die supply company on Merton Street, he executed his dinghy designs as a labour of love for which he would accept no financial compensation. Although Charlie had a bad heart, he would go out on the club support launch *Victor* with Max and Don Croucher every Thursday and Saturday to watch us race. His first molded plywood design was manufactured by his good friend, stockbroker Harvey Bongard shortly after World War II, using the technology that had been developed to build Spitfires. Like Charlie, Harvey was an enthusiastic supporter of dinghy sailing.

While they were building his new dinghy, John gave me *Sunflower KC 41*. He sat on the shore while I sailed, but finally, with the season well along, his new boat *Sunshower KC 141* was delivered. I raced against him in his first race in his new boat. I was on port tack and John on starboard coming to the windward mark. He had the right-of-way, but I miscalculated and as I bore off to miss him, I hit his gunwale six inches from the stern, leaving a big scar in his new boat. I sailed immediately into the dock. It was one of the worst days of my life. John did not talk to me for weeks.

Sunflower was a great boat and I sailed if for three years. We were able to do quite well, especially in light weather. In heavier weather we would get to the upwind mark, often in first place, and then let one of the new planing hulls pass. We became very adapt at sitting on the other boat's stern wave, being dragged along just like a surfer on a wave. This skill held us in good stead in all our future sailing.

Skip Lennox was a young 13-year-old sailor who lived on the Island and had quite a spark. John asked him to be his new crew. Skip didn't weigh very much and was like a cat in the boat, but John compensated with his own size and strength. They did very well together. During the Canadian Dinghy Championship held at the RCYC early in August 1954, there was a hurricane that backed up from the Atlantic. The Race Committee cancelled the races due to the high winds. John was furious—the harder it blew the more he liked it.

Along with Bill Gooderham, a great Olympic and International sailor, John convinced the Race Committee to sail the prestigious Governor General's Race in Toronto Bay and not out on the open lake. Most sailors were too scared and stayed on shore. Skip and John won easily.

Skip's family cared more about school attendance than ours did, and there were times when Skip was not allowed to travel to regattas, so I would play hooky and crew with John. We won the Connecticut Cup together at the Essex Yacht Club in Long Island Sound off Fenwick, Connecticut, in 1952.

John also loved Bermuda because the wind often blew hard and the Bermudians were such characters. Sydney Greet ran the supermarket in Bermuda called the "Stop and Shop," but he usually referred to it as the "Stop and Steal." Whenever there were light winds, he and De Forest (Shorty) Trimingham would perform a strange ritual. They had a porcelain black pig and would dip its bottom into the sea, all the while chanting, *"Black Pig! Black Pig! Black Pig!"* More often than not it blew like hell the next day.

Chapter 4:
Fulfilling John's Dream for Sailing

On a cold Thursday night in January 1956—the night before John was killed—we had been out five-pin bowling. Back home again, I sat down on his bed while he composed a letter, all the while lecturing me about what we must do for sailing in Toronto and in all of Canada. The letter was to the Canadian Yachting Association demanding they send a two-person dinghy crew to the 1956 Melbourne Olympics. John looked forward to the Olympic trials, because Melbourne was known for heavy winds. As it turned out, Canada did send a team to Melbourne. Second, since the RCYC was on the Island, John said we needed a dinghy launching facility on the city side so we could extend our season beyond the current five months and allow competitive sailors to travel to regattas. Carrying the idea further, he said that a city club would also serve as a focal point, allowing everyone to keep together year round. He noted ruefully that the RCYC was not family-friendly, as sailors usually left the club once they were married.

John left a hand-written will in which he gave all his possessions to our mother, except for his 14-foot dinghy and Skip Lennox, both of which he left to me. Thus I inherited Skip and for 10 years we sailed more than 2,000 races together. He was great fun to sail with and, in my opinion, was the best crew ever. We ended our career together representing Canada in the 1964 Tokyo Olympics in the two-person Flying Dutchman Dinghy. The city launching facility was delivered with the founding of The Water Rat in 1968 and the acquisition of the city launching crane, first at the foot of Jarvis Street and later at Parliament Street. The 1974 merger of the RCYC with the Carlton Club led within seven years to the erection of the new RCYC City Club. Although I did not consciously focus on my brother's dreams, I like to think that in some way, I helped bring them into reality.

Charlie Bourke had become a great friend and mentor of my

brother. He was some 40 years older than we were and it seemed that he wanted to impart all his worldly knowledge to us. He would call me every Friday and Monday morning to review our races. If he started the conversation with "Paul," I knew we had sailed well. If he began with "Mister," I knew we had screwed up. We usually finished well because of Skip's ability to maneuver downwind flying the spinnaker. Charlie analyzed each segment of the race, not just the finish. He phoned one Friday after we had been slow going into the wind and said, *"Mister! Put your centreboard down as far as you can."* The next Thursday we were no better upwind and I got the usual call, *"Mister, pull your centreboard up more."* I was confused. *"But Sir,"* I said, *"last week you told me to put it down. What is right?"* *"When you are going as slow as you are, try anything."* Such was Charlie Bourke's Irish wisdom.

One Friday in 1958 he phoned and, starting with "Paul," asked if I could have lunch with him downtown, as he had not talked to me face to face for a while. I could not go due to some crisis in the plumbing business. He went by subway downtown and, walking up the stairs to lunch at the Ontario Club, suffered a heart attack and died. At 23 I had lost my two great mentors, my brother and Charlie Bourke.

Skip and His Tricks

Skip and I sailed everywhere we could and had a wonderful time winning the USA National Championship in Buzzard's Bay and again in Rochester, New York, where Lennox grandstanded as usual. There were two races the first day. We won the first race in a strong breeze. As we crossed the finish line, they fired a gun. Skip let go of the spinnaker and, standing on the gunwale, pirouetted down to the stern collapsing in the water as though shot. He was a good swimmer, but not stupid. He swam over to the committee boat where our good friend Frank Shumway, chair of the Race Committee, dragged him aboard. Lennox reclined in a deck chair eating a sumptuous lunch while I flogged around alone, waiting for the next race. He thought it was funny, as he did most of his capers.

When we went to regattas, Lennox and I usually drove all night because we had to ration his time away from the Glidden Paint Company, where he worked as Technical Engineer. We always tried to go to the Connecticut Cup off Fenwick. The members of the Essex Yacht Club presented a trophy in memory of my brother John who was the first Canadian to compete in that race. It now hangs in the RCYC city club.

The recently completed New York Thruway reduced the trip to about 12 hours from the original 20. I picked up Lennox at work at about 3:00 p.m. and we drove all night, arriving in Fenwick in pitch black about 3:00 a.m. We pulled up to the side of the road and went to sleep not realizing we were in the middle of a golf course. At about 7:30 there came a tremendous banging on the roof of our van. We woke up to face a rather annoyed redhead who informed us in no uncertain terms that we were blocking her tee shot. It was Katharine Hepburn. We sailed well and won the trophies.

Skip made good friends with Don Doyle from the Essex Yacht Club, and they were always trying to one up each other. It was during the Cold War and we were sailing at Stu Walker's Severn Sailing Association in Annapolis, Maryland, in front of the U.S. Naval Academy. In a pseudo-military exercise Skip stole Doyle's mainsail and took it to a local sail maker to have the letters "SR" sewn on after the letters "US," which were in use by the USA at that time. Doyle had to sail the whole regatta with "USSR" on his mainsail. While it was a great laugh and we sailed well again, I was anxious that Doyle would retaliate. There was no doubt in my mind that he would do something to get even with Lennox, especially since everyone was acting overly friendly as we left.

We always had a complete cover enclosing the hull to protect it from road tar and debris during the long drive back home. The customs officer at the Peace Bridge border crossing in Fort Erie asked us to pull over for an inspection. When we opened the covers we saw that our boat had been filled with used tires. Doyle had struck.

Fortunately, the customs officer had a sense of humour and let us through.

Canadian Team Race Team in Cowes

The 1958 World 14-foot Dinghy Team Races were held in August at Cowes, Isle of Wight, U.K. Canada had an excellent team and I was asked to be the spare crew. We went to compete against the U.K., USA and New Zealand. It was the first time I had been overseas.

The team consisted of:

Paul McLaughlin (skipper) Olympic sailor, father of Olympic medalists Terry and Frank;

Jim Stephens (crew) brutally strong, my personal lawyer for years;

Bud Whittaker (skipper) excellent sailor and squash partner;

Doug Roberts (crew) from Toronto;

Bruce Kirby (skipper) from Ottawa, Olympic sailor and designer of the Laser dinghy; and

Harry Jemmett (crew) a founder of the Canadian Olympic Regatta Kingston (CORK).

We arrived at Malton Airport (now Pearson International Airport) and were waiting to board our flight to London when Harvey Bongard arrived in his blue blazer to wish us luck, a *Globe and Mail* tucked under his arm. Harvey was about 65, and his wife had died just a few months earlier. As we were about to board the plane, Bruce Kirby said to him, *"Harvey! The team needs a manager. You're not doing anything. Come with us?"* Harvey went up to the Air Canada ticket agent and bought a first class ticket—without any luggage or passport. My God, how travel has changed! It was never publicized who had paid for our trip, paid for the RCYC dinghy sheds, or funded our Olympic teams, but I can tell you now that it was Harvey Bongard. He was great fun, and totally committed to the sport. Alongside dinghy sailing, Harvey's other great passion in life was iceboating.

When we arrived in London, we were met by the paragon of U.K. dinghy sailors Stewart Morris, who had won an Olympic gold medal in the 1948 games. He was a hops merchant and his London telephone number was HOPS—simple life in those days, even in London. We stayed at the original Royal Thames Yacht Club in Kensington across the street from Harrods, in the centre of London. That night Stewart picked us up in his lorry. We all piled in and off we went to the risqué Eve's cabaret. The show's centerpiece was a tableau of beautiful nude girls posing as still life. (I thought this a bit tame, since on a number of memorable Friday nights back in Toronto while I was studying engineering, Billy Wilson and I would drive to the Palace Burlesque in Buffalo to see women like "Tempest Storm" shaking it. But these beautiful girls merely posed. I never understood why until I saw Dame Judi Dench in the film *Mrs. Henderson Presents*, about the Windmill Theatre and how she got young ladies to pose nude on stage.)

The next day, Stewart drove us to Itchenor in the south of England, where we picked up our boats. Then it was off to Cowes, Isle of Wight. We stayed at the Royal Corinthian Yacht Club, where crews from all teams slept on cots in a dormitory named "Boys Town." The skippers, however, had private rooms. Harvey Bongard stayed at York House, a nice bed-and-breakfast where he became well acquainted with the owner's statuesque daughter, whom he named "The Duchess of York."

What a great time we had in "Boys Town." The Kiwis (New Zealanders) were a unique group and the Brits and Yanks also were great fun. One night Ralph Roberts from Auckland led the boys in a pillow fight, with the Brits and Yanks against the Kiwis and Canucks. I had a scissors leg grip around the neck of American sailor George Moffat, when Ralph hit him over the head with a pillow. His chin hit my knee and it knocked him out cold, bringing the pillow fight to an abrupt end. George left sailing a few years later and took up gliding where he still holds a number of world records. He explained that gliding was just "three dimensional sailing." One of the Kiwi skippers was "Shorty" Pryde, who was killed in a glider accident some years later in New Zealand. His brother is Neil Pryde of Windsurfer fame.

Ralph Roberts was the first to announce—at the prize giving, no less—that I was going bald. To this day he remains an influential sailor in New Zealand and around the world. I still communicate with Ralph and his wife Penny at least once a month.

Bungy McRae

The most memorable Kiwi crew was a Maori from Rotorura, Bungy McRae. A very powerful man, Bungy was uncomfortable in this milieu mostly because it was his first time out of his homeland. He wore a hei-tiki which his wife had given him to protect him on his long trip. Bungy was renowned in New Zealand for his sailing skills and was a wonderful addition to their team. When he found out that I was a plumber and was traveling overseas for the first time myself, he bonded with me. We went everywhere together. Bungy was over 50 and, I am told, had 18 children. I was still wet behind the ears and 23, with very pale skin. It was a hot, sunny summer in the south of England that year. He said to me once, when we were out in the noonday sun, *"Hendison, you burn and I shine!"*

Our first dinner in Cowes was a formal reception at the Royal Corinthian Yacht Club with all the Sirs, Ladies, Dukes and Duchesses the Brits could muster, plus the famous dinghy designer and resident of the docksides of Cowes, the bizarre Uffa Fox. All teams were asked to sing for their supper. Bungy, in a beautiful resonant voice, sang the Maori farewell, *Now is the Hour*. The Canadian Team sang *Alouette*. The Americans sang *God Bless America* with their hands over their hearts. Uffa Fox sang, with the many verses that only he knew, *"Oh! Dear what can the matter be? Three old ladies were locked in the lavatory."*

Sitting opposite to me at the table was "Sir Somebody or Other," escorting a striking, young blond lady with swept back hair and a nice cleavage. I was fascinated by her and was sure I had met her before, but as I had been in the U.K. for only a week at that time, I was puzzled. I pondered and pondered, wracking my brain to remember where I might have seen her before. Finally at dessert, the light bulb went on and I blurted out, *"You're the head nude at Eve's?"* To which she replied, *"Did you like the show?"*

A few nights later we were all invited to another formal dinner at the Royal Yacht Squadron (RYS). The invitation was quite specific, right down to insisting that we all wear blazers, grey trousers and black shoes. The RYS is such an exclusive club that it refused Sir Thomas Lipton membership because he traded. Being a tradesman myself, I was worried that I might not be allowed in the front door. Ralph Roberts was an electrician so he was also suspect. We all got dressed and started down the hill to the dinner. I walked by Bungy's bunk and he was lying there undressed.

"Bungy!" I called out. *"What the hell are you doing?"*

"I'm not going, Hendison. I'm not going there," he explained.

"Yes you are, and I'm waiting for you to get dressed."

Bungy finally agreed and the two of us walked together through the front door of the RYS, just as the last person was going in to dinner. At the RYS, one enters for dinner in order of your club number, which means that the oldest go first and the most junior, last. Bungy and I were in our proper places entering last. Each table was round and seated ten. By the time we got inside there were only two seats left and they were at the centre table where our host, Sir Peter Scott, was sitting and Bungy and I duly took our seats. Son of the famous Antarctic explorer Robert F. Scott, Sir Peter was an excellent sailor. At that time he was President of the International Yacht Racing Union, an office I myself would hold some 30 years later. He was a painter of wild fowl and marine subjects, and had been appointed "Keeper of the Royal Swans." Many Christmas cards featuring scenes with wild fowl were painted either by Sir Peter Scott or by Keith Shackleton.

The room was rather musty with photos of past commodores hung on the wall, alongside several tapestries depicting royalty. The club had not been refurbished after World War II and the ceiling was cracked and water-stained. As happens at most noisy banquets, there is a quiet time when port is usually served. During one of these lulls, Bungy's stentorian voice could be heard to exclaim, *"Hendison! I am the first Maori ever to be in this place and by the look of the ceiling you are the first plumber!"* I almost threw up.

The Canadian team won the team race series, beating the Kiwis in the finals. Geoff Smale and Ralph Roberts, from Takapuna, New Zealand, won the prestigious Prince of Wales Trophy, the first foreigners ever to do so. Paul McLaughlin and Jim Stephens were second.

Thirty years later, Mary and I went to an IYRU meeting in Auckland and decided to travel the length and breadth of the wonderful country of New Zealand, which has been prolific in its production of the most successful racing sailors in our sport. One of our stops was Rotorura, the capital city of the Maoris. I had heard that Bungy McRae had died a few years earlier and I told Mary that I wanted to visit his family, but I had no idea how to make contact after all this time. Next to the hotel, a bridge crosses over to the traditional Maori village where many of the older Maoris sit and talk. Brashly I walked up to them and asked if they knew Bungy McRae. They were less than friendly and I suppose apprehensive about this interloper. *"Why do you ask? He has died,"* one of the men replied.

I then explained how I had known him from sailing and that I wanted to say hello to his wife and family on this my first visit to New Zealand. They immediately became exceptionally friendly and called a taxi-driving friend to escort me, paying the fare. We were taken to a well loved house a few miles away. I knocked on the door and a nice lady answered. It was one of Bungy's many daughters. I told her who I was and she invited me in. The walls were covered with pictures from Bekin of Cowes. Prominently displayed was a photo of Bungy and me saying goodbye. She demanded that I go and see her mother, who was at that moment involved in a very important meeting with the government down at the Maori Meeting House. Mary and I boldly walked into what was evidently an intense meeting between English government officials and Maori chiefs. It was obvious we were not welcome. A self-important English official intercepted us: *"You are intruding. What do you want?"*

Recovering quickly I replied, "*I am a Canadian sailor and sailed against Bungy McRae in 1958 in Cowes. I would like to say hello to his wife.*"

The distinguished leader of the Maoris stood up at attention. I am sure he was one of Bungy's relatives. With his hands clasped behind his back and in a resonant voice that called my old friend to mind, he announced to the crowd: "*Any friend of Bungy McRae is a friend of ours. By the way, our yachties are better than your yachties.*" With that there was a shuffling in the back of the hall and a small, elegant lady came forward with tears streaming down her face. We went outside and hugged one another. Bungy's wife said that he had talked about Cowes and his Canadian friend many times over the years.

Bermuda

In 1958 we went to Bermuda again and stayed with our good friends the Butterfields at their home, *Edelweiss*. Billy Wilson was my crew. His mother, who ran the Penny Wise antique shop in Thornhill, a northern suburb of Toronto, had gone to Branksome Hall, Toronto's elite girls' boarding school, with Mrs. Butterfield. Everyone called her "Coach" and her husband Arthur was known as "Pop."

Billy was sure that Bermuda was very English. Dressed in a grey flannel suit and bowler hat he strode off the plane with his "brollie," looking the proper Fleet Street gentleman. An elegant man dressed in the ubiquitous Bermuda shorts and knee socks walked up to him and said, "*Hey Mon! Where did you get that bullshit outfit?*" Billy took it all in stride.

That year John Hartley Watlington and Walter Jones won the Princess Elizabeth Trophy, one of the most elegant trophies anywhere, in the Bermuda National Championship. Hartley gave the best winning speech I ever heard. He had been shot down over France in World War II and had been harboured by the Resistance. He had walked through France to Spain dressed as a deaf-mute priest, not speaking for nine months. He had never said more than a few words before and was even more reticent afterward. When he did hold forth, his speech was interspersed with salty four-letter words. He was most appropriately nicknamed "Mumbles." (His wife Faith had grown up on Toronto Island, proving that Hartley was very wise indeed for a Bermudian.) The presentation was held on the front lawn of the Royal Bermuda Yacht Club with all the beautiful people and dignitaries in attendance, including the Governor and the Prime Minister. Hartley was presented with the trophy, then turned around to leave without saying a word. *"Speech, Hartley! Speech! Speech!"* we all yelled. Very uneasily, John Hartley Watlington turned and went slowly back to the microphone and mumbled, *"I sailed well and deserved to win."*

The next year, 1959, Skip Lennox was able to come to Bermuda. The Bermuda National Championship was held in April each year and therefore would be our first race after the six-month winter hiatus. We had only one day before the first race to practise. It was one of those spectacular, warm Bermuda days with not a cloud in the sky, but it was blowing a gale. Any sailing could be hazardous and no one wanted to risk breaking gear before the official races started. We were all sitting on the front lawn at the yacht club, many with a rum swizzle in hand. Lennox and I did not drink, but we sat listening to the yarns being spun by some of the other sailors as the day wore on. We were in the company of RCYC Commodore Paul Phelan, owner of Cara Foods, and a Dragon sailor. A Dragon is a stable keelboat, needing a good breeze just to move it. We watched enthralled as a Dragon sailor ventured forth in the strong wind with only a jib set. The other Dragon sailors on the lawn pointed out that this was a true sailing ship and could handle any weather conditions. At this Skip turned to me and, in customary form urged, *"Fat Boy, let's go!"* *"Yeah,"* I replied, *"I have to pay the bills when you break up my boat and blow out my sails."*

As usual, Skip prevailed and we sailed gingerly across Hamilton Harbour, with full sails up under the high cliffs on the sheltered shore. *"See,"* Lennox pointed out, *"there's not much wind. Up spinnaker!"*

So up went our spinnaker and we screamed across

Hamilton Harbour as fast as I have ever gone. Arriving at the launching dock, Lennox performed one of his skillful maneuvers, dousing the spinnaker, jumping out of the boat and fending it off as though it was routine. Commodore Phelan, when asked who these nuts were sailing a 14-foot dinghy in this gale, merely replied, *"Oh that's Henderson and Lennox from the RCYC."*

Going into the final race for the Princess Elizabeth Trophy it was again blowing very hard, about 25 knots. We had to win the race and have Glen Foster, who would eventually capture an Olympic Gold Medal for the United States in 1976, well down the fleet. Glen was dismasted at the start, so that part of the puzzle was solved for us. We got to the first upwind mark ahead and rounded with a few others very close behind. Lennox gave his usual command, *"Up spinnaker!"* *"You've got to be kidding!"* I replied. *"Up spinnaker!"* he shouted again, more forcefully.

Up went the spinnaker and we took off down the reach. About halfway down the leg I looked aft and saw no one there. They had all tried to hoist their spinnakers and capsized. *"Lennox!"* I yelled. *"Look behind!"* He took a quick look back and immediately instructed, *"Down spinnaker!"*

We won the race and the Princess Elizabeth Trophy and had no idea how this grandstand performance would impact our lives. The evolution of 14-footers continued apace, but we no longer had Charlie Bourke to keep up with the new designs coming out of the U.K. Jack Wright, lawyer for the well known Tannenbaums in Toronto, bought a new Ian Proctor design from the U.K. He knew he was too old to sail dinghies, being over 50 at the time and not in strong health, but he liked to tinker with boats. He worked most of the summer putting it together and fine tuning it, but never raced it. He asked me if I wanted to buy it. Being more than anxious to do so, I sold John's boat *KC141* and was able to get *KC241*. It was a rocket ship! In the summer of 1961, Lennox and I never lost a race in this beautiful boat. The team races were again held at the RCYC with the international teams competing. When they came together it was in all aspects but name the world championship, and there were more than 80 boats on the starting line. Skip had to work in the morning so Bruce Brymer filled in, but Skip was there for the afternoon races. We won every race including the Governor General's Long Distance Race and captured the Bourke Trophy. Our lives were about to change again but we didn't realize it at the time.

Outer Harbour Dinghy Sailing

In 2000, Juan Antonio Samaranch, President of the International Olympic Committee, appointed me as an International Federation representative to the IOC Sport and Environment Commission. I went to several conventions on the environment representing the IOC, and I categorized the environmental activists I met in two groups:

- the constructive ones who focused on a problem and tried to find a solution;
- those who seemed to be a little out of touch with reality, wanting to rid the world of people, it seemed to me, in order to leave it unspoiled for the birds, animals and trees.

From my point of view, sailing is a sport which relies totally on the environment. Sailors use a renewable resource—wind—for our power. Our boats sail across lakes and oceans, and we do not scar the surface. Sailors are extremely concerned about the environment. In fact, one of our 1972 Olympic medalists, Paul Cote, was a founder of Greenpeace.

I first became aware of environmental issues in 1966 when I was invited to a luncheon at the Argonaut Rowing Club organized by Gordon Norton and Bill Cox with Jack Jones, the forward thinking chief engineer of the Toronto Port Authority. Jack had built Ontario Place and other marinas along Toronto's waterfront using landfill. Toronto was going through a dynamic construction boom with a number of large office buildings going up in the downtown core. This required digging large foundations to house subterranean parking lots and shopping concourses, and the earth had to be dumped somewhere. Jack's solution was to build a large spit out into Lake Ontario at the foot of Leslie Street, which he justified by saying that all this earth had once been under the lake before it receded centuries earlier. Lake Ontario is a huge body of fresh water about 400 kilometres long, 100 kilometres wide and 200 metres deep. There is a ledge east of Toronto Harbour where the lake is only 10 metres deep, and this was where the spit would be constructed. Some three kilometres offshore, the lake bed drops off dramatically to about 100 metres.

An environmental lobby tried to stop construction of the spit on the grounds that it would ruin the natural mating ground of the soft-shelled crab. Sounding a different alarm, a left-leaning New Democrat Party (NDP) city councilor said that the spit would take up some of the surface area of the lake. I could not believe this uninformed rhetoric—Lake Ontario pulsates minute by minute due to small changes in atmospheric pressure. The lake is also subject to strong east and west winds and depending on wind direction, the water piles up at one end and then runs the other way. The surface area of the lake is constantly changing, and the 200 acres of the proposed spit would have a negligible impact on its overall surface area.

At the luncheon, Jack Jones rolled out his engineering plans for the spit and informed us that they had poured a small test area about 100 metres long at the east end of Cherry Beach to test whether it would be subject to erosion by winter storms. They found that this test spit built up as sand collected along its edge. Jack suggested that we should grab it to ensure a footprint for recreational sailing in the waters to be protected by the spit, which would come to be known as the Outer Harbour. We needed to come up with a reason to convince our friends at the Toronto Port Authority to allow us to use it. It so happens that the Hearn Generating Station used water from the lake to cool their generators, returning the slightly warmer water back into the Outer Harbour. This kept the area ice-free during the winter. We prepared a letter asking that sailors be allowed to use the test spit for winter sailing, and the Toronto Port Authority gave us a temporary permit to do so for six months in 1968. We purchased eight Sunfish dinghies and sailed almost every weekend all winter long (see photo). It was a very bleak, treeless area housing derelict fuel tanks, salt piles, mounds of aggregate and scrap yards, but it gave us our much needed access to the water. The sailors are still there.

The Water Rat

We needed a name for our new venture. Gordon Norton was quite politically astute. He observed that since the Toronto city council had been taken over by the left-leaning NDP, it would be ill advised to use the words "Yacht Club" because he felt these words would carry connotations of privilege to the proletarian-minded NDP. Norton believed we should call it "The Water Rat" after the famous line in Kenneth Grahame's *The Wind In the Willows* where the water rat says to the mole,

"Believe me, my young friend, there is NOTHING— absolutely nothing—half so much worth doing as simply messing about in boats. Simply messing . . . ."

Norton also decreed that we should not have a commodore but a "head cheese," and the always helpful Bill Gooderham was so named. One day I went down to the barren Outer Harbour and saw Bill planting a dozen willow trees which he had purchased. If you go down there today, the 25-year-old trees are very grand.

So The Water Rat was founded. We needed a fence to enclose the area to protect our boats, which we left on the shore but The Water Rat had no money. Colonel Frank Ovens, our mentor and manager of the RCYC, allowed Cox and me to access the membership roll and send letters to our RCYC friends asking each for $100 to underwrite the cost of the fence. This raised the required $10,000. Sailing was now possible in Toronto all year round. The print media that first winter were very supportive.

Thanks to the Port Authority, which was breaking up old lake freighters, we inherited the captain's cabin and wheelhouse of the *Victorious* and converted them into a unique clubhouse. The structure was detached with cutting torches, loaded with the Port Authority's unusually large crane onto a truck, and installed at The Water Rat. We also needed a dock. Commodore Grant, who owned Overland Transport, donated a flat-bed from a semi truck, and it still serves as a very functional dock.

Maury Edwards, also from the RCYC, was CEO of McCord's Concrete. He said that most nights they had leftover concrete in their trucks and were dumping it out at the spit. If we would meet the trucks at The Water Rat, we could get free concrete for our boat park and thus secure the land. We had a detail of members worked out, and when McCord's called we would all hurry down to The Water Rat with our rakes, shovels and hip waders. As luck would have it, one night the concrete pumps broke at one of the big building sites downtown, and we got seven trucks each carrying 12 cubic yards of concrete. The Brymer boys, Stu Green and, as usual, my Mary were there to help. That is a hell of a lot of concrete to spread!

Norton was right. At a city council meeting, NDP leader Jack Layton stood up and announced that The Water Rat was the type of recreational facility Toronto should foster, as opposed to the "royal" yachting clubs. He demanded that The Water Rat be designated on new city maps. We were now kosher! I never told Layton that The Water Rat had been founded and funded by members of the Royal Canadian Yacht Club, which over the years has been the glue that holds all sailing together in this region. The Water Rat has since been turned over to its present users with no strings attached. I trust they remember that it was the RCYC sailors, together with the vision of Jack Jones, who made it all happen, and that it has allowed many entry level sailors to enjoy sailing on Lake Ontario.

Outer Harbour Sailing Federation

In 1972 there was a very close federal election. Prime Minister Pierre Trudeau was fighting for his political life. I am not a card-carrying anything, and I usually vote for people I know. I am an entrepreneurial businessman with a social conscience, and am equally as concerned about where tax money comes from as I am about where it is being distributed.

Mary's good friend Ruth Hutchinson was married to the Honourable Donald Macdonald, M.P., who represented the federal riding of Rosedale where we live. Summoned to a policy meeting for the election, I asked Don what he wanted me to do. *"Work for the opposition,"* was his tongue in cheek reply.

His advisers felt that the election would be very close and that the densely populated high-rise apartment buildings of Toronto's St. James Town would be key to the outcome of the election. I had an idea. The St. James Town YMCA had ushered in a new concept for community sailing to introduce newcomers to Toronto, aged 20 to 40, to the sport. It had proved so successful that it spawned similar projects out of the Westwood YMCA, North Toronto YMCA and Mooredale House, all operating out of the Toronto Island Marina. The City of Toronto, which owned the marina, was in the process of evicting them, however, and they had no place to go. Two of these clubs were in Macdonald's Rosedale riding, as was The Water Rat— Port Authority land is a federal jurisdiction. I suggested that if Macdonald would promise to allow the community sailing clubs to operate on the unused Port Authority wasteland east of The Water Rat, he would be doing a great service to the community.

I told him that the next Wednesday I would be giving one of my monologues on sailing to the St. James Town and Mooredale community sailing clubs and that he should make an appearance at the meeting. I would introduce him and he could make the commitment publicly to give them a new home. My own involvement with these initiatives came about as a result of the established sailing clubs' refusal to allow these new community clubs to race with them, ostensibly because they had a long-standing exclusive racing alliance. Bill Gooderham and I made it a practice to enter all the keen racers from the community clubs at no charge under the aegis of the RCYC, and in this way we were finally able to break the stalemate. The community programs have in fact proven to be excellent feeders to the established clubs.

At the Wednesday meeting, Macdonald signed up 30 residents of St. James Town to canvass voters on his behalf. The Trudeau Liberals won the election by one seat. Macdonald carried the St. James Town polls by 600 votes, which proved decisive in the Liberals' extremely narrow margin of victory in Rosedale—he hung on to the riding by only 400 votes! By virtue of our modest initiative, Trudeau carried the country.

True to his word, Macdonald delivered the land east of The Water Rat. Peter Van Buskirk, then manager of the RCYC, became the first president of the Outer Harbour Sailing Federation, guiding it through its early years, and was especially skillful in his dealings with the Port Authority.

For some reason the North Toronto YMCA did not take up its slot, so the Hanlan Rowing Club took over, adding a new aspect to the use of the Outer Harbour. Over the years they have tended to act as if theirs is the controlling use, and occasionally I feel compelled to remind them of Olympic rower Marnie McBean's observation that rowers sit on their ass and look backwards.

The Spit

Looking back, the continuing environmental story of the Leslie Street Spit is almost humourous. As the landfill piled up and rose through the water, debate began over who owns or governs the spit. It is attached to city land but water lots are under federal jurisdiction. Above the water, the land is under the jurisdiction of the Province of Ontario. It's a typically Canadian, ridiculous, bureaucratic snafu. Due to seemingly endless legal arguments and the tireless environmental lobbying, the spit has just sat there. As the landfill got close to the western end, gulls began to nest, and their copious droppings fertilized the land. Trees have grown up and Torontonians are now seeing birds nesting out there that have not been seen in 100 years. The same people who fought the spit now say it is the natural mating ground of all these birds. Sometimes it seems to me that the lobby group "Friends of the Spit" was created only for birds and birdwatchers. Another group was founded advocating that all the lands attached to the spit be left as wilderness, and that a small forest comprising a unique stand of trees about an acre in size must not be touched. I wonder if Bill Gooderham planted those trees, too.

Now a scourge of cormorants has come upon us destroying trees and scaring away other birds, to say nothing of all the fish they eat. I can scarcely believe that yet another environmental group has come out of the woodwork, intent on protecting the cormorants and allowing the havoc they wreak to continue unchecked. Surely a couple of fox families living out there on the spit could rapidly cull those pests.

In 2001 I was once again asked to try to secure a rowing course in Toronto. The establishment of such a course would have made for a beautiful urban park on the land north of The Water Rat from Cherry Street to Leslie Street, encompassing existing bicycle and jogging paths that make up the Martin Goodman Trail. It would have been economical to dig out the sand that was pumped there in 1900, leaving natural sand shoulders with small marshes for birds. Since we the people own all the land, I was optimistic when I went to see Robert Fung of the Toronto Waterfront Revitalization Corporation, but his advice was to forget about it because the political quagmire was so difficult to negotiate. It will be sad if short sighted politicians wall in this area in with condominiums or turn it into a parking lot for some other non-water use as they have done with other parts of my beloved Toronto waterfront.

City Crane

After the failed Toronto/Ontario Olympic Council (TOOC) bid in 1990, Hiram Walker and Sons, Ltd., who owned the Gooderham and Worts Distillery at the foot of Parliament Street and was an active TOOC sponsor, held a reception and dinner for the 1996 Olympic bid in their pub. Gooderham and Worts also owned a strategic piece of land on the north shore of Toronto Harbour where they brought in their barges carrying molasses for making rum. The RCYC had rented this land from the distillery for years to launch our racing boats using the requisite crane and dinghy launching ramps. (The RCYC lets all sailors use this facility because it is the only one in the harbour.)

At the dinner, I was sitting beside a Gooderham and Worts vice-president who explained that they would be closing down the distillery and turning the land over to their union pension fund for development or other uses. A light bulb went on in my head and I asked if the RCYC could buy the spare piece of land on the waterfront. He said he thought that would be possible, but only at full market value. Fortunately Roger Wilson, a senior partner at the Fasken Martineau law firm, was in London at the time and negotiated the purchase with Allied Lyons, the parent company of Gooderham and Worts.

Toronto Bay is unique in Eastern Canada in that it is ice free for almost 10 months of the year. This means the season for dedicated small boat sailing is quite long, especially since the introduction of self-rescuing boats and the sailors' use of wet-suits in colder weather. I hope the RCYC will be allowed to install a national sailing centre here to welcome sailors from all clubs to train as they have done in years gone by. Toronto Harbour is evolving as an exciting recreational area now that shipping and port usages have been substantially reduced.

RCYC City Club

For almost two decades, Bill Cox and I had been looking at options for a RCYC city club. Now fate took over and dropped the city club on us. Here's how it happened: In 1974, I was president of the Toronto Racquet Club, the oldest squash racquet club in North America. There are now many squash clubs in the Toronto region, with an active inter-club league. I was playing at the Carlton Club, an old and revered establishment, with the club's president Peter Ferguson, who also happened to be an old friend from university .

Originally from Woodstock, Peter was one of Canada's greatest badminton players. After he had beaten me handily, we sat down for a sandwich and beer, and the subject quickly turned to the health of various clubs. He explained that membership in the Carlton Club had shrunk to around 200, and the club was losing about $10,000 a month. The bank was about to foreclose. On top of all this, Toronto Mayor David Crombie had imposed a city-wide 45-foot height limitation in order to curtail uncontrolled development. This meant effectively that the Carlton Club could not be sold for a fair price. I proposed a solution, which was to merge the Carlton Club with the 2,500-strong RCYC. Peter immediately jumped at the idea and the merger was completed six months later with almost 90 per cent support from both clubs.

The Carlton Club had a swimming pool, four squash courts, three badminton courts and social amenities on an acre of land on Hayden Street within two blocks of Toronto's main intersection at Yonge and Bloor. The club was in an advanced state of disrepair, however; Ferguson described it as *"held together by the termites linking arms."*

The RCYC assumed the Carleton Club's debt of some $400,000 and gave memberships in the newly structured club to all 200 of its members. Peter Ferguson was always very helpful. Right from the start he had said that we must keep the new club running until we could sell the real estate to a developer. I started to work on getting the one acre rezoned under Mayor Crombie's new city planning criteria. Most sites in the city had been downgraded, but because our land was adjoined to abutting properties, its value had tripled.

Around this time, my old friend Jim Crang and his partner George Boake bought the Medical Arts Building on Bloor Street about a mile west of the Carlton Club. The 22 doctors who had originally owned the building had also bought a large mansion across the street in order to tear it down to create the space for their parking lot. R.G. Henderson had done the plumbing at the Medical Arts Building, so it was natural for me to go to Jim and George to tell them that we wished to sell the Carlton Club property when real estate values heated up again. I also told them that we had our eye on the doctors' parking lot as the new location for the RCYC

City Club. The local ratepayers had four requests, to which we readily acceded:

1) that we keep the new building lower than 45 feet (although a height of 90 feet was legally permissible);
2) that we clad the building in red brick;
3) that we slope the roof; and
4) that we not exceed the allowed square footage in building the new club.

The RCYC then sat back and waited for an upswing in the Toronto real estate market, which took off wildly from 1979 to 1981. We heard rumblings that the Crown Life Insurance Company, which owned land across the street from the Carlton Club, was looking to expand and wanted to acquire the club's property and adjacent lands to build a substantial office tower. The board of the RCYC thought that we might get $4 million—maximum—for the old club. Although several commodores seemed to think they were real estate experts and knew best how to proceed, I demanded that we engage the services of the highly respected commercial realtor J.J. Barnicke. Crown Life's first offer came in at $4 million. The board said we should take it. Joe Barnicke gave me a great piece of advice: *"Good deals take patience!"*

It was a very stressful time for me as I was caught in the middle, but I trusted Joe Barnicke. When the offer got to $9 million, Joe said we were close to making a deal. A meeting was convened between Crown Life and the representatives of the RCYC, Commodore Charles Parmalee, lawyer Roger Wilson and myself, with Joe Barnicke on the phone. The deal was done toward the end of August 1981 for $11 million, with payments spread over three years. In my wildest dreams I never thought we would be in that range. The RCYC was able to secure the doctors' parking lot and all systems were "Go." A month later the Toronto real estate bubble burst and we couldn't have got even $4 million for the property.

Toronto Historical Society

During the construction of the new city club, I received a call from the Toronto Historical Society. They had received a donation of 23 ship half-models which appeared to have been scorched in a fire. I phoned George Cuthbertson, the well known yacht designer and club historian, to go with me to look at them. George couldn't believe what he saw.

These models had been in the devastating RCYC fire of 1918, which destroyed the island club. Since then, the models had been known to the club only through poor quality photographs and a few scant written accounts. It seems the commodore of that day had gone through the debris of the fire and, finding these scorched remains, had taken them home and never gave them back to the club. His grandson had inherited them and, not really wanting to keep them, had donated them to the Toronto Historical Society.

The RCYC was very happy to get them back. We had a proper model room outfitted in the new city club, and we refinished the scorched models, some of which continue to hang there to this day. If you go over into the southeast corner, you will see one which was not refinished—it is left mottled as a reminder that it survived the fire. The curator of the Toronto Historical Society was not surprised that they showed up 75 years after disappearing. He explained that it often happens that the third generation has no idea of the significance of old items that are handed down, and so they eventually reappear.

In 1976, the annual meeting of the North American Yacht Racing Union (NAYRU) took place at the new RCYC City Club. The NAYRU had run sailing in both the U.S.A. and Canada, but the Olympics were becoming more and more nationalistic and each country now had to sail under a separate national yachting authority. The Canadian Yachting Association was already in place, but the Americans had been slow to change and continued racing under the aegis of the NAYRU. Paul Phelan, at the time president of both organizations, convinced the Americans to organize their own body, the United States Yacht Racing Union (USYRU). Thus, as fate would have it, the United States Yacht Racing Union was inaugurated in Canada at the Royal Canadian Yacht Club.

Chapter 4:
Flying Dutchman Sailing

≋≋≋

Tokyo Olympic Games 1964

In July 1961, I got a call from Commodore Paul J. Phelan, affectionately referred to by young and old alike as "P.J," asking me to have lunch with him at the RCYC on Toronto Island. The whole Club knew the reason except me. Before going to lunch, P.J. said, *"Let's go down to the dinghy docks."*

There, sitting on the docks were two brand new, 21-foot Olympic-Class Flying Dutchman dinghies—FDs—the most beautiful and enjoyable boat I ever sailed. One was purchased by P.J. for Skip Lennox and I to campaign and the other was purchased by Commodore T.K. Wade for John Eastwood, who was an excellent sailor. They were Italian Alpa-built fiberglass boats, exact copies of the Gold Medal winner from the 1960 Olympic Games in Rome. The FD was the first dinghy to allow the use of the trapeze, although that had been tried by the English on the 14-foot dinghy in the 1930s and subsequently outlawed. The crew was attached by a wire to the upper mast for support, which allowed them to stand outstretched with feet on the gunwale. It was spectacular and allowed us to grandstand even more than usual. P.J.'s only instructions were, "Make the 1964 Canadian Olympic Team."

Over a protracted lunch, P.J. explained that our grandstand performance in Bermuda the previous year had sparked the idea to help get us to the Olympics. Neither Skip nor my family had the money to achieve this goal, so the next few years required rather difficult maneuvering. We discussed insuring the boat, but P.J. decided we did not need to as it was new and a fine yacht. Skip and I trained all that summer while still racing our 14-foot dinghy.

Demolition

The 1962 Flying Dutchman World Championship was held in January in St. Petersburg, Florida. Skip was studying engineering at the University of Waterloo and could not travel to crew for me, so I asked Jim Stephens to go instead. Jim was the most physically powerful man I had ever met, yet he didn't know his own strength.

The greatest collection of world-class sailors imaginable was there, and I still keep in touch with many of them. It was blowing hard almost the whole week—so hard that some days we couldn't race. During the fifth race we were going upwind when I noticed that the lee deck was awash. I told Jim that the buoyancy tanks were leaking and we were sinking. *"Drive the Goddam boat!"* Jim yelled from the trapeze. So I did, and we filled up more and more. This boat was double-skinned, so we could not bail or even tell how much water was accumulating between the skins. It put such extreme pressure on the rig that the mast finally collapsed, punching a hole through the hull large enough to walk through and totally destroying the boat.

We brought the boat back to Toronto and I went to see P.J.

"Do you want the good news or the bad news?" I asked.

"Oh! The cut and thrust of life! Give me the bad news. I like to end with good news."

I started, *"You know the Alpa FD you bought me? Well we totally destroyed it in Florida."* *"Oh my God!"* was P.J.'s reaction. I continued, *"You must remember that you did not agree to insure the boat and it is a total write-off."* P.J. responded, *"Did I say that? That is terrible! Tell me the good news."*

"Well, the good news is that my dad would not allow me to sail your boat without insurance, so we insured it against your instructions. We bought the damaged boat for next to nothing from the insurance company and Skip has refinished it. Although it is no longer good for top racing, we have a buyer in cottage country."

P.J. was his most vibrant self. *"We must get a new boat. This time let's buy a molded plywood boat from Holland and get on with the project."*

The new boat was ordered from Van Duisburg in Loosdrecht, Holland, for delivery in July, just before the major Dutch and European championships. Our first regatta was at the little lakes, really dugout peat bogs, near Loosdrecht. It was an amazing experience for us, because World War II being still fresh in the minds of the Dutch, we Canadians were treated like royalty. This was especially true at the yacht club as Commodore Huisken's son had emigrated to Canada and it happened that I knew him very well. Skip and I drank copious amounts of Applesap.

Syndi

Flying Dutchman *KC 41* was named *Syndi,* short for "Syndicate," honouring all the people who had helped us. It was the most beautiful mahogany boat ever built. As is not unusual in boatbuilding, she was not totally finished when we took delivery; therefore we could not sail in the practice races. When she was almost finished, we wheeled her down the main street of Loosdrecht and launched *Syndi* just in time for the first official race.

Due to the configuration of the bogs in Loosdrecht, races start on a planing reach, and the marks are everywhere. As a result, we had no idea what course was to be sailed. I was engrossed in steering and pulling the new ropes. I yelled at Skip on the trapeze, *"Lennox! How the hell are we doing?"* *"Fat boy!"* he replied, *"Whatever you are doing, keep it up. We're first."*

We had been told that the team to watch was the Dutch World Champions, the Kraan Brothers, who were palingrocers—purveyors of smoked eel. When we got to the end of the first leg, we had to stop and wait for the Kraans to round because we had no idea of the course to be sailed—that was the only time I ever waited for anyone. We followed the Kraans and finished third in that race, having been slow upwind, which probably meant that our mast was not in the optimum position. When the fleet had come in for lunch and everyone was eating, we took our spinnaker pole and measured exactly where the Kraans' mast was. We then adjusted ours accordingly. In the afternoon we went out and won both races. That night as we left the boat park in ecstasy, we looked around just in time to see the Kraans measuring the position of our mast with their spinnaker pole! We finished second to them in that regatta and went to race the next week on the Ijsselmeer (Zuider Zee) at Muiden. The Kraans promised that if we beat them, they would supply a barrel of the best gourmet smoked eel and beer for the celebration. When we won the Dutch Open Championship, the Kraans threw a great party.

We were allowed to sail in the European Championship, and even though we were not scored, we won several races. In any event, we had to leave before the end because Skip had to get back to school and I had to return to work. We were very fast downwind, blindingly fast, under spinnaker. The teams from the U.S.S.R. were dedicated to winning, and were accompanied by KGB security. Their coaches followed us around the race-course filming us, no doubt trying to discover how Skip was creating so much speed. We were only doing what we had learned in Toronto Bay sailing 14-foot dinghies.

Harry "Buddy" Melges

We spent the summer of 1963 sailing in North America. In my sailing career there were two skippers who were in a league of their own. Harry "Buddy" Melges was one of them. The other was Paul "The Great Dane" Elvstrom, whom I met and sailed against later. Buddy Melges came from Zenda, Wisconsin—population 50, most of whom worked at the Melges Boat Works. Zenda is close to Lake Geneva, which is only about a mile wide by five miles long. The inland Wisconsin lakes have produced many fine sailors, but Buddy was the best, winning Olympic Gold and the America's Cup, plus almost every other championship. Buddy was an icon in the USA and had a very erudite crew in Bill Bentsen. A university professor, Bill was nicknamed "Hemingway" because he did all the paperwork. He attended skippers' meetings and would brief both Buddy and me. After winning both Bronze and Gold Medals at the Olympics, Bentsen served the sailing world for years as the ISAF racing rules guru, following in the footsteps of Lynn Watters from Montreal.

We were sailing in the 1963 North American Flying Dutchman Championship in Lavallette, New Jersey. It was a nice place to sail when New York City heated up and the heat bubble rose, sucking in the wind. One day the bubble over New York did not rise and we were sitting around the club waiting for the wind to come in. Entering the boat park, Lennox had picked up a large, discarded brassiere. He immediately went over and hoisted it up Buddy's mast where it stayed as we waited until about 3:00 p.m. for the wind to come in. When we were finally able to start racing, Buddy was first and I was second at the first weather mark in a fleet of over 60 boats. As we rounded, I notice that Melges and Bentsen had stopped without launching their spinnaker. Instead, they just sat there looking back at us. This was the North American Championship, a serious ranking regatta, so we knew something was up.

"Up spinnaker!" Skip barked as usual. And then Buddy broke up because sewn to the bottom of our spinnaker was the largest pair of silk bloomers you ever saw, with our number *KC 41* neatly embroidered by Mother Melges, as we all affectionately called Buddy's wife Gloria. Buddy won that regatta and we were second.

A Little Liver Problem

Around that time, I noticed that whenever I got emotionally excited, either giving a speech—which I did whether I was asked to or not—or in a fit of passion, I would break out in a rash that started in the palms of my hands and then spread to my neck and face. During a meeting at the Royal St. Lawrence Yacht Club, I ran into Dr. Archie Cameron in the washroom. He took one look at me and said, *"You are yellow. Go see a doctor."*

Our family doctor sent me to a specialist who, fortunately for me, was quite thorough. She put me through blood tests that indicated some abnormality in my liver functions. This pointed in turn to my gall bladder and she scheduled me for surgery to have it removed. Three days before the operation I underwent more tests. The specialist concluded that the problem was not my gall bladder but something else. The next test was a liver biopsy, which in those days was not a particularly pleasant thing to have to undergo. It consisted of shoving a small metal straw through your ribs and having it fill up with liver tissue. You would have to lie there on your stomach for 24 hours. One time she shoved the tube through my ribs and announced, *"Missed! Did not get any liver tissue that time."* *"What did the hell **did** you get?"* I asked.

When the results came back, the doctor said I had cirrhosis of the liver and asked whether I was a clandestine drinker, since my liver looked like that of someone who drank three cases of beer a day for 30 years. At that time I had never had any alcohol in my life, so there was no obvious reason for my condition. I was subjected to seven more liver biopsies over the following weeks which, if nothing else, should have landed me in *The Guinness Book of Records*. The doctor kept at me, trying to discover the cause of my symptoms, which were consistent with some sort of ingested drug reaction. That night when she came in to check on me, I casually mentioned that the only thing I could think of was that I used a prescription hair shampoo containing selenium—back when I had begun to lose my hair, my mother had sent me to a dermatologist in the Medical Arts Building who had prescribed a hair shampoo containing a high level of selenium. I had been using it at least once a week for seven years, continually renewing the prescription.

"My God!" she replied. *"That's it! Your illness is consistent with what miners get in Sudbury when they are overexposed to selenium in the nickel mines."*

The liver specialist really let me have it, saying that I should have read the directions. It was to be used only once a month under normal conditions and the prescription should definitely not have been renewed. By a stroke of luck—or foresight—I had held onto the original prescription from the dermatologist, that said to use it every time I shampooed and to have it renewed as required. She was furious and demanded that I bring the doctor to task.

I tried, but quickly learned that you never take on the medical fraternity; they closed ranks behind the incompetent dermatologist until I abandoned the attempt to bring charges against him. The truth is, all I ever wanted to do was to get better and go sailing.

I was bed-ridden for most of April and May of 1964. Every Thursday, Buddy Melges would phone and give me the news from Zenda. Mary McLeod, whom I had met a little over a year earlier, came most days and helped my mother look after me, probably the only bald person ever to contract cirrhosis of the liver from a hair shampoo. I was put on a strict but wonderful fat-free diet of lean roast beef and skim milk and, fortunately, my liver regenerated itself. Had the situation been left unchecked much longer, I would have been in deep trouble. During the period of my infirmity, however, I should have been training hard for the upcoming Olympics. I have never used that as an excuse for not doing well in Tokyo, but the fact is I was out of commission for more than four months while everyone else was sailing in Europe.

In 1964, the U.S. Olympic Trials were held at Red Bank, New Jersey, across the river from Manhattan. It was really hot with no wind. Buddy suggested we get out of there and rent a private plane to fly up to Newport, Rhode Island, to see the America's Cup trials. He explained how he knew Gardiner Cox, brother of *American Eagle* skipper Bill Cox—not my friend from Toronto—and he could get us on board *American Eagle*. We flew in a five-seat Piper Cub to Newport. *American Eagle* was out on a pier under very tight security. Buddy got in touch with Gardiner and after a half-hour wait, Bill Cox came down the pier.

He walked right past Buddy without acknowledging him at all, stuck out his hand and said, *"Paul, how are you? You don't remember me, but I sailed against you when you won the Connecticut Cup in International 14-foot dinghies."*

Walking down the dock with Bill Cox, with my friends Buddy Melges and Bill Bentsen bringing up the rear, turned that day into one of the greatest in my life.

Ted Turner

Like sportsmen almost everywhere, sailors have to bear the curse of nicknames. Mine was "Curly," Elvstrom was "the Great Dane," Harry Melges III was "Buddy," James Schoonmaker "Ding," and Ted Turner was "Terrible"—until he won the America's Cup in the 12-metre *Courageous* when he became "Captain Outrageous." Although perhaps somewhat eccentric in his business career, Ted was one of the most honest sportsmen on the water.

The best insight into his character arises from an incident at Alamitos Bay, California, in 1967 when we were sailing in the tough Finn Dinghy North American Championships. At the end of the last race, we were packing up our boats and three of us—Ding, Terrible Ted and I—were standing on the tarmac, where it must have been 120 degrees Fahrenheit. Ding pointed out that the prizes were only for the top five in the fleet of some 50 boats.

"I think I finished fifth or sixth," he said. *"If it's sixth, let's go to a nice air-conditioned restaurant for dinner instead of the hot clubhouse for rubber chicken."* "I finished eighth," I replied. "I finished thirty-third," drawled Ted. *"I'm going to the banquet—somebody has to cheer."*

Ted could not beat Buddy Melges—but then who could?—to represent the USA in Tokyo, so he decided to compete for the America's Cup. He sailed an old but fast boat named *Courageous*. Ted and his upstart crew won the right to defend the cup for the USA in September, 1978. I was invited by IYRU President Beppe Croce and New York Yacht Club Commodores George Hinman Sr. and Harry Anderson to view the final race on the Commodore's Yacht when Ted won the America's Cup in Newport, Rhode Island.

Ted got rather drunk after his victory and passed out at the press conference. He slid under the table, much to the dismay of the establishment, although the press seemed to be amused. Prior to that, Ted had come aboard the Commodore's Yacht to thank the New York Yacht Club for allowing his crew to sail under the NYYC burgee. He was already a little under the influence when he arrived. He saw me over in the corner and, leaving the beautiful people behind, said, *"Hey Curly! How is your liver?"*

"Better than yours is going to be," I shot back, surprised at his memory.

The 1967 World Flying Dutchman Championship was held in Montreal. In his usual way, Ted got himself in trouble, and he phoned me and asked if I could help him solve his dilemma. While the exact circumstances will remain between Ted and me, it's enough to say that I thought I could help him, and I did. He was appreciative and asked how he might repay me. I told him that it was my practice to keep a list and I would call my marker later—much later as it turned out, 13 years to be precise.

In 1980, Canada's Olympic sailors needed new boats. I asked Jim Crang, a very good sailor and successful architect, what we should do. We needed to raise $50,000 so we threw a fundraising dinner at the RCYC. Jim set the price at $500 a plate, which I thought was a lot of money. We had to find a dinner speaker to attract the deep pockets, but we couldn't afford to pay someone at that elite level. Crang had sailed against Ted in the 5.5 metre class and suggested that he was the man, Ted having just won the America's Cup. He had also recently launched the revolutionary CNN television network. There was no doubt about it—Ted Turner would be the perfect drawing card.

I phoned his well known secretary Dee Woods in Atlanta and explained who I was.

"I am a sailor from Toronto and I know Ted well," I began.

"Stop!" Dee butted in. *"Are you going to ask him to speak at a sailing banquet?"*

"Yes, that is why I'm calling."

"Sorry, Ted is not doing that. He has moved on to his business interests and accepts no speaking engagements for sailing banquets," she explained.

"Can I write a one-line letter addressed to you, and would you put it on top of his correspondence file?" I pleaded.

"Yes," she replied. *"I'll do that."*

I sent the following letter:

"Terrible,

I am calling my marker from 1967 and you will speak at the Royal Canadian Yacht Club in September 1980, on a day of your choice.

Regards,

Curly"

About two weeks later my phone rang. It was Dee. *"You sure must have something on Ted,"* she said.

"I sure do," I replied.

"He will come on September 20."

When Ted arrived, I picked him up at the airport and we had a nice discussion driving in.

"How are things going with CNN, Ted?"

"I am either going to be the next Rockefeller or lose the ass out of my pants," he said. Continuing to make conversation, I asked: *"What are you going to do next?" "Buy MGM,"* he answered. *"I have to own* Gone with the Wind.*"*

This he did shortly thereafter, and acquired an incredible motion picture archive. This just shows how far his brain was out in front of everyone else's.

Ted drew a great crowd for the dinner, and we raised $80,000 in one night. The round tables were set up with eight seats each. I seated Commodore R.D. "Bob" Grant, one of my great mentors and supporters, at Ted's table. Ted dominated the discussion, as he considers himself a history buff, especially on the U.S. Civil War, even down to naming his children Rhett and Beau. Turning from that subject, Turner weighed in on the subject of D-Day and how the U.S. attacked the beaches of Normandy. Bob Grant let him rant on awhile and then swayed back in his chair. *"With all due respect Mr. Turner,"* he said, *"you are full of it!"*

"If you are so knowledgeable, what is your experience?" Ted enquired. *"I was in the first wave of*

Canadian tanks ashore on D-Day, part of Fort Garry Horse," Grant stuck it to Ted. Regrouping quickly, Ted blurted out, *"I defer to greater knowledge."*

Ted owned the Atlanta Braves, who played against the Toronto Blue Jays in the 1992 World Series. He had married Jane Fonda, and Toronto society had been abuzz at the prospect of these two stars arriving in their midst. Ted Rogers, the most successful cable entrepreneur in Canada, hosted a luncheon at the Sutton Place Hotel for one hundred of Toronto's most influential people. It was a hot ticket affair. A few days before the luncheon, I received a call from Dee asking if I would go to the luncheon, as Ted wanted at least one person there whom he knew. Naturally, I was excited to attend (see photo).

The Sutton Place banquet room is on the second floor, so most of the guests came up by escalator. I arrived early and stood in one corner out of the way of the crush surging to meet the celebrated guests. Ted and Jane came up the escalator with Ted Rogers, the Mayor of Toronto, the Lieutenant Governor and the Premier of Ontario. His quick eyes darted around the room as he searched the crowd. He spotted me over in the corner and bellowed, *"Hey Curly! How are you?"* I yelled back, *"Great, Terrible! How are you?"* He immediately left the entourage, strode over to the plumber in the corner, and introduced me to Jane Fonda. She said, *"I know why they call you Curly, but why do you call him Terrible?"* *"Jane, pleasure to meet you,"* I said, *"but I have known Ted a lot longer than you have."* We then went into the luncheon, where Ted spoke.

Everyone was on tenterhooks waiting to hear about Jane, CNN, MGM and the World Series. Ted devoted a good portion of his speech talking about sailing against me in Flying Dutchman dinghies.

It might sound from all this that I am one of his closest friends, but I'm not. We met many years ago and run into each other only every five years at best, but he is a very loyal person who remembers old friends. Anyone who doesn't like Ted Turner doesn't really know him.

Preparing for the Tokyo Olympics

The 1963 Flying Dutchman World Championships were held in Bavaria, Germany, during the Oktoberfest beer festival. The Royal Canadian Yacht Club had set up a members' fund to help defray the Olympic sailors' travel costs. Club members have always comprised over half the Canadian Olympic sailing team, and most of them grew up on Toronto Island. We had already sent *Syndi* on ahead to Europe by freighter when we learned that the club's management had cut our funding, directing our allotment to some other club function. On hearing the news, Fred McKenzie, one of our stalwart supporters, immediately went out to the bowlers on the bowling green in front of the RCYC clubhouse, and hit ten of them up right then and there for $100 each, and off we went.

The regatta took place on Starnberg See, a mountain lake near the small town Tutzing. At the Canadian Championship earlier that year in Montreal, we had finished second to Ward McKim of Ottawa in a light wind regatta. In Bavaria, Ward sailed in the 20-boat Worlds, an event that allowed only one boat per country. We raced with the rest of the 100-boat fleet and finished second to Norm Freeman of the USA. Due to the large number of participants, the fleet was split into four groups, so it was a double round robin. Although we beat Norm both times that we raced him, we had one bad race against the other divisions and he did not. Nonetheless, we thought it was a good finish.

From the regatta in Bavaria in October 1963 until the Olympics in September 1964, we sailed at home. In Europe, however, it was a very intense season since fewer weekend sailors and more full-time professionals were trying out for their respective Olympic teams. The Canadian Olympic trials were held in Kingston in late June, 1964. We won easily, beating out Ward McKim, Tony Zegers from Montreal, and the Lemieuxs from Edmonton, among others. Immediately after the trials, *Syndi* was shipped to Tokyo.

The departure point for Tokyo for Olympians from Eastern Canada was Toronto's Malton Airport. Proudly attired in our Canadian Olympic blazers, we were in the process of boarding the airplane when all of a sudden a Cara food truck, owned by Paul "P.J." Phelan and driven by Ben Collenbrander, pulled up to the side of the airplane. Out of the truck spilled the Imperial Poona Yacht Club band dressed in their brass-buttoned blazers, white pith helmets, yellow Bermuda shorts and red knee socks. Down the plane they marched, making one hell of a racket. They had decided we needed an "Imperial" send-off. Air Canada was finally able to get rid of these nuts, and we departed in peace to collect the western contingent of the Olympic team in Vancouver en route to Japan. I remember how different in size the Olympians were. The gymnasts were tiny, but Roger Jackson and George Hungerford (rowing) as well as Doug Rogers (judo) were immense.

Japanese Sailors

Earlier that summer, four young Japanese students from Waseda University, who were in Canada sailing Snipe dinghies in Oakville, had visited the RCYC. A young Japanese fellow whom I had befriended in Tutzing had sent them to me—since they spoke hardly any English, he asked me to look after them. We housed them for about three weeks at the RCYC. One of my more mischievous colleagues taught them that "shitty" means "nice." They had a great time at the stately RCYC saying that everything was "shitty."

When we arrived in Tokyo, they were there to meet Skip and me. I didn't realize it then, but in 1964, if you sailed in Japanese sailing society, it was inconceivable that you worked in the plumbing trade. They had set up special events for us in Japan. One of their families owned a major department store in the Ginza. He took us shopping and then to his family home for dinner. It was a great honour, as Japanese people tend not to entertain in their homes. His mother was a niece of the Emperor. I remember the dinner very clearly, and to this day I love tempura, which I tasted then for the very first time. His father was a successful businessman and organized a visit to his special geisha house for the entire Canadian sailing team. No wonder I did not sail well!

Olympic Games Tokyo 1964

The sailing events were held in Enoshima. The sailors had wonderful accommodation in a Five-Star resort hotel right on the Pacific Ocean with Mount Fuji in the background. The other athletes were billeted in an old army barracks in the middle of Tokyo, three to a room. Skip and I roomed with Canadian Finn sailor Bruce Kirby, who later designed the Laser Class (see photo), and I still hear from Kirby over 40 years later, usually bad jokes that he signs, "Roomie." The hospitality at the Olympic sailing village was excellent. In those days there were no women's events, so it was all male except for the two wives of the Dragon-class skipper from Thailand, Prince Bera. One crewed for him, but I am not sure what the other did. Working at the reception desk was a beautiful Japanese girl. All the sailors tried to chat her up without apparent success, so she became known for the duration as "The Dragon Lady."

The American team was extremely well organized, and they raised the bar higher than any of us had seen before. They stayed in a separate hotel in order to focus on the regatta. The Olympic marina at Enoshima was overwhelmingly large with bigger facilities and more equipment than we had ever seen. After launching each of our boats down a large concrete ramp, the Japanese support crews would hold the boat in the water as we just stood there watching. Then they would carry us out to our boats like emperors, carefully placing us aboard so we wouldn't even get our feet wet.

The Tokyo Olympics, like the Mexico City Games in 1964 and Seoul in 1988, were held in late September after the Pacific typhoon season. A powerful storm hit before the Games began, however, and then doubled back on itself, blowing hard and wet. Ralph Roberts, from the Cowes regatta days, arrived as coach of the Kiwi Team yet again. His very unusual skipper Donald St. Clair Brown was team manager, and their bright pink boat served as the training boat for the Kiwi Flying Dutchman team. The Kiwis won the practice race and to this day, Don Brown, recently passed away at 94 and was still racing, says they would have won

Gold if they had been allowed to race in the *Pink Lady*.

On the day of the opening ceremonies, the skies cleared on a beautiful day. We were loaded into buses for the trip from Enoshima to the Tokyo Olympic Village, which usually took three hours on the small roads. The police cleared all the roads for us, however, and it was an exciting journey as. We traveled at speeds up to 100 kilometres per hour through the winding streets and arrived in only an hour. The Japanese had a manual that covered every eventuality, with complete instructions to be followed in all situations. When we arrived at our specified gate into the Olympic Village, the bus could not get through, being a couple of centimetres too high. Rather than risk a break with protocol, our driver got out, let most of the air out of the tires to lower the bus, then got back in and drove us through the gate.

We joined our national teams to march into the Olympic Stadium, which seated over 100,000 spectators. The athletes marched about two kilometres along a wide avenue before entering the stadium. Another 100,000 people stood on the curbs cheering, and made it indisputably one of the greatest days in our lives. I am sure this could be arranged at most Games, but it hasn't been done since out of concern for security. The Canadian team marched in and the stands came alive with thousands of fans chanting, "Canada! Canada! Canada!" My God, what an experience for a kid from Toronto Island!

The racing started in Enoshima two days later. It was blowing very hard and the seas were quite confused. Buddy Melges and Bill Bentsen, representing the USA, came around the first mark and hoisted their spinnaker. Their rudder snapped and they capsized. The same thing had happened to Skip and me in Germany, which cost us the regatta and the prestigious Manfred Curry Prize. After that disaster, we always carried two rudders. In Japan in those days, there were no racing boat builders, and although Buddy was a boat builder, he did not have a spare. Skip and I fetched our spare and offered it to Buddy and Bentsen who sailed well with it and came in third. We never won any medals in the Olympics, but our rudder won Bronze.

The New Zealand Flying Dutchman sailors, Earle Wells and Helmer Pedersen, had a bad first race and were disqualified in the second. Donald St. Clair Brown and Ralph Roberts decided that something had to be done. They also noticed that Skip and I were in the middle of the fleet and not sailing up to expectations. Don Brown decided that everyone should go to the Turkish baths, now known simply as a bath house. Lennox declined to go, but I went. As it turned out, the bath house experience did not help, as we stayed back in the middle of the fleet, but it sure helped the Kiwis. They sailed brilliantly and won a Gold Medal. New Zealand has since become the best sailing nation in the World, with only 3 million people—and 50 million sheep. I believe it all started in the Turkish baths in Enoshima, and I was there to witness the event.

Donald St. Clair Brown became an icon in New Zealand. "Brownie" was an extremely successful entrepreneur who detests endless bureaucratic processes, profligacy and ostentatiousness, one reason we were friends now for half a century. He has quietly funded most Kiwi youth and international sailing endeavors over the years. In 2002, with the encouragement and support of Ralph Roberts and Hal Wagstaff, the ISAF presented Donald St. Clair Brown its Gold Medal for his great contributions to sailing.

After the Games I had five days to see the country before we were to be flown home. Skip was homesick and did not want to accompany me, but one of the Japanese Flying Dutchman sailors, whom I nicknamed "Sake" because his family owned a sake brewery and because I couldn't pronounce his name, picked me up and we traveled by bullet train to Kyoto. That night he took me to a 300-year-old restaurant in an old monastery in the middle of Kyoto. I was suffering from tight hamstrings, which made sitting on the floor more than a little uncomfortable. We were having a great time when I heard "clink, clink, clink" coming down the corridor. It was Sake's father with a bag full of bottles. Sake—rice wine—is said to be best when freshly brewed, and he had come with the very latest batch. The second night in Kyoto, Sake's father took me to his traditional geisha house, where I had a great time. The next day, the geisha picked me up at the Japanese Inn where I was staying and took me to the famous Kyoto Kabuki theatre. The third day, I was picked up by Norio Wakamatsu, another young Snipe sailor, who took me to the ancient Shinto shrine in Ise. Norio's family owned a traditional Japanese Inn called the Futamikan on the beach in Ise. It was one of approximately twenty Japanese Inns where the Emperor would stay when he moved each year from Kyoto to Ido. I was given a traditional Japanese room and attended by a beautiful kimono-attired lady. Being from a rather conservative Scottish-Canadian background, I found it quite a change in custom to be undressed—and totally bathed—by this lady. She gave me a kimono, then Norio's mother entered and personally served me a wonderful dinner. I loved every second at the Futamikan. As I left to catch the train back to Tokyo, Norio's parents came to me with a tray of Mikimoto cultured pearl pins and told me to pick one for my mother. Mom wore it proudly for years, and now my wife Mary does.

When I arrived at the Tokyo Airport to go home with the rest of the Canadian team, I was walking through the departure area when I saw my Flying Dutchman sailing friends from Trinidad, the Barrow Brothers, Rawle and Cordel. Cordel looked terrible—completely worn out and not his usual handsome self. I asked him what was wrong. He turned around and, pointing to a lovely girl, replied, "The Dragon Lady." Also looking unwell were Hungerford and Jackson, who had won Gold in the pairs rowing. They slept most of the way home.

When we landed in Vancouver, the press was all there to welcome them home. The team leader demanded that they be dressed in their complete Canadian team uniforms, including the white Stetsons. Roger Jackson had lost or given his away on the Ginza. I lent him mine, and it appears in all the photos of their triumphant return.

Back in Canada: P.J. Phelan, RCYC Crane and Toronto Bay

When we got home from Tokyo, Cox and I turned our attention to establishing the facilities necessary to sail and train properly in Toronto. This theme of endeavoring to establish facilities for all sports in Toronto and throughout the Province of Ontario has run like an obbligato through my life. It remains a major focus for me because the facilities are still pathetic. Toronto's sailing season is much longer than many might realize. There is open, protected water in Toronto Bay from early March to December, but access to the water has always been very difficult. Toronto Bay lies relatively unused except for the 12 weeks from June 15 until Labour Day. Sailing and racing are good activities for the other months. Modern self-righting boats and wet-suits make it feasible, and most people like to see sailboats out on the lake, as they do not contribute to noise or pollution. There are only a few places in all of Canada where sailing is possible nine months of the year, and almost none of them are in Eastern Canada.

As my brother had pointed out the night before his untimely death, Toronto sailors needed a launching facility with a crane on the city side. At the foot of Jarvis Street, the shipping channel adjoined a piece of unused, available land. We had good friends at the Toronto Harbour Commission in CEO Ernie Griffith and Chief Engineer Jack Jones, and they leased it to us for a one dollar a year. P.J. Phelan was campaigning his elegant Dragon Class boat, which he transported on the top of a Cara truck instead of hauling it by trailer, and this meant we needed a crane somewhat taller than usual. P.J. offered to sponsor the installation substantially provided that we made the crane high enough, and we did.

P.J.'s Dragon was transported by Ben Collenbrander, an opinionated and resourceful Dutch-Canadian sailor. Like many other young Europeans, Ben came to Canada after World War II. Ben recalls driving the Cara truck, with the boat and mast on top, down a narrow street in Newport, Rhode Island, the famed New England sailing town which hosted the America's Cup for almost a century. Threading the truck down the narrow street to the launching area, Ben encountered a very tight T-intersection and found he could not make the turn without hitting a house. He needed another three feet to turn the corner with his long load. Resourceful fellow that he is, Ben figured out a way to solve the problem. When the lady of the house answered his knock on the door, Ben asked if she would kindly open her bathroom window. She was taken aback but—being a sailor herself—she did as he asked and Ben completed the turn with the mast swinging through her open window.

P.J. Phelan

From the time I was old enough to ride past his cottage on the lakeshore until he died in September 2002, Paul "P.J." Phelan, accompanied by his equally impressive wife Helen, was always there as a remarkable influence in my life.

In 1993, P.J. and I hosted the International Yacht Racing Union's annual general meeting in Toronto, the first time the AGM was held outside Europe. P.J. had hosted a great party for the 1971 Finn Gold Cup in a tent raised over his tennis court. I went to P.J. and asked that he and Helen host a similar event for the AGM. The negotiations went like this:

"P.J., we should host the IYRU delegates at your house."

"Oh Paully, that would be okay, but Helen will not allow more than 100 for a sit-down dinner. You must make out the guest list and get her approval."

I went to Helen with the list. She reworked it, asking that some of her friends be included, which raised the number to 125. *"But don't tell Paul,"* she admonished me.

A week later, I phoned P.J. and told him Helen had agreed to the guest list. He then said that he had checked the list himself, and had to add all his old crews, which now got the number up to 150. *"But don't tell Helen,"* he said.

The Phelans relied on Shannon Howard to organize their events. I met with Shannon and Helen about three weeks before the event to set the menu and the program for the evening. Helen said that she had

had to invite all her executive board from the Women's College Hospital, which she chaired at the time, to meet the Royals. We were now up to 175. *"But don't tell Paul."*

When I went to see him about who would make the speeches and toasts, he informed me that all the Royal Canadian Yacht Club's past commodores must be invited with their wives, which now brought the total to well over 200. *"But don't tell Helen!"* he adjured me.

Three days before the dinner I was beside myself. I phoned Shannon Howard and told her we had to meet with Helen and explain the situation which, through my eyes, was now totally out of control. We went to see Helen and finally got around to the point: the original 100 had risen to more than 200. With her unique smile and wonderful giggle Helen replied, *"That is just fine, as I have just ordered 250 chairs."*

What a great party it was! King Harald and King Constantine stood all night at the oyster bar. The lovely Catherine McKinnon from Nova Scotia sang sea shanties, and everyone held hands dancing around the tables. P.J. sat in his living room holding court and reveling in the aura of the evening.

When he died, I was accorded the great honour of delivering the eulogy at his funeral. I am not adverse to or intimidated by public speaking, but I was shaking. I had to do this for a man who had had such a profound impact on my life. The service was held at the Roman Catholic Holy Rosary Church, and it was filled to capacity. As usual, P.J. had had a hand in orchestrating the event: because he loved the gold vestments and trappings in church at Christmas, he had instructed that it be decked out like Christmas for his funeral. Who could refuse P.J. Phelan?

It is not customary to bestow praise on mortals in places such as this, but in P.J.'s case they made an exception. I trembled as I delivered his eulogy, my voice cracking under the weight of the emotion I felt.

Eulogy to Commodore Paul J. Phelan: delivered September. 9, 2002 by Paul Henderson

Commodore Paul J. Phelan! Everyone calls him P.J., no matter what their age. That was the greatest tribute all Youth could give him. P.J. was everyone's friend. P.J., like Elvis, or Tiger or Gretzky, no other name was needed, just P.J.

P.J. was awarded the highest honour the international sailing world could give, the Beppe Croce Trophy. It is given to those who have contributed unselfishly to our beloved sport of sailing. At the presentation, with his always present nervous giggle, he pointed to me, saying he remembered me riding my bike along the Toronto Island boardwalk with short pants, lunch bucket and a silly sailor's hat—which my mother made me wear—to the Royal Canadian Yacht Club Junior Club.

During his years as commodore of the RCYC, he lent many of his Cara staff to making the club work, and the club never operated better than during those years. As Bobby Grant always said, *"P.J. had more good ideas before breakfast than most people had in a lifetime."*

But as commodore, P.J. still had fun; to him that was what life was about. The English International 14-foot dinghy team came to the RCYC to challenge Canada and after the closing banquet, we were in the RCYC Annex making a terrible racket. We had sailed in Bermuda that spring and we decided that limbo dancing at midnight on the second floor of the Annex would be an appropriate tradition to continue.

Colonel Ovens, the revered club manager, appeared at the staircase and said the noise was deafening and that the police had been notified. *"Would you children stop!"* Holding the limbo pole was Bruce Kirby, designer of the Laser and P.J.'s America's Cup boat, and Stewart Morris, O.B.E., captain of the English team. Going under the limbo pole at exactly that moment was Commodore P.J. Phelan. The Colonel stomped away mumbling, *"Keep the noise down."*

Mia was P.J.'s beautiful Dragon, which he sailed often with

his beloved Helen as crew. One Thursday night, the rumour started that after the race we had to go to the bar of the RCYC as it was some Phelan anniversary or other. It was a light wind race, which P.J. hated. As everyone knows, he had a great command of all aspects of the English language and an Irish temper to go with it. Helen had put a tape recorder under the skipper's seat and recorded the whole race. When we got to the bar after the race, Helen put the tape on the RCYC P.A. system. P.J. was sitting in his usual armchair with his ever present giggle, saying, *"Oh Helen! I promise I will never say those things again. Oh Helen!"*

Everyone who came to the club in those days marveled at the height of the launching crane. P.J. had Ben Collenbrander design it so that they could drive the Cara truck underneath it with Mia, his Dragon, on top. P.J. had the dream of going to the 1968 Mexico Olympics, but sadly, placed second behind a young team from Vancouver. Typical of P.J., after losing a very close finish, he went to the young B.C. team and said, *"Take Mia and all the equipment and represent Canada well."*

Marvin McDill, a Calgary lawyer who knew nothing about sailing, decided to prepare a Canadian challenge for the America's Cup. His eyes were bigger than his pocket book and he approached P.J. for help. A dinner was set up at the RCYC and Marvin McDill came to town. P.J. was like Muhammad Ali going to a prize fight with his entourage, Commodores Gord Norton, Ced Gyles, R.D. Grant, and David Howard, legal beagle Larry Hynes, and me. About four o'clock in the afternoon, I got a call from Marvin McDill. He had been advised by some friends in Calgary that I knew P.J. very well and did I have any advice. The whole Canada 1 America's Cup project rested on getting P.J. involved. I responded, *"No matter how much is consumed at the dinner or how late it goes, P.J. is still smarter than you."*

Well, the dinner went as expected and P.J., with his Irish blarney, manipulated Marvin. It was a joy to watch. *"Oh the cut and thrust of life,"* P.J. kept saying, *"I like chattels, Marvin, chattels."* At midnight, walking down the RCYC dock, Marvin whispered, *"I wish I had listened to your advice."*

P.J. put forth Canada's two America's Cup challenges with great dignity. Marvin McDill and P.J. became great friends.

Last week, I got letter from a well-known New Zealand sailor, Ralph Roberts, who reminded me that P.J. had been the first chairman of the IYRU Youth Committee. P.J. had started the IYRU Youth Championship, held for the thirtieth time in Lunenburg, Nova Scotia, this summer. Ralph and others started a youth trust to give scholarships to young sailors from emerging nations to compete at the Youth Worlds. He waited for the appropriate time to ask P.J. to contribute. He chose the IYRU annual black tie dinner at the Royal Thames Yacht Club in London. Ralph explained the youth trust to P.J. and asked if P.J. would like to contribute.

"No," P.J. responded. Ralph dejectedly turned away. He was totally taken aback. *"Where are you going? Ralph, Come back here."* P.J. then said, *"Ralph, I promised Helen that I would always say 'No' to any more requests for money. I now have filled that obligation. How much do you need?"*

Every Tuesday of the IYRU Meetings in London, P.J. and Helen would invite people for dinner and it became a tradition. P.J. and Helen would agree before leaving Toronto that no more than 10 people would be invited, and I was given the list to extend the invitations.

Helen had to invite a few friends like Sir Gordon and Lady Smith, *"But do not tell Paul,"* she insisted. Then P.J. would invite the kings as, *"They do add a special atmosphere you know, and do not tell Helen,"* and on and on, ending up with around 40 invitees. We always went to Brown's or the Ritz or Claridges, as you would expect.

One year we went to the Holiday Inn Marble Arch. It took till about dessert before Julius Blankstein, P.J.'s friend from Israel and also a major contributor to the youth trust, to finally ask, *"We always go to the Ritz or Claridges. Why the Holiday Inn?"* "*Helen and her brother George Gardiner own it!"* I replied. He astutely changed the subject and asked, *"Why is such an unusual character as Paul Phelan so successful in business and other pursuits?"* I responded, *"P.J. has a unique ability to pick dedicated, honest and loyal people."* Many of you who are here today were astutely picked by P.J.

Commodore Paul J. Phelan!

P.J., thanks for taking a kid from Toronto Island in short pants with a lunch bucket and a silly sailor's hat, and showing him how to climb up the world ladder to a rung much higher than he ever deserved.

On behalf of all the young sailors you befriended, thank you P.J.

Thank you!

Chapter 6:
Mary McLeod

From the time my brother died in 1956 until 1964, life was very busy as I tried to juggle my obsession with sailing, running the plumbing business, working toward my Master Plumber's ticket and supporting my mother and father.

Every weekend in the winters, we went skiing in Collingwood. We stayed at Johnny Johnstone's BeaconGlo Inn, which we called the "Palace of Comfort." It cost twenty dollars for two nights, including two breakfasts and Saturday dinner. Bending beer caps at midnight was not included in the price. We always went there for New Year's Eve. In 1962, Billy Wilson invited a young acquaintance of his from Beaverton, a certain Mary McLeod, to join us as a spare lady. She had just returned from a year in Europe where she had become as excellent skier. She did not sail, which to me was an added bonus because the last thing I wanted to do was mix my social life with my obsession. I later justified this to myself by noting that Bobby Orr never played hockey with his wife. Mary was also a good golfer, and had even competed in the Canadian Open. This meant that she understood sport, but more importantly that she understood someone like me. Thus began a controlled romance that has now lasted over forty years.

Mary's mother Maude McKenzie came from the prolific McKenzie/Mackenzie clan of Beaverton and Kirkfield, descendants of Sir William MacKenzie, the railway baron who, along with Sir Donald Mann, built the Canadian Northern Railway (CNR). Mary's grandfather, "Big Archie" McKenzie (a Protestant and no relation to Sir William, a Catholic) married Minnie MacKenzie, Sir William's niece. Confusing, eh?

Big Archie and Sandy Mann, a brother of Sir Donald, built the Canadian Ontario Northern Railway. Big Archie died of a heart attack while opening another of his projects, the Shoal Lake water filtration plant that feeds Winnipeg. As was common in those days, the railroad had to find names for its new train stops all across the country. Camrose, Alberta, and Rosetown, Saskatchewan, were named after Mary's uncle Cameron and her aunt Rose.

Mary's dad Norman enlisted in the artillery when World War II broke out and although he was really too old to go, he fought in the Italian campaign. He refused to be promoted to major, preferring to remain a captain because he wanted to stay with his troops. Maude went back to Beaverton during the war to raise Mary. As the town brat, she had complete run of Beaverton from the age of five until she turned 10. Her cousin Judy tells the story of Mary going to church on Sunday with a straw hat that her mother insisted she wear. Mary thought it would look better floating down the Beaver River. As she walked over the bridge on her way to church one Sunday, she threw it in. Mary would have—and eventually did—fit in well on Toronto Island. Both Mary and Maude loved letters and would write each other twice a week, about what I never could fathom. It was easy to remember the McLeods' address—Box 1, Beaverton, Ontario.

Mary and I courted for three years, but my life was focused on making the 1964 Olympic team. I lived at home because the food was good, the rent was cheap and my mother would do my laundry. She was exerting great pressure on me to get married. Like everyone else, she was very fond of Mary. The pressure was intense and I had to do something, so I told my Victorian Church-of-England mother that Mary was Roman Catholic and that she was older than me—Mary had gone elegantly grey in her mid-20s. This relieved the pressure for a few months until one Sunday night at dinner, my mother had the nerve to ask Mary, *"What religion are you?"*

"Church of England. I went to Bishop Strachan School," Mary honestly replied.

The next question was obvious. *"How old are you?"*

"Eighteen months younger than Paul."

Needless to say, this landed me in deep trouble.

Married in Beaverton

During a fit of great passion, I said to Mary that if she was still around after the Tokyo Olympics we should get married. How romantic! Well, I came back from the Olympics and she announced, *"I am still here."* Being a man of my word, I suggested we get married on Labour Day, 1965. To this day it is one of the major arguments in our relationship. Mary insists we got married on September 6, but I celebrate our anniversary on Labour Day as that is easier for me to remember. Once every six years we are at peace.

The Imperial Poona Band marched that day in their outrageous uniforms of brass-buttoned blazers, yellow Bermuda shorts, red knee socks and white pith helmets, carrying brollies and numerous flags designating various constituencies (see photos). Billy Wilson was my best man. He discovered in church that he had lost the ring, but managed to find it on his person after I told him, in a voice no one could fail to hear, *"Hey you stupid S.O.B., it's in your breast pocket!"* The ceremony was saved.

In those days there was no traffic bypass around Beaverton, so all the traffic coming down from the northern lakes had to go right through the middle of town past Mary's house, where we were carrying on the party after our formal wedding lunch. Billy Wilson stood out in the middle of traffic dressed in his bizarre Poona garb, his white pith helmet looking very official. Holding the Poona flag, he directed all the oncoming traffic down a dead-end side street. Even locals who had lived there all their lives made the turn. Normie was laughing so hard he had to go to the back porch and sit down with Robert "Rabbit" Hague. God, it was funny! After directing about 100 cars down the dead end, Billy left his post and went into the house for another drink. Within minutes, the Ontario Provincial Police came to the door. Normie answered. They had received a complaint about what had gone on. Normie pleaded ignorance, and as he personally knew all the police, they left. For months afterward, it was a great laugh in Beaverton.

Honeymoon

As we honeymooned at the Brock Hotel in Niagara Falls, we felt disconcertingly old. The United States government had just initiated a draft for single men aged 18 and up to go to fight in Vietnam, and married men were excluded. Niagara Falls was teeming with newlyweds still in their teens. But there was method in my Labour Day madness. The next day we drove to Buffalo to catch a flight to Italy so I could compete in the Olympic Flying Dutchman World Championship. At the boat park in Alassio and San Remo on the Italian Rivera, all my sailing friends gathered around to meet the poor woman who had married Henderson. We had a great honeymoon there. We stayed right on the beach in the Lido Hotel and enjoyed the best pasta ever at the Alassio Yacht Club. Unfortunately, I sailed badly, which was no reflection on the skill of my new crew John Wright, the future National Hockey League player. His father Jack had prepared our terrifically fast 14-foot dinghy years before. After the regatta Mary and I traveled to Trieste and drove directly north through Tito, Yugoslavia. We stayed in a comfortable hotel in Bled before going on to Salzburg, Austria.

Aspen, Colorado

I have had the best marriage contract ever: if I promised to take Mary to Aspen, Colorado, for ten days each year, I could do whatever I wanted the rest of the year, or so Mary led me to believe. Mary had graduated from the University of Toronto in 1958 as a physical and occupational therapist. She had started to ski at Collingwood north of Toronto, and then went to Bad Gastien and St. Anton in Austria on the famous Margesson Tours. In 1962, with six friends stuffed into a Chevy along with their skis and other paraphernalia, she drove 33 hours to Aspen. After that trip she never wanted to ski anywhere else, a fact which alone shows what a classy lady I had married. In 1962 Aspen was a ski bums' haven, and we saw it evolve into the most upscale town in the USA. We tried several other ski areas but to us Aspen was nirvana.

The first year, we took Billy Wilson and my sister Sandra. Billy was a great skier but, although I could get down the hill, I wasn't very good at it. We stayed on the main street at the Snowflake Inn run by the Goodenoughs, well educated ski bums who, having come for one winter, decided to remain indefinitely. The Snowflake Inn was geared to skiers, not snow bunnies.

Mary and Billy thought we should go to ski school, which started each morning at 10:00 a.m. at the top of Ajax Mountain. Ajax is a reverse mountain, which means that when you stand at the bottom, it scares the hell out of you because the steepest slopes are the ones furthest from the top. The slopes behind and above are among the loveliest and friendliest ski hills possible. I was intent on making it into the same class as Mary and Billy, which was a challenge. I snuck out of the Snowflake and got on the first morning lift, the old Number 1A, to practise. I skied for an hour before ski school started before realizing that I was in the wrong area. I had to ski cross-country, cracking through trees, to where the members of the ski school were congregating. I made it with my ass dragging just as they were testing to see who would go in which class. Billy and Mary had already selected the instructor they wanted, an Austrian named Dieter, and they had conned him into accepting me. What a great week we had.

There are things about that week I will never forget. In those days there was no super grooming of the hills, a more recent innovation that I and my backside would have much appreciated. As one grows older, jumping off cliffs and pumping down moguls become part of the remembrance of one's youth. Dieter took us down Ruthie's Run, which in those days had moguls so large that you could disappear in them. When you fell, Dieter would say, *"Damn mogul-mice!"*

"What do you mean Mogul Mice?" we would dutifully ask.

"Mogul-mice are mischievous little animals that live in moguls and pop up unsuspectingly, undo your bindings and make you fall on your ass."

In those days if you told the barflies at the Mother Lode, Red Onion or Souper that you had skied Ruthie's Run, you were a skier. I made sure to let everyone know exactly where I had skied.

Dieter gave us his favorite piece of advice after he had skied down a reasonable distance and come to a stop, standing with his skis crossed watching the class come down. We would stop in a line waiting for the next instruction.

"To get a good tan, Stein Erickson always says, 'Face the sun!'" This was an important piece of advice because most of us, being very white Easterners, wanted to go back home looking fried so that all our friends would ask, *"Where have you been, Florida?"* "No—*Aspen Colorado, skiing Ajax Mountain!"* was a much more satisfying reply.

Dieter took us down the Face of Bell, which has to be the greatest ski hill anywhere. It is long and steep with moguls and trees all over it. Only my launderer will know how scared I was looking down from the top of Bell Mountain that day. The day finished with Dieter going down the Corkscrew. The first turn is more like ski jumping, but we survived. It is why most average skiers prefer Snowmass.

After the Goodenoughs sold the Snowflake Inn, we moved to the condominiums at the Gant. This meant we could walk to the hills and never have to set foot in a car the entire time we were in Aspen. The Gant was close to the new Bell Mountain cable car lift, which improved the skiing there considerably, especially for us at our age. We could ski the top, Copper Bowl and Ruthie's Run, riding down in the cable car at night and viewing the treacherous lower slopes, remembering how good we once were.

A must-see in Aspen is the Crystal Palace theatre restaurant. Aspen legend Ruth Whyte first took us there. She was a generous contributor to the USA ski team and the Aspen Historical Society. She told us how she had served as a judge at a local talent show back in 1962 and had placed singer Henry John Deutschendorf Jr. third in the competition. How was she to know that, encouraged by his showing, he would go on to become the world famous singer-songwriter John Denver? Going to the Crystal Palace with Ruth over a span of some 40 years ensured that we always got the best table. How we loved to hear Mead Metcalf sing *With a Lump of Peanut Butter on My Chin, Old Farts on Wheels, There's a Fairy in the Fire House* and *Felt up at the Airport,* among other classics. The food was good and the show beyond compare.

We skied Snowmass before it was developed and you had to ski there with a Bombardier SnoCat. The powder snow was magnificent, but I handled it badly. When you fell you had to spit to know whether you were facing up or down. In later years, we would spend a day at the new mega-resort that Snowmass has become, but we always returned to Ajax Mountain—our mountain.

Family Grows

For about two years after our wedding, it seemed that Mary's only remark to me was, *"I am pregnant."* John McLeod Henderson was born on November 11, 1966. Eighteen months later on April 24, 1968, Martha Mary Lynn arrived.

Summerhill Avenue

Our first home together was a duplex on May Street and there little John was installed. When Martha was about to enter the world, I decided we needed a house. Driving along Summerhill Avenue about a block from the plumbing shop, I noticed a real estate agent putting a 'For Sale' sign on a lawn. I stopped and bought it on the spot without even showing it to Mary. Her friends could not believe it. She simply told them, *"Why should I see it? Paul is in the construction business. It will be totally changed."*

It was an incredible place if only because the old woman who had lived in it for over 60 years had done nothing to it. The lights were activated by pull-strings hanging from the ceiling. The wallpaper was turn-of-the-century. The plumbing was out of the ark and the heating was still coal-fired. My father and mother were appalled—they had fought all their lives to get out of places like this. Their university-educated son and daughter-in-law had moved into what my father called "Bugs' Row." What they didn't realize was that this was a very trendy part of Toronto that was definitely on the upswing.

All the tradesmen with whom my dad had worked for years demanded that they be involved in renovating the house. The tile job in the kitchen and bathrooms was done to the highest possible standard. The plasterer was from the old school and, with a skill now long forgotten, hand-ran the cornice moldings. Most houses have three-eighths-inch water supplies. We had two-inch pipes, which made filling the bath a matter of seconds, not hours. I was sailing a Finn dinghy at the time, so I had a big door installed into the basement in order to I could store it there.

Mary went to the hospital to deliver Martha, the timing of which I believe she orchestrated so she would not have to be involved in the move from May Street. I moved us into our new home while she was in the hospital. Needless to say, she had to rearrange most things when she got back home.

An elderly lady lived next door to us. John and Martha named her "Mrs. Bow Wow" because she was always grumpy. One day when Mary was wheeling Martha in her carriage, Mrs. Bow Wow said to her, *"I feel very sorry for you and your husband."*

Mary was taken aback. *"Why?"* she enquired.

"Well, you have had that Henderson plumbing truck out in front of your house for three months now, every day. They are the most expensive company in Toronto."

Mary replied, *"I am Mrs. Henderson."*

John was always a morning person, waking before the rest of the family. One morning we came downstairs to find breadcrumbs everywhere. We had learned with John never to assume why he did things, because he usually had a logical reason.

"I am feeding the ducks," he told us.

This was a typical young Toronto Islander's activity. We loved to walk through the parks intertwined in that area and John, overly active as he was, would always be way out in front. Martha would drag behind and, even on the coldest day, would discard her gloves.

We have many fond memories of Summerhill Avenue. I think Mary would like to have stayed there, as she loved the neighbourhood. In 1972, I started to sail Solings, much bigger boats than the Finns. I had no place to work on it so I decided, while Mary was on the Island for the summer, to buy a new house where I could build a big garage. I found it a short distance away and phoned her to come and see it. She came, but was upset that I had made her come into the city. Mary was indifferent because she knew the house would not remain very long in its original configuration, and it has indeed evolved substantially over the years. Now whenever I suggest we move, she plugs her ears.

Sailing the Albacore

When Martha was 11 she came to me and said that she wanted to learn to be a racing sailor. She had decided to crew with one of the best known sailors at the RCYC. I was 45 at the time and thought my competitive sailing career was over. Going back that night on the RCYC ferry, I sat beside Brian Gooderham, of the well known sailing family. Brian and I talked about what I was going to do and, out of the blue, he suggested that I buy an Albacore racing dinghy and sail with Martha. He himself had been racing with his father Bill for several years. False modesty aside, I decided that Martha had better learn from the best, and her father was not yet ready to retire (see photo).

For 10 years, Martha and I sailed all over Ontario, competing in more than 500 races. It was as enjoyable a period as ever I had in sailing. We became very close—maybe too close. We won many regattas and Martha spoke at most of them, accepting on our behalf. She became a competent young lady but, like her father she was independent and opinionated. I think our best performance was when we came fourth in the World Championship against some of the best sailors from the USA, U.K., Ireland and Canada when she was 13. We won two races against more than 70 competitors. We could have won the championship, but I screwed up in the last race.

The most enjoyable regattas were at the community sailing clubs in Toronto's Outer Harbour. Their members are mostly enthusiasts who came to sailing as adults. There are several clubs out there that were originally fostered by the YMCAs. The most dominant is St. James Town with its famous Klinger half model trophies. Martha and I won several times, and I was very proud when they made me an honorary member of the St. James Town Sailing Club.

Martha made all of us so proud as she made the 2008 Canadian Olympic Sailing Team representing Canada in the Yngling Class 3 person keel boat, with Jen Provan and Katie Abbott racing in Qingdoa, China after finishing 3rd in the Open World Championship.

Hans Fogh

While we were in Italy, Roger Green and I had a long talk with the well known Danish sailor Hans Fogh and his wife Kirsten, about immigrating to Canada. In 1960, Hans had won a Silver Medal at the Rome Olympics in Naples. He was an accomplished sail maker, the kind of craftsman we sorely needed in Toronto. In those days, Canadians had to buy most of their racing sails from the USA. Many of us smuggled the sails into Canada because of oppressive import duties. Every so often, the RCMP would show up demanding payment.

Hans had learned his sailing and sail making skills from Paul "the Great Dane" Elvstrom, who had won Gold Medals in four straight Olympics in the single-handed Finn Class. Packing everything up and moving to Canada was not easy for Hans, as he was a sailing icon in Denmark, but he wanted to be his own man and Kirsten was pushing him to go. It took a couple of years to convince him, but we kept at it. Hans came to Toronto in January, 1969. Kirsten and their son Morten followed in March. When we went to see an immigration officer, the conversation went like this:

"Mr. Fogh, you want to come to Canada? What job will you do to support yourself?"

"I am a sail maker," Hans replied nervously.

"*SALE MAKER,*" spelled the officer, thumbing through his large manual. "We have no category for that."

"*SAIL MAKER,*" I immediately spelled out, as Hans speaks no known language.

"*SAIL MAKER,*" spelled out the officer. "*Canada has no need for that trade either.*"

Thinking quickly and realizing that the Canadian bureaucracy was at work here, I butted in, "*Mr. Fogh apprenticed as a gardener.*"

"*GARDENER,*" he again looked up. "*Oh yes, Mr. Fogh, Canada has a need for gardeners.*"

Hans became a Canadian citizen and won a Bronze Medal for Canada in the 1984 Olympics in the Soling Class. To this day, I still call Hans Fogh a gardener. He had taken out a $10,000 mortgage on his house in Denmark to start his business, and single-handedly reversed the trend of Canadians importing sails from the USA. He eventually grew his company to more than 60 employees. His two sons have followed his lead, and each has built a thriving boating business.

In 1969, Hans gave me one of his Flying Dutchman dinghies to sail in the North American Championship. He did not like it himself because while it was fine on starboard tack, he found it to be very slow on port. I checked the whole boat out because I found the same thing. When I took out the aluminum centreboard, it was easy to see the problem—one side was not properly curved. I installed a new centreboard and sailed the boat to victory with Richard Zimmerman in Toledo, Ohio, at the North American Flying Dutchman Championship. Hans borrowed it back and won the Flying Dutchman World Championship in Rochester, New York, the next year.

Following our honeymoon in Italy, I returned home with no idea what to sail next. The 1966 Canadian Nationals in the Flying Dutchman class were to be held in Vancouver's English Bay. I decided to compete partly because I had never sailed there before, and partly because, Mary being six months pregnant at the time, I knew my life was about to change significantly very soon. Billy Wilson agreed to crew with me, and we won handily, which made my decision that much easier to sell the beautiful *Syndi* while I was still in Vancouver. I felt I could then focus completely on the new arrival in our family.

Finn Dinghy

Mary was not sure, however, that she liked me not competing. Whenever she was asked if she raced with me, her answer was always direct: *"Oh no, sailing is the greatest husband-sitter there is. I take him down to his little boat and shove him out to sea where he drifts around all day. He then comes home tired, while I go off and inspect the art galleries."*

I had no crew and was now 32 years old. The Olympic-class single-person dinghy is the Finn. There was a competitive fleet in Toronto, so I bought one. The Finn is physically the toughest boat to sail. I was really too small and too old to start, but it was great fun and the fraternity of sailors was unparalleled. I would go out to Lake Ontario to race and come in through the Eastern Gap, where Mary would hand me our infant son John so that I could sail with him back to the club. One day during the 1967 Miami Mid-Winters when I was out sailing the Finn, Mary was pushing John in the baby carriage along the dock at the Coral Reef Yacht Club, her elegant grey hair blowing in the wind. One of the young Finn sailors' girlfriends asked Mary if her son was sailing in the regatta, observing that John was a handsome grandson. Mary broke up.

I started with the idea of just having fun—no surprise to anyone—but eventually became quite competitive, so much so that I had a chance to make the 1968 Mexico City Olympics, sailing in Acapulco. My main competition was Dr. John Clarke, a very fit, tough and accomplished dinghy sailor. I could beat Clarke in flat water and light-to-medium conditions, but he ground me under in stronger winds. Fortunately for me, it was a light wind summer and I qualified for the Olympics.

Canadian Olympic Regatta Kingston: CORK

I won the Canadian Finn Championship in 1967 on the

Lake of Two Mountains in Montreal in light winds, earning the right to go to Europe and sail in the famous Keilerwoche in Keil, Germany. Roger and Stewart Green were there sailing Flying Dutchman dinghies.

All of us stayed at a nice little farm house *pension*. It usually blows like hell in the Keil Fjord and that year it really did. I was in agony, so thoroughly bruised I thought I was going bad. After one rather trying race, Roger Green burst into my room and told me that when we got back to Canada, we had to inaugurate the same sort of high level regatta. Many of us had talked about it for years, but we had never followed through. Roger can be very demanding and on the flight home, we set up the plan. We figured that Montreal would never accept the event being held in Toronto, and Toronto would never accept Montreal. Nobody wanted to go to Ottawa, either.

We zeroed in on Kingston. Equidistant from the three other cities, it is really the best place to sail. We had great friends in Kingston—Barty Dalton, Sam Lazier, Harry Jemmett, Cam Jones and Michael Davies—and convinced them to host the regatta. President George Goodfellow and financial control expert Russell Scrim, both from Montreal, controlled the Canadian Yachting Association at that time, along with the ever present racing rules guru Lynn Watters. Watters owned a large printing company and was able to get everything printed that might be needed to support the regatta. Judge Livius Sherwood and Rod Miller from Ottawa were put in charge of the race committees. Terry Phillips named the regatta CORK— Canadian Olympic Regatta Kingston—and the event was off to a great start. It is reassuring to see that it is still vibrant to this day.

In August 1969, three weeks before the first event, Russell Scrim informed me that CORK would be cancelled unless we raised $5,000 immediately. The City of Kingston refused to pick up the impending deficit. Russell never minced words—his letters were in bold 14-type and never more than 30 words in length. You never had to read what he wrote twice. I have always tried to emulate his method of communication.

Bob Hawkes, a 14-foot dinghy sailor, was president of

Rothmans Inc., tobacco manufacturers. I phoned him in a panic and asked if Rothmans could help. Bob took no more than 24 hours to reply that Rothmans would step in with sponsorship of the event, and they sustained CORK for years. Without their help, CORK simply would never have happened.

Paul Elvstrom: "The Great Dane"

Although I had met him earlier, my first real exposure to Paul Elvstrom came sailing the Finn. "The Great Dane" went to his first Olympic Games in London in 1948 when he was an 18-year-old bricklayer. For better or worse, sailing has always had an aura of elitism, and the Danish Yachting Association at that time did not want to send a tradesman to represent Denmark in the first Games following World War II. Elvstrom was a dedicated and determined man, and after he won the right to represent his country at the Games, he won the Gold Medal in the Firefly dinghy single-handed class. (Boats sailed by one person are said to be single-handed; sailed by two they are double-handed. The unique language of sailing is rarely intuitive.)

A new boat was designed for the 1952 Helsinki Olympics, aptly christened the Finn dinghy. Elvstrom sailed it to a Gold Medal finish. He went on to win Gold again in Melbourne in 1956 and yet again in 1960 in Naples at the Rome Olympics, a four-Games championship string unmatched in Olympic history.

In the 1960s there were talented sailors in Puerto Rico, one of the finest places for sailing—especially in Fajardo, where the trade winds blow every day. Sailors love wind, and sailing is one of the few sports outside of kite flying that embrace the wind. Our hosts in Fajardo were Gary Hoyt, who has designed many boats and who was then head of Young and Rubicon for the Caribbean region; Lee Gentile, a construction business owner from Texas; and Juan Turreula, a lawyer who was later named a judge of the US Appellate Court. They had great influence in Puerto Rico and would invite Finn sailors to come there to sail, including Paul Elvstrom, myself and many others.

One year we were sailing off a beach in San Juan. Because I had had to stay in Toronto to work, I arrived only the day before the regatta was scheduled to begin. Most of the others were out practising, having been there for days. I was on shore putting my boat together when I noticed a Finn coming into the beach through the dangerous surf. The skipper jumped out on the shore-side between the waves and his boat. A wave picked up the boat and smashed it into his leg, shattering it. We ran down the beach and pulled him out of the surf. It was Paul Elvstrom. Fortunately, Puerto Rico was well prepared to handle such problems and they had ambulances stationed at every beach. After we had poured Elvstrom into an ambulance, I went back to putting my boat together and went sailing. I learned later that he had come into shore to get a stiffer mast because his was too limber.

Later that day, I went to the hospital to check on him. I walked into Paul's room only to see him all trussed up with his leg in an immense cast. Two sailors' wives from the USA were also there, and had evidently been chattering away all afternoon oblivious to my friend's condition. When Elvstrom saw me, a bemused smile spread over his face, and he said in perfect English: *"Paul, this morning my mast was too limber and now my leg is too stiff."* The two women were incredulous at this display of perfectly enunciated English. One stammered, *"Mr. Elvstrom, you speak English?"* "Yes," Paul replied *"I speak it well ... but sometimes I do not listen."*

In 1967, I was sent to sail in the pre-Olympics in Acapulco. Once again, the sailors were given the best accommodations. All the other athletes had been billeted in an army camp in Mexico City, but the sailors were housed in luxury in the five star Caleta Hotel on the beach in Acapulco. Elvstrom also came to sail in that regatta.

Conditions for the first race were a 15-knot breeze with the usual Pacific swell. I started to leeward of Elvstrom, thinking that if I could hang with him it would prove my speed was good, and I did. The problem was that the wind was slowly and constantly moving clockwise. This meant we were sailing the great circle route, with the result that he was second to last and I was last at the first mark. The first-place sailors were usually followers and were unaccustomed to leading. The shifting wind had completely disoriented the fleet, and 10 kilometres out at sea there are no buildings from which to get your bearings. The first boats sailed off to the wrong mark on another course over three kilometres away. The rest of the fleet followed like lemmings.

Elvstrom, the Old Man of the Sea, knew exactly where to go. He turned around to me and yelled, *"Henderson! Do you want to finish second?" "Sure do!"* I replied—to what most sailors would consider an insult. *"Wait, and jibe when I jibe,"* he instructed. (Jibe is a 90-degree turn to leeward.)

We followed the first boats and at exactly the right moment, Elvstrom yelled at me to jibe. The two of us sailed to the correct mark as the others sailed off the end of the world. Elvstrom waited at the finish line, making everyone stop. When the whole fleet had finished, we had an impromptu race back home. Our finish was as he had predicted, and now we had a marvelous, Pacific wave driven, 10-kilometre planing reach, in an 18-knot breeze back to the Acapulco Yacht Club. Elvstrom disappeared over the horizon, showing all of us how to sail a Finn.

Paul Elvstrom still lives in the house where he was born, in the suburb of Hellerup outside Copenhagen. His wife gave him four daughters, and he lives today surrounded by his grandchildren. I visit him as often as I can. He is a fine raconteur of great stories, filled with warmth and humour. In 2002, I was present at the Olympic Museum in Lausanne when he presented his Gold Medal Finn dinghy to the Olympic Museum.

Stan Leibel

In 1965 I got a call from my good friend Stan Leibel, a member of the Island Yacht Club, which had a predominately Jewish membership. The members of the Leibel family are great sports people. Stan's brother Jack owned the Gibraltar clothing company that provided our first stretch fabric ski pants, and was a Canadian squash champion. His other brother, Bernard Sol, is a renowned diabetes researcher whose son Allan is the best amateur sailor I ever competed against. Stan's son Lorne is an accomplished sailor and crewed for Allan at the 1976 Montreal Games. Stan's daughter Terry was a world-class equestrian and is now an accomplished television sports commentator. Stan once told me that horses are more expensive than boats, and assessed the cost of horses by the leg because that made them appear cheaper.

Stan was dedicated to making the 1968 Olympic team in the 5.5 Metre Class. (This illustrates more of the sometimes confusing terminology of sailing. A "Metre Boat" has nothing to do with length; rather, it is the name of the "rule." The length, beam, displacement, and sail area are entered into a formula, and if the numbers come out less than 5.5 it is a "5.5 Metre Class Boat." The length of the boat actually comes in at about 10 metres, or some 35 feet. If the numbers in the formula come out less than 12, then the boat is called a "12 Metre Class Boat" even though it may be almost 25 metres long.)

The RCYC had the only crane to launch boats on the city side of Toronto Bay. Stan asked if I would go to the Board of the RCYC and ask if he could use the crane for a fee. I told him, *"Stan, it's easy. Just join the RCYC and use it like all members do."* The RCYC would have let him use it for nothing, but Stan always paid his share and more.

"I'm Jewish," Stan replied.

"Oh Stan! I didn't know that," was my facetious response. *"What the hell has that got to do with it? You're a sailor and should be a member of the RCYC."*

Due to my rather uncomplicated upbringing and working in the plumbing business, where we had many Jewish clients, I knew that there was racial prejudice in Toronto, but never knew to what degree. Stan agreed to put his membership forward so he could use the crane. Billy Cox, Gordon Norton and I proposed him for membership. The RCYC commodore was R.D. Grant, whose close friend Eddie Goodman established the law firm of which Stan's nephew Allan became a managing partner.

About a month later I got a call from Stan. Sounding very uptight, he asked if I could meet him for lunch at a delicatessen on Spadina Avenue.

"*Switzer's?*" I asked.

"*How do you know that restaurant?*" he wanted to know.

"*We do their plumbing,*" I told him.

Stan drove his classic Lincoln Continental to Switzer's and, after the usual small talk, came straight to the point. He had learned that his membership application was scheduled for consideration at the RCYC Board meeting that night, and he wanted his application withdrawn. Stan is a much understated person—in no way did he wish to lead any activist movement.

"*Paul, I have not been forthright with you,*" he explained. "*Not only am I Jewish, but I practise and support my religion. I do not want to cause any problems.*"

"*What the hell has that got to do with your ability to sail?*" I shot back. "*If the RCYC does not want you, I do not want to be a member.*"

I did not withdraw his membership and it went through with only one comment at the meeting. Commodore R.D. Grant in his remarks to the Board said, "*Stan Leibel is the quality member the RCYC requires. I am proud that he has decided to join.*"

Stan went on to represent Canada at the 1968 Mexico Olympics. His nephew Allan made the 1972 and 1976 Canadian Olympic teams from his base at the RCYC, and would have gone in 1980 as well, had Canada not boycotted the Games.

Chapter 7:
Olympic Games 1968 – 1984

Acapulco 1968

The Mexico Olympic Games were held in late September to avoid the typhoon and rainy season in the Pacific Ocean, with the sailing events in Acapulco. Commodore Grant lent us a semi-trailer in which we transported all our boats. Ken Greig, also an Islander and one of our younger RCYC members, volunteered to drive the rig from Toronto to Acapulco a month before the Games were due to begin. It was still the rainy season and that year it was very wet in Mexico. Ken made a point of calling Cox—or me if Cox was unavailable—every day to report on his progress. He got through customs at Detroit easily enough, although he was initially stopped by a customs officer because the paper work was not all in order. A second officer happened to be a sailor, however, and waved him through with wishes of good luck for the team. The Mexican border was no problem at all, as the Mexicans wanted everyone to have a good time at their Olympic Games.

When Ken got to a small village near Guadalajara, he found himself up against an extremely serious situation. When he called, the anxiety in his voice was palpable.

"Hey Boss! It's raining like hell here. I am on the north side of a dangerously swollen river. The locals say the bridge is about to collapse and they warn me about driving over it. The problem is that if I turn around I'll have to go all the way back to the US border, and who knows what will happen. If I make it over the bridge, I'm in good shape to get to Acapulco. What do you want me to do?"

"What do you think?" I asked.

Ken was an Islander, being rather adventurous and not at all deterred by small problems. *"I am prepared to risk it as long as you take the blame,"* he offered.

"Phone me as soon as you can after you cross, and good luck!" I demanded. I sweated bullets waiting for his next call. It took two hours because all the phone lines were washed out. Finally the phone rang.

"Hey Boss! The good news is that I made it driving like hell. The bad news is that the semi started the bridge swaying. When I got to the other side I looked back and saw it collapsing behind me."

Ken arrived in Acapulco and unloaded the boats, then got into the tequila. He put the semi into a ditch the night before we arrived. Cox's first job was to get Ken out of jail.

We still see Ken quite regularly as he has served superbly as manager of the Mimico Cruising Yacht Club now for over 20 years. We enjoy going there for lunch and rehashing all the old stories.

I won the right to sail the Finn for Canada at those 1968 Games by being the top Canadian in 12 of the 17 regattas held that year, and winning the Canadian Finn Championship. It was a light wind summer and, being small and now 34 years old, I wanted light winds. The Finn dinghy is very hard on the knees and back, and this makes it a young man's boat, especially for those stupid enough to like pain. Nonetheless, the best sailors in the world, at one time or another, have all sailed Finns.

The Olympic Finn boats, masts and sails were supplied for us in those days, so we had little latitude in adjusting the rig for our size. The equipment was designed by North Sails in San Diego, where the winds are light. The rigs were powerful, so if it blew hard the little guys like Carl Van Dyne (USA), Gary Hoyt (Puerto Rico), and Jacques Rogge (Belgium) were at a disadvantage. That summer it blew hard, with a big Pacific Ocean swell.

I finished in the middle of the fleet, but managed to beat Rogge, now president of the IOC. He is always reminding me that I sat on his wind all the way up the first leg of the first race. My answer is always the same: *"Jacques! You cannot sit on anyone when you are behind."*

As usual, the sailors had the best accommodations.

Since there is no water in Mexico City, the sailing events were held in Acapulco. The press had been hyping that the altitude and thin air in Mexico City would make it very difficult for the athletes. It was hot and humid in Acapulco, however, so after each day's racing, we congregated around the swimming pool. One day, two women from the USA were complaining about how uncomfortable they were. *"My God,"* said one, *"It's hard to breathe at this altitude."* It was all I could do to keep my mouth shut—they were sitting one metre above sea level!

The Olympic Village for sailing was the five star Caleta Hotel, right on the beach within easy walking distance of our marina. The Mexico City Athletes' Village was situated on a military base. Sailors lucked in again (as we deserve!). Billy Cox, my RCYC Junior Club co-conspirator, had been appointed team manager and he was completely organized and supportive. His job was to supply everything we needed. He worked on the theory that had he been a better sailor, he would be out sailing. He had appointed Gordon Norton as his assistant. Cox always sat in the same place and wore very colourful red outfits so we always knew where he was. Before leaving Toronto, he had purchased various gifts, such as Canadian pins and cufflinks, which he could use to influence the Mexican organizers. He employed some of these inducements to procure the hotel's opulent penthouse rooms for us, where the evening breezes were cool and refreshing.

The organizers had intended to bus the 400 sailors to the opening ceremonies in Mexico City. It would have taken us at least 12 hours traveling there all night and then back to Acapulco the next evening in time for racing the following morning. Billy led the fight to get us an airplane. At first, the organizers said there were no planes available, but they later relented. They scheduled five flights, starting at midnight. The teams would leave in alphabetical order. How Cox got the Canadians on the last and most leisurely flight at 11:00 a.m., I never knew. The entire Canadian delegation was allotted only 50 tickets for the opening ceremonies, but Billy himself had 30. Since he was responsible for looking after our wives, he took all of them with him to Mexico City, along with the coaches and spares. He also convinced the organizers to give him extra seats on the airplane for free. The Mexicans named him "Señor Fox."

Studying the organization was Otto Schlenzka, the well known race official from Kiel Germany, who was slated to run the 1972 Olympic regatta. The Germans had not looked after Otto and he was about to be left behind in Acapulco. Looking ahead to 1972, Billy gave Otto a ticket for the opening ceremonies and found a place for him on our flight to Mexico City. Otto later spoke of how he went to the opening ceremonies as a Canadian Team wife. Billy called in the favour by getting our 1972 team the best rooms in the Kiel Olympic Village. I am invariably perplexed at the way Canadians believe they will be treated fairly just by being nice and not by manipulating the system like everyone else.

Acapulco Medal Ceremonies

The Medal Ceremonies in Acapulco were impressive. John Eastwood, Gordon Norton and I decided we had to do something to honour Billy Cox. Norton orchestrated a clandestine maneuver. The flags of the 40 nations were flown in an oval circle around the podium set up for the medal ceremonies, at the conclusion of which they were lowered with military precision, folded, and marched out of the compound by the Mexican Army. All this was done to the rhythms of one of the ubiquitous mariachi bands. Norton and Eastwood were to create a diversion so that I could steal the Canadian flag unnoticed. Out came the soldiers and I could see the folded flag with bits of white and red showing. I grabbed it and ran. Everything had worked out as planned.

When we got back to the Caleta Hotel, we found that we did not have a key. Norton would never allow any challenge to stop him. Like a cat he climbed up an eaves trough to the roof eight floors above the sea, and swung over the edge down to the balcony of our room. He opened the door for us and there we waited for Cox. In a solemn and tear-jerking presentation, we gave Billy the flag in his honor. Billy unfolded it, greatly touched, thus becoming the owner of the largest Swiss flag in Canada. I had stolen the wrong one.

Ben Lexcen

The night of the medal ceremonies is usually great fun with the Irish and Aussies trying to outdo each other. On the Aussie team was the well known sailor and designer Bob Miller. An orphan from the streets of Sydney, Bob was a true genius but a bad businessman. When his company went bankrupt, he said his name was not really Miller—that was merely the name that had been assigned to him by the adoption agency. He chose for himself the name Ben Lexcen instead. His close friends were allowed to call him "Ben Bob."

He always wore the worst clothes possible, which he usually purchased at Goodwill, a second-hand charity thrift shop. On the closing night in Acapulco, Ben wore a flowered Hawaii shirt, green Bermuda shorts and sandals. He thought the Aussie party was losing steam even though the room was crammed. Having imbided and knowing I did not drink, he commandeered one of the Acapulco Pink Jeeps and I drove him down to the Tequila-A-Go-Go in the middle of town. Ben went in and hired the seven-piece mariachi band. He piled them into the back of the Jeep with all their instruments.

We drove through Security quickly and with little trouble. Ben took his band up to the hallway outside the Aussie room, where he had planned to conduct like John Philip Sousa. The security officers, who were by then aware that something untoward was about to happen, reacted, demanding that Ben's band leave, much to his disgust. He found me again and announced, *"I am going to see Buddy Melges. Take me to the airport!"*

I tried to point out that the hour was well advanced and there were likely no flights scheduled out of Acapulco until morning. Melges had not competed in 1968 and was back home in Zenda, Wisconsin. Ben insisted, however, so I drove him, attired as he was, directly to the airport. At the desk, he announced to the ticket agent that he wanted to book a flight then and there.

"To where?" she enquired.

"Anywhere," Ben replied.

"There is only one flight left tonight and you must hurry," she said. Ben bought a ticket and disappeared through the gate with no baggage.

When I arrived back in Toronto three days later, I was still worrying about him. I phoned Melges to see if he had heard anything from Ben Bob.

"Buddy have you seen Ben Lexcen?" I asked.

"Yeah, he is right here. Do you want to speak to him?" The flight Ben had boarded in Acapulco was destined for Bogotá, Colombia. He connected from there to Miami, and from Miami to Dallas, arriving finally at O'Hare Airport in Chicago where Buddy met him and took him home. Not all my friends were as bizarre as Ben Bob, but many came close.

Years later, Ben Lexcen conceived the winged keel for the Aussies' successful America's Cup Challenge in 1983, when the USA was defeated for the first time in over a century off Newport, Rhode Island. As an IYRU vice-president at the time, I was involved in the dispute over the winged keel. The IYRU had to make the final decision before the race as to whether or not it was legal. IYRU chief measurer Tony Watts was responsible for all technical aspects and rulings on such innovations. Since boats are always measured in an upright position, Tony decreed that the winged keel was legal. The USA defenders argued that the boat should be measured heeling with the winged keel hanging further down, which would have made it illegal. The week before I was to fly to London to hear the arguments, I was sailing in the Star Class World Championship at Marina del Rey, California. I was asked to attend a confidential breakfast with the USA America's Cup syndicates, who lobbied me to vote against the Aussies. They had taken pictures of the winged keel and figured that the boat was very fast. As their final point, they argued that if the Cup went to Australia and was not kept in

Newport, the America's Cup would die. I explained to my American friends that I supported the decision of the IYRU chief measurer. IYRU President Beppe Croce let it be known that he was of the same mind. The day before the flight to London, the Americans withdrew their appeal and the Cup went on as scheduled. The Aussies won in an exciting series. Since that victory, the America's Cup has been held in Fremantle, Australia; San Diego, California; Auckland, New Zealand; and Valencia, Spain. It is now more popular than ever, but it was Ben Lexcen's revolutionary winged keel that changed the course of racing history. Ben died of a heart attack in his 50s, much too young.

The Other Paul Henderson

I have not infrequently found myself confronted by situations over which I have no control. The emergence of another Paul Henderson was one of them. There are almost as many Hendersons in the Toronto region as Smiths, Joneses or Wongs. Paul is a very common name, so it is not surprising to find a number of men named Paul Henderson in the city.

Hockey is like a cult in Canada. We live and die by the international results of our national game, also by who wins the Stanley Cup, and the depressing antics of the Toronto Maple Leafs, now well into the fifth decade since they last won Lord Stanley's coveted prize. In the 1960s and 1970s, Canada's supremacy was being challenged by the Soviets, but our professional players were not allowed to play in the Olympics or World Championships. The Soviet players were all well paid members of the Red Army, the American players were all on substantial college scholarships, but a Canadian player who was openly paid $100 a week was considered to be a professional. This was sport hypocrisy at its worst.

Canada's pros were finally allowed to play against the USSR in 1972. Expert opinion was that Canada would win easily. On the team was a talented player named Paul Henderson. He was a good skater and shooter, skills which stood him in good stead on the larger international ice surface. The first four games were played in Canada, at the end of which Canada trailed two games to one, with one game tied. They then went to Moscow where they lost the first game 5-4, so now Canada was down 3-1. This meant Canada had to win all three remaining games. They won the first two, edging the Soviets in each game by one goal, the winning goal being scored in each game by Paul Henderson. The final, decisive game was tied with only seconds left on the clock when Paul Henderson again scored the tie-breaker at 19:26 of the third period. It was the greatest day in the history of Canadian sport.

Immediately, my telephone started to ring off the hook with young girls wanting to meet the hockey star. He has long curly black hair and an athletic shape. By contrast, I am bald, short and squat. I had to change my listing in the telephone book to P. Henderson, but even to this day, fans phone all the listings in the book asking for him.

I have also used it to my advantage. When I phone a business and state my name, asking to be put through to a senior executive, the receptionist quite often asks, *"Are you **the** Paul Henderson?"*

My answer is always the same: *"I sure am!"*

Coming through customs at Pearson Airport in Toronto, the customs officer, on reading the name on my passport, invariably welcomes me home and whisks me through without any problem.

There are many stories I could tell about being mistaken for this Canadian hockey icon. During the Olympic bid process, I was invited to the Conn Smythe dinner, a fund-raising event held each year for Easter Seals, a charity which supports crippled children. I was asked to sit at the celebrities' table with two rows of sport dignitaries. The high-profile athletes sat in the back row—Darryl Sittler, Pinball Clemons, Ernie Whitt, Ken Dryden, Marnie McBean and many others. I was seated in the lower row and, like the others, had a name card in front of me. At the end of the dinner, a rather matronly lady sashayed up to my seat. *"You are my husband's hero after the goal in 1972. He will be so happy, because he has lost his hair also. Would you sign my program for him?"* she asked. I did, and I always do, because it is easier than disillusioning the fans.

I was invited to attend the opening of the Hockey Hall of Fame in Toronto. All the legends of hockey were there and it was a great privilege to stand among them. Carl Brewer, the legendary Toronto Maple Leafs player from the great 1960s cup-winning dynasty, was very erudite and marched to his own drummer. He was bald and had the same shape as me. I was walking through the exhibits when a cub reporter stopped me and asked, *"Are you Carl Brewer?"* *"No! I am Paul Henderson,"* I replied. The poor reporter was speechless.

At a golf tournament during the Olympic bid process, hockey's Paul Henderson said that he would be glad when the Olympic bid was over, because he was sick and tired of being asked for tickets to the opening ceremonies.

I have met him several times and have no problem carrying the same name. He is an elegant contributor to the community and to the lives of athletes. He is now a minister of the church and is involved in the Campus Crusade for Christ.

Munich 1972

For the 1972 Munich Olympics, Billy Cox was again manager of the Canadian team, Gordon Norton was assistant manager, and I was asked to be the coach. The sailing events were held in the Kielerfjord in northern Germany, because Munich itself had no water. The venue in Kiel was awe-inspiring. The organizers had used the occasion of the Olympics to revitalize an entire section of their waterfront with an extensive new marina and housing complex. The Olympic Village was comprised of a number of high-rise apartments, but they were severely lacking in elevators. Cox had researched this beforehand, however, and was able to obtain accommodations for the Canadian team on the third floor. This was high enough to be quiet, but low enough so we could walk up easily. Thanks to Cox, the Canadian sailors were again well situated.

Germany was intent on hosting the world in the friendliest Games ever. I have always said that the Mexicans had tried to prove to the world in 1968 that they were as efficient as the Germans, and that the Germans in 1972 had tried to prove to the world they were as laid back and friendly as the Mexicans. The food was by far the best ever and the ambience very friendly. The security was relaxed—so much so that the wives of some of the Australian sailors were able to pole-vault over the fence to be with their husbands. (One of them was Rasa Bertrand, whose husband John won a Bronze Medal in the Finn class and went on to skipper Australia to its first America's Cup victory.)

Opening Ceremonies: Munich

As usual, Cox had extra tickets to the opening ceremonies, but not enough to take all the spares and the wives. He was three or four tickets short. Norton worked out a system to allocate the tickets: each team member was called into Cox's room and offered a ticket for $200. If the sailor reneged and said he did not want to pay that much to take his wife, the offer was withdrawn. If the sailor was prepared to pay, Billy gave him the ticket for free. His logic was that if you weren't prepared to pay for your wife's ticket, then clearly it was not a priority for you. Off we went to Munich, and it was a great experience for us all.

Olympic Sailing Regatta: Kiel

Kiel and the Baltic are known for storms and high winds, so everyone had trained for such conditions. In 1972, however, it was hotter in the Baltic than it in the Mediterranean. While the bikinis—or lack thereof—on the beach were enticing, the unusual weather caused a problem for all the sailors in that there is simply no wind when it is that hot. The 1972 Olympics proved to be the only Games where some of the sailing races were not completed, proving the adage that the wind conditions at the Olympics have historically been almost exactly the opposite of pre-Games forecasts.

On the day before the first race, I went down to the boat park as the kindly old coach and asked all the Canadian sailors what wind conditions they wanted. The Soling crew from Vancouver answered, *"We couldn't care less—let's just get racing!"* I knew that skipper Dave Miller and crew John Ekels and Paul Cote were ready, and they proved it by winning a Bronze Medal (see photo).

Greenpeace

Paul Cote is a large and powerful man with an unusual sense of humour and a great social conscience. His father was chancellor of Simon Fraser University. As law students, Paul and a few of his friends were disturbed by the French nuclear tests in the open air of the Aleutian Islands.

They begged for donations on the streets of Vancouver and raised enough money to buy an old fishing trawler. Cote, recently married and with a new child, hosted a meeting of the group in the basement of his house. During a heated debate over the proposed name of their endeavour, Cote's wife looked up from her ironing and suggested, *"Why don't you call it what it is—Greenpeace."*

They sailed the trawler up the British Columbia coast and sat under the French bomber yelling, *"Don't drop that bloody thing!"* I am very proud that a Canadian Olympic medalist sailor started "Greenpeace." Sailors are environmentalists almost by the definition, since we use the sea and the wind as we find them.

Tall Ships

On the middle Sunday of the Games, the organizers scheduled the "Parade of the Tall Ships," with more than 100 square-riggers and other ships sailing down the Kielerfjord. Some two million people lined the shore in the early morning haze that heralded a marvelous sunny day.

The Canadian team had rented a small 20-foot Swedish motor boat as our equipment boat. Cox had obtained some food containers and quietly filled them for our lunch from the breakfast buffet. Norton had brought a Canadian flag so large that when it flew it was longer than our boat. We had asked P.J. Phelan to come with us to Kiel, and he served as commander of the escapade. I was the boat boy and driver. Out we went to sea with our wives and the Canadian Consul General in the small boat, the oversized Canadian flag flying proudly from a spare mast that had been hijacked from Ian Bruce's Star boat.

It was a spectacular day. The *Christian Radich, Danmark, Dar Pomorza, Eagle, Gorch Fock, Winston Churchill* and about a hundred other classic sailing ships emerged out of the mist. P.J. took over: *"Oh, the cut and thrust of life! Paully, get closer!"* So I drove the small boat to within 100 metres of the parade of ships. *"Paully, I want to get closer,"* P.J. demanded, so I drove to within 50 metres. The US Navy *Eagle* came past. Taken from Germany after World War II by the USA in war reparations, she was the sister ship of the *Gorch Fock*, and had been used since then as their cadet training ship. *"Get closer, Paully. I want to see the sailors on board the Eagle,"* P.J. again demanded. So I drove our little twenty-foot boat right under the bowsprit of the *Eagle*, our big Canadian flag billowing out in the wind. P.J. was very happy. As we came out the lee side, we noticed that the captain of the *Eagle* had hoisted naval signal flags up in the rigging that telegraphed for all to see: "Carry on Canada." What a great day that was!

Black Tuesday

Then came Black Tuesday and the massacre of the Israeli athletes. By Wednesday morning, we were all aware of the tragedy. What had been a festive atmosphere suddenly changed, and we found ourselves in a deep depression. Cox, Norton and I were sitting in our team room when a call came from the Canadian Olympic team manager in Munich. The IOC was asking us to poll our athletes on what should be done. They gave us three alternatives:

Cancel the Games and go home;

Cancel all events in which Israeli athletes had been scheduled to compete;

Hold three days of mourning and then continue with a limited schedule.

I was delegated to poll the Canadian sailors and report

back. I had no idea what we should do. I looked out the third floor window and saw our Dragon skipper, Allan Leibel, sitting alone. I thought that Allan, being Jewish, was likely the only person with the sensitivity and insight to know what we should do. I went down and sat beside him, and asked his advice. He immediately replied, *"We should be racing today, for if we do not, the terrorists win."* That became the official position of the Canadian sailing team. The next day the IOC resumed the Games.

[Years later, as president of the International Sailing Federation (ISAF), I had to make a tough decision, and Allan Leibel's insight at Kiel governed my thinking. ISAF had scheduled the 1999 Windsurfing World Championship in Haifa, Israel. Terrorists were blowing up buses at that time and many countries did not want to send their teams. I announced that as ISAF president, I was going to be there at the opening ceremonies and I hoped that all the teams would join me. As it turned out, all but a few came and the event was a great success.

I really did not understand the political issues of the region. In my naivety, I decided to visit Beirut, Lebanon, on my way to Haifa. On the map, Beirut looked to me to be only a few miles from Haifa. While Beirut had been largely destroyed, I found its people friendly, the food superb, and the women most elegantly dressed. Traveling to Haifa from Beirut was not easy, however. I was told not to let anyone know I had been in Lebanon or was going to Israel, and I was warned not to get my passport stamped. My Lebanese hosts advised me to fly to Amman, Jordan, and from there to travel by taxi to Israel. As I left Beirut, I was presented with a five-foot wide carving of cedar from Lebanon in recognition of my visit.

When I finally arrived at the new bridge to cross the river into Israel, I carried the cedar carving under my arm, dragging my small carry-on bag with me. The Israeli border official never asked where I had been. I was extremely happy to see Zvi Ziblatt, who drove me to the regatta. At the reception, I told the story of the Munich Games and Allan Leibel's advice, much to the delight of the appreciative Israeli officials. IOC Israeli member Alex Gilady then drove me to Tel

Aviv, where he took me to his office to show me a map of his mother's amazing trek on foot from Russia to Israel. Then he pointed out the place where she gave birth to him along the way.]

Closing Ceremonies

The closing ceremonies in Kiel were friendly. The athletes were finally able to enjoy their accomplishments and one another's friendship. Cote and Don Barnes, one of the spare boatmen, were walking from the customary Aussie party over to the obligatory Irish party when somebody from the seventh floor of one of the residences threw a bucket of water on them. That both Barnes and Cote were patently large, tough men made the bucket-throw seem imprudent and ill advised, to say the least. They took the elevator to the seventh floor. When the perpetrator saw them coming down the hall, he hurriedly locked himself in his room. Cote and Barnes applied their large shoulders to the door, causing the door and the frame to cave in, along with everything that had been attached to it. Cowering in his room with his girlfriend was a small, sparsely clad member of the French team. They were scared out of their wits. Barnes and Cote looked around and saw that the lovers had been enjoying a bottle of fine Napoleon, which, they allowed, must have contributed in no small measure to the giddy Frenchman's momentary lapse of judgment. Giving him the benefit of the doubt, they sat down and graciously accepted the snifters of cognac politely proffered by the penitent prankster.

Montreal 1976: Sailing at Kingston, Ontario

In 1970, Montreal was awarded the 1976 Olympic Games. I was appointed Canadian delegate to the International Yacht Racing Union, and would be actively involved in the organization of the Olympic sailing event. Due to the resounding success of the Canadian Olympic Regatta Kingston (CORK) and the availability of the residences at Queen's University during the summer, Kingston was designated the sailing venue. Since this would be the only Olympic venue outside the Province of Quebec, a group was formed to ensure that the sailing events would not be forgotten. Doug Keary, Bill Cox, Gordon Norton and I comprised the group's Toronto contingent, and coincidentally—or so it seemed—we all happened to be political activists. The group's members from Kingston, Montreal and Ottawa, on the other hand, were the nice guys who would be running the events.

Kingston Mayor Val Swain hosted a reception in 1971 to announce the project. Montreal Mayor Jean Drapeau was in attendance, but nobody had to announce his arrival because there was something about the aura that surrounded him that made everyone aware of his presence. Drapeau played a very disturbing card—he would not confirm that Kingston would be the venue for the sailing events. When he returned to Montreal, he told the press that he wanted everything in Quebec and announced that the sailing events would be held at Lac St Jean. In fact, he delayed making a decision on the venue because his budget for sailing was only one million dollars. He wanted the Government of Ontario to pick up the rest of the tab.

Doug Keary was not only a competitive sailor, but as owner of the construction and development company InterNorth, he was also experienced in cost analysis and project management. Doug was concerned about Drapeau's announcement, and convinced our group to engage Project Planning Associates of Toronto, led by Martin Dake and George Yost, to do a feasibility study that would define the options for the sailing venue. Fortunately Cam Jones, one of the leaders at the Kingston Yacht Club, was director of engineering facilities at Queen's University, and he agreed with Keary's assessment. In fact, without Cam Jones the Kingston Olympic sailing regatta would most likely never have happened.

In 1971, a number of our group traveled to Kiel, Germany, to study the organization required for the 1972 Olympic regatta. The German organizers revealed everything to us, including all costs and staffing requirements. Hanna-Marie Bense and Otto Schlenzka, our friend from Acapulco, were extremely helpful. We were staggered at the requirements. Anyone who claims to know how to run the Olympic Games—especially the sailing—is a fool. Seated beside me on the flight back home was Barty Dalton, elder statesman of the sailing fraternity in Kingston. When we were over Bremerhaven, he told me that the last time he flew here it had been on a mission to bomb the city. I told him I never understood World War II—or any war, for that matter.

Project Planning Associates completed their analysis of all potential venues in and around Kingston. There were several available, but Mayor Swain demanded that we select one within the boundaries of the city. (Political decisions tend to have an impact on Olympic decisions.) One of the proposed sites was Portsmouth Harbour, an ugly, unused marsh abutting the Kingston penitentiary with several derelict boats awash in the bog. I must admit that I thought it was a terrible place. Considering all possible sites, did we have to put the Olympic harbour beside a penitentiary? The local residents were used to the penitentiary, however, and were quite amenable to Portsmouth Harbour. Keary suggested that windows be installed in the large grey walls so the inmates could add to the number of spectators.

In the end, Portsmouth Harbour was selected. It was an excellent choice in that it left Kingston a great legacy and has become one of the great regatta centres anywhere in the world. Whenever I am asked by cities now bidding for the Olympics whom they should copy, I always say Portsmouth Harbour. The sailing venues at Kingston, Ontario; Barcelona, Spain; Kiel, Germany; Enoshima, Japan; Busan, Korea; and Athens, Greece, are the most profitable and well used venues of any Olympic Games installations. Los Angeles, Savannah (Atlanta) and Sydney, which built temporary sites, left no legacy either to the sport or to their citizens—they just threw money away. Sydney was the most upsetting to me, because Sydney Harbour and the Aussie sailors really needed the legacy of a first class sailing facility.

Once Portsmouth Harbour had been selected, Doug Keary, Cam Jones and Project Planning Associates worked on the budget, setting it at $24 million. This may seem like a lot of money, but the total Montreal budget was over $2 billion. [Savannah's temporary 1996 facility proved even more costly.] Drapeau still refused to anoint Kingston and continued to delay his decision with just 24 months left before the Games. Keary and Jones were beside themselves, and the Toronto tough guys were strident in urging Mayors Drapeau and Swain to get on with the job.

At that time, Canada was in the grip of a major steel shortage. The steel companies had warned that, unless the steel was ordered and delivered immediately, they could not supply enough to build the installation at Portsmouth Harbour. Cam Jones, an understated, quiet, happy and dedicated man, swung into action. He issued a purchase order for the steel through his position at Queen's University, hiding the order in the requisitions for some proposed new building on campus. The steel was delivered and stored at the university while we worked on the Government of Ontario for financial support. Ontario came through, negotiating with Drapeau for more than the one million dollar budget. Val Swain went to Drapeau and finally struck a deal, but in return Drapeau demanded that the Toronto group be sidelined. For this reason, Keary, Cox, Project Planning Associates and I were not involved in the final push. Kingston was confirmed and Cam Jones brought the Portsmouth Harbour project in on time and on budget at $24 million as we had projected. I am sure the citizens of Montreal were wishing that the rest of their Olympic venues had met their respective budgets in similar fashion.

Before the Toronto group withdrew, we acted on a critical lesson we learned from our German friends in Kiel. It is fairly commonplace that major lawsuits are filed after the completion of the Olympics. In order to protect ourselves, we convinced Canadian Yachting Association President David Yule, who also happened to be my accountant, that the CYA should be indemnified against any liability arising out of or in the course of the Olympic Games. When Mayors Swain and Drapeau asked the CYA to sign binding documents, Yule refused, much to their dismay. With all the lawsuits being slapped hither and yon after the excellent Montreal Games of 1976, this proved to be an astute move. As a result, the CYA's contribution to the success of the Games was not formally recognized even though it was the CYA's skilled members who volunteered and made the sailing events run smoothly.

The Canadian sailing fraternity should be very proud of the 1976 Kingston Olympic regatta, as volunteers from all clubs in Canada came together and made it happen. The three race courses were managed and equipped from race committees assembled in Montreal, Ottawa and Toronto, with Chief Race Officer Judge Livius Sherwood from Ottawa presiding. The Kingston sailors and their friends took care of most of the onerous onshore volunteer logistics. Carry On Canada, indeed!

Soling

After Montreal, I was somewhat at a loose end, so I decided to try again to make the Olympic team for the 1976 Games. This time I would compete in the Soling class, which is a three person keelboat. There were excellent crew available in Dennis Toews and John Kerr, who had sailed with Hans Fogh. I had never sailed what dinghy sailors call "a lead mine" (because of the keels), so I had to learn how to handle the broaches or "wipe outs" that occur in heavy winds under spinnaker. What happens is that the boat loses stability and rounds up violently as the keel tries to get higher than the mast.

I asked Dennis what I should do if this happened. *"Don't worry,"* he replied, *"Kerrsey and I will help you."* In the first heavy weather race, I came around the weather mark, set the spinnaker and, when the first major squall hit, reacted like it was a dinghy. We broached and I was thrown into the boat, ending up awash in the leeward scupper. When the boat finally righted itself, we got the rig and sails back together and continued in the race. Dennis turned to me and said, *"Skipper, you handled that very well."*

A number of highly talented crews were trying to make the one spot that was available to Canada, among them Paul

Louie from Vancouver. While sitting around the boat park one day, Paul and I discovered that our ancestors' stories were remarkably alike. He explained how in 1880, his grandfather, then a young man, came all the way from China to help build Canada's railroads, essentially as a slave. His uncle later became a very influential leader of the Chinese community in Vancouver. I told him that the same year that his grandfather had been sent to Canada, my grandfather, at the tender age of eight, was put on a boat in Scotland and sent to Canada alone to work on the farms in a similar lowly capacity. And here we were almost a century later, both proud to have the singular opportunity to strive to represent Canada at the 1976 Olympic Games.

It was a very close trial series between Peter Hall from Montreal, Glen Dexter from Halifax and our team. Going into the last race, the three of us were in a virtual dead heat with only one point separating each team. As luck would have it, the last race was never completed due to a lack of wind and the Race Committee had to go back to work. The Halifax crew was selected, being just ahead of us. They went on to represent Canada and sailed well in the Games.

Star Sailing

After the Kingston Games, I thought it would be fun to sail the classic Star boat, so I asked my old crew Bruce Brymer from the 14-foot Dinghy days to sail with me. He was built like a fireplug, tough as nails, and enjoyed life to the fullest. He was a good Finn sailor and owned his own plumbing supply business. I was starting to reap the rewards of the plumbing business myself and no longer needed to beg for support. Bruce was in the same situation and always paid his own way. We won the Canadian Championships and finished third in both the Bacardi Cup and North Americans against some of the best known sailors. We enjoyed an incredible victory in the last race of the 1978 World Championship in San Francisco in a 25-knot breeze against 108 competitors.

We were using a special sail that Buddy Melges had developed for small crews sailing in just those conditions. It was a joyous day for us as we went right over the top of well known USA America's Cup winner Dennis Connors on a planing reach. We broke our boom vang, which holds the boom level and is crucial in a Star boat racing downwind in such a heavy breeze. Bruce sat on the boom to hold it down in the treacherous conditions, and demanded that I sail the fastest course and not play it safe. This gave us a five-boat length lead that we never relinquished.

Our main Canadian competition was Allan Leibel, with crew David Shaw from Calgary. Weighing in at 250 pounds and six feet seven inches tall, Shaw was the opposite of Brymer, who was a good foot shorter. Shaw was in the house moving business, and I believed he could do the job all by himself. He was a real character, usually decked out in high heeled cowboy boots and a ten gallon hat that made him look immense.

At one club race when Bruce Brymer could not make it, my daughter Martha convinced me to race with her as crew. She was about 14 at the time, two feet shorter and 150 pounds lighter than Shaw, so our boat was much lighter than theirs. On the last leg we hit a corner, gained the wind shift and won. Shaw insisted that Martha was the reason we had bested them, and walking beside her explained that as crews they must stick together. It was typical of this mountain of a man that he let everyone back at the club know how Martha had won.

Buddy Melges' crew, Andreas Josenhans from Halifax, who was a little over six feet tall and tipped the scales at 225 pounds, once made the mistake of poking fun at Shaw's cowboy boots. Shaw grabbed him by the shoulders, lifted him up, and plunked him down on the roof of a car. He made Andreas stay up there until he was good and ready to let him get down.

The winners of the 1980 Canadian Olympic trials were decided by the total points accumulated from the North Americans in Seattle, the Bacardi in Miami and the Spring series in Nassau, Bahamas. We just edged out Leibel and Shaw in both of the first two series.

Moscow 1980: Boycott by a Peanut Farmer

The US-led boycott of the Moscow Games in 1980 marked a very dark moment for the Olympic movement. I could not believe what happened. It is what has made me distrustful of politicians and cynical about their motives. I have learned never to trust their machinations and lack of forthrightness. To this day I feel that politicians mislead us; nevertheless, I still try to cope with their methods. Hope springs eternal! That they use sport and athletes to pursue their own political ends was never more apparent than in the boycott of the Moscow Olympics orchestrated by US President Jimmy Carter and supported by Canada's Prime Minister Pierre Trudeau.

After the Bacardi Cup in January, 1980, all hell broke loose. The Soviet Union attacked Afghanistan and Moscow was to host the 1980 Olympics. President Carter, a peanut farmer from Atlanta, Georgia, was up for re-election that year. His Democrats were lagging in the polls and he needed to show that he was in control. He did it— immorally, in my view—on the backs of Olympic athletes by demanding that the USA boycott the Moscow Games. For some unknown political reason, Pierre Trudeau backed him.

Trudeau threatened the Canadian Olympic Association (COA) that if they did not join the boycott, all funding for elite sport in Canada would be withdrawn. The Olympic Trust of Canada, the COA's private funding arm centred in the Toronto business community and led primarily by men who had fought in World War II, insisted that the COA support the US president and Canada's prime minister. I naively believed that this was just political posturing and that the governments would eventually find a solution and back down from their entrenched position. I could not believe that the politicians would take away a generation's chance to compete in the Olympic Games for crass, political self-interest. I reluctantly supported the position of the Olympic Trust, even as I realized that this would be the last Olympics in which I myself could compete. This was not as disastrous to me as it was to those athletes who had trained for years for this one chance to become an Olympian, but it is without doubt the greatest mistake I have ever made.

At a COA meeting in Montreal, COA President Richard Pound was adamant that Canada must go to Moscow. He felt that the Olympic movement must be shown to be above political maneuvering. Pound demanded that the COA should stand strong against Trudeau. It was a brutal debate. Athletes who had recently immigrated to Canada from the Soviet bloc demanded that Canada support the USA against the USSR. In the end, the COA voted to boycott the Games.

The sailing venue for the 1980 Games was in Tallin, Estonia. While Canadian athletes were stuck at home, Canadian freighters were unloading Canadian wheat at the docks there. Jimmy Carter never stopped American business from trading with the Soviets. Yet Carter and Trudeau shattered the dreams of a generation of American and Canadian athletes. I felt strongly that Pound was right, but his voice was unheeded in the Canadian Olympic wilderness.

When the last sailing trials were held in Nassau, we knew we were not going to be allowed to go. Allan Leibel accumulated more total points there and beat us easily.

On the day of the opening ceremonies in Moscow, we ran a mock ceremony in the back yard of the Zimmerman's home in Toronto that was attended by the disenfranchised Canadian team. It was a blast in more ways than one. I was asked to construct the pseudo-Olympic flame, so I rigged it up with an acetylene tank from my plumbing business. I did not test it out beforehand. Jay Cross, who with Tam Matthews had finished second in the Worlds that year, was a definite Medal contender, so he was chosen to run in with the Olympic torch that Ken Greig had stolen in Mexico back in 1968. Jay climbed the ladder to the apparatus, but when I turned on the gas, he was almost blown into orbit. He survived to build Toronto's new Air Canada Centre, home of the Maple Leafs and the Raptors, then became president of the Miami Heat basketball team, and later president of the New York Jets NFL football team.

As vice-president of the International Yacht Racing Union, I was accredited to go to Moscow, but I could not bring myself to attend while our athletes were forbidden to compete. I did not agree with or approve of the many officials and politicians from Canada and the USA who accepted their free trips to Moscow. I will give them the benefit of the doubt, however, that they justified it in their own minds by convincing themselves of their country's need to be properly represented on the many international commissions and sport bodies.

I have never have been able to come to grips with the final blow on this issue that came when the IOC awarded the 1996 Games to Atlanta over Toronto. How they could do this after the 1980 Moscow boycott led by Atlanta's renowned citizen, Jimmy Carter, I will never be able to fathom.

Los Angeles 1984

Good news: Jimmy Carter lost the US presidential election. I want to believe that boycotting the Moscow Games in 1980 helped in his defeat.

Bad news: Jimmy Carter's US-led boycott ensured that the Eastern bloc would boycott the Los Angeles Games in 1984, thus depriving another generation of athletes of the opportunity to become Olympians.

I sailed in the Canadian Olympic trials Star-class with Dennis Toews as crew. We finished third. I had thus competed in the trials for every Olympic Games from 1952 until 1984, and I enjoyed all of them immensely.

At the age of 50, my life was turning in other directions. Martha had decided at the ripe age of 11 that she liked sailing. We sailed an Albacore dinghy together during this period and until she was 21. It was a great experience for an aging sailor to sail with his daughter. I had also been elected a vice-president of the International Yacht Racing Union (IYRU), and Beppe Croce, IYRU President, has appointed me technical delegate to the 1984 Games.

Sailing Test Events

Most of the time, we and our American friends work well together, but there are times when it seems to me that they are less than fair with their northern neighbours. I usually get their backs up when I say, *"Cold air may come from Canada, but the hot air comes from the USA."* Every sport holds a test event before the Games to evaluate the organization and train volunteers. Sailing invariably has two, however, and they are held at the same time of year as the Games, but 12 months earlier. Test events attract many more competitors than do the Olympics—only one entry is allowed per country per class in the Olympics, but more are welcomed in the test events, if only for the much needed entry fees that accrue to the organizing committees.

In the lead up to the Montreal Olympics, the test event was held in Kingston in the summer of 1975, with the entries limited to three per nation. I received a call from Sam Merrick, head of the US Olympic Sailing Committee and a Washington, D.C., lobbyist. Sam seemed to look at the world through the jaundiced eyes of a lawyer. He asked if Canada would allow the USA to double its entries in the light of the support they had extended to our Canadian Olympic Regatta Kingston. I acceded to his request because I knew that some countries would be unable to fill their allotments, and that it would not be inappropriate to offset this by increasing the number of entries from the USA and Canada. We generously allowed them six entries and matched that with six of our own. None of the other countries asked for more than three.

Fast-forward to 1983: Los Angeles held a test event prior to the 1984 Games and limited the entries to two per country. Due to the Eastern bloc boycott, there were many openings available. Sam Merrick was still the power in the US Olympic Sailing Committee, so I phoned him and said, *"Sam, at the Kingston pre-Olympic events, Canada doubled your entries from three to six. How about returning the favour and doubling Canada's entries from two to four?"*

Sam laughed at me. *"We are winning Gold for the USA,*

not Canada. No!" he said and hung up. I have told that story to the embarrassment of many American sailors, but it did happen that Sam filled the test event with some 15 Californian teams to make up the required numbers.

The opening quotation in Peter Ueberroth's book *Made in America* explains the policy he instituted, and as an entrepreneurial businessman I agree with him completely. It explains why I am at odds with left-wing Canadian and Toronto politicians who focus only on spending money but not where it comes from. The quotation is from Winston Churchill:

> *"Some see private enterprise as the predatory target to be shot, others as a cow to be milked, but few are those who see it as a sturdy horse pulling the wagon."*

Los Angeles was at times a trying experience for me as the IYRU technical delegate. The atmosphere was volatile. It followed Montreal, which had lost millions of dollars, and then the unfortunate Moscow boycott. Montreal had demonstrated new sources of income for the Olympics but had let construction costs run wild. L.A. augmented the Montreal income schemes and then pushed every dollar through a strainer.

The L.A. plan was to use existing and temporary installations wherever possible. I fully agree with the use of existing facilities for the Games, but temporary facilities leave no legacy whatsoever. While they may be less expensive to build, the money spent on temporary facilities is money thrown away. If the venues are to leave a lasting legacy, the facilities must be permanent. On the other hand, if it is clear that the venues will lie unused after the Games, they should be temporary. After the financial success of L.A., the IOC started judging bid cities by the yardstick of compactness, showing little concern for the projected use of the facilities after the Games or the "white elephants" that might be left at considerable cost to local taxpayers. Fortunately there now appears to be a new concept emerging at the IOC where bids are judged on sustainability. I trust that will become the major criteria in judging bid cities.

Most L.A. residents were ambivalent about the Games. Tickets sales were lagging, and that made the financial projections suspect, but three months before the opening ceremonies, local residents caught the Olympic bug and began lining up for tickets. New kiosks were opened all over California. In the final weeks, ticket sales topped $300 million, which put the Games into the black. Ueberroth not only had to make L.A. work, however; if the 1984 Games had failed, the Olympics might have disappeared altogether. History proved Los Angeles to be a great success, both artistically and financially.

Long Beach

The sailing events were a challenge. Ted Hinshaw was responsible for delivering the sailing venue. I was on the other side, working on behalf of the IYRU and the sailors. Many people did not get along with Ted, but coming from the construction business, I understood that his mandate was to deliver an acceptable event under the constraints of a limited budget. L.A. originally promised to build a regatta venue that would leave a much needed legacy to sailing on the West Coast, similar to what Canada had delivered in Kingston, but in the end it didn't happen.

The location of the L.A. venue kept changing. Finally, Hinshaw said the regatta would be run from a temporary facility in Long Beach. I remember one meeting with him when a European vice-president complained that this was unacceptable because of rain. Hinshaw told him that it does not rain in L.A. in August, and it didn't. Every day during the Games, we would wake up to a grey haze that burned off so that the sun shone by 10:00 a.m.

Ueberroth had instructed all his venue managers to be completely open with regard to budgets and costs. At every meeting, Ted would open his spreadsheets and show what money was available. If the IYRU wanted something, we had to delete something else.

The L.A. sailing venue was unique—the lack of rain and the warm water allowed for a number of innovations, but we were afraid at first that they might not work as planned. For one thing, instead of expensive docks and seawalls, the designers brought in the used artificial turf from the Los Angeles Coliseum and laid it on the beach and out into the gently sloping seabed. This made for a very cheap 100-metre-long launching ramp in place of the usual congested ramp only 20 metres in length, and it worked extremely well.

The second innovation replaced the large clubhouses complete with lockers and showers that were usually constructed for the sailors. These facilities had never really worked well, the lockers usually being far too small to accommodate all the sailing equipment, and the overflow creating an obvious security problem. The L.A. organizers placed long rows of used 40-foot shipping containers on the beach, allocating separate units to each team, with two or even three for the larger teams. All equipment could be locked up securely in the containers each night. The teams were responsible for looking after their own equipment.

Although they were functional, the containers were quite ugly. I think it was the Aussies who started the competition to see who could transform them into the most spectacular sites. During the boring two weeks before the first races, when everyone was waiting for the Games to start—specially the support teams who had little to do—picket fences and deck chairs appeared, and the sites were festooned with flowers. Canopies made from used sails stretched out from the front of the containers. The sailors painted the ugly containers in the colours of their countries. They erected makeshift flag poles from unused masts, and national flags flew everywhere over the beach. This innovative concept was much maligned when it was first proposed, but has since become *de rigeur* for all teams at major regattas. most countries now have fully equipped containers which they ship around the world, thus relieving the organizers of construction expenses. All that is required is a large parking lot and a way to launch the boats.

Canada won three sailing medals in Los Angeles. Hans Fogh, John Kerr and Steve Calder won Silver in the Soling class, and Terry Neilson won Bronze in the Finn. Terry McLaughlin and Everett Bastet competed in the Flying Dutchman class. Canada and the USA were running first and second—whoever beat the other won Gold. The race committees in those days were all from the host country. In the last race, there was a major dispute when the Canadians were called for a premature start. The television helicopter cameras showed that this was a questionable call, but this evidence was not allowed and McLaughlin and Bastet had to settle for Silver. Complaints of bias continually pop up in sport, and the perception of unfairness must be minimized whenever possible. When I became ISAF president, I initiated several policies in an effort to eliminate any perception of bias or favouritism.

Chapter 8:
Toronto 1996 Olympic Bid 1996 "TOOC"

We called the project "Toronto/Ontario Olympic Committee" (TOOC) in recognition of the fact that the City of Toronto had (and still has) no money; consequently, the Province of Ontario would underwrite the Games and that had to be recognized. I believe that awarding the Games to a city is ridiculous in today's world. The Games are so large that they must be underwritten by a state and/or federal government and venues are spread over a much larger area than the boundaries of any major city. After the success of Los Angeles, it became popular to bid for the Olympic Games and bidding became big business. At first there were no IOC guidelines for bidding; then even when they did impose some regulations, it seemed that the goalposts were continually being moved. The IOC appears also not to recognize what a bid city requires to promote both at home and internationally.

Overview:

The five years I spent leading Toronto's first bid to host the Olympic Games had a major influence on my life. I was exposed to the inner workings of the Olympic movement and came into direct contact with the three levels of Canadian politics—municipal, provincial and federal. It was an experience that left me with an even more jaundiced view of politicians than I had going in. It is not that I personally dislike them but I am appalled at how they prostitute their integrity just to get elected.

As a volunteer I was not paid. Mary and I often spent money out of our own pockets, and we gave wholeheartedly of our time. In retrospect, it was the most exciting and challenging period of my life. I have few regrets, although I do carry some deep wounds, most of which were self-inflicted.

The 1984 Los Angeles Olympics showed the Olympic movement how to run the Games as a financial success. During those Games, three of us—Bill Cox, George Gross and myself, all Toronto boosters—used to breakfast together at the L.A. Olympic hotel. It was during one of those early morning meetings that someone first breathed the idea to have Toronto bid for the 1996 Olympics.

Bill Cox, my Island friend since we were 10 years old, was then assistant *chef de mission* of the Canadian Olympic team. Billy did all that work looking after the Canadian team as assistant because the Chef de Mission was busy socializing and attending receptions. George Gross was sports director of *The Toronto Sun* and a great promoter of Toronto sport. It is difficult to become George's friend, but having achieved that goal I find it impossible to get rid of him. I talked to George every week until he quietly passed away in 2007. As IYRU vice-president, I was technical director of the 1984 L.A. sailing events.

Once the idea was floated to have Toronto bid for the 1996 Games, we took a serious look at the situation to determine whether it might be possible for Toronto to win. For one thing, 1996 was to be the one-hundredth anniversary of the first modern Olympics, and it looked like the Games might well go to Athens. If Athens did win, then Toronto might contend for the 2000 Millennium Games. We felt that if Athens did not win the 1996 bid, however, then the Games would come to North America.

We believed that if Toronto won, the city would be left with an incredible legacy:

- Facilities for sport were woefully inadequate in Toronto and indeed, all of Ontario (and still are). More than 150 new installations would be constructed throughout the Greater Toronto Area, including upgrades to school gyms and municipal parks.
- Toronto's industrial wastelands—the Portlands—would be revitalized as had those in Barcelona when the Olympic Village and Olympic Marina were built.
- A much needed recreation centre for south-east Toronto

would be created along with the Olympic swimming
facilities.

- After the Games, the Athletes' and Press Villages would
  be converted to assisted social housing.
- The Olympics would create 80,000 people-years of jobs.
- The Games would serve as a cohesive force uniting
  Toronto's many diverse ethnic communities.
- Public transit facilities would be upgraded as they were
  in Montreal, Calgary and now Vancouver.
- Overall Toronto would benefit from a 10 billion dollar
  injection as a direct result of hosting the Games.

To this day, members of the international Olympic family still tell me
that the Toronto 1996 bid was excellent and technically the best.

Olympic Bid Politics

In my opinion, Toronto lost to Atlanta primarily because of the
negative publicity generated by the left-wing political group *Bread not
Circuses* led by Toronto's New Democrat Party leader Jack Layton,
defeated NDP candidate Michael Shapcott, Layton's mayoralty
campaign co-chairman David Kidd and the Communist Party of
Metro Toronto. *Bread not Circuses* protested not just against the
Olympic bid, but many civic initiatives, including the domed stadium
(now the Rogers Centre), opera house (now the Four Seasons Centre
for the Performing Arts) and the World's Fair bid, which Toronto also
lost. To my mind, NDP means "Never Debate Positively" and now,
some 15 years later, Toronto is firmly in the grip of socialist
reactionaries. I find it almost amusing that David Kidd ran for the
leadership of the Communist Party of Metro Toronto, but lost because
he was too radical.

From 1989 until 1994, North America experienced the worst
economic downturn I have ever witnessed. Small entrepreneurial
businessmen like me had to scrape and claw to survive. Many Toronto
businesses went under or were sold to foreign interests. Economic
growth stalled in just about every city in North America except

Atlanta, which grew seven per cent each year. Why? Because Atlanta won the Olympic Games.

Many of our best media and sports brains traveled to Atlanta to help run the Games. Some never came back. Toronto has lost more than 100,000 jobs since 1992 and, at this writing, the Portlands are still an industrial wasteland. The various levels of government have made their customary election promises for the Portlands but have delivered very little but consultants' studies at a cost of some 100 million dollars. A small housing project is nearing completion on the site of our proposed Olympic Press Village. The site of the Olympic Athletes' Village, on the other hand, is being developed as a towering, upscale condominium project instead of the low-rise subsidized housing community we had envisioned for it.

During my participation in the Olympics during the 1960s, Ontario produced three out of every five Olympic athletes. Now, Ontario is lucky to have one in four. Ontario suffers from a great dearth of sport facilities for our youth, and has not hosted a major sporting event since Hamilton ran the 1932 British Empire Games. In 2000, the federal Liberal government promised to turn an unused part of Downsview Airport in the north end of Toronto into a national sport institute, but little has been done with the exception of more consultants' studies. (Toronto has now won the right to host the 2015 Pan Am Games which I started and will be a keen observer of the sport legacies finally delivered.)

Some cite the Montreal Olympic deficit and Vancouver cost overruns to support their negative stance on hosting the Games. Remember, however, that Montreal got a new subway line to service their eastern most communities, along with major arterial roads. British Columbia is finally building the Sea-to-Sky Highway from Vancouver to Whistler, and is undertaking local highway improvements. Vancouver is the first Canadian City to get a fast train service from the middle of the city to their airport—all done because of the Olympics. These infrastructure enhancements should not be lumped into the cost of the Games. Rather they should be understood as legacies to the city. Toronto traffic is grinding to a stop in a constant state of gridlock, hopefully the 2015 Pan Am Games will be the catalyst to bring much needed transportation upgrades. Hosting the Olympic Games puts a deadline on delivering promises. Politicians and bureaucrats cannot dither—they must deliver.

When Barcelona was awarded the 1992 Games, U.K. Labour MP Chris Chataway (who had run as the pacer "rabbit" when Roger Bannister broke the four-minute mile in 1954) observed, *"Now Barcelona has the ability to do 30 years of urban renewal in six."* Barcelona did just that, as will London with the industrially depressed Lea Valley for the 2012 Summer Games.

In my view, the only way to get our taxpayers' money invested in the greater Toronto region is to secure a mega-event and then essentially blackmail all levels of government to pay for it. Montreal, Vancouver, Calgary, Winnipeg and Victoria have all seen that the only way to put their politicians' feet to the fire to secure major urban renewal is to host a mega-event. The citizens of Toronto have turned their backs on such initiatives with the shallow retort, *"We do not want our taxes spent on the Olympics, a World's Fair or an opera house."*

The rest of Canada can then say, *"Terrific! We will spend Toronto taxpayers' money instead."* And they do, since Toronto is a major contributor to they country's economy. It has been said that Canada is a country tied together by a universal hatred of all things Toronto, and we Torontonians are our own worst enemies, since we have hosted nothing but seemingly endless negative debates.

Toronto 1996 Olympic Bid

In the fall of 1984, we held several meetings to discuss mounting an Olympic bid. Early on we conscripted another old friend, Basil Rodomar, who became our number one gopher and we quietly went to work. I put together the preliminary technical venue plan while Basil worked on the publications. Billy Cox felt out the Canadian Olympic Association and his corporate friends at the Olympic Trust. George

Gross made some inquiries on the viability of the Toronto bid through his international contacts in the media.

In June 1985, I was contacted by one of my wife's friends who was chairing a fundraising and awareness dinner at the Royal York Hotel to stop acid rain. They had engaged Senator Teddy Kennedy from Massachusetts to give the keynote address. Kennedy asked if he could bring along his 16-year-old son to go racing on Lake Ontario and then to a private fishing lodge on one of Ontario's northern lakes. I asked Paul Phelan to supply the well known Canadian yacht *Red Jacket* and asked Jim Crang of Crang and Boake Architects to invite the Kennedy entourage to the Griffith Island fishing camp. Kennedy's visit occurred during a very difficult time in his career and he was terribly demanding of everyone there. He also failed to show for the race, and it was with a great sigh of relief that I poured him onto a private jet to fly him home in time for a New England Patriots football game.

At the acid rain reception in the library at the Royal York Hotel, Billy Cox and I met with Toronto Mayor Art Eggleton and briefly pitched the idea of a Toronto Olympic bid. He indicated some interest so we set up a meeting for the following week.

I asked Jim Crang for help, and he produced three six-foot-square cardboard "venue boards" of the City of Toronto, the greater Toronto region and Ontario. David Angus, another sailing friend in the advertising business, supplied stick-on pictograms of the sports and other venues required. I stuck them on in the appropriate places, moving them around when necessary. The total cost of this presentation was 50 dollars, and off we went to see Mayor Eggleton. The Mayor was intrigued and demanded that we do an intense feasibility study before he would commit to the project—but with the following caveats:

1. That there be no request for City of Toronto money; but they reserved the right to exercise a veto on any issue. This was typical of municipal political positioning.
2. That the City of Toronto and the Mayor would be front

and centre in all aspects. This would permit them to take credit without responsibility.

3. That we must pitch all the city councilors and get them onside.

4. That Metropolitan Toronto and the other municipalities would have only minor influence.

5. That TOOC would be responsible for getting the provincial and federal governments to back the project.

Our acceding to these conditions proved a big political mistake. Every time any of the elected officials said jump, I would ask, *"How high?"* and run off trying to deliver whatever mundane request they had thought up. The more we proceeded to deliver the project, the more the politicians demanded. The more we tried to deliver, the less they did. We were treated like real estate developers, not volunteers trying to sell Toronto to the world. We should have had a list of what we would do and a list of what the politicians would be responsible for, and we should have held them to it.

Sponsors

The first challenge was the feasibility study. Christopher Lang, who had orchestrated the incredible success of the Petro Canada Calgary Olympic Torch Relay, came up with the successful concept for our fundraising. The plan had four principles:

There would be no corporate exclusives since we could not guarantee that for the Games.

Most CEOs had a discretionary limit of 50 thousand dollars. We decided to ask for contributions of 35 thousand dollars every six months during the bid period.

The money must be considered sponsorship and it must come from the corporate marketing budgets, not from their charitable donation budgets. TOOC was not a charity. TOOC would not—and did not—give tax receipts to anyone.

A corporation could opt out at any time.

With the 50-dollar venue boards, I pitched the corporations and raised the first half-million dollars. In those days, I knew someone either at the top of every corporation or who could get me to the top. This may sound arrogant, but it is true. Sailing, squash, university— if one of those was not the entrée, being plumber to the carriage trade was. TOOC secured five banks, four breweries, three automobile manufacturers and 60 other corporations as sponsors. On top of this, we got an equal contribution from in-kind companies including Air Canada and Canadian Airlines, along with a number of hotels, restaurants and limousine services. At the first meeting of the sponsors, whom we called the "TOOC Brigade," one asked why they all appeared in our agenda in the order listed, as they were not in alphabetical order. I responded that since I came from the plumbing business, the corporations were listed as their cheques had come across my desk.

Two things stick in my mind from this period. I was scheduled to pitch General Motors in Oshawa on a Thursday morning of one month when they hear various pleas for money. I waited outside with the others, being on tap for my half-hour. GM President George Peeples was present when I walked in with my 50-dollar boards and went through the Olympic presentation. When I finished he said, *"GM is with you."*

"That was easy," I said with surprise. *"What did I do that was so good?"*

"Well," he said *"GM gets many presentations. Just before you, the Salvation Army was here with a slick and professional 250 thousand-dollar audio-visual presentation asking for money for the poor. You walk in with these basic boards and pitch from the heart, knowing what you are talking about."*

I was not ready for this, but it was very gratifying.

Billy Cox knew a vice-president of Air Canada in Montreal so he, Basil Rodomar and I took our boards to Montreal to pitch Air Canada President Pierre Jeanniot and four of his vice-presidents. Their board boom was furnished with a big round table with an empty space in the middle like a donut. There was no place to display the boards so I jumped over the desk into the middle and pitched from there. Jeanniot was momentarily taken aback, but at the end of the presentation he said, *"How many free Air Canada tickets do you want?"* *"Eight hundred and seventy-nine,"* I immediately shot back. *"Please give us a breakdown and we will take a look at it,"* he said.

We were walking down Sherbrooke Street when Basil asked, *"Where did you get 879 from?"* *"Seemed like a good number at the time, but I have no idea how many we need,"* I confessed.

In the end, Air Canada was the most important sponsor TOOC had and gave us exactly 879 free airline tickets.

All in all, Canadian corporations supplied six million dollars for the bid in cash and matched that with the same amount in-kind. The provincial and federal governments each contributed two million dollars. The five-year bid cost a total of 16 million dollars. The City of Toronto contributed nothing except employ a bureaucracy who did nothing but get in our way.

I instructed our finance team of Ron Bertram, David Wishart, David Yule of Ernst and Young, Peter Baker of Beaver Lumber, Norman Seagram of Molsons, and Roger Wilson of Fasken Martineau that, no matter how irate and unreasonable I might become, under no circumstances was TOOC to spend more money than we had. At the end when we closed the books, TOOC was in the black by 10 thousand dollars. We gave five thousand dollars to the Canadian women's hockey team and the same amount to the Canadian women's volleyball team. Neither group had the money to go to its World Championship. This is consistent with the meager support given athletes to this day by the Government of Canada through Sport Canada.

Ontario Provincial Government

I made an appointment to pitch Ontario Premier David Peterson. I did not know him, but I played squash with his brother Tim at the Toronto Racquet Club and Tim set up the interview. In I went with the boards and went through the pitch. The Premier said he was intrigued, but needed time to look into the situation. At a meeting two weeks later, Peterson confirmed that Ontario was onside and asked whether I knew what they had been doing for the last two weeks. I replied that I had no idea. The Premier informed me that they had the Ontario Provincial Police and RCMP checking me out and they could discover no way in which I could benefit personally from the Olympic bid. This was a great compliment. Gordon Ashworth was given the Ontario Olympic portfolio and while he was there, everything went smoothly. His advice was invaluable and he kept all politicos under control.

Peterson gave us the heads-up that he had been advised by Robert Nixon, Member of Provincial Parliament from South Western Ontario, that it was politically unwise to support major projects for Toronto. Nixon confirmed this much later, after the defeat of the Peterson Government when he was serving as Ontario's high commissioner in London. My daughter Martha happened to be working there and met Nixon at a reception at Ontario House. *"I guess we should have supported the Toronto Olympic Bid more,"* he admitted. Martha turned on her heel and left the reception, a true Henderson!

Federal Government

Dealing with the federal government was much easier. The Conservative government under Brian Mulroney had appointed a separate minister for sport, the famous Canadian athlete Otto Jelinek. Otto was a champion for all sport and was always available. George Gross, who like Jelinek hailed originally from Czechoslovakia, had a direct pipeline to the new minister. It is a travesty that more recent federal governments have not put a similar focus on sport by appointing an independent minister who at least knows something about sport and is not encumbered by more pressing portfolios.

Toronto City Council

TOOC pitched every one of the 21 city councilors and all the municipalities that were then part of Metropolitan

Toronto, including the adjoining regions from Hamilton to Oshawa and north to Barrie, an area known as the Golden Horseshoe. If Toronto had won the bid, the 1996 Games would have been the most compact Olympics ever run and would have left a legacy to many communities in the Golden Horseshoe. The city councilors were a diverse group, to say the least. In 1987, the council was fairly well balanced with the left, middle and right almost equally represented. A few of the key players stand out in my memory.

Barbara Hall, who succeeded Art Eggleton as mayor of Toronto, was very diligent and supportive. She traveled to Los Angeles and spoke with local community groups to gain a first-hand idea of the impact of the Games. L.A. residents were very positive in their remarks. Barbara was able to keep the left-of-centre councilors under control until *Bread not Circuses* arrived on the scene.

Chris Korwin Kryshinski, affectionately known as KK, was always a great cheerleader. He would invariably show up at bid-related events with great enthusiasm. Michael Walker, who represented the constituency where I live, played an interesting game. He would not support the Olympic bid unless there was something in it for his constituents. Walker demanded that CN Real Estate give the old, disused Belt Line rail corridor south of Davisville Avenue as a park for joggers. The City had been unable to deliver it as a park for years. Walker demanded that the TOOC deliver the Belt Line as a park or he would vote against the bid. This had nothing to do with the bid; nevertheless, that was the price he set for his positive vote. I mentioned this to Senator Trevor Eyton, who had played football with Cox in their student days at Jarvis Collegiate Institute. Trevor and I went to see CN Vice-president Doug Tipple and asked for CN's support. After much negotiation by Trevor, CN deeded the corridor to the City, which promptly renamed it Kay Gardiner Belt Line Park, in honour of one of their own. Michael Walker has never acknowledged that this was a legacy of the Olympic bid, or that it was really Senator Trevor Eyton and CN Real Estate who made it happen.

My first meeting with NDP Councilor Jack Layton was a

memorable one. He was very positive and told us how he had once swum against Richard Pound, IOC member in Canada, at the exclusive Montreal Amateur Athletic Club. (Jack hails from among Montreal's old English elite.) He said that he spent most of his time looking at Pound's feet. He stated clearly that while the NDP is continually accused of being negative on just about every issue, the Olympic bid was one project his party must strongly support. He wanted to sit on the city council Olympic board, and was immediately appointed to it. I take great credit for being one of the few people ever to get Layton to be positive on any issue, even if it was only for a few months. It did not take long for Layton to flip flop, however, and begin working to destroy Toronto's chances for the sake of his own political agenda.

TOOC produced a complete, in-depth feasibility study and presented it to the City. The vote at City Council in the spring of 1988 was unanimous, carrying by a margin of 21 to zero. TOOC went forward assuming we had their complete support. We agreed and contracted that TOOC would do the international lobbying while the politicians elected to City Council were charged with raising public awareness of the bid.

Toronto's surrounding municipalities were positive and wanted to be involved, with only one exception. Scarborough Mayor Joyce Trimmer was always there when we needed her, especially when the IOC evaluation commissions came to Toronto. Etobicoke Mayor Bruce Sinclair and Mayor Dave Johnson of East York were also onside. Mississauga Mayor Hazel McCallion was a joy to be with. Hamilton Mayor Bob Morrow was a great help. Markham would have taken the whole Olympics if they could have. The cities of Oshawa, Sudbury, Ottawa, Barrie, King and London all wanted venues and were scheduled to host events.

North York Mayor Mel Lastman sounded the sole negative note. Lastman said he wanted no part of anything in Toronto and wanted no events in North York either—not even at York University. (York wanted the subway extended to their campus, but Lastman wanted the next subway line to run through his municipality east along Sheppard Avenue. Lastman's Sheppard line is now known as the "subway to nowhere." The cost of the more sensible extension to York University, if it is ever to proceed, is projected to be in the billions of dollars.)

To my mind, what Lastman did when the IOC Evaluation Commission came in early 1990 was crass political posturing in the extreme. The IOC schedule for the committee's week-long technical visit specified Wednesday as the day when the committee would meet our local politicians at Toronto City Hall, a facility shared by both the City of Toronto and the Municipality of Metropolitan Toronto that encompassed all the surrounding municipalities. The bid was from the City of Toronto, however, because that was IOC protocol. The Wednesday visit fell on a day which was routinely scheduled for a Metro Toronto Council meeting. Lastman refused to allow the IOC and TOOC to come into Toronto City Hall on that day, and he held the right of veto. Can anyone in his right mind believe that the proponents of Toronto's Olympic bid were not permitted to go into their own city hall?

We needed a token city hall so we met at the Scarborough Town Centre. Many members of the Toronto City Council were in attendance as Mayor Joyce Trimmer put on a great show for the Evaluation Commission. Dennis Flynn and Alan Tonks, the appointed chairs of Metropolitan Toronto, were supportive of TOOC and the 1996 bid, but they could not corral or muzzle Lastman. Lastman later became mayor of the newly amalgamated City of Toronto and made a show of supporting Toronto's 2008 bid, which was a slam dunk for Beijing. In my opinion, Lastman's uncouth performance on the international stage was nothing short of a world-class embarrassment to the city.

The membership of the Toronto/Ontario Olympic Committee included: Thomas and Sonia Bata, Marina Baturinskya, Ron and Betsy Bertram, Sue Bolender, Bill Cox, Julie Carter, Fred Doucet, Jean Dupre, Suzanne Drapeau, Senator Trevor Eyton, M. El Farnawani, Tamara Gabnai, Carlos Garcia, Paul Godfrey, George and Elizabeth Gross,

Sam Guerra, Joe Halstead, Hagood and Martha Hardy, Martha Henderson, John Henderson, Alex Henderson, Sue Holloway, Greg Joy, Fraser Kelley, Ana Kirkham, Marjorie La Tour, Lisa Lyn, Andrea Martin, Maria MacDonald, Ray McNeil, Doris Mohrhardt, Monica O'Neil, Julie Osborne, Anne O'Connor, Susan Puff, Dan Pulgiese, Grace Polski, Hans and Eva Pracht, Dan Poyntz, Cheryl Price-Evans, Diane Radnik, Basil Rodomar, John Rogers, Norman and Joyce Seagram, Joe Seagram, Bill and Meredith Saunderson, Rick Seifeddine, Chris Simpson, Gina Stephens, Horacio Toledo, Pat Valde, Rita Wong, Roger Wilson, David Wishart, James and Brigitta Worrall, and David Yule.

It is patently obvious from this long list of luminaries that, although I was occasionally accused of being a one-man band, it was more a case of my being the music man leading 76 trombones.

As president and premier spokesman for Toronto's 1996 Olympic bid, I was in charge of securing the sponsorship dollars. I removed myself from the expenditure and hiring processes, delegating these responsibilities to the finance committee. The Reichmanns, through Senator Trevor Eyton, donated our office space on the waterfront at the Terminal Warehouse Building. As a volunteer, however, I still had to work, and operated out of my regular office uptown at R.G. Henderson plumbing.

I needed someone who could coordinate my oppressive schedule and try to keep me sane. Norman Seagram had had a wonderful assistant at Molson's in Sue Bolender, an elegant lady who always wore vibrant red lipstick, and he suggested her for the job. She would take great joy in planting a big kiss on my bald head, leaving her marker for everyone to see. I could not have survived without her.

At Cox's suggestion, we "recruited" York University lecturer Carol Anne Letheren, who also brought along her old friend Dr. Bryce Taylor, York's head of physical education and the author of a valuable text on First Nations customs and dances. Bryce in turn recruited members of York University's women's volleyball and field hockey teams to work as volunteers at

TOOC. At various times during the bid period we had about 15 of them with us, and I found them to be outstanding, motivated young people who were a real joy to work with. I still hear from many of them, and they keep me up to date on their growing families.

As a volunteer in the early stages when we were starting up, Carol Anne Letheren proved invaluable to us, and without her the administrative load would have been almost unbearably onerous. She worked hard to keep up with the endless demands for one report after another. When we opened our official office in February 1987, she told us that she and Taylor must be put on the payroll. It seemed to be the logical thing to do, so the finance committee negotiated terms, which proved to be quite favourable to them and binding on TOOC, as I later discovered to my dismay. Carol Anne was responsible for all communications, including publications, videos, and other promotional and marketing initiatives. Bryce Taylor was hired as general manager.

It did not take me long, however, to notice her excessive spending and repeated hiring of outside consultants for almost every phase of the project. TOOC was on the verge of being out of control financially, so we brought in Ron Bertram to act as chief operating officer. David Yule engaged the volunteer services of chartered accountant David Wishart, who had just retired from Ernst and Young, and he came on board with Bertram in the early summer of 1987. They were instructed to keep the finances in order and they did.

In November I received a call from Bertram summoning me to the TOOC office. The concern in his voice was palpable. There was apparently some urgent matter that David Yule and Norman Seagram needed to discuss with me. I knew that TOOC's books were totally open to scrutiny and that all transactions were transparent, because TOOC was audited every three months by city, province and federal auditors.

Toronto's Chief Financial Officer Jack Rubinovitch had just spent two days checking our books and his report was devastating. Rubinovitch demanded that I address the financial concerns with

Letheren and Taylor. The TOOC financecommittee agreed. They also advised me to hang on to all supporting documentary evidence, and I still have it to this day. Rubinovitch filed a full report for the City archives on the matter.

This was a delicate situation for me because Letheren was about to become president of the Canadian Olympic Association (COA) and was being proposed for membership on the IOC. Taylor was very well connected in the Canadian sport hierarchy, and if they both left, it would cause a major dislocation, to say nothing of the negative repercussions that might echo throughout the Canadian sports community. Letheren was out of town when I called Taylor into my office. We had a constructive and gentlemanly discussion in which he explained that business was not his area of expertise and he had been hoping that I would allow him to return to York University. He also told me that he suffered from major heart problems and the stress of TOOC was getting to him. We parted amicably, and not long after, he accompanied a group of us to Calgary for the 1988 Winter Games. Sadly, Bryce died a short time later from heart failure.

At the end of November 1987, Carol Anne Letheren returned and we met in my office. I was well prepared for the meeting, having made up my mind to talk softly while carrying a big stick. I laid all the cards on the table and then told her that she would no longer have any discretionary spending power. Henceforth, all expenditures would be authorized and vetted by Bertram and Wishart. This did not go down well with her.

"You do not understand the business of consultants," she said. This was, in fact, a magnificent grasp of the obvious with which I wholeheartedly agreed. She then said, *"I am going to spend three weeks in the Dominican Republic over Christmas. I will give you my response when I return."*

In January, I received a formal lawyer's letter to the effect that Carol Anne Letheren could not continue under the constraints I had imposed. She demanded—and received—full severance according to the terms of her contract. She went on to become president of the COA and was appointed an IOC member in 1990, in Tokyo. Two years later, she converted her volunteer position as COA president to a paid one as COA executive director, a move which did not surprise me in the least, considering her history at TOOC.

During the 1987 Pan American Games and the 1988 Calgary Olympics, it became obvious from discussions with IOC members that the 1996 Games were not going to Athens. Toronto was well positioned. Seeing that the Toronto bid was strong and that Athens was not a slam dunk, the USA decided to put Atlanta forward for the 1996 Games just before the deadline passed for committing to bid. The Americans seldom support Canada in these situations since they believe that if Canada gets the Games, the USA will be delayed for consideration in the future.

James "Jim" Worrall Gala

Jim Worrall had the great honour of being Canada's flag bearer at the 1936 Berlin Olympics and marching past Adolf Hitler. An active member of the COA, Jim was made an IOC member in Canada in 1967. He was born in 1914 on June 23, which just happens to be World Olympic Day. Fittingly, the Games have had an impact on his whole life.

When we started the bid process, Jim was one of the first people we contacted. His insights into the protocol and language of the IOC were invaluable, and he gently corrected us often. Another skill he brought to TOOC was spelling, and he became responsible for checking all our documents.

In 1989, TOOC honoured Jim with a special night at Roy Thomson Hall in celebration of his seventy-fifth birthday. Hagood Hardy offered to produce the evening. He asked Jim whom he would like to see perform at his gala. Naturally, Jim asked Hagood to play, and also for the Canadian Brass and concert pianist Hae-Jung Kim, the daughter of Korean IOC member Dr. Un Yung Kim. Hagood also engaged classical guitarist Liona Boyd and Canada's world-renowned opera singers Maureen Forrester and Ermano Florio. Some 1,500 guests attended from all walks of Toronto life. Beside Hagood, masters of ceremonies included Olympic diver Sylvie Bernier and crazy Canuck skiers Ken Read and Steve Podborski.

Jim was one of the most likeable and respected IOC member so we decided to kill two birds with one stone and invite all IOC members to come to Toronto for the gala—and to see our proposals for the Games. More than 40 IOC members and their wives attended. It was a great three day event kicked off on the first night with an evening reception at Queen's Park hosted by the Honourable Lincoln M. Alexander, Lieutenant Governor of Ontario.

The IOC members were in awe of Variety Village and the physically challenged kids who put on a great show there with a basketball game, swimming and arts and crafts. This was followed by a special exhibition of sport at the Ontario Science Centre that our visitors liked so much and stayed so long to watch that they were late for dinner. We also took the IOC members for a sail around Toronto Bay, with a stop at the RCYC. A number of Torontonians took them to their homes for dinner. The Blue Jays gave us free tickets to the ball game where the sponsors entertained our guests in their boxes. The visitors loved it and so did Jim Worrall. The TOOC staff worked around the clock to make it all come together. They were a great team. TOOC was able to get many of the costs covered in-kind. Ford and General Motors gave us cars to squire the visitors around, and the hotels offered us special rates.

The only sour note was sounded by Michael Shapcott, who showed up with 15 *Bread not Circuses* supporters yelling negative slogans at our visitors. This was the first time these people embarrassed Toronto on the world stage but, sad to say, it was not the last. Frank King had sent me newspaper clippings of some articles Shapcott wrote while a journalist for *The Calgary Herald*, including some that were highly supportive of the 1988 Calgary Winter Games. I went outside and confronted Shapcott, asking him why he supported Calgary yet was such an embarrassment to his recently adopted City of Toronto. *"Different city! Different times! Different political agenda!"* he replied glibly.

The IOC members were scheduled to fly to Puerto Rico after the gala for the annual IOC session. TOOC flew them on an Air Canada charter out of Hamilton International Airport, and their compliments about Toronto were most gratifying. TOOC rented two cabanas at the San Juan Hilton, the IOC session hotel, and we took along volunteer chefs from Centro's Restaurant and Joe Brancatella from Grazie's on Yonge Street. Loblaws donated Canadian meat and other goodies. Our little hospitality area was a great success. Returning home I saw that *Sports Illustrated* had ranked Toronto in the lead for the 1996 Games, but Jack Layton and Michael Shapcott had other ideas. From that time forward, the enemy was within.

Bread not Circuses

The November 1988 City of Toronto election saw the balance of power shift dramatically from the middle of the road to the left. New Democratic Party sympathizers were in control under the leadership of Jack Layton. This proved disastrous for TOOC. Eventually this group took credit for defeating Toronto's Olympic bid.

Liz Amers was elected from Toronto Island. I had known her since we were children; as a teenager Liz had been a great athlete. During her campaign for city council, Liz held a reception for all Olympic athletes who had been born on Toronto Island. I never thought she would sell herself out to Jack Layton, but political allegiances clearly run deeper than mere decency.

Early one morning in February 1989, my telephone rang off the hook. First to call was *The Toronto Star's* Olympic journalist Jim Byers. He was very hyper and asked what I knew about the *Bread not Circuses* press conference opposing the Olympic bid. Layton and Shapcott were the main speakers. I said I had never heard of Shapcott and asked Jim to fax me their press release. I was shocked when I read it. Not only did they oppose the Olympic bid, but also the World's Fair, new opera house, domed stadium and just about every other civic initiative. At the bottom of their letterhead were listed as supporters Jack Layton, Marilyn Churley, Liz Amers, Roger Hollander and the Communist Party of Metro Toronto, over the signatures of Michael Shapcott and John Metson.

I could not believe that in 1989 these politicians would list the Communist Party as their supporting political base. It was even more shocking to me that some of these political ideologues even manage to get elected in Toronto. The Berlin Wall had come down, eastern Europe was in chaos and they, without compunction, were allowing their names to be associated with a political system that was not only passé, but also offensive to everyone who had escaped to Canada and freedom. I find it disturbing to see how many Canadian left-wing politicians spent their formative years in academic retreats in the USA, or arrived here during the Vietnam War, and use Canada as a soap box for their political anti-USA biases.

As is my style, as soon as I heard about *Bread not Circuses,* I picked up the telephone and phoned Michael Shapcott, whose name up to then had been unfamiliar to me. He explained that his father, a doctor, had left England for Toronto when socialized medicine was instituted there. About the time that Canada adopted socialized medicine, his family moved to Denver, Colorado. When the Vietnam War escalated, Michael fled the USA for Calgary, where he worked as a journalist with *The Calgary Herald* and lauded the Olympics. Due to family problems, he moved to Toronto. He told me he had led the 1988 left-wing campaign opposing Toronto's middle-of-the-road Mayor Art Eggleton, orchestrating this movement out of the Christian Resource Centre, which served a subsidized housing initiative in Regent Park and operated out of a United Church building there. Shapcott admitted there was a much greater political agenda in *Bread not Circuses.* Seeing Layton elected mayor was the final chapter in their bid to help the militant left wing take over Toronto. It was obvious to me that he was acting not for the poor and those without bread at all, but from his own crass political motives.

I then phoned Layton, who was his usual mushy self.

He hid the truth, saying that *Bread not Circuses* was really nothing to be worried about, but that he had some concerns about the bid. After that I met Liz Amers by chance walking along the Toronto waterfront. She apologized but said that since she still lived on Toronto Island, she had to support Layton and the leftists because they had helped her save the Toronto Island community from expropriation and eviction from their homes. She also confirmed that she and her colleagues were not involved in a personal vendetta against the Olympics, but rather in a political movement to take over Toronto.

Bread not Circuses protested every meeting we held. A newspaper man, Shapcott knew how to play and excite the press. He produced numerous pamphlets attacking both the bid and me personally, and did it all out of the Christian Resource Centre at the United Church. *Bread not Circuses* even had the nerve to offer tax receipts for donations funneled through the Church. The group's backroom leaders were David Kidd and John Piper, who became Layton's campaign co-chairs for his run for mayor. Kidd is the brother of Canada's famous Olympic runner Bruce Kidd; Piper is one of Layton's remaining high school friends from upscale Hudson Heights in Montreal.

Jack Layton

Layton created a major disruption to the bid process after the NDP-controlled city council was elected. He demanded that TOOC organize and pay for community consultation and intervention and that no plans be finalized until this was done. TOOC had been working for three years with 95 per cent of the work already in place. From the outset, Layton had sat on the City's Olympic committee but had waited until now to show his hand.

TOOC's position was that we were constituted to promote the bid internationally and that the City, with its large committee of politicians, was responsible for community consultation. But that is not how politicians work when they are ambitiously seeking to attain higher office. They want photo-opportunities and media attention.

Layton pointed the finger at TOOC because that was the highest flagpole in Toronto on which he could hoist his personal flag of ambition. He demanded we hold eight public meetings at TOOC's expense, each with a different subject. TOOC had to pay the protesters to do their research to attack us, and they called this "intervener funding."

Only about a dozen people showed up at any of the meetings. There were more TOOC members than so-called "stakeholders" in attendance. It was always the same speakers with the same biases, no matter the subject. If the meeting was purportedly about transit issues, then activists for the homeless or animals spoke. The City reserved the right to decide who would get intervener funding. TOOC had to pay one such recipient 10 thousand dollars. He was a newly minted York University professor who had recently arrived in Canada from the USA. The professor had his students do the research for nothing and then pocketed the money. The total four-month delay cost TOOC sponsors about one million dollars. Layton sought continual media exposure though his negative position, all to raise his profile for his eventual run for mayor.

The COA and TOOC had organized a promotion at Toronto City Hall for June 23, 1989—World Olympic Day. Hundreds of school children arrived to participate in races. When I got up on the stage to speak, I could hardly believe my eyes. I saw Jack Layton hiding behind the Peace Garden in Nathan Phillips Square at Toronto City Hall. As soon as I got off the stage, I went down and congratulated him for showing up. He confessed, *"It's my day to look after my son and his school class is competing."* Layton was *forced* to come to the World Olympic Day celebration with his young son from a previous marriage, yet apparently had not had the courage to show his face publicly.

Street Kids International

In 1990, TOOC was summoned to City Council to justify why, after four years of dedicated volunteer work, they should continue to support the bid. This was another of Layton's ploys to create a negative vote, shoving yet another stick in the spokes of the wheel of Toronto's bid.

One of our presenters was David Wilson, a volunteer worker with *Street Kids International*. David had graduated from Upper Canada College and Dalhousie University, where he had been awarded the Terry Fox Humanitarian Award for his work with underprivileged young people in Halifax. The mandate of *Street Kids International* is to work with young people who drop out of society and end up on the streets to motivate them to get back into society. We felt that David was well qualified to give his perspective to bear on Toronto's Olympic bid.

City Council had limited all presentations to five minutes each, but they sat in rapt silence as David—all six-feet, five inches of him—held their attention for 15 minutes with his first-hand experiences with youth on the streets. He explained why he was opposed to the rhetoric of *Bread not Circuses* who purported to speak for the underprivileged. David said that the greatest challenge to those trying to get kids off the street is just to get them to fill out an application for a job—any job. The Skydome (later renamed the Rogers Centre) was about to open and many of Toronto's street kids were excited to take just about any job there. Some 200 of them had completed applications to work as hot dog and soft drink vendors. In the eyes of *Street Kids International,* this was a major accomplishment.

Sport is the one activity most youth understand, and there are many activities in which you do not have to be a star to be involved. Every time I see Wayne Gretzky's pal with Down's Syndrome who helps with the Edmonton Oilers, or the young autistic man from Rochester, New York, who shot all those baskets supported by his entire high school, I am moved almost to tears. Canada was so proud of our first Vancouver Gold Medal won by Alexandre Bilodeau and his wonderful brother Frédéric with cerebral palsy cheering so enthusiastically.

David told of his work with young people in Africa, where there was perhaps one television set every 100 miles or so. The inhabitants of the entire region would gather around the set to watch their famous runners or soccer players. I found it interesting that the video London used in its Olympic bid against Paris focused exactly on this—how the motivated youth of a small village in Kenya were dreaming to come to London for the Games in 2012.

David Wilson asked Toronto City Council to realize the value of sport to underprivileged young people, stressing that hosting the Olympics in Toronto would motivate even the most disenfranchised youth of the city to apply for a job.

Final Push

Every two weeks, Mayor Eggleton held a breakfast meeting in his office which I attended in order to brief city councilors and staff on our progress with the bid. We had to produce a bid book for the IOC and deliver it no later than February 15, 1990. It was a detailed 1,500 page document covering all aspects of the bid including financial guarantees and venue proposals.

In order to give us time to set the type, edit and print it, the City had agreed that October 30, 1989 would be the drop-dead date for changes. In late October, Layton walked into one of the meetings to demand that no venue be situated east of Yonge Street—which splits Toronto down the middle—or on City-owned land. He did not want any Olympic facilities in the geographical area of his political base. I was in shock.

Two years earlier, we had asked city planner Ken Rosenberg where the swimming complex should be situated. Ken said that the lower east end of Toronto desperately needed a community sport and social complex for the East Riverdale, St James Town and Regent Park low-cost housing communities. Following Ken's recommendation, this is exactly where TOOC had planned to locate it, and we had held an open design competition for the facility. It had been well publicized and all city councilors had been fully briefed. It would have been the greatest legacy of the Games for

Toronto. Eggleton and Layton were now locked in a political fight to see who was going to be the next mayor. Eggleton demanded that I submit to all of Jack's requests, for a reason that only politicians understand. So Jack Layton killed the swimming complex.

TOOC did not have time to explore other alternatives. We needed a new location for the facility and the to revamp the bid book. I phoned Premier David Peterson to brief him on the crisis. Our proposed solution was to situate the facility on the waterfront at Ontario Place, which is owned by the Province. It took Peterson about two seconds to say okay. In early December, 1989, I demanded a meeting with Eggleton and David Peterson at Queen's Park at which I resigned from TOOC, saying that the constant problems and lack of leadership by Eggleton and interference from his staff, led by Herb Pirk, meant that they should carry the torch to the finish line. I told them that as an unpaid volunteer, I had taken the bid as far as I could and should be replaced. Eggleton was taken aback and just fidgeted nervously. Peterson, in his customary abrupt fashion, immediately responded, *"You are in too deep. Resignation rejected. Mr. Mayor, get off your ass and support TOOC, not Layton!"*

Layton was not through with his sabotage. In 1990, he demanded almost constant debate at City Hall, saying that the 1987 unanimous vote of the previous council was not binding. He was able to schedule another vote in April 1990, only four months before the final vote on the bids in Tokyo.

The changes to the bid book, intervening meetings and constant debates diverted TOOC from presenting Toronto positively to the IOC. Every other week from January to April, city council debated the bid. Atlanta, a one-newspaper town, was coming on strong. Bert Roughton, a reporter with *The Atlanta Journal Constitution*, which was a financial sponsor of their bid, attended every City of Toronto debate. The negatives were headlined in their newspaper and circulated to all IOC voters. Layton was getting the exposure he craved.

Howard Levine, a member of Layton's New Democratic Party,

said he was against the bid, but for personal reasons that he would not disclose. I asked Councilor Barbara Hall about this and she explained confidentially, *"Levine is gay."*

"So what?" I replied.

Barbara went on, *"It is due to what the IOC did in San Francisco."* *"The Games were in L.A., not San Francisco,"* I pointed out. *"No, it is the IOC opposition to the San Francisco Gay and Lesbian Olympic Games,"* she said. I could not believe that a mature Toronto city councilor would hide behind this.

In any event, the decision was made not be the IOC but by the United States Olympic Committee (USOC). Games that focus on unique athletes, who cannot otherwise compete in the Olympic Games, can use the word "Olympics" or a variant in their titles. There are the Paralympics for disabled athletes and the Special Olympics for mentally challenged athletes. There are a good number of gay and lesbian Gold Medal winners in the Olympic Games—sexual orientation or preference does not exclude them from competing. The USOC was right not to allow the use of the name for the Gay and Lesbian Games. The USA was not homophobic, as alleged. The USOC took the San Francisco organizers to the United States Supreme Court, asking that the Gay and Lesbian Games drop the use of the word "Olympics" and won. Levine turned his back on Toronto and voted against our bid because of his support of his gay friends in San Francisco, and was quite the obstructionist.

In April 1990, Layton made an impassioned speech at city council to kill the Toronto bid after three years of diligent work on the part of TOOC. Even though the vote was positively in our favour, the damage had been done. TOOC had responded to every one of Layton's requests, even ensuring, as much as we could, that 60 per cent of the Olympic and Press Villages would be converted to social housing. We moved the venues out of his area of Toronto as he had requested. He had nothing left to attack, so he hung his NDP ("Never Debate Positively") hat on his distrust of the guarantees supplied by the federal Conservative government.

He uses this reason for his militancy to this day. The federal guarantees were exactly the same as they gave Calgary in 1988 and Vancouver for 2010. That was not good enough for Layton and his run for mayor, however. The Mulroney Conservative government was in power at that time and had given us letters from all federal agencies supporting the Toronto bid.

The Conservative Member of Parliament for Pointe Claire, Quebec, and head of the Privy Council was the Honorable Robert Layton, Jack's father. Jack Layton's distrust of the commitments of the Mulroney federal Conservative government meant in essence that he did not trust his father.

WASP

During one of his irate speeches at city council, Jack lashed out at TOOC and attacked me racially for leading a "WASP TOOC." At about 9:00 o'clock that night, I received a call from the research assistant to the Canadian Broadcast Corporation's Joe Coté, host of the radio program *Metro Morning*. The assistant asked if I would be available for Joe Coté to interview me in the morning. *"Sure,"* I replied, *"but I will not lower myself to the level of the racist Mr. Layton and respond to the 'WASP' venom spit out by this man."* She promised me that was not to be brought up. By this time I had become acutely aware of how the media works. Just before going to bed, I told Mary I knew how to handle Coté.

The telephone rang at 7:00 a.m. and it was him. The first question he asked was, *"Paul, what is your reaction to being called a WASP by Jack Layton?"* Prepared, I answered, *"WASP, WASP, WASP—does that mean 'Wily, Aggressive, St. Clair Plumber'?"*

Coté really lost it and, very agitated, lashed out, *"You know what it means."*

"Well, that is what it means to me. What does it mean to you, Joe?" *"White, Anglo-Saxon Protestant,"* he said.

"Oh! I am one of those too," I replied, proud of myself even though I am a Celt, having only Scottish and Irish ancestors.

Gallery of Photos

Royal Canadian Yacht Club: Circa 1910

North American Jr. Championship, Aphrodite Cup,
1950 Montreal with Harry Bruce as crew.

"Simply Messing Around in Boats" at age 18.

Helping Brother John rig his first 14ft Dinghy 1952.

Crewing with brother John in the 14ft Dinghy Bermuda 1954.

International 14 Ft. Dinghy Team Races in Cowes, Isle of Wight, UK. 1958 L-R: Gerald Parks, Geoff Smale (NZ), Bud Whittaker, CAN), "Bungy" McCrae (NZ), Uffa Fox (UK), Harry Jemmet (CAN), Jim Stephens (CAN), Ian Pryde (NZ), ???, Bruce Kirby (CAN), Stewart Morris (UK), Michael Pope (UK), Mike Peacock (UK), Ray Simich (NZ), Keith Shackleton (UK), Ralph Roberts (NZ), Doug Roberts (CAN), Ron Watson(NZ), Harvey Bongard (CAN), Paul Henderson (CAN),

Skip Lennox and me with the Flying Dutchman "Syndi" Marina, 1963 at North Americans, Lavalette,N.J.

"Syndi", Skip Lennox, and me at Enoshima Tokyo Olympic Games 1964.

Blasting across Toronto Harbour in "Syndi", 30kts (50 km), breeze.
Only Skip's head peering through the spray on the trapeze.

The Imperial Poona Yacht Club (Non-Revolting Repulsive Colonial Outpost) was headquartered at the Annex of the RCYC. In 1996, The Poona chartered the Toronto Harbour Com. Tug "J.G. Langton" for the Annual RCYC Sailpast. The Poona flag was dipped in honour of the RCYC Commodore as the Poona Marching Band sailed past. Aft of the wheelhouse is *Bill Gooderham, (Repulsive Commode), John Langton (Triangle), *John Eastwood (Snare Drum), Bill Wilson (Cymbals), *Paul Henderson (Tuba), Joe Prendergast (Trumpet), *Bill Cox (Pump Organ) and Gerry Pangman (Slide Whistle).

(*designates Canadian Olympic Team Members.)

Imperial Poona Yacht Club sahibs performing the "Whistling Beetles". Bill Cox, Bill Wilson, Barclay Livingston, Peter Van Buskirk.

Leaving the church in Beaverton, Labour Day 1965, with the Poona Colour Guard, with Brollies and Poona Flag.

Attacking "Ruthie's Run", Aspen Colorado, with Mary waiting to pick me up.

Gordon Norton and Bill Cox, Founders of The Water Rat,
preparing to sail a Sunfish at the inaugural Water Rat Regatta
December 1970. This shows how the Toronto Outer Harbour
looked when we started to use it. The rocks were there to protect
the erosion of the shore which was happening before "The Spit"
was built, planned by Jack Jones. The barren wasteland, with no
trees, is where the community sailing, rowing and windsurfing
clubs now operate. The land was allocated by the Hon. Donald
MacDonald. The Martin Goodman Trail now winds between the
Water Rat and the Hearn Power Generating Station. More
recently, the same group has tried to get a rowing/dragon boat
course dug out north of the Water Rat to save it for recreational
use. Bill Gooderham, Head Cheese of the Water Rat, planted the
first trees there. Gordon Norton, Bill Cox and I are proud of the
fact that we started the recreational use of this industrial wasteland
guided by the vision of Jack Jones of the Toronto Harbour
Commission.

1972 Canadian Olympic Soling Bronze Medal Crew
L-R, *Paul Henderson (Coach), Don Barnes (Trainer),*
David Miller (Skipper), John Ekels (Crew), Dr. Jack Balmer,
Bill Cox (Team Manager), Paul Cote (Crew, Founder Greenpeace).

Racing with Martha at the Albacore Worlds 1982. Great crew. 12 years of
enjoyable competition.

The lovely Mary in her "Hanbok" during the 1988 Seoul Olympic Games. Left is Miss Lee our hostess and the right is Miss Kim, Tallberg's hostess.

Brian Williams, Canadian Olympic TV Host, about to be interviewed.

IOC President, Juan Antonio Samaranch, visiting Toronto 1988 during the Olympic Bid.

Construction of the Rogers Centre (SkyDome) 1989.

xii

*George Gross and me getting
ready for another adventure*

*Basil Rodomar sailing in Toronto Bay
with IOC Members.*

*Hagood Hardy playing in
Tokyo with a jazz friend.*

Step into my office! Goran Petersson, now ISAF President, Ken Ryan, Michael Jackson taken by Tom Webster. Barrier Island originally proposed by Atlanta for the Savannah Olympic Regatta awash during the fortunate Hurricane of 1995 forcing the OCOG to listen to those who knew reality.

Ted Turner with Jane Fonda talking to Ted Rogers. '93 World Series between the Atlanta Braves and Toronto Blue Jays.

Andy Donato's cartoon, Toronto Sun, during the Atlanta '96 Olympic Games.

*Paul Elvstrom, "The Great Dane" four time
Olympic Gold Medal Winner. Visiting RCYC 1999.*

Crewing with Raimondo Tonelli on Lago de Garda, Italy 1998. Age 65.

xvi

Credit Mark Dadswell /Allsport

Johanson and Jarvi, Finland, sailing to Gold, Barker and Hiscocks, UK, sailing to Silver, McKee Bros. Mckee, USA, sailing to Bronze in the 49er Class at Rushcutters Bay of the Sydney 2000 Olympic Games, Australia.

Athens' Security Team getting ready for the races in George Andreadis' speed boat at the Olympic Marina.

The Canadian 2008 Olympic Women's Yngling Crew Left to Right: Jen Provan, Katie Abbott, Martha Henderson.

Helen Stewart, Gilbert Felli, Bob Elphinston, Frankie Fredericks, Philippe Bovy, Sophie Willatts

Jaqueline Barrett, Paul Henderson, Els Van Breda Vriesman, Simon Balderstone, Patrick Jarvis, José Luis Marco

Sam Ramsamy, Nawel El Moutawakel, The Queen, The Duke of Edinburgh, The Princess Royal, Mustapha Larfaoui, Ser Miang Ng

Nawal El Moutawakel and Gilbert Felli. Our beloved IOC 2012 Evaluation Commission leaders.

IOC 2012 E.C. visit Élysée Palace, Paris, with Jacques Chirac, IOC
Members Jean-Claude Killy and Maurice Herzog.

IOC 2012 Evaluation Commission meeting at the Kremlin in the Cabinet
Rotunda with President Vladimir Putin (left of Nawal) and other Russian
Officials including Vaicheslav Fetisov. (8 in from right)

*Celebrating Commodore R.D. Grants 90th Birthday
November 16th 2005.
L-R: David Howard, Gerry Rochon, Richard Grant,
Commodore R.D. Grant, Michael Grant, Daphne Grant Peacock,
Geoffrey Zimmerman, Basil Rodomar.*

*At the end of my time at ISAF and the IOC.
What a great ride it has been for a kid from
Toronto Island.*

Robert "Grandpa Bob" Grant Henderson, Founder of R.G. Henderson and Son Ltd. Company Sargeant Major, The 48th Highlanders of Canada.

Albert "Ab" John Grant Henderson. It is obvious looking at Dad why he always said I looked like the milkman.

Edythe Henderson's, "Mom", favorite photo with HRH Prince Phillip during his 1981 visit to the RCYC.

*Sandra Mary Henderson on graduation
from the University of Toronto. "Sister
Sandra" is a very close friend of both
Mary and her brother and this is a
compliment to her patience.*

*Maude and Norman McLeod boarding a tramp
steamer in Halifax on one of their Caribbean
trips.*

Mary walking with her three children in 1974.

*John, on his graduation from
George Brown College in Business.*

Martha's graduation from Western University.

I wish one day would pass without someone asking how lovely Mary puts up with me. Now for over 40 years.

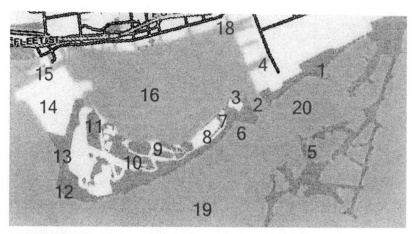

Toronto Island and Surrounding Waters

1) Water Rat and Outer Harbour Sailing Clubs
2) Eastern Gap
3) Clapp's Cove and Henderson Cottage
4) Cherry St. Bridge and Ship Channel Airport
5) "The Spit"
6) Ward's Island Beach
7) Ward's Island
8) Algonquin Island
9) Royal Canadian Yacht Club
10) Centre Island

11) Mugg's Island
12) Gibralter Point
13) Hanlan's Point
14) Toronto Island

15) Western Gap
16) Toronto Bay
17) CN Tower and Roger's Centre
18) RCYC City Crane
19) Lake Ontario
20) Outer Harbour

Sabot

Brutal Beast

Finn Dinghy

Tornado Catamaran

Yngling

Laser Class

Star Class

Owen Churchill's "Angelita" won the Eight Meter series for the U.S.A. in the 1932 Olympics at Los Angeles

America's Cup Class   *Dragon Class*

Final Straw

The final straw in the Jack Layton charade was the letter he wrote to his colleagues at City Hall on September 19, 1990, one day after we lost in Tokyo due to his sabotage of Toronto's 1996 bid. This self-serving politician had the nerve to open his letter as follows:

"Dear Colleagues,

We have an opportunity to recognize the hard work of those many Torontonians who worked on the Olympic proposal to achieve the goals we set for ourselves when we approved the Olympic Commitment... Specifically, the commitment was focused on achieving the following objectives: a more equitable city, an environmentally healthy city, and a financially sound city. The Toronto Olympic Commitment was proposed as a 'covenant' between the City Council and the people of the city, providing Torontonians with the foundation principles upon which a Toronto Olympics would be staged.

We should renew that covenant now.

Signed,

Jack Layton, Councilor"

Richard Petty, general manager of the City of Toronto housing department, answered Layton's diatribe with an open letter to city council, listing what had been lost with Toronto's defeat at Layton's hands:

1) provincial allocation of 1,000 social housing units;
2) definite schedule for development and faster build-out— five years instead of 10 to 15 years;
3) financial support from senior levels of government to offset the cost of developing a fully serviced community;
4) provision of an opportunity to deck the CN rail corridor;
5) potentially earlier reconfiguration of the Gardiner Expressway-Lakeshore Boulevard corridor;
6) financial loss of TOOC rental to offset capital costs.

I found Olivia Chow, Jack Layton's wife, to be equally as racist as her husband, or at least prepared to play the race card against a "WASP" if required. Jack ran for mayor against Eggleton in 1991. I was very bitter at what he had done, and obviously still am, as I witness the continued decay of my Toronto. At every all-candidates meeting, I would sit at the front, my bald head shining, and stare at candidate Layton. I was easily noticed, but never spoke at any of the meetings. I did not need to—someone in the audience would always bring up his sabotage of the Toronto Olympic bid. One of these meetings was hosted by the Chinese business community at the University of Toronto's Koffler Hall. The meeting was attended by a cross-section of Toronto's multicultural communities, although Chinese Canadians were in the majority. As I walked by Olivia's seat in the back, she lashed out, *"You are not welcome here. This is for the Chinese community."*

I did not answer, but knew I was getting to the Laytons. I sat at the front on the aisle. Olivia came and sat right behind. Leaning over, she demanded that I leave as this was only for the Chinese and First Nations Torontonians. I responded, *"Well, if I wait long enough, maybe you will include the WASPs who live in Toronto."*

The confrontation was noticed by a number of those present, and a few days later I got a letter from the chair, William Wen Jr., apologizing on behalf of the Chinese business community for the rudeness of Olivia Chow. He added that everyone was welcome at their meetings.

The left-wing hordes were diverted for a short time, as Layton and Levine lost the 1992 mayoralty election, but they and their ilk achieved their goal with the election of David Miller as mayor. They are in complete control of a once great city that I hope will withstand this disastrous period in its political life and again strive to be great.

Jack Layton is now leader of the federal New Democratic Party. His wife Olivia Chow was elected as an NDP federal Member of Parliament (MP). Marilyn Churley was elected a Member of Provincial Parliament (MPP) but lost as a federal candidate. Shapcott worked his way into various government bureaucracies and ran twice unsuccessfully as a federal NDP candidate in the riding where I live. Liz Amers was dropped by her NDP colleagues and continues to live on Toronto Island. Peter Tabuns, another member of Layton's NDP, was recently elected an MPP in Ontario.

My biggest objection to these academic left-wing ideologues is that they dishonestly say they represent working people, especially union members and tradesmen with whom I have spent my working life. The tradesmen who built Toronto are generally hardworking family members who have bought their own homes, pay their mortgages and love sport. They are so far removed in lifestyle and outlook from these career politicians that it is insulting to them to be used in this way.

It is my hope that Canadians will see through this group who have brought the once dynamic City of Toronto to its knees and are now spreading out through the parliaments of Ontario and Canada. When people such as Buzz Hargrove, leader of the Canadian Auto Workers Union, and Bob Rae, former Ontario NDP premier, desert these destructive demagogues and their political ideology, it should serve as a wake-up call to all Canadian voters to abandon the academic-driven socialist ship.

Tokyo Vote, September 1990

There were six bidders in the competition: Athens, Atlanta, Melbourne, Belgrade, Manchester and Toronto. Hope springs eternal, but I knew at the start of the summer that Toronto's bid was in deep trouble, having been sabotaged by the local protests and manifest lack of political will at all three levels of government. The final blow was delivered by Premier David Peterson when he called an Ontario provincial election for September 8, 1990—10 days before the IOC vote on the bids in Tokyo. Peterson went into the election with an overwhelming majority, but it eroded quickly. Ontario elected its first ever left-wing NDP government under Bob Rae. Rae freely admits that he was unprepared to govern. One of his influential constituencies was Jack Layton's *Bread not Circuses*, which had Rae's ear. With only a few days left to the IOC vote, we had no time to brief the new government fully. Layton, Shapcott and *Bread not Circuses* had an inside track with a direct entrée to the premier's office. Rae almost cancelled the bid outright, but decided to let it go to the finish.

I was in London, England, promoting the bid on the day of the election and returned home to a crisis meeting with TOOC. We contacted the new premier and asked him to send to Tokyo Mrs. Zanana Akande, an NDP candidate who had just been elected to the new legislature. She had been actively involved in the bid with her husband and had entertained African IOC members in their home. She was an elegant and articulate force in the Afro-Canadian community. Rae appointed her a minister in his new government, but refused to send her to Tokyo as TOOC requested.

At Layton and Shapcott's urging, Premier Rae opted instead to support the *Bread not Circuses* sabotage of the bid by sending as his official representatives "Pink" Floyd Laughren from Sudbury, and John Piper. At the first meeting with Laughren in Tokyo, he was less than supportive of our efforts. He admitted that he was not sure why he had been sent, since it was well known that he did not believe in the Olympics and, being from Sudbury, was not a great fan of Toronto. I suggested that he use the taxpayers' money to see Japan and keep out of our way, which he did—for the most part.

I had no idea who Piper was, but I soon discovered that he was Layton's schoolboy friend from Montreal who was working on Jack's campaign for mayor of Toronto and had been sent at Layton's request to embarrass Toronto. He was a consultant to Hill and Knowlton, an American public relations firm that had been retained by Atlanta to do the PR work for their bid. I have met with Bob Rae several times over the years since then and, although he has never apologized, he has said that if he had thought more about it he would have acted differently.

One of the volunteers working for the Atlanta bid was an old friend whom I had taught to sail at the RCYC before he moved south. He asked to speak to me because he was very disturbed by what he had heard. Every morning, the TOOC team got together to plan our lobbying activities for the day and go over the previous day's results. He said that all our strategies and information were being passed on through Piper to Atlanta and that we should ensure that he was isolated. From that point on, we never again spoke with either Piper or Laughren.

My Atlanta friend explained that copies of *The Toronto Sun* from the day after the Ontario election were stacked in the lobby of the Atlanta hospitality house. The headline read, "Ontario Turns Socialist." Atlanta believed this was a significant negative for Toronto, because ever since the Berlin Wall fell, the Eastern Bloc countries were going the other way.

Before leaving Toronto, I had heard rumblings that Layton and *Bread not Circuses* were going to physically disrupt Toronto's bid in Tokyo. We had heard that two protestors were in fact already in Tokyo living with Japanese anarchists. We believed that since they had no accreditation, they would not get past security into the IOC hotel. We went ahead oblivious of John Piper and the shenanigans he was orchestrating.

We discovered that the two *Bread not Circuses* protestors were David Kidd and Jan Borowy. Kidd, whose brother Bruce had competed in Olympic track events, was a member of the Ontario Communist Party and co-chaired Jack Layton's mayoralty campaign with John Piper. Jan Borowy had been a good field hockey player at York University and was slated to be on the 1988 Olympic team. Just weeks before the Games, however, she was cut from the team. Understandably, this left her with a deep scar and she turned against the Olympics.

The IOC Session runs for three days. Members are cloistered in a large hall for their discussions, breaking at noon for lunch. As they came down the hotel stairway from the second floor convention rooms at lunch time, they were met by a small teepee that had been quickly erected in the lobby where, dressed in rags, Kidd and Borowy were beating aluminum pots with wooden spoons and shouting, *"No games for Toronto! Feed the poor! Only profit for the rich!"*

The IOC members were appalled. Atlanta had 30 youngsters singing *God Bless America* and *Georgia*. Toronto had these *Bread not Circuses* nuts. It was not only a disgrace, but also a boil on the back of our great city. The hotel management did not know what to do because of John Piper. His role in the affair was to plant himself in the hotel manager's office to delay any action, arguing that it was standard operating procedure in Canada for protestors to act this way. He told the hotel management that the Japanese would be perceived as insulting Canada if he threw these nuts out of the hotel. Piper was able to delay their expulsion for over half an hour, but by then the damage was done.

I could not believe it. Basil Rodomar, Ray McNeil and Norman Seagram were dispatched to make sure I did not explode. Otto Jelinek was so furious he started to run at David Kidd to punch him out, which he could have easily done. Joe Halstead, Deputy Minister of Tourism in the Ontario cabinet—and a very burly man—tackled Jelinek and carried him away. Joe was a great supporter of TOOC, but he did the right thing. A fist fight with Jelinek was just the sort of thing Kidd was hoping for to create more negative press coverage and disgrace Toronto even more than Jack Layton and his gang of dissidents had already done.

That afternoon, we rehearsed our one-hour presentation to the IOC members. On behalf of the federal government, former Prime Minister Joe Clarke started to read a speech that had been prepared for him but immediately called time. *"This is crap!"* Joe announced, and demanded a coffee break. He then wrote his own speech which was far better. Joe was excellent. We had also received a fax from Toronto saying that the TOOCers left at home had received more than 75,000 telegrams of support from the citizens of Toronto.

The next day, we lined up to march into the presentation. All of us were very uptight. Joe Clarke went to the front of the line with a smile on his face, announcing that, as he was known as a great marcher, everyone should follow his lead. We all broke up—as any Canadian knows, Joe's gait is one unique to him. In we went and presented Toronto's bid with style and class befitting a great city.

The vote was unusual and had a strange twist. In the first round, Belgrade was discarded with Athens leading and Atlanta just ahead of Toronto and Melbourne, but all very close. In the second round, Manchester fell by the wayside with fewer than half the votes than they had in the first round. Melbourne jumped up by nine votes, just ahead of Atlanta with Athens still in the lead. In the third round, Toronto jumped ahead of Melbourne whose vote fell, much to their dismay. Toronto needed to pick up most of the Melbourne vote in order to beat Atlanta. It was obvious that Athens was not going to win. The Melbourne vote split, however, and Toronto was dropped. Atlanta won the right to host the Olympic Games of 1996.

At the announcement, there were 20,000 Torontonians assembled at the SkyDome. They were deflated when Samaranch announced, *"Atlanta."* The CBC had set up a camera in a *Bread not Circuses* supporter's home. On the announcement of "Atlanta," they broke into *God Bless America*. They were proud of having destroyed 80,000 people-years of jobs and a 10 billion dollar economic impact for Toronto which, at the time, was plunging into a severe economic depression. The decision greatly affected not only sport and business, but all aspects of Toronto's once vibrant cultural mosaic.

I thought that Athens would get the emotional vote and win in the end. Their bid showed that they could run the Games. I did not factor in the repercussions of the fall of the Berlin Wall in 1988, before which most of the 14 Eastern Bloc votes were slated to go with Athens, as they had harboured anti-American sentiments all through the cold war. After the Wall came down, these countries were all in chaos; most of the Eastern Bloc voters were unsure of their future. With Toronto's bid disrupted, the USA was the only meaningful choice left to them.

Mary and I returned home with the TOOCers the next day, proud of the way in which we had tried to put Toronto forward in a stylish and honest manner despite the efforts of ambitious, elected officials to drag their city through the mud.

The next period of my life was equally as exciting and challenging. My first priority was to ensure that my plumbing company survived in the entrenched economic recession of the 1990s. I withdrew from public life and watched from the sidelines as left-wing ideologues strengthened their hold on city hall.

Bidding Experiences In Toronto

When I reflect on Toronto's 1996 bidding experience, I do so fondly because it was an incredible five years for Mary and me. I knew some of the 100 IOC members before the bid due to my involvement in international sailing, but I came to know them all to a greater or lesser degree during the bid period. Some visited Toronto and we in turn visited them in their homes. I struck up a number of friendships, many of which endure to this day.

Don German Rieckehoff: Puerto Rico

There was never an IOC Member who so loved his country and was so intent on ensuring that the Olympic Movement was enshrined there than Don German Rieckehoff from Puerto Rico. It is amazing what he accomplished in his lifetime, and it is an embarrassment to the wealthy Province of Ontario that we have not been able to follow his lead. An engaging and true Olympian, he personally developed the Albergue Olimpico, a great training facility with basic accommodation for athletes. Such a facility is exactly what we want for the National Sports Institute in Toronto.

Don German also wanted the youth of Puerto Rico to be exposed to Olympic athletes—he needed to draw them to his dream. To the waterslides and playing fields of the Albergue he wanted to add a zoo as another attraction even though it was difficult to justify the expense. He and his gracious wife came to visit Toronto during the

Royal Winter Fair, the world renowned agricultural fair and horse show. At the fair he stopped beside a unique display of various chickens breeds. He could not believe the number of different varieties, more than 100 of them. Some resembled poodles, others ostriches, but they were all chickens. Don German thought that if he could get a few eggs donated, he could hatch them in Puerto Rico and inaugurate a very exotic but cheap zoo. At his request, we sent him the mailing addresses of all the egg producers. If you visit the Albergue Olimpico today, you will see a most wonderful display of chickens. The eggs were all donated from Toronto.

Prince Albert: Monaco

Prince Albert of Monaco visited Toronto on a stopover during one of his trips to the USA, homeland of his mother, Princess Grace. He always enjoyed spending time with active athletes. During the Worrall gala, we left him in the company of Sue Holloway, Olympian in both Summer (kayaking Silver medalist) and Winter Games, and her husband Greg Joy (Olympic Silver medalist in high jumping). We took him to a Blue Jays baseball game when John Cerutti was pitching. Prince Albert and Cerutti had attended prep school together. At the end of the game, Prince Albert went down onto the field and out to second base. Standing in the cavernous SkyDome, the three of them yelled, *"Where's Curly?"* (I would respectfully suggest to Monaco's head of state that he look no further than his own mirror.)

Phil Coles: Australia

Phil Coles, a personable member of the IOC from Bondi Beach in Sydney, Australia, was an Olympic kayaker, so we left him with Sue Holloway during his visit to Toronto. They went kayaking up the Rouge River. Phil had not been paddling for years. He had put on a little weight and his shorts were too short, leaving a rather exposed expanse of bottom skin. He wore the skin off his derrière and could not sit down for weeks. Phil spent most of his time in Toronto standing. He never declines an invitation and becomes a good friend to the bid cities and sport federations. With the recent implementation of somewhat draconian ethical guidelines by the IOC, he has come under some criticism, but he is one of those IOC members who appreciate the responsibility to promote sport and the Olympic movement.

Tay Wilson: New Zealand

Tay Wilson, a bear of a man from Auckland, New Zealand, has all the usual bravado of a Kiwi rower—they tend not to listen and by brute strength and seeming ignorance believe they can accomplish anything. Toronto's bid was, for the most part, centred on the waterfront. We did not need to use helicopters or limousines under police escort. TOOC took Tay and a few other IOC members sailing in Basil Rodomar's 30-foot Nonsuch catboat. (For non-sailors, a catboat has a high mast set at the bow with only one sail.) I was confident that I could instruct the IOC members how to sail. I let them steer, even though some of them had never sailed before. I gave all of them the same instruction: *"When the boom comes flying over on a jibe, duck. Do not grab anything!"*

In true Kiwi fashion, Tay did not listen and with his tough rower's hands grabbed the mainsheet (that's rope, to landlubbers). He wished, and so did I, that he had not done that. He peeled the skin off both hands, leaving him with a painful memory of Toronto, but we are both able to laugh at that today.

The Raja Balendra Singh: India

The Raja Balendra Singh from Patiala in the Punjab was a large man with an infectious smile and laugh. He told me that the Patiala turban is the finest in the world. I have great fun going up to Sikhs I meet in Toronto, and opening with the line, *"Is that a Patiala turban?"* Their initial confusion usually gives way to a warm smile and friendly conversation about Patiala.

In 1989, the Raja explained that there were great difficulties in the Punjab and he could bring only 600 dollars out of India. That

TOOC would have to subsidize his trip was a source of great embarrassment to him. He said he would come only if Mary and I would in turn visit Delhi and Patiala in order that he might return the hospitality. We stayed at the home of his son, Raja Rhandir Singh, who later became secretary-general of the Olympic Committee of India and an IOC member. The Punjab was closed, but the Raja wanted to take us to Patiala, north of Delhi, where he was born. Rhandir rapped my bald head in one of his elegant turbans and off we went through several police checkpoints to Patiala.

We were taken on an inner tour of the Maharajah's palace, a splendiferous estate, which few in the outside world have ever seen. The Maharajah, his father, had four wives, each with a separate abode and 250 concubines, some of whom still live in the palace. As we walked through, they turned their heads so that we could not see their faces. In the depths of the palace we came upon an indoor swimming pool with a gazebo in the middle and a swing strung from the ceiling. The Raja explained that the girls would swing over the pool to the gazebo, where they would land in front of the Maharajah.

The kitchens were spectacular. The Maharajah loved French cooking and imported a bevy of French chefs to Patiala. The Raja loved to cook and would spend hours learning from the chefs. Poor people from the village were always welcome to come and eat at the palace kitchens.

The Raja told me that when Mountbatten came to Patiala as viceroy after World War II, the Maharajah, who loved to stick it to the English, entertained him on the palace's front porch. The porch is so immense that it spans the three large cricket fields onto which it fronts, and which the Maharajah covered with his collection of Oriental rugs. As he sat with Mountbatten, a bizarre parade passed in front of them—a multitude of nannies dressed in nurse's uniforms each wheeled a baby carriage. *"What is this?"* Mountbatten inquired.

"This year's production!" the Maharajah proudly replied.

The Maharajah died in his forties—I guess with a smile on his face. The new Maharajah, the eldest son, donated the palace to sport in India and became one of the most revered and involved statesmen in the Punjab.

At one point during the 1990 bid process, the Raja called to ask if I would meet him at the Toronto Cricket Curling and Skating Club. He had come on his own, not under the auspices of TOOC. He explained that one of his children who lived in Toronto was in some sort of crisis and asked for our help, which we gladly supplied. By way of thanks, he offered to prepare a wonderful dinner in our house for ten of my closest friends, but warned that we would be eating late, as he was interested in the quality of the food and not in the timing. The feast was to be held on a Saturday night. The Raja came early in the morning so that Mary could take him down to the local Indian market where he would personally select all the ingredients. At 3:00 p.m. he started to cook, fortified by the Scotch that he preferred to drink neat. The air was redolent of the sweet and pungent aroma of exotic Eastern cuisine. I am sure the neighbours wondered what the hell was going on. The guests arrived around 7:00 p.m. He had also invited his two daughters, one of whom—Chotu—traveled everywhere with him and tied his turbans. The kitchen was in chaos as the Raja held court, entertaining us all with his wonderful stories. At midnight, dinner was served. It was beyond description. What a great man he was!

Jan Staubo: Norway

Jan Staubo had a great affinity for Canada, especially Toronto. He had first come here as a young man at the start of World War II, to train as a fighter pilot at Little Norway, now the Toronto Island Airport. I suppose he was one of the flyers we had given cookies to years before. He took great pleasure in relating that he had been in more jails in more countries than any Olympian. Staubo was shot down over Dieppe during the doomed Canadian raid early in the war. He was captured and interned in various German prisoner-of-war camps, and was one of the organizers of the Great Escape at Stalag 17. His captors' suspicions were aroused, however, and he was relocated to another camp just days before the escape. After the war, he came to Halifax to recuperate. Jan was a fine tennis player, winning many tournaments in Eastern Canada.

In 1989, to commemorate the fiftieth anniversary of the Norwegians' air training at Toronto Island Airport, the Canadian government designated as a public park the land on the edge of "Little Norway" where the barracks had stood. It would be deemed Norwegian land with the Canadian and Norwegian flags flying together. His Majesty King Olav V and some 250 Norwegian fliers from World War II came to dedicate the land. The king, an accomplished sailor, invited me to accompany him to the ceremony. It was rumoured that around that time, a number of Toronto matrons about the same age as the Norwegians sent their husbands to the Muskoka Lakes, and took advantage of the opportunity to renew old acquaintances.

I had lunch with the King and Jan Staubo and, as the stories began to flow, Staubo said, *"I will not go to the Royal York Hotel because they do not like Norwegians."*

Stepping into the trap, I asked, *"Why?"*

"When we got our wings, we always went to the Royal York to celebrate," Staubo related. *"When we threw the furniture out of the bedroom windows, they put the hotel off limits."*

"Jan your memory is failing," intervened the king. *"It was not when you threw the furniture out of the windows. It was when you broke the beds and threw them out that caused the ban."*

The Norwegians—especially the King and Jan—had a wonderful time at the reunion and, I suspect, so did the Toronto ladies.

Sam Ramsamy: South Africa

I had met Sam Ramsamy several years earlier in London, where he was exiled by the apartheid South African government. Sam is a very short man with a tenacious heart who was the leader of the opposition to apartheid in sport in South Africa. He was dedicated to this one issue since he believed that sport should be for all and done together, no matter an athlete's colour, race or religion. When Sam came to Toronto, a number of political activists wanted to corral him. I made the mistake of setting up a meeting, after which Sam took me aside and in his quiet way explained that he was upset because these activists were advancing their skewed political agendas on the back of sport. That was not his motivation, however. Anti-apartheid in sport was a separate focus for Sam, not to be confused with other issues.

Along with Nelson Mandela, Sam has been honoured with a park in South Africa bearing his name. We took him on our customary sailing tour and, as is my fashion, I kidded Sam that his wife Helga was a more accomplished sailor.

Kevan Gosper: Australia

Kevan Gosper, who had been a senior official with Shell Oil, arrived with the singular mission of inspecting our sports venues with a view to how transit would work. He asked to travel to some of the venues in the same way the spectators would. For this reason, TOOC took him on the Toronto subway system, and not in limousines. We took him to a baseball game at the SkyDome (now the Rogers Centre), where he went down onto the field before the start of the game. He had never seen artificial turf before. Amazed, he stomped on the turf and at exactly that moment, the warning sirens rang out and the spectacular SkyDome roof began to open. He was incredulous. To this day, I call him "God Gosper."

One episode in particular demonstrates Kevan's integrity and sense of propriety: TOOC always supplied the airline tickets to our visitors. When Kevan returned home to Melbourne, Australia, he took his ticket to his travel agent, obtained a refund and sent the money back to us.

Roque Napoleón Pena: Dominican Republic

Another good news story concerns Roque Napoleón Pena from the Dominican Republic. TOOC worked with other bid cities and we all got along well, helping each other where we could. Roque was a rather quiet person with a lovely sense of humour. He told the bidding cities that he wanted to travel from the Dominican Republic to Atlanta, then to Toronto, Manchester and Melbourne, arriving in Tokyo in time for the vote. He wanted to do this all in two weeks. We spent a good deal of time on the telephone with the other bid cities, setting up the trip and sharing the cost. When the ticket was ready, we sent it to Roque. He stared in shock at the cost printed on the ticket then took it to his travel agent who was able to arrange a ticket at half the price we had all orchestrated. He then sent us back the excess money.

Pirjo Haggman: Finland

Peter Tallberg and Pirjo Haggman, IOC members in Finland, had been my friends for years. Peter and I had both sailed in the 1964, 1968 and 1972 Olympics. We were both IYRU vice-presidents; he became president in 1986, and I succeeded him in 1994. His three sons lived with us at various times, one in the early 1980s and another in 1984—both before the TOOC bid. The third visited us in 1990 after the bid. The middle son invited Mary and me to his wedding to Helsinki in 1987. While we were there, Peter asked me to have lunch with Pirjo Haggman and her husband Bjarne.

Pirjo was one of Europe's great Olympic runners, a truly fine and attractive person who grew up in a small town in the middle of the country. Bjarne was a forestry expert. From one good look at a forest he could determine the value of the timber stand. Bjarne had spent time in Ottawa and other parts of Ontario on a Finland-Canada forestry exchange program a few years earlier. Both the Province of Ontario and the Government of Canada had publicized job openings for Finns with his special skill. There were 250 practitioners in Finland and a great need for them in Canada. When Bjarne's application to work in Canada was accepted, he came to Ontario with their two young sons. Tallberg wanted me to look out for them when they arrived, and I said I would.

Both Pirjo and I went separately to clear their arrival with IOC President Juan Antonio Samaranch. We did not want allegations of a conflict of interest to be thrown up against the Toronto bid or give the appearance that I was doing them a favour in exchange for their votes in Tokyo. Samaranch agreed that it was all right. The Haggmans were scheduled to arrive just after school ended in June, 1998, but Pirjo's mother took quite ill and they stayed in Finland until her mother died. They rescheduled their arrival for Christmas week.

I had no idea what the Ontario government was doing with the forestry department. In their wisdom, they had decided to move the bureaucracy from Toronto to Sault Ste. Marie in Northern Ontario just months before the Haggmans were to arrive. The forestry department staff and their families were uprooted as they had to leave behind their schools, friends and lifestyles. They were not a happy group. On my journey home from a Canadian Olympic Committee meeting in Winnipeg, I stopped in Sault Ste. Marie and met with senior staff members of the forestry department to review arrangements for the arrival of the Haggmans. I wanted to make sure they would be properly looked after.

The office manager told me that housing in Sault Ste. Marie was tight because of all the relocations, and that the government would engage the services of A.E. LePage Realtor to find appropriate accommodation for the Haggmans. He assured me that they would be welcomed with open arms. The government did in fact find them a rather unpretentious frame house.

I was in Florida with my family over Christmas when I got a panic call from the TOOC office. The landlord of the house in Sault Ste. Marie refused to accept a lease or cheque signed by a foreigner from Finland. There was a metre of snow piled high and it was 15 degrees below zero. The Haggmans were taken into a hotel until their only friend in Canada—Henderson—could sort it out. I told the TOOC staff to issue the cheque and sign the lease. After all, the Government of Ontario had hired Bjarne Haggman and had found him the rental house. All the bureaucrats who were involved were away on Christmas holidays.

The rent payment was entered into the TOOC books as an account receivable, as were all TOOC expenditures. It took months to resolve because of the foot-dragging inherent in all government bureaucracy and the animosity that had built up against the government by those who had been relocated to Sault Ste. Marie. TOOC and the Haggmans were caught in the middle. The rent for the house was 600 dollars per month, a sum indicative of the modesty of the accommodation for a family of four. Bjarne's salary was 25,000 dollars a year, which was 25 per cent below the remuneration paid to Ontario citizens for the same job.

The Government of Ontario realized that in Pirjo they had a famous athlete in their midst. They had created an initiative to encourage young women to become involved in sport, promoting participation and fitness. They asked Pirjo if she would accept a paid position as a speaker at schools and seminars on the subject of women in sport. She agreed to do so only as an unpaid volunteer because it was against the Olympic charter for her to accept a fee.

I was in Melbourne at the 1999 sailing world championship when the infamous "Olympic Bid Scandal" broke loose in Salt Lake City. Richard Pound reported that the Salt Lake officials were pointing the finger at Toronto's bid and Pirjo Haggman. I could not believe it. Spending two years counting trees and living in Sault Ste. Marie in the winter is nobody's idea of luxury. Salt Lake City was trying to obfuscate their scandalous actions by shifting the spotlight to Toronto.

I immediately flew home to the media frenzy. On my first night home, I answered my doorbell to find a rather attractive woman standing at my door holding a book. I had said no more than hello when a man with a TV camera stepped out from behind a big tree and the woman started into an aggressive interview, the microphone hidden in her book. I slammed the door in her face, but it was too late. It had all been taped ready to play across the nation on television. This so-called investigative reporter then went to Sault Ste. Marie and again on national television waved what she called a TOOC cheque. It was not a cheque, however; it was only a receipt from the landlord's books with no signature and no record of who had signed it. Soon afterward, the CEO of the TV network called me to apologize for the actions of this woman, and she was subsequently dismissed.

Back in Finland, the press was on fire against Pirjo. I thought the Toronto press was difficult, but the Finnish press makes them look like Sunday school teachers. They harassed Pirjo to the point were she resigned because of the trauma it put her through. She had no reason to resign and would have eventually been vindicated. I phoned Samaranch and was very forceful—to say the least—urging him to protect this great athlete. He said he could do nothing because she had resigned. I asked both Samaranch and Jacques Rogge to reopen the Pirjo Haggman issue, but they would not. In my view, the Finnish press should apologize to Pirjo, a great Finnish athlete, for such unwarranted character assassination.

IOC Members

TOOC's motto was: "Everyone in the world has a relative in Toronto." We have more than 200 community organizations representing and honouring their native countries. Most IOC members are well known in their countries and many are sports heroes. When they came to Toronto we asked the respective community associations to host them, which they did proudly and with enthusiasm, and it was great for the citizens of Toronto. TOOC left the IOC members in the company of their respective communities without our supervision. Raja Balendra Singh was hosted at the Sikh Temple in Markham. Pal Schmitt, multiple Olympic Gold Medal winner in fencing, disappeared for two days with our Hungarian community. Sam Ramsamy, anti-apartheid sport activist from South Africa and colleague of Nelson Mandela, was actively involved with Toronto's African community. Dr. Kevin O'Flanagan, multiple sports hero, was taken over by the zealous Irish. Venezuelan equestrian Flor Isava, who competed many times in show jumping at the Royal Winter Fair, was very popular. Anton Geesink, Gold Medal winner in judo, visited several judo clubs giving seminars during his stay with Toronto's large Dutch community. Poland's Irena Szewinska spent a full day at the Polish Hall on Beverly Street. Fernando Lima Bello from Portugal arrived during the visit of their famous marathon runner Rosa Mota, and his wife sang with the Toronto Mendelssohn Choir.

These were just a few of the wonderful visitors from the Olympic family to whom we had the opportunity to expose Toronto. *Bread not Circuses* and its leaders should realize that Toronto's citizens were involved with the bid on many, many levels, and not just superficially in the political arena.

Observation:

As the Salt Lake media frenzy grew more and more animated it became quite childish. Admittedly there were half a dozen IOC members out of more than 100 from every corner of the world who should have been and were disciplined, but most of the allegations of wrongdoing were unwarranted. Within any organization of 120 individuals, be they priests, doctors, lawyers, journalists or athletes, you will no doubt find a few questionable characters among the delegates.

IOC Meetings

From 1985 to 1990, bidding for the 1996 Games required that we travel extensively to meet with the IOC members in their homes, at IOC sessions and at major sporting events. Since the IOC instituted a ban on members' visits to bidding cities in 1990, direct contact with the IOC voters now must be done more or less clandestinely by going to where the members are. The irony is that members of the Olympic press corps are allowed to make paid visits traveling business class to bidding cities, but the voters themselves are prohibited from going. I made many a trip during the bid process and more than a few of them were unforgettable.

IOC Session 1986 Lausanne

My first exposure to the Olympic family came in 1986

when I traveled to Lausanne for the final vote on the 1992 bids. Back then, the IOC held both the Summer and Winter Games during the same year. All the 1992 bid cities had arranged impressive hospitality suites at the Beau Rivage Hotel, one of the truly upscale hotels in the world, with promotion booths at the Palais Beaulieu Convention Centre. This was an eye-opener for me—I could see what lay in store for Toronto. The bidding commitments have escalated dramatically every four years to the point where bid expenditures for the 2012 Games are at least five times what TOOC spent for the 1996 Olympic bid, yet the IOC says they have curtailed bidding costs. How naïve of them!

The best part of the 1986 extravaganza in Lausanne was that the bid cities provided concerts throughout the session. Barcelona staged a brilliant performance from their magnificent opera diva Cabral Montserrat at the cathedral in Lausanne. Mary and I were in the best seats in the cathedral as most of the IOC members were cloistered in meetings.

ASOIF Belgrade

The 1990 annual general meeting of the Association of Summer Olympic International Federations (ASOIF), including the IOC executive meeting, was held in Belgrade. This was to be the last IOC meeting TOOC would attend before the vote in Tokyo in September. The IOC asked the bid cities to provide the cultural program at the opening ceremonies. TOOC was running a tight financial ship at that time and we did not know what to do. Ron Bertram came up with the idea of inviting our good friend and well known jazz composer Hagood Hardy from Toronto. Hagood had offered to help in any way he could, and agreed to perform without fee as his contribution—as long as he could bring his wife Martha with him. Martha hails from one of Canada's best known sailing families and had been his teenage sweetheart.

On the day of the performance I was in a panic because Hagood had disappeared. I kept asking Martha, *"Where is Hagood?"* She reassured me that he never missed a performance or a golf game. Hagood was almost a scratch golfer. We entered the concert hall and still no Hagood. My stomach was flipping. Melbourne's performer was a statuesque young lady attired in a body stocking—presumably to excite the aging IOC—and playing classical violin. Atlanta had imported an opera diva who bellowed loudly. Athens presented a singer performing Greek folk songs, and Manchester a concert pianist. The master of ceremonies announced, *"Toronto!"* and the curtain opened on Hagood with a drummer and bass player. He had just arrived from the local jazz club where he had been getting them up to speed. Because Hagood was so respected in the jazz world from his days with George Shearing, the Yugoslavs would hardly let him leave the club. He put on a spectacular show. As we were leaving, IOC Director François Carrard, who was also chairman of the Beau Rivage in Lausanne and a jazz fan, told me, *"Toronto was by far the best, and Hagood Hardy is a celebrity in the jazz world."* Sadly, Hagood was taken away much too young after a courageous fight with stomach cancer. What a loss of a great Canadian!

TOOC Bid Book

It was customary in those days to hand-deliver the bid books to IOC members in their homes to give them a personal briefing on Toronto's ideas. George Gross and Basil Rodomar covered Eastern Europe; Joe Halstead looked after Africa, Julie Osborne the Carribean, Bill Saunderson Scandanavia, Carlos Garcia South America, and Mahmoud El Farnawani the Middle East. I took care of the remainder of the deliveries. Most of our travel was completed using the free airline tickets provided by Air Canada.

Three years in the making and running to some 1,500 pages, the bid book was the most outstanding promotional vehicle ever produced for Toronto. With production coordinated by Grace Polsky, it was a brilliant piece of work. Thirty bound copies had to be delivered to the IOC by February 15, 1990. On January 6, just as we were going to press, Richard Pound—on behalf of the IOC—unilaterally changed the framework for the financial projections of the bids. Without notice, he demanded that the IOC receive a larger slice of the television revenues, and levied a 10 per cent tax on any declared profit. The TV share was reduced from 70 to 60 per cent for the organizers. He also changed the rules, stating that capital costs could not be written off against the Games. This changed all TOOC's financial projections and meant revising the bid book's financial section only a month before the delivery deadline.

I phoned Pound, a Montreal tax lawyer, and we had one of our more memorable shoot-outs. The new directive was ridiculous. I explained to Pound that accounting is an art form, not an exact science. The IOC was forcing organizers to be "creative" in their accounting instead of transparent. In order to avoid paying the 10 per cent tax, no organizer would show a profit. Instead, all capital installations would simply be held by a separate corporation and rented back to the organizers. Pound told me that if Toronto did not like it, we should withdraw. He later became chair of the IOC coordination commission for the Atlanta Games. This type of accounting is exactly what they did—and with his approval.

The legal entity in Atlanta was his idea and was contrary to what the IOC had demanded from other bid cities. On behalf of the IOC, Pound demanded that all bidders have the Games fully underwritten by all levels of government. This was part of the 1996 host city agreement that all bidders were supposed to sign. In Toronto's case it meant having the Games underwritten by the city, provincial and federal governments. It took months for us to accomplish this as bureaucrats at all three levels of government did their usual dance. It was the same for Melbourne and Manchester, but the IOC permitted Atlanta to bid without this tripartite guarantee. The IOC waived the requirement, allowing that due to the laws of the USA, Atlanta simply could not provide these government guarantees. Pound permitted Atlanta to establish its structure as a private corporation without state or federal underwriting. While TOOC was tearing our guts out with public hearings and endless city council debates, Atlanta was reporting that Toronto and the others did not have the required support that they themselves had from their elected officials. It was obvious why—we had to get open and transparent government commitments and Atlanta did not. We were not bidding on a level playing field.

As a result of its experience in Atlanta, however, the IOC now requires all bidding cities to secure underwriting of the Games from all levels of government. The IOC still awards the Games to a city even though the guarantees come from higher levels of government. In many cases, very few facilities are under the jurisdiction of the host city. As a Scot, I believe that "he who pays the piper should call the tune."

The packaging of our bid book was brilliant. Roots Canada donated 100 leather backpacks tastefully emblazoned with the TOOC logo. To this day IOC members say they or their grandchildren still use them. Most other bid books I have seen are packaged in an expensive cardboard slipcase covered with avant garde graphics. The worst one was encased in a metal box that gouged the rich wooden desks of some of the IOC voters, thus serving as an unpleasant reminder of that bidder's lack of foresight, if not downright incompetence. Adhering to Pound's directive, TOOC revised the bid book at great expense, copies were dispatched to the IOC in Lausanne, and we prepared to deliver copies to voters around the world.

Central America

Off I flew with the bid books in an attempt to get to at least one IOC member a day. As a result, I spent most of my time in airplanes. I flew first to Los Angeles, then to Mexico City, and then on to Guatemala. I went to sleep in my hotel room in Guatemala City, only to be rudely awoken at 5:00 a.m. by what I thought was machinegun fire. My first reaction was that I was going to be killed in a revolution. After about ten minutes, I got up enough nerve to peak out the window and saw, much to my relief, that the fireworks factory on the next street was exploding. That day I spent traveling to Antiqua, Guatemala, with IOC member Willi Kaltschmitt.

It was a relaxing side trip, especially our dinner in a unique restaurant in that historic town. Every IOC member I visited seized the opportunity to return at their own expense the hospitality we had offered them in Toronto. Sadly, the press never seems to report on the more positive actions of the IOC membership.

The next day I was scheduled to travel to Panama to meet Virgilio de Leon and his devastatingly beautiful daughter, who was Panama's entry in the Miss World contest. Panama was under martial law—General Manuel Antonio Noriega had just been deposed and the US Military was in control. The flight was a milk run. We took off from Guatemala, bounced down the runway in Nicaragua, flew to El Salvador and slid down the runway, then when we landed again—and it was really a horrendous landing—I was shell shocked from all the abuse. With no announcement except in Spanish, I assumed I was in Panama. Walking into the terminal, however, I realized to my dismay that I was in Costa Rica. I looked around to see my airplane taxiing down the runway. I always travel with only carry-on luggage so that part of it was all right, but I was worried about how I would get to Panama.

I explained my dilemma to a helpful young man at the TACA Airlines desk. He noticed my TOOC pin and asked if I was from Toronto. He told me his sister lived just west of Toronto in Mississauga, and hoped that he too could come to Canada. He closed down his station then drove me about five kilometres to a private airport where he knew a charter pilot. His friend offered to fly me over the mountains to Panama in his single engine Piper Cub. Panama City was just over the mountains about an hour away. It was a spectacular flight. Half-way there the pilot explained that he did not have a permit to land in Panama. Since it was under martial law, the US Air Force would most likely force us down. If we were lucky they would make us land at our preferred airfield. Then I would be on my own. Well, that is exactly what happened.

When we landed, soldiers in US military vehicles surrounded us, machine guns at the ready. We were escorted briskly to the commander.

I explained how foolish I had been, but I had the right documents and visas for Panama. The commander was a keen athlete; after I gave him an extra copy of the Toronto bid book, he let me stay but explained that under martial law, I had to be off the streets by 10:00 p.m. or risk being shot. He also ordered that my wonderful pilot be escorted out of Panama in his Piper Cub by US Air Force jet fighters.

I had to be back in Toronto by noon the next day to address the city council. The commander said that any flight arriving in Panama was suspect and that schedules were uncertain, but he had noticed that a flight from Bolivia landed around midnight most nights en route to Miami.

It was now about 6:00 p.m. and de Leon was waiting for me. I pitched Toronto over dinner then took a taxi to the airport, arriving totally exhausted just before the 10:00 p.m. curfew. I worried that the flight might not come at midnight as expected and that even if it did, I might fall asleep in the airport and miss it. Fortunately, I managed to stay awake long enough to see the flight arrive. At Miami I caught an Air Canada flight back to Toronto. I want to go back to Panama one day, but I think I will go by cruise ship through the canal next time.

Morocco

It was customary for bid cities to present their proposals to the various continental Olympic associations. We flew to Rabat, Morocco, to present to the National Olympic Committees of Africa. We had learned that it was essential to have multilingual capabilities. Our entourage included the attractive and capable Julie Osborne who spoke English, French and Spanish; the Honourable Lincoln Alexander, Ontario's Deputy Minister of Sport Joe Halstead; Molson's President Norman Seagram; and me.

Representatives from all over Africa jammed the hall. Julie introduced Lincoln Alexander, the elegant black Lieutenant Governor of Ontario, who gave an impassioned and heart rending speech in his always impeccable English. Then up stepped Norman Seagram, his bald head shining under the lights, to give an equally emotional speech in which he praised the virtues of Toronto. The Africans started to shuffle their feet, then they began whispering to one another and suddenly broke into applause. Norman, who had spent five years in Kenya, was addressing them in Swahili. The Africans loved it.

Peru

During his visit to Toronto, Ivan Dibos, IOC member in Peru, struck up a friendship with Mayor Art Eggleton over their shared interest in municipal governance—Dibos was also a member of the Lima city government. He asked that Eggleton accompany us when TOOC came to visit him in Lima. Art and I attended the National Olympic Committees annual general meeting in Mexico City, and then flew on to Peru.

Mayor Eggleton made a point of visiting one of the large shanty towns outside Lima. We met a Canadian International Development Agency (CIDA) volunteer who was helping to build a proper sewage and water system in this very downtrodden community. He told Eggleton that the biggest single problem these people faced was that, while they wanted to work, the 10-kilometre trek into Lima could only be done on foot, regardless of the weather. The Canadian volunteer asked if Toronto had any old buses they were scrapping that the mayor might be able to donate. It did not matter what condition they were in because these people could repair anything mechanical. Eggleton said he would do something.

I was sailing out the Eastern Gap of Toronto Bay a few months later when I looked over at the shipping pier and saw two old TTC buses destined for Lima. The mayor had come through without telling anybody. In today's world of the holier-than-thou media frenzy and the imprecations of the IOC ethics commission, this would be reason enough to censure Toronto. What nonsense! This is what concerned Canadians do, especially Olympians. I am proud that Mayor Eggleton delivered on his promise to Peru. And I trust that the old Toronto buses are still running.

Eastern Europe

The trip to Eastern Europe was most exciting. The Communist governments were overthrown either while I was there or within days of my departure. The Berlin Wall came down two weeks after I left East Berlin. I was in Hungary the day they declared independence. The same happened in Czechoslovakia, although it was a few years before it split into the Czech Republic and Slovakia. During my visit to Poland, my sailing friend Tomas Holc introduced me to Lech Walesa.

My visit to the USSR was an eye opener. I visited Vitaly Smirnov, who had been a senior member of the IOC for many years. Moscow was in dire straits at the time. I noticed the long lineups at stores and realized the people were lining up for food rations. That night Smirnov picked me up in a black automobile and took me to a nondescript grey building devoid of signage. Upstairs was an elegant French restaurant with an extensive menu and a bar stocked with just about every type of liquor known to man. I realized how fortunate I was to have been born in a free Canada.

When I returned to Moscow in February, 2005 as a member of the IOC 2012 Olympic evaluation commission, I was pleased to see the advances that had been made toward a more open society. There were long lineups at the new McDonalds and Kentucky Fried Chicken restaurants, and people could buy what they wanted.

Around the World

The longest and most trying trip I took to deliver copies of the bid book started with a leg to Los Angeles, where I met with Anita DeFrantz over dinner at the California Yacht Club. The next day I flew to Samoa Occidental and stayed at the well known Aggie Grey's Inn. A day later, I traveled to the 1990 Commonwealth Games in Auckland, New Zealand, and caught up with a number of my sailing friends. Mary and my son John met me there.

From New Zealand, we all went to Sydney, Australia, where we were taken by Phil Coles for a delicious seafood lunch on the boat of one of his friends. From Sydney I flew to

Paris for a one-day IOC meeting, and then I was off to Lausanne for a presentation to several IOC members resident there. Two days later, I flew to Hong Kong to meet up with Mary, whom I had last seen in Australia barely a week before. En route, we landed in Bahrain but I did not get off the plane. A large Scotsman with red hair and a bushy beard boarded the flight. I discovered that he worked in the oil fields and was traveling to Hong Kong for some rest and relaxation. I naïvely commented, *"It is good to see that peace in the Middle East is at hand."*

He broke up at that. *"You have to be kidding. The Muslim world is set to explode. It will encompass the whole land mass from Turkey through the oil fields, including the soft underbelly of the Soviet Union, and all the way to China."*

These days I recall that 1990 conversation often, in view of the military, ethnic and religious disruptions that are so prevalent there now.

Mary met me in Hong Kong and we immediately departed for the Philippines to meet IOC member Francisco Elizalde, who happens to be a fan of the New York Yankees. From there we flew to Taiwan to pitch C. K. Wu, then to Delhi to meet Ashwini Kumar and our great friend the Raja Balendra Singh. The next day we flew to Lahore, Pakistan to meet with Wajid Ali, who entertained us at his home with his multitude of offspring. I did not expect much of Lahore, but found it to be a uniquely impressive city, especially with all the lights strewn everywhere. From Lahore we caught a flight to Frankfurt where I met with the German IOC members.

I did this all in less than 18 days. The psychological impact this had on me is what I call the "Hostage Syndrome." You get so attached to your airplane seat with food, movies, sleeping, music and attention from the flight attendants that you become almost captive to the airplane environment. I had met more than 40 IOC members on this trip and it had become obvious that the Games would not be going to Athens. It was therefore a contest between Toronto and Atlanta. To this day, many IOC members say that Toronto had the best technical bid and that our bid book was excellent.

Back in Toronto

After I returned home in late March, reality set in. Toronto's left wing, led by Jack Layton and the *Bread not Circuses* adherents, were in full negative flight doing everything possible to embarrass Toronto and sabotage the bid. Being so opposed to their ideology, I did not handle the Toronto political obstructionists well. As we got closer and closer to Tokyo, the TOOC members hunkered down and tried to put Toronto's best foot forward. I am very proud of them all.

Olympic Bidding Observations:

One result of being designated host city for the Olympic Games is that the city is catapulted onto the world stage for almost a decade. This has several major benefits. The cost of hosting the Games is about four billion dollars, but this is more than offset by the 80,000 people-years of jobs created and the ensuing 10 billion dollar economic benefit. It also serves to force politicians to meet deadlines. They must act, and if they act properly—as was done in Barcelona—it revitalizes a city. This is one reason that so many forward-thinking cities are so intent on hosting the Games. Bidding cities tend to be centred in the most dynamic regions on every continent.

Several procedural changes affected the 1996 bid process:

- IOC President Juan Antonio Samaranch expanded the size of the IOC by appointing members on every continent.
- In 1987, on the advice of Horst Dassler of Adidas, the Summer Games and Winter Games were split. They are now held two years apart, instead of during the same year. The bidding cycle has therefore become more or less continuous, allowing for more sponsorship dollars to accrue to the IOC.
- Under the leadership of Peter Ueberroth, Los Angeles showed everyone how to run the Games at a profit, thus enticing major cities to bid for the right to host the Olympics. Up to that time, it was questionable whether

anyone really wanted them.

- Revenues from television were escalating, as were the opportunities for countries to promote themselves as tourist destinations.

In the media frenzy over the Salt Lake City scandals, the practice of IOC member visits to the bidding cities was called into question. How shallow! Putting a stop to the visits does not end greed and corruption. Human nature governs. There will always be a few bad apples in the barrel. Due to the cessation of this procedure, however, the cost of bidding has escalated dramatically. Toronto's 1996 bid cost eight million dollars in cash and an equal amount in kind. The Atlanta and Melbourne 1996 bids cost about the same. Toronto's 2008 bid cost almost 60 million dollars, two-thirds of which was cash, the remainder in kind. The London and Paris 2012 bids were reported to be in the vicinity of 100 million dollars, accounting for both cash and in-kind contributions.

After the 1990 bid process ended, President Samaranch asked each city to present its experiences and recommendations on enhancing procedures. Toronto gave a full written report to the IOC executive board, who acted on only a few of our suggestions. Had more of our recommendations been implemented, the Salt Lake City scandals may well have been averted. In time, however, most of the recommendations were adopted. When the US Senate report on Salt Lake was tabled, the TOOC report was included as an exhibit.

The escalation can be attributed largely to the no-visit policy and the resulting under-the-table lobbying expenses—there is now a perception that it is essential to employ Olympic lobbyists or "consultants" to present the bidders to IOC members. There are a myriad of consultants who embellish their résumés and are hired by the more naïve bid cities. The fees charged by these consultants are exorbitant.

Olympic consultants fall into three groups:

1) Former journalists who, having followed the IOC family, can now earn much more working as lobbyists on behalf

of bid cities.

2) Former Olympic organizing committee employees who, finding themselves newly unemployed, hire out their services for the next round of Games. At least four teams of consultants from this group say they were actively involved in the inside workings in Sydney. One such "consultant" is now employed as a senior sports official in Canada. His résumé says he was active in the Sydney organizing committee (SOCOG). On checking, I discovered that he was a volunteer at the beach volleyball site. In no way can this be construed as bestowing on him any in depth insight into the organization of the Sydney Olympics.

3) Former bid city employees and volunteers looking for work. A large group from London 2012 recently appeared on the scene. If you check their references with the leaders of this outstanding bid, however, their connection to the bid appears tenuous at best; in fact, most are simply unknown.

It is disconcerting to see the multitude of Olympic lobbyists sitting interminably in the IOC hotel lobbies, waiting for the chance to pander to the Olympic family, or feeding rumours and gossip to the bid committees. Their misinformation costs the bid committees mega-dollars.

The IOC must address this ridiculous situation.

Order of Canada

After the 1996 bid, several bid leaders were honored for putting their cities on the world stage. Manchester's bid leader became Sir Bob Scott. The top bidders in Melbourne received the Order of Australia. A statue of Billy Payne was erected in Atlanta's Olympic Park.

In my country, awarding of the Order of Canada is a secret procedure, one supposedly above political influence. I had no idea that Senator Trevor Eyton, Norman Seagram and

John Rogers were putting my name forward for this honour until I received a telephone call from Trevor explaining that my award was being held up by Prime Minister Brian Mulroney because of something I had said that was reported in *The Globe and Mail*. Mulroney had been pushing strongly for the North American Free Trade Agreement with the USA. When asked to comment on this, I said that I was apprehensive about it not because of the object of the agreement but because I did not think that Canadians had the spine to stand up to the USA on the disputes that would doubtless arise.

Trevor asked me to write a letter of apology to the Prime Minister. I said I would write a letter, but I wouldn't apologize because my concern was well founded—indeed, it was rooted in my own business experiences dealing with Canadian branches of American corporations. I also pointed out that my statement should have nothing to do with my being considered for the Order of Canada, because I had led the bid as an unpaid volunteer and that had nothing to do with my plumbing business. Needless to say, Mulroney did flex his backroom muscle to ensure that I was not admitted to the Order.

Twice more my name was put forward. In the first instance, I was nominated as the first Canadian ever to become president of an Olympic sport federation; in the second, it was as one of the few Canadians to become a member of the International Olympic Committee. On both occasions I was passed over, most likely because I refuse to kowtow to the canons of political correctness if they run counter to what I believe to be true.

Gilbert and Sullivan put this in perspective in *H.M.S. Pinafore*: "*I polished the brass so carefully that now I am the ruler of the Queen's navy!*" Personally, I much prefer to follow Shakespeare in determining the course of my actions: "*To thine own self be true, and it must follow, as the night the day, thou canst not then be false to any man.*"

Chapter 9:
Winter Games

Mary and I like the Winter Games very much, and for several reasons:

1) We attend all events as spectators, unlike the Summer Games where sailing events occupy 14 of the 16 days and we work from 8:00 a.m. to midnight on most of them.

2) As a Canadian I understand all winter sports. I often take my IOC colleagues to events and explain the intricacies of the sport to those who do not come from lands of ice and snow.

3) Canadians tend to do well at the Winter Games, so I can be very patriotic and proud.

Calgary 1988

In my opinion, the Calgary 1988 Winter Games were the best run Olympics ever—Summer or Winter. They made a profit for the organizers, as had Los Angeles. Calgary left a great legacy of facilities for Canadian winter athletes, as well as an Olympic-standard swimming pool, and produced a legacy fund to help maintain the facilities. This legacy allowed our Canadian winter athletes to perform well in Turino in 2006 and Vancouver 2010.

It was frigid at the opening ceremonies, but as we sat in the stands we could clearly see the telltale grey horseshoe over the mountain pass that signaled the imminent arrival of the Chinook. The temperature went from minus 20 degrees Celsius at midnight to plus 20 by noon the next day and stayed there for the rest of the Games. The sun shone and the temperature was quite balmy. I met Frank King and Bill Pratt at the Paliser Hotel after one of their difficult discussions with the IOC and asked what they were going to do about the weather and lack of snow. They explained that they did not want snow—snow would screw up the schedule and it cost a lot to plow it away. Calgary had been storing snow in the woods and it was much easier just to shovel it out to where it was needed.

The opening ceremonies were excellent. Calgary tried to show off its unique culture with many Canadians performing, including a number of First Nations people. The rodeo and chuck wagon demonstrations delighted the crowd, as did performances by k. d. lang and Ian Tyson. Calgary came up with the idea to involve ordinary citizens in the medal ceremonies. They introduced a medal plaza downtown and each night thousands could come to see their heroes. It was a great innovation. After some gentle prodding, the IOC accepted the new concept and the medal plaza is now an institution at all Olympic Games.

Samaranch told a great story about his volunteer driver. One day they arrived back from the cross-country skiing competition at Canmore at about 4:00 p.m. when the driver asked, *"Mr. President, when do you need me tonight?"*

Samaranch replied, *"I will go to the figure skating final, which means not till 10:00 p.m."*

"Good!" said the driver, *"that will allow me to go to the hospital."*

"Are you not feeling well, or is a member of your family sick?" inquired Samaranch, concerned.

"No!" explained the driver. *"I am the senior neurosurgeon at the Foothills Hospital. There has been a major traffic accident and I have to oversee the operation. I will be back by 10:00 p.m."*

Lillehammer 1994

At Lillehammer in 1994, a unique and wonderful Winter Games, the Norwegians cheered for everyone. Lillehammer is a mountain village with one main street to which everyone gravitated at 4:00 p.m. after the day's events and before the evening ones. I was walking down the crowded street admiring the beautiful Norwegian women when I felt a strong thump on my back. I turned around to see His Majesty King Juan Carlos of Spain enjoying a stroll. I do not know why kings always thump me on the back, but that appears to be their calling card.

IOC member Peter Tallberg asked if I wanted to be listed on the ISAF accreditation with a guest. (Mary did not go so I had an extra guest accreditation.) My daughter Martha found out that Elvis Stojko, Canada's great skater and Olympic Silver Medal winner, was refused accreditation for his choreographer Uschi Kessler. Elvis needed her badly so I took her as my guest. This did not go down well with Skate Canada, since with my IOC accreditation she could get special cars and entry into all events and they could not. Martha was responsible for looking after the Canadian Television Network (CTV) entourage and obtained a special airfare and hotel for me. This meant I had to put up with Paul Beeston of Toronto Blue Jays fame and his wife Kaye, who are also Olympic Winter Games groupies.

The day of the opening ceremonies, I went over to the IOC hotel to see a few people. (I was not staying there myself.) Standing guard outside one of the convention rooms were two Norwegian military attachés. I knew them from several sailing meetings where they had accompanied His Majesty King Harald. They asked me to wait outside as the King was meeting with Hillary and Chelsea Clinton. When the King strode out of the meeting, he was clearly surprised to see me.

"What are you doing here?" he asked.

"I thought the Olympic Games were going on. Have I come to the wrong place?"

As Uschi and I were leaving for the opening ceremonies that night, Donna Brown, Richard Pound's efficient secretary, handed me a bunch of warming pads to slip into my boots and gloves, because it was colder than "the hell of the Eskimos." The reason I like women so much is that all the women in my life have spoiled me, but that night they saved my life. Uschi had a big fur coat that I snuggled into, and if you know Uschi, you'll know that was enjoyable. We walked up the hill to the ski jumping venue where the opening ceremonies were to be held and took our seats in the third row. King Harald sat in the first row with his family. The second row was empty until just before the ceremonies got under way, when six burly security guards—definitely from the USA—came and stood right in front of us, ushering in Hillary and Chelsea Clinton. It was obvious that they fully intended to stand there for the whole evening. I was intent on making sure they did not. In my finest Canadian accent, I forcefully said, *"Whoever you are, would you please move as I want to see the opening ceremonies."*

One of the big men turned around and strongly rebuffed me. *"You are showing great disrespect for the wife of your president."*

"As a Canadian, we do not have a president," I replied. *"Please move."* At that, Hillary told them to leave, and we had a great evening.

The Norwegians had been lobbied to hire a Hollywood producer to orchestrate their opening ceremonies, but refused and did it their own way, putting on a terrific show that featured trolls and other figures from traditional Norwegian culture. The Olympic flame was skied down the ski jump and handed to Crown Prince Haakon, who lit the flame. I have always believed that the opening ceremonies should reflect the culture of the host country and not be a carbon copy of some other country's hype. The president of the OCOG was Gerhard Heiberg, who became a member of the IOC and one of my most respected friends.

I was supposed to stay only for the first week, but I was having such a great time and trying never to miss an event that I completely lost track of what day it was and ended up missing my flight home. To this day, Paul Beeston talks about how absent-minded I am. I tell him that I came out on top, as he had to go home and the Blue Jays were not even playing baseball! I attended the men's downhill skiing, watched Canada play another hockey game, and saw Elvis Stojko free skate. On top of that, Martha persuaded Canadian Airlines to honour my ticket a day late, so it all worked out perfectly for me.

Nagano 1998

During my term as ISAF president (1994-2004) I had my own

accreditation for the Games. Julie Osborne was responsible for the IOC sponsors' hospitality suite. When I went over to see how she was doing, she told me to hang around as there was going to be a special recognition of Jean-Claude Killy in commemoration of the thirtieth anniversary of his triple Gold Medal accomplishment in Grenoble in 1968.

Samaranch arrived with his entourage and gave a warm speech highlighting Jean-Claude's successful career in the Olympics and later in business, along with his contributions to the IOC. A down-to-earth and wonderful Olympian, Jean-Claude has a great sense of humour. He told the story of Albertville's first, unsuccessful bid to host the Winter Games. After the loss, Jean-Claude went to see Samaranch, disillusioned. He told Samaranch that he would never have anything to do with such a demeaning process again. Samaranch replied: *"I bet you 100 Swiss francs that you come back again."* Four years later, Jean-Claude showed up again in Samaranch's office and announced that Albertville was going to try again and bid for the 1992 Winter Games. Samaranch replied, *"Where are my 100 Swiss francs?"* Killy offered to pay up, never expecting Samaranch to accept, but Samaranch took the money and everyone—including Jean-Claude and Samaranch—laughed heartily. Albertville won the bid to host the 1992 Games. Jean-Claude Killy later became president of the organizing committee (OCOG) for Lillehammer.

Nagano did a great job. All the facilities were excellent, including the wonderful bullet train ride from Tokyo to the mountain city. The Nagano Games were the first in which curling was featured as an Olympic sport, one in which Canadians usually win medals.

Salt Lake 2002

The Olympic experience in Salt Lake City was outstanding—much to our surprise. We had all been apprehensive about what might happen after the scandals that had plagued the bid process. Together with the rumours we had heard about Mormon religious restrictions (about which most of us knew nothing), our anxiety tempered our optimism regarding the atmosphere surrounding the 2002 Winter Olympic Games. As it turned out, however, we had nothing to fear and the Games were excellent. The people were courteous and friendly and could not do enough to make our stay meaningful. Most American citizens never travel outside their own region, let alone their country, but in Utah it's different. In their early twenties, Mormons are sent to foreign countries for up to two years to preach the Mormon gospel.

Our driver Melanie Armstrong was an energetic young woman who had spent two years in Poland after graduating from Brigham Young University. She was a modern Mormon, respecting her religion but understanding that she must accommodate to the modern world, discarding that which no longer fits. She knew Utah well and never needed to consult a map. She did not follow the set travel patterns, which meant that we traveled to all the venues quickly and without the customary Olympic hassles. She educated us on her religion and its history, and in all aspects made our stay very enjoyable.

The excellent Little America Hotel was situated so that we could walk to all the downtown events. The State of Utah should be proud of its volunteers. The leadership shown by Governor Mitt Romney added a degree of stability to the Games that filtered down to everyone involved.

David Yule and Jean-Claude Killy

In 2000 when I sold the plumbing business, David Yule was there to advise me on what to do. David had helped me in all my endeavors in his capacity as a chartered accountant and senior partner of Ernst and Young. I had known the Yule Family since my teens, as their father was a dinghy sailor. David would not accept a fee for his services so I asked his sister Leslie Rogan what I might give him as a present. In her direct manner she replied, *"David doesn't need anything. Why don't you take him on one of your trips?"*

I invited him to accompany me as my guest to the Salt Lake Olympics and he readily accepted. An active curler and skier, David never missed an event, starting with curling at 9:00 a.m., then going to skiing and ending up at the various skating events at night. Halfway through the Games he announced, *"Everything I complain about regarding the IOC, I am doing! I love every minute of it."*

One night, after the Canadian women's hockey game, we went to the IOC sponsors' facility in the historic Union Pacific Railway Station, opposite the Medal Plaza where all the Olympic family congregated. Being a bean counter, David tends to be frugal and it may well have been for this reason that he was wearing a very old, yellow Jean Claude Killy ski jacket. When we entered I asked him, *"Would you like to meet Jean-Claude?"*

With great enthusiasm he replied, *"Sure would!"*

I took him over to where Killy was sitting with some friends and said, *"Jean-Claude, this poor Canadian bought one of your jackets."* Killy immediately pointed out, *"It is one of the first ones we ever made and it is a great design. I always buy a drink for anyone who has had a coat that long, especially at the free bar."*

Killy stood up and took David Yule over to the bar where they talked for a good twenty minutes. David was in seventh heaven.

Figure Skating Scandal: Jamie Salé and David Pelletier

The major dispute at the Salt Lake Olympic Games was, of course, the figure skating rhubarb over the judging of the pairs final. A French judge, Marie-Reine Le Gougne, dishonestly awarded first place to the Russian pair, Elena Berezhnaya and Anton Sikharulidze, having worked out a deal in advance to bolster them in exchange for Russia's support of the French skaters in the ice dancing competition. She thus assured that the Canadian pair, Jamie Salé and David Pelletier, would finish no better than second no matter how well they performed.

The event took place on the first Monday night of the Games. Mary and I had arrived early and were sitting in the first row of VIP seats immediately above the judges. The Canadians skated flawlessly, clearly outperforming the

Russians, who were also excellent but not quite up to the level of the Canadians that night.

When the scores were posted, all hell broke loose. The boos were deafening from the mostly American fans, but particularly from the press. On the podium, the Canadians handled the situation with dignity, smiling through their disappointment, surely knowing they had been robbed. The Russian pair also handled it well and with restraint, suspecting that something was not right.

I turned to Mary and said this was the same sort of dishonesty we had seen in Calgary in 1988, when Elizabeth Manley clearly outskated Katarina Witt, but was awarded only the Silver Medal. We walked out of the arena carrying our Canadian flags, and everyone we met apologized for the travesty and unfairness of the scoring system.

The next day the frenzy among the press corps was escalating. We could not get through the lobby of the hotel without being subjected to the intense media scrum asking for my thoughts on the controversy. I told them I was a sailor and had little knowledge of the workings of figure skating, which wasn't quite true. Most Canadians are keen observers of any skating sport. By Wednesday, the frenzy was completely out of control. I tried to ignore the issue with the press because the controversy was beginning to overshadow the rest of the Olympic Games.

On Thursday morning at 5:00 a.m. the phone rang in our room. The hotel operator apologized for waking us, but said she had a very determined man on the line from Toronto. He said he was a close friend named Pat Marsden and that it was a very important matter. I told her to put him on—Pat was indeed a close friend and had been a strong supporter of Toronto's bid for the 1996 Games. The call was live on the air for *The FAN 590* sports radio talk show that Pat hosted. *"Marsden!"* I began, *"What the hell are you doing phoning me at 5:00 a.m.?!"*

"Sorry Paul, but it is 7:00 a.m. in Toronto and you should be up. Canada is under attack and you're the only one who can do

anything." He was playing on my well-known patriotism—and short attention span.

"I am only a sailor and have little to do with the Winter Olympics except as a spectator," I said.

Marsden berated me, telling me to go and see IOC President Jacques Rogge, who was also a sailor. We had competed against each other in the 1968 Olympics. Marsden was sure I could get Rogge's attention. *"Henderson, do something or you're not the man I know,"* he said. Pat sure knew how to jerk my chain.

I told Mary I had to do something. I went to breakfast and met Bob Storey, president of the International Bobsled Federation, who was from Ottawa. We discussed several possible courses of action and decided to call Mike Chambers, president of the Canadian Olympic Committee. I said I would do it. I was scheduled to go to Soldier's Hollow with Mary and a couple of friends to watch the cross-country skiing. It was a good 90 minutes away so we bundled into Melanie's car and started on the trip. I phoned Chambers and asked in a very controlled voice what he and the COC were doing about the figure skating fiasco.

He replied, *"We have hired an Ottawa law firm to prepare a brief."* I was taken aback—what did an Ottawa law firm know about figure skating and international sports politics? Still under control, I offered the assistance of Bob Storey and myself in editing the brief since we, both presidents of international sports federations, were familiar with the format and language used by such bodies. I also asked Chambers what advice he had heard from Dick Pound, Canada's member on the IOC. Chambers said he had talked to Pound for only a minute, but Pound was advising him to wait until after the Games to make any formal complaint.

This was not acceptable. Something needed to be done to quell the escalating media outcry that had stolen the focus from every other aspect of the Games.

Chambers then really got my dander up when he said, *"The Canadian Olympic Committee must be very careful*

because the Canadian chef de mission [Sally Rehorick] is running for
a senior position at the International Skating Union, which is very
political, and she does not want to upset her colleagues by pushing for
the Canadians, Salé and Pelletier." This was typically Canadian. No
other country in the world would work this way for its athletes.
Canadians bend over backwards to appear to be fair, and in so doing
our athletes, whom we should be supporting, suffer the consequences.
I hung up on Chambers and realized Marsden was right. I must stand
up.

I discussed it in the car with my friends and the light went on—
officials take an oath at the Opening Ceremonies to officiate fairly and
with integrity. If the French judge had sold her vote, something must
be done and it was up to the IOC to act. We arrived at cross-country
skiing and I was totally in orbit by this time. I dropped everyone off
and told Melanie to get me back to Salt Lake City. I had to speak to
Rogge. (By leaving I missed Becky Scott winning her Bronze Medal,
which was later upgraded to Gold, the two Russians who beat her
having been disqualified as drug cheats.)

I arrived back at the Olympic hotel at 11:00 a.m. and went to
IOC Director General François Carrard for advice. He advised me to
go immediately to talk to President Rogge. I left Carrard and went and
sat outside Rogge's office. It was now noon on Thursday and nearly
three days had passed since the event. Within 15 minutes, Jacques
came by and asked me into his office. The first thing he said to me set
the tone for the conversation.

"Let's talk about Salé and Pelletier, which is why you are here.
You are the first Canadian who has come to see me. I am surprised
that your Olympic team officials have not contacted me earlier,"
Rogge said. This just about floored me. I could not believe that with
all the COC officials in Salt Lake, I was the first to show concern
directly to the president—and it was nearly three days since the
incident. This shows just how unprepared the COC is to handle issues
at the top levels of Olympic sport; they seldom ask for help from those
of us who have served their apprenticeships at the highest level.

"If the IOC stuck its nose into sailing issues, you, as ISAF president, would give me hell for interfering," Rogge told me.

"Yes I would, and I have," I replied. *"But then you would tell me forcefully what you thought and then we would settle down and agree on how to solve the problem."*

We talked for another half-hour, after which Jacques asked me to tell Octavio Cinquanta, president of the International Skating Union, exactly what we had discussed, which I did as soon as I left the meeting. Octavio is a respected colleague with whom I have always enjoyed a meaningful discourse. As I left the meeting with Rogge, who is much taller than me, he put his arm around my shoulders and said, *"Paul, I will call a press conference for tomorrow at 10:00 a.m. and make an announcement. Thanks for coming."*

It was obvious to me that he had made up his mind and that my intervention had only reinforced what he had already decided to do. I was in the hospitality tent at the bobsled competition the next day with Bob Storey and some friends when Rogge appeared live on television to announce that the IOC had decided to award two Gold Medals for pairs figure skating, to the Russians and to the Canadians. It was a very proud day for Canada. Jacques Rogge had shown great leadership in acting as he did and moving the Games forward on a positive note, That night we were proud to see Toronto's Bare Naked Ladies performing at the Medal Plaza.

Turino 2006

There were many concerns about Turino, but at the end of the day it was a great success. I found the city charming and the people very friendly. It was a picturesque half-hour walk from the Olympic hotel—a converted Fiat car assembly plant—along the river to the hockey arena or to other venues, including the spectacular Medal Plaza. Usually the locals inflate their prices, but not in Turino. Taxi drivers charged normal fares and the excellent restaurants did not overcharge their guests. One of the most enjoyable trips was through the Italian countryside to the curling venue in Pinerolo with a driver who knew the back roads and kept off the highways. The hockey arenas were quite the opposite, however. The old arena had friendly volunteers, but the ice was terrible, one possible reason that the Canadian men's team did so poorly. They were heavy and their skates sank into the slush. The faster, lighter teams made them look inept. In the newer arena the ice was good, but the administration cold. Canada's women's team was overpowering. Experienced players such as Hayley Wickenheiser, Cassie Campbell, Vicky Sunohara, Sami Jo Small and Danielle Goyette were still the heart of the team. Mary was proud to watch Syl Apps' skilled granddaughter Gillian, as he had been captain of the Toronto Maple Leafs. The sad thing is that she, along with many other Canadian athletes, had to go to the USA on athletic scholarships instead of staying in Canada and acting as role models for our youth.

It was a long trip up the valleys to the skiing, but no further than at any other Winter Games. One day there was a heavy snow storm and some of the IOC members who were trapped up the mountains complained bitterly. What did they expect? I would ask them to experience Toronto when a winter storm hits. That is the challenge and joy of living in a region where the weather plays a deciding role on one's activities. Mary and I enjoyed Turino very much.

Vancouver 2010

Mary and I have just returned from the Vancouver Winter Games. The IOC's lasting impression of these games will be how the citizens of Canada embraced their Games. The city was overrun with millions of people walking around wanting to be part of the Olympic experience. The real Gold Medal winners were the 30,000 volunteers who efficiently and graciously welcomed all visitors. Canada's Olympic Athletes performed to an unprecedented high standard winning 14 Gold Medals and 26 in total. The COC Officials realized half way through the Games that their motto to "Own the Podium" was ill-conceived. They wisely changed course and zeroed in on the individual athletes achievements which made all of Canada proud. In fact any athlete who has the honour to represent Canada in the Olympic Games makes Canada proud.

Chapter 10:
Seoul 1988 and Barcelona 1992

During the Toronto 1996 bid process, Ben Johnson held the highest profile of any track athlete in the world. He appeared to me to be a young man whose only desire was to run fast in a straight line, leaving all the rest up to his handlers. I attended a number of track meets in Europe where Ben ran and I worried that he was not being properly managed, especially with regard to his finances.

I mentioned my concern to George Gross of *The Toronto Sun*. George set up a meeting with Lincoln Alexander, Lieutenant Governor of Ontario, who invited Ben, George and me to a private luncheon at "The Residence" in the Ontario parliament buildings. Ben was in awe of the Lieutenant Governor, both men having roots in Jamaica. Lincoln offered all the help he could, suggesting that he could get one of his many friends at the top of Canada's corporate community to ensure personally that Ben's money was invested prudently.

Ben agreed to get back to Lincoln, but never did. A short time later, TOOC received a contract from Ben's lawyer stipulating a large sum to be paid to Ben for promoting Toronto's bid. TOOC turned it down. It was our policy that, although TOOC would pay expenses for those who acted as ambassadors, we would not pay lobbyists' fees. TOOC did not use Ben again, which saddened me.

George Gross was deeply involved in the Association Internationale de la Presse Sportive (AIPS) as vice-president. In July 1988, he asked me to go to Disentis, a historic town in Switzerland's Romanesque region, as his tennis partner in the AIPS tennis championship and to promote Toronto 1996. About the third day, we were sitting on the front patio of the auberge where we all stayed, when an Austrian journalist sat down and produced two pictures of Ben Johnson taken 18 months apart. He showed how Ben had bulked up and how his complexion had changed, indicating steroid use. The

Austrian warned us that Ben was going to be caught at the Seoul Olympics that coming September. We were very concerned.

On returning to Toronto, I phoned Canadian Olympic Committee President Carol Anne Letheren to explain that the European press believed that Ben was juiced up. I suggested that the COC should test Ben before going to Seoul to make sure he was clean. She responded that it was none of COC's business, being under the purview of Athletics Canada, which had in turn shifted responsibility onto the shoulders of the athletes and their coaches. I had done all I could and informed George Gross of COC's position.

I attended the Seoul Olympics as the technical delegate for the sailing event, held in the remote venue of Busan. Peter Tallberg, then president of ISAF and IOC member from Finland, spent most of his time in Seoul discharging his IOC duties. I watched the 100-metre race on television and was elated when Ben Johnson won Gold. About 6:00 a.m. the next day, however, Jim Worrall, IOC member in Canada, woke me up to tell me that Ben had tested positive for steroids. Chaos was descending on the Canadian team. He pointed out that this would have a negative impact on Toronto's 1996 bid and that I should get to Seoul immediately to help in the damage control. The performance of Carol Anne Letheren and other COC executives on television was something of a charade as they endeavoured to spin that they were unaware of what would become the greatest blight on Canadian Olympic sport.

Sailing in Busan

When Seoul was awarded the 1988 Games, everyone was surprised because the country was still emerging from the Korean War. Since none of the IYRU executive committee had been eager to go there, IYRU President Beppe Croce had sent me to check it out in the summer of 1983. I had no idea what to expect but always stood by the policy of "when in Rome, do as the Romans do."

I arrived in Seoul from Vancouver via Tokyo. The proposed sailing venue in Busan was an hour's flight from

Seoul. I was met at the Seoul airport by a proper Korean man who announced in perfect English, *"My name is Kim Bong-Sik. You can call me Bob."* Bob became a great friend and served as my eyes and ears in Asia when I became ISAF president in 1994. (His history explained his excellent English: during the Korean War, Bob had left his family behind in North Korea and had walked south from his home. Having taught himself to speak English, he became one of General Douglas MacArthur's interpreters. Together with Admiral Ko, who ran Daewoo Shipyards and was president of the Korean Yachting Association, Bob made my time in Korea very enjoyable.)

Bob and I flew south to Busan where I checked into the Chosun Beach Hotel. The hotel overlooks the sea and the view from my room was straight down the long promenade of the beach. I was jet-lagged and unable to sleep, being 12 hours out of sync with my body clock. In Korea, nothing seems to get going until the sun goes down, which Bob told me was due to the cultural notion that ladies with paler skin are more beautiful, so they try to keep out of the sun. Sure enough, the promenade came alive at dusk. Carts opened up into full restaurants and the air was redolent with the exotic aroma of gimchi. Try as I might I couldn't fall asleep, so I did the only reasonable thing and went for a walk along the promenade. That apparently served only to stimulate me further because when I got back to the hotel, I was even more awake then before. So began a cycle of walking up and down the promenade, then going back to bed, then out again for another walk.

On the third night, I answered a call in my room to hear the voice of a nice young lady. She was upset. *"Mr. Henderson, I am very tired. Would you please phone me when you decide to leave your room? My partner and I are worn out."*

I had no idea what she was getting at and asked, *"Why?"*

"Every time you leave the hotel there are two women walking a few steps behind. We are your security officers."

"I have not noticed but I will phone from now on," I assured her.

At most Games, especially where there are language difficulties, executives are provided with hostesses who make sure we get to where we must go. My hostess in Busan was an outstanding 23-year-old young woman named Miss Lee. To differentiate her from the myriad of other Miss Lees, I named her "Now Famous Miss Lee," which reduced to "NFML." She was extremely efficient and proud of being Korean. One day when I was not being cooperative, she loudly announced to everyone within earshot, *"Frankly speaking, Mr. Henderson! If you would be on time for your appointments, you would make my life much easier!"*

For years afterward, a few sailing officials who had heard this directive would address me in debates with the introduction, *"Frankly speaking, Mr. Henderson...."*

A Korean national holiday similar to our Thanksgiving fell during the Games on September 28. Our hosts had invited us to a gala evening hosted by Daewoo. The hostesses brought their mothers' traditional colourful hanboks for the wives of the ISAF executive committee members to wear to the party. They all refused except for Mary, who thought it would be fun and respectful. "NFML" was so proud. A photo of Mary in her multi-coloured Korean dress was featured on the front page of all the Busan newspapers (see photo).

One evening at dusk, Mary and I were strolling down the promenade along the beach from the hotel when, about halfway along, we ran into the excellent Portuguese sailor Patrick DeBarros, dripping wet and very upset. He had seen a young Korean girl walking into the surf intending to drown herself. Nobody seemed to care but Patrick, who immediately dove into the sea. She struggled so hard against him that he had to knock her out, then drag her limp body to shore. She was revived and taken to hospital. As it turned out, Patrick was awarded a special citation for this act of bravery by IOC President Juan Antonio Samaranch.

The weather conditions were predicted to be light winds, which everyone trained for. ISAF scheduled races every day so we could get them all off. As happens at almost every Olympic regatta, however, the conditions were exactly opposite to what all the competitors had trained for and it blew like hell. Due to the current coming down the river, the strong shore current and very high tides, it was like sailing in a washing machine.

Whenever there was concern about anything in sailing, I would get a call from President Samaranch. At 8:00 a.m. on the third day of racing, my telephone rang. *"This is Juan Antonio. You must never allow racing in such conditions again."*

"Why? What is the problem, Mr. President?" I replied, surprised. *"All the press is getting seasick, rolling around out there,"* he explained.

Thinking quickly I said, *"Sir, let me put it in context of a sport you know well, like skiing."* He knew all sports but skiing was the best I could think of. *"What is the toughest downhill ski race?"*

"Kitzbuhl!" he replied emphatically.

"Well sir, sailing in Busan is like a downhill ski race in Kitzbuhl. The sailors love it and the best sailors are winning," I offered by way of analogy.

"Thank you," he said and hung up.

The next morning, all the newspapers quoted Samaranch's response to the media question about them all being seasick and uncomfortable in Busan: *"It's like a Kitzbuhl ski race. The best sailors are winning in Busan and they love it."*

Martha Henderson has always said that sailing will never get the press coverage it deserves until we first solve the media seasickness problem.

Due to the fact that the races did come off as scheduled, the spare days were not needed and the racing was over on the Monday. The Koreans had scheduled the medal presentations and Closing Ceremonies for Wednesday. Samaranch phoned to demand that the ceremonies be moved up to Tuesday because it would be easier for him to travel to Busan then. I discussed it with Bob Kim and together we went to see the official in charge. He absolutely refused to change the schedule. When we got outside, Bob explained the reason for his intransigence: Busan City was invariably in conflict with Seoul, and this was their day in the sun. They had hired the best bands and rock stars from around Korea to entertain the sailors and the event could not be rescheduled at such short notice. It went on as scheduled on the Wednesday and I caught hell from Samaranch.

Frank McLaughlin won a Bronze Medal with John Milne as crew. They were both from the RCYC and, naturally, Toronto Island. Frank's father Paul and his sister Madeline were in Korea to see Frank race. Paul McLaughlin proudly wore his 1948 Canadian Olympic blazer at the medal ceremonies. I told Madeline I would look after them, but she was anxious, constantly demanding to know where they were going to sit. I told her to take a Valium. At the last minute, I went into the crowd, picked them both up and seated them on the main stage just behind Samaranch and Queen Sofia of Spain. It is important to look after Toronto Islanders. They were very proud.

Barcelona 1992

Our beloved IYRU President Beppe Croce died in the Spring of 1986. Peter Tallberg and I agreed that Peter should be ratified as the next president that November. In June, Barcelona was chosen over Paris to host the 1992 Games. Barcelona bid with two sailing venues, Barcelona and Palma, Majorca. Tallberg designated me a committee of one to study the proposals and report to the executive with a strong directive to pick Palma.

Barcelona Mayor Pasqual Maragall i Mira put extreme pressure on me to select his city. He asked me to meet with their Olympic engineering department and inspect their plans for the Olympic Village. Maragall proposed that the sailing venue be in the old port, which was heavily polluted. I informed him that it was unacceptable. I also explained that the sailing waters off Barcelona needed to be cleaned of the raw sewage that was flowing directly into the Mediterranean. On my visit to the engineering department, I was shown a detailed maquette of the plans for the Olympic Village. It was to be built to revitalize an old industrial wasteland facing onto the Mediterranean. They had planned a long walking pier out into the sea with a tower and restaurant, and promenades along the waterfront. As usual, I put my foot in my mouth when I off-handedly threw out a suggestion to the engineers: *"Why don't you just square off the pier and enclose an Olympic harbour inside?"*

I returned to my hotel room and within minutes my phone rang. It was Mayor Maragall. *"I am sending a car to pick you up. Please be in my office as soon as possible."*

When I arrived at his office, he immediately came to the point. *"Did you say you would put the Olympic sailing regatta in Barcelona if we built the marina where the long pier is proposed?"*

"Yes sir," I dutifully responded.

"It will be done and Barcelona expects you to deliver on your word," Maragall pronounced.

"What about the sewage in the sea?" I countered.

"We will do everything to clean that up also," Maragall promised—and he did deliver.

My report to the IYRU executive strongly favoured Barcelona. They went along with my recommendation in choosing Barcelona.

Tallberg appointed me to oversee the marina installation. I was actively involved with the architects and engineers in the brilliant design of the facility, the projected cost of which was some 250 million dollars. The Catalans, renowned as great businessmen, added condominiums to the boat slips and onshore restaurants, and sold the whole project for 350 million dollars, turning the sailing venue into the most profitable and utilized facility of the Barcelona Games. Carlos Ferrer, the late IOC member in Spain, facetiously named it "Henderson Harbour." As an added tribute to Toronto citizens, a large sculpture of a fish by Frank Gehry overlooks the venue.

In 2005, I had the privilege of sitting on the IOC commission evaluating the bids for the 2012 Olympic Games, including Madrid's. The engineer planning the new harbour proposed for Palma looked directly at me during his presentation and said, *"Henderson Harbour in Barcelona is so successful that we are doubling its size. The new one in Palma will be equally as successful. Thank you for your vision, Paul."*

He was one of the engineers I had met in Barcelona 20 years before. At my age, it is nice when someone remembers what happened.

City planners come from all over the world to see the Barcelona Olympic Harbour and what it did to revitalize their waterfront. The mayor of Toronto took a very large contingent to see it recently, in view of the fact that Toronto's Portlands area remains an industrial wasteland. I was not invited. It's tough being a prophet in your own land!

The Barcelona waterfront is a prime example of what can be achieved as a legacy to citizens as a result of hosting the Olympics. It is sad to see that the naysayers dwell only on costs, never allowing that the Games permit a city to achieve 30 years of urban renewal in seven. Barcelona ranks first among the exemplars of this economic and cultural reality—it is an indisputable fact that the 1992 Olympics were the key to Barcelona's transformation into one of the great cities of modern Europe. The forward thinking Maragall was a pleasure to deal with when he was Barcelona's mayor, and it did not surprise me that he was later elected president of Catalonia.

Chapter 11:
ISAF Presidency, 1994-2004

Peter Tallberg retired from the IYRU in 1994 at the end of his eight-year term. There is still some confusion over the name change from International Yacht Racing Union (IYRU) to International Sailing Federation (ISAF), a change that I did not support. "Yachting" is a good marketing word and had been in the name of the federation for almost 100 years. It also had the added bonus of appearing last in the alphabetical list in any multi-sport games—it made the results easy to find. Tallberg and IYRU Executive Director Mike Evans felt that sailing had to become more modern, however, and renamed the federation. "ISF" was already used by the International Softball Federation so we had to use the letters ISAF instead. I am continually asked what the "A" stands for and I have never been able to come up with a good answer. I did not like dropping the word "Racing" from our name either, because that is what the Federation was about. (The UN forces in Afghanistan also use the acronym ISAF.)

It was becoming obvious to me by 1992 that I was not going to be nominated to replace Peter, who had appointed himself chair of the nominating committee. Their first choice to be the next ISAF president was Jacques Rogge, an Olympic sailor and past president of the Finn Class. Jacques said he was not interested, as he was then president of the European National Olympic Committees and was the front runner to replace Samaranch at the IOC. The well qualified Brazilian lawyer Peter Dirk Siemsen, who was a good friend and very capable administrator, was now emerging as the heir apparent.

When the nomination slate came out, Peter Siemsen was chosen and my name did not appear. I was not sure what to do because there had never been an election before. Mary put the steel in my back to run from the floor for the presidency. She pointed out that I never backed away from what I thought was right and should put my name forward, so I did.

It was a lively campaign. I did not get any support from the European establishment. My support came from the Caribbean, South America, North America and Asia—thanks to Bob Kim. Much lobbying was done on my behalf by the international classes, especially the Finn sailors. My travels to the emerging sailing nations that Beppe Croce had sent me on during my 16 years as IYRU vice-president served me well and I won the vote 43 to 36. On hearing the result, Samaranch phoned me to say he knew I would win. I thanked him profusely. The sad thing was that the ISAF lost Peter Siemsen, a solid contributor with a much needed Latin American focus.

At a pub around the corner from the London Hilton Hotel, my old crew Dennis Toews grabbed the spotlight and announced to the gathering, *"Dammit, I wish Henderson had been elected Pope! Then I would only have to kiss his ring."* And thus was born my nickname, "the Pope of sailing."

A change in the voting date from the middle of the Olympic cycle to the end added two years to the nominal eight-year term, and I enjoyed an exciting decade as ISAF president—albeit a challenging one. I felt it incumbent on me to bring the sport of sailing from the exclusive age of blue blazers and traditional clubs into the modern age, and to ensure that women felt the federation was inclusive. At regattas, I always enjoyed walking through the boat park debating various issues with the sailors. With the advent of the Internet and email, it became possible to throw out ideas and receive immediate responses. If nothing else, I encouraged communication and put a transparent face on the previously remote and staid ISAF. I also attempted to consolidate the fractious divisions of our sport within ISAF, to bring all sailors into the same family.

First Months as ISAF President

The first months of my presidency were very challenging, but in the long run rewarding. The most serious problem concerned finances. We had a competent honorary treasurer in Brian Southcott, who had looked after our finances superbly. He had grown concerned because ISAF was spending our Olympic revenue before we received it. Southcott pointed out that ISAF was spending five years' revenue in four. ISAF had to pull in its wings and live within our means, spending only the money we already had in the bank. The IYRU Audit Committee led by Joe Butterfield of New Zealand announced that unless we reorganized, ISAF would go bankrupt within three years. This was simply because ISAF was budgeting on a yearly basis when, like most Olympic sports, 60 per cent of our revenue comes in installments every four years after the Olympic Games. Switching to a four-year budget cycle was instrumental in solving the problem.

I had met the secretary general of the Norwegian Yachting Association (NYA), Arve Sundheim, at the Lillehammer Games where he helped in running the Olympic Village. I thought he would make a good secretary general for ISAF. I wanted a non-English person, but one who thought like the English. Before I asked him to apply, I consulted with H.M. King Harald to apprise him of my interest in hiring Arve. The King was an accomplished sailor and took great interest in the NYA. The King wrote me back what I am sure was the harshest letter ever written by a monarch. He accused me of subverting the NYA, because Arve was the only person who kept that organization financially solvent. He added that it was totally inappropriate for ISAF to undermine a member national authority. I wrote him back and thanked him for the best possible endorsement of the candidate. H.M. King Harald replied that it was a great honour for Norway to have Arve selected as the first Norwegian to serve as secretary general in any international Olympic sport federation.

The next problem was even more serious. I insisted that all of the federation's financial affairs be completely transparent and open to scrutiny, including that from the UK Internal Revenue Department. The problem was that the Olympic monies, which had become substantial, and all our subscriptions were potentially subject to taxation as if they had all been earned in the UK. This is the reason that most sport federations have moved out of the UK to Switzerland or Monaco. Because of the traditions of sailing, I wanted to see if we could work it out and remain in the UK. It was complicated and took a large amount of time and money, but we did accomplish it. Now all interested parties can check the ISAF books as they wish.

Internet

Within a month of taking the helm, I received a call from Bernie Stegmeier, president of the Swiss Yachting Association, who rather forcefully demanded that I bring ISAF into the emerging world of the Internet. As Director of IBM in Switzerland, Bernie knew what he was talking about. He said that the Internet was made for sailing. He convinced me that it was the future even though email and the Internet were then in their infancy. The launching of **www.sailing.org** was not easy in the staid and traditional fraternity of sailors. We asked for bids from UK Internet companies to build our website. The resulting proposals were in the range of one million dollars (US), a ridiculous sum. On top of that, ISAF staff members were not up to speed and were suspicious of the value of the Internet to our activities. At the February, 1995, ISAF executive meeting, Bernie and I tried to convince ISAF to jump into the Internet with both feet. The ISAF vice-presidents were not receptive to the idea, however, and refused to allocate funds to the project. One member was not even on fax yet, so the Internet understandably represented a quantum leap for his brain.

As usual, fate took over. I was having my customary delightful conversation with Peter Harken, the bizarre genius and inventor of sailing hardware from Pewaukee, Wisconsin, when he told me about his discovery of programmer David McCreary from Ithaca, New York, who had produced a website for Peter at a fraction of what it would normally have cost. I contacted McCreary and he turned out to be all Harken had said and more. Working out of the basement of his house, McCreary said he would construct the entire website for an initial fee of 30 thousand dollars, which was a long way from the million dollar quote in the UK. In four days,

McCreary had developed a mock-up of the website that I presented to the next executive meeting in May, 1995. The ISAF executive committee members remained unconvinced, however, and allocated no budget to support it. I was determined to get it up and running and paid the 30 thousand dollars to McCreary out of my own pocket. I contributed additional funds over the next 12 months to keep the website going until everyone woke up, but I was never reimbursed.

Each morning for the next two years, Bernie and I edited everything from our respective offices in Switzerland and Toronto before authorizing McCreary to send it into cyberspace. Nobody worked harder than David McCreary. A fantastic vehicle for promoting sailing and the most significant legacy to the sport during my presidency, **www.sailing.org** has been selected several times as the most advanced sport website by a number of independent agencies. Without David and Bernie behind it, however, it would never have got off the ground.

ISAF Administration and Governance

With finances on a secure footing, Arve's strong hand on administration, and the Internet proving to be everything Bernie had predicted—and then some—ISAF was well positioned to sail exuberantly out of its storied past into the Twenty-First Century. Of those who came onside and made my life as president enjoyable, windsurfer Luissa Smith from Itchenor, England, was the most dedicated and competent staff contributor. She looked after almost all areas of ISAF diligently and with a smile. Jerome Pels, a lawyer and Olympic coach in Holland, also joined ISAF and immediately courted Fleur Ainslie in the ISAF office. Fleur is the sister of the famous UK sailor and Olympic Gold medalist Ben Ainslie. And into his fourth decade of service in ISAF's technical department, Simon Forbes remained one of the federation's longest serving stalwarts.

When I became ISAF president, I needed protection—mostly from myself. I asked Toronto lawyer John Tinker to come to ISAF and lead the constitution committee. His instructions were never to allow me to do anything that was not on the up and up. This was a ridiculous directive as John Tinker would never impugn his integrity even for a friend. Mary liked him and he would often come to dinner. Our son John could never understand the intense arguments that Tinker and I would get into, and believed we did not like each other.

It was entirely to John Tinker that nothing was done at ISAF during this decade that could not withstand open scrutiny. At the 2004 annual general meeting, Tinker retired with me and gave me his typical advice on some important subject: *"On the one hand, if you do this, here are the consequences and on the other hand, if you do this, the result will be as follows."*

I observed, *"I wish I could find a one handed lawyer!"*

Before the gathered throng, Tinker replied, *"Henderson you do not want a one-handed lawyer. You want a two-fisted lawyer!"*

As I was leaving, a woman from the British Virgin Islands came up to me and said, *"This is my first meeting. I had heard about you two Canucks and I am sad I will not see you continuing to perform and lead ISAF with such dedication and humour."*

I was sad that Tinker and I had to leave, but all things eventually come to an end.

I found one of the most enjoyable duties of my presidency to be traveling to various sailing nations, especially the emerging sailing countries, where my arrival meant something to them. This was also characteristic of my attendance at the various regional multi-sport games.

Offshore Racing Council (ORC)

One of the first countries I was invited to visit was Iceland, which was slated to host the 1995 Games of the Small Nations of Europe. Ten sports are admitted to these games and nine had already been chosen. The tenth slot was up for grabs between judo and sailing. At the behest of the Icelandic Sailing Association, I traveled there in February 1995 to lobby the minister of sport to include sailing, an effort in which I happily succeeded. It was a wonderful trip to a very unusual place. Iceland is famous for its horses that are renowned for their stamina—in spite of their less-than-handsome features—and some of the most beautiful women in the world.

In my hotel there hung a photo of Reykjavik in the early 1930s, the air polluted almost beyond belief. All its energy was supplied by coal imported from Scotland. During World War II, however, coal supplies became scarce. An innovative engineer developed the idea of driving pipes into the ground to exploit geothermal energy. The US Navy arrived with a boat-load of pipe, and in short order the concept was proven both sound and feasible. The geothermal energy of Iceland was tapped. Reykjavik is now pollution-free using the world's most envied geothermal technology.

My visit left me with many fond memories, including a wonderful seafood dinner at the small sailing club. The sailors complimented ISAF on the website, saying it allowed them to keep in touch with what was happening in the rest of the sailing world. They added that every summer, they were visited by sailors from Norway, Denmark and Scotland wishing to compete in their weekend races and asked if there was some way they could get an online handicap system up quickly and cheaply. I thought it was feasible.

Shortly afterward, Karel Bauer asked me to go to Prague to talk to the re-emerging Czech sailing fraternity. Karel took me to see Lake Lipno, a man-made lake some 30 kilometres long and 10 kilometres wide. He explained how, in the 1950s the Soviets had built a power dam in what was then a mountain valley, and flooded it creating this lake. After the creation of the Czech Republic, Karel acquired an impressive piece of land on the shore for a sailing club. If Prague is awarded the Olympic Games, this will be the sailing venue. Karel is an energetic enthusiast who usually gets things done. We drove back to Prague where I addressed the members of the traditional yacht club on the river. During the question period, a young Czech sailor spoke highly of the ISAF website and asked why ISAF could not get an inexpensive yacht handicap system up and running online.

I had now received two requests from emerging nations to do this. It was feasible with the ISAF's new Internet capability, so I wrote an editorial suggesting ISAF should provide this service to the small nations and, for that matter, to any group who wanted a cheap handicap system. All hell broke loose when the Offshore Racing Council (ORC) maintained that they had a franchise monopoly from ISAF to govern independently the "offshore" division of sailing, which they defined as encompassing "any boat with a bed," a ridiculous assertion. IYRU President Beppe Croce had told me that the worst mistake he had ever made at IYRU was forming the ORC in 1967. The last time I spoke with him before he died, he told me to correct the mistake and bring the ORC back into the fold because sailors were sailors, regardless of whether the boat had a keel or a centreboard, or for that matter a bed.

I had not intended this confrontation, but the ORC demanded their exclusivity on this important part of the sailing spectrum. Robin Aisher, an ISAF vice-president and ORC council member, came to me and said the ORC was on a course to start a new International Offshore Federation and that I must act decisively. Aisher knew what he was talking about.

During this debate I attended the US Sailing (USSA) meeting in Newport, Rhode Island, and stayed at the most peaceful place in the sailing world, the New York Yacht Club, Harbor Court. Mary and I were enjoying breakfast when the revered Olin Stephens walked by. Olin was then in his 80s and very sharp. Olin was the designer of many racing yachts, including America's Cup defenders. He was an outspoken supporter of the fact that offshore sailing should be organized in a separate federation under the ORC, distinct from ISAF. I went up to him and introduced myself:

"Mr. Stephens, I am Paul Henderson president of ISAF."

"I know, and I do not like you," he replied and left.

Later that day, I found Olin sitting by himself in the lobby. I went over and sat down beside him, and we had a great talk. He explained handicap rules. I asked about the

International Measurement System (IMS), and he lectured me on it, ending with the insight that the USA/IMS scoring method does not work well in waters where there are large tides or currents. I pointed out that perhaps this was why the English do not like it. The Solent, where most of their racing takes place, has brutal tides. I left believing I had opened up a dialogue with this wonderful man.

By 2002, the ORC was in disarray. They had constantly changed their rules, confusing the sailors. I received a personal letter from Olin asking me to try to resolve ORC's problems, as he believed I was the only one tough enough to address the dilemma in Offshore Racing. It was perhaps the greatest compliment I have ever received. When I retired in 2004, he sent me a beautiful letter apologizing for having given me such a hard time earlier. Olin Stephens never has to apologize to anyone, least of all to me.

The Royal Ocean Racing Club, a division of the Royal Yachting Association (RYA), had another handicap system based on the IRC rule. It was simple and inexpensive, costing less than 100 dollars to get a rating. It was exactly what I thought could be done over the Internet. Robin Aisher tells the story of how the original IRC rule was started. It was then called the CHS, which most people believed was an acronym of "Channel Handicap System." Aisher says it started one night when the English and French got together and went out on the town in Paris—CHS actually stands for "Crazy Horse Saloon."

Along with Ken Ellis of the Royal Yachting Association, I worked very hard to get the RYA/IRC rule endorsed by ISAF as an alternative bona fide system for handicapping various racing yachts. Finally in 2002, after eight years of work, ISAF adopted the IRC rule against the strident debates put forward by the exclusive ORC supporters. Today, even the New York Yacht Club and San Francisco's St. Francis Yacht Club have adopted the IRC rule for most of their club racing.

America's Cup

It proved to be quite a challenge to encourage the America's Cup fraternity to respect the structure and services ISAF provided. Founded in 1851, the America's Cup is a group of elite sailors who have long considered themselves to be outside the purview of ISAF, yet able to cherry pick ISAF services without contributing financially to the administration of the sport. I had to remind the America's Cup adherents that ISAF was founded in 1907 and after 100 years had served the sport well. One hundred and thirty nations recognized ISAF as the single governing body for sailing in all its forms. The America's Cup syndicates were prepared to recognize ISAF as long as they could avail themselves of its services for free. This is consistent with what I had discovered in the plumbing business, that those with the most money were the poorest to pay—which I suppose is why they have so much.

In the 1980s, sailboats were still free of advertising. Sailing was imagined to be an amateur sport pursued by gentlemen from wealthy clubs. This indicates how far behind the real world the leaders of the sport were. In 1985, the Aussies, Kiwis and Danes petitioned ISAF to allow advertising on hulls and sails, believing it to be the only way they could compete against the wealth of the USA. They petitioned the ISAF that, if ISAF allowed advertising on boats, they were prepared to pay a fee back to ISAF and to the national authorities for the development of sailing. Their recommendation at the time was a payment of 10 per cent of their total sponsorship. It was a very difficult negotiation led by Peter Siemsen (Brazil), Judge Livius Sherwood (Canada) and Tom Ehman (USA) on behalf of ISAF. After two years of work amid roadblocks thrown up by US Sailing, who did not want any commercialism of the sport, the Advertising Code was passed. It appears that the implementation of the Advertising Code had a positive impact on the ability of other countries to compete after all.

In 1995, New Zealand won the America's Cup, with their defense scheduled for 1999. Sir Peter Blake led the Kiwi defense along with his sidekick Alan Sefton and lawyers Russell Green and Hamish Ross. Blake was a big, rawboned man, as tough a customer as I have ever had to deal with. I was intent on getting a sensible fee as originally promised by the America's Cup Syndicates in 1988. The letters that went back and forth were brutal on all sides and are best forgotten.

ISAF developed racing rules specifically for America's Cup match racing, trained all the judges and referees, and governed the system that produced the sailors, most of whom were Olympic sailors. It was only fair that ISAF be reimbursed by those who benefited from the services it provided.

The total cost to field an America's Cup syndicate was, at the low end, 50 million dollars (US); some syndicates spend more than thrice that. There were to be 10 syndicates, for an overall expenditure of some one billion dollars. ISAF delegated Vice-presidents Goran Petersson and Ken Ryan to negotiate the fee and all other aspects of the 1999 America's Cup. They went to Auckland and met with Blake, Sefton and their lawyers. On returning to Europe, Petersson and Ryan reported that they did not like to negotiate money and that dealing with the Kiwis was not something they relished. They asked me to assume the negotiations, a prime example of the sign on Harry Truman's desk, "The Buck Stops Here!"

I was appalled at the first formal offer of 10 thousand New Zealand dollars (about five thousand US dollars), which was to cover all payments to ISAF and the relevant national authorities with entries. This was an extreme insult, inconsistent with their original commitment to ISAF in return for its having allowed advertising. This was less than five hundred dollars per boat. I sent back a request that the fee should be two million dollars (US). Blake and Sefton attacked me in the press, but I was resolute. It should be noted that the Opti, a youth training sailboat costing two thousand dollars per boat, had been responsible for paying more into the work of ISAF in one year than any multi-million dollar America's Cup campaign. I threw it back at the America's Cup syndicates that they should be ashamed to have been subsidized by the youth of the sport.

Finally a meeting was called, and all sides met with their lawyers in the ISAF offices in Southampton. John Tinker was present as ISAF legal adviser. Thankfully, Commodore Robert James of the New York Yacht Club was there. A senior advertising executive, he understood the situation. The meeting became somewhat heated with Blake and his Kiwi lawyers stonewalling most of the debate. Commodore James called a time-out, suggesting we all caucus separately for an hour. He then called the ISAF delegation back in and said they had an offer to make, which was one million dollars (US) to be split 50 per cent to ISAF, 25 per cent to the New Zealand Yachting Association, and the remainder to be split equally among the other nations with entries. ISAF accepted immediately and I thanked Commodore James. Peter Blake put his arm around me and we left together for a drink. Sadly, he was murdered while exploring the Amazon on behalf of the Cousteau Foundation. Blake was a unique and driven character. I really like his type.

I decided that I would hand-deliver subsequent ISAF requirements to all the syndicates in Auckland during the Cup. When I arrived in Auckland, Dyer Jones, past commodore of the New York Yacht Club, informed me that the Royal New Zealand Yacht Squadron (RNZYS) had refused to allow me to meet in their club because of the protracted debate on fees. I responded with two observations: I told him that in view of the fact that the RNZYS had given me an honorary membership only the year before, this was indeed a strange way to treat a new member. I then observed with no little irony that when you start with an offer of 10 thousand New Zealand dollars and end up with one million US dollars, you cannot expect to be universally loved. Blake and the Kiwis won the America's Cup for the second time, but the standard for the ISAF fee had been set for the future.

The real talent responsible for the Kiwi victories lay with Russell Coutts and Brad Butterworth, the most experienced and formidable team ever to have competed in the America's Cup. They abandoned the Kiwi ship for the next challenge, however, because of problems caused by the Kiwi lawyers who had now taken over the next defense. They sailed for Switzerland in the

2003 Cup, which they won sailing *Alinghi* with Ernesto Bertarelli as the major backer. Butterworth, then working and living in Switzerland, met with me during the Spring of 2004 in Geneva to conclude the ISAF agreement for the 2007 Cup. The whole negotiation took less than an hour. As we went to lunch, Brad said that had we done the deal together years earlier, there would have been no problem.

In Athens for the Olympic Games, we were lining up to board the bus for the Opening Ceremonies when Jacques Rogge walked by and, seeing me, told me that Ernesto Bertarelli was at the back of the line-up and wanted to talk with me. I had met Ernesto two or three times before, but could not say I really knew him. I left Mary and went back to see him. Bertarelli lectured me on the fact that the America's Cup is the top of the sailing pyramid and therefore must be respected by ISAF. I replied, *"We look at this issue differently. You believe sailing is a pyramid with the America's Cup as the pinnacle. I believe sailing is like the Himalayan Mountains. There are many peaks, some higher than others. All divisions of the sailing spectrum are important."*

The America's Cup is the one sailing event that transcends the normal sailing fraternity and which I hope will rise to the level of other elite sporting events such as Wimbledon, Roland Garros, and the Masters. There are very few such events and I sincerely hope the America's Cup will reach that exalted level.

Women's Sailing

Women's sailing was another focus of my presidency, one that included trying to break the ISAF old boys' club mentality. In the sailing events in the 1996 Olympics, women accounted for only 19 per cent of the participants, the poorest showing in any dual gender sport. In Athens, the women's participation rose to 37 per cent. This was achieved by securing additional events for women at a time when the IOC was cutting back, thanks to the support of His Majesty King Constantine and Juan Antonio Samaranch.

I believe it is a simple matter—if women are sailing then the men will be there, and if men are sailing the women will be there also and the whole sport will grow. The traditional clubs and regattas must buy into the reality of today's culture. It is essential to go overboard to make women feel accepted and comfortable in the clubs, involving them in all aspects of the organization of the sport.

In 1994, the ISAF executive and the 39-seat council were exclusively male-dominated. It should not have been required in today's world, but it is only by decree that ISAF could force intransigent males to give up their sinecures. The first thing I did was to demand that one of the seven ISAF vice-presidents be female. The usual nonsensical debate followed, but the measure was passed and Italy's Nucci Novi Ceppellini became the first female vice-president. ISAF added another special seat on its council for women. The first woman ever to sit at council was Venezuela's Teresa Lara, an alternate replacement nominated by Bobby Symonette from the Bahamas. I had met Teresa in the Dominican Republic when she managed her team there during the Caribbean Games. I challenged her to get involved in ISAF, and she too became an ISAF vice-president. Teresa is a good friend of Flor Isava, the first woman ever to become an IOC member.

I didn't stop there, however. The year before my retirement when people were lobbying to be elected themselves, I militantly orchestrated that at least two of the seven vice-presidents be women and further that women account for at least 20 per cent of the council. The sitting council said this just could not be, so I allocated the number of women required by each continent and got it all through before most council members woke up to the impact this would have. The elections were held on my last day in office and to everyone's surprise, three women out of seven were elected to the executive. Women failed to account for 20 per cent of the council women, however, and the primary culprit was Europe: two European women had been elected to the executive, and they needed one more to meet their quota of three out of 19 European seats. They tried to renege by refusing to nominate any women from Europe for the council, but I stood fast. They finally put forth Nazli Imre from Turkey who had entertained Mary and me on our wonderful visits to Istanbul.

Because of my militancy on women's issues, Anita DeFrantz of the USA asked me to sit on the IOC Women and Sport Commission. Only 10 per cent of the 120 members of the IOC are women. I attended a meeting in Morocco and berated the women's executive that they must be militant and demand their rights. I recommended that a resolution be passed demanding that the IOC—really Jacques Rogge—must appoint one woman for every man appointed until there were a minimum of 25 women on the IOC. I was shocked at the women's response. They were afraid to act because the IOC would not like it. This was a disturbing but understandable response because most of the women had become paid consultants on issues relating to women in sports in their respective countries. I find this mentality everywhere. Those who are paid consultants do not rock the boat on any issue because they like to continue being paid.

Joint World Championship of Olympic Classes

It was always the dream to have all Olympic classes hold their world championships at one time in one venue the year before the Olympics. This was to be the major qualification regatta for the Olympic Games. For 2003, ISAF finally endorsed and led the concept for the Joint World Championship of Olympic Classes and wisely chose Cadiz in Spain. It was an excellent venue as it has dependable wind conditions. The onshore facilities are as fine as those found anywhere else in the world, while the hotels and rental accommodations are varied and reasonably priced.

It was a resounding success. There were over 1,500 competitors and 300 accredited media in attendance. As I walked through the boat park talking with the sailors, they all commented on the excellent wind conditions. Europe had had a summer of no-wind regattas and Cadiz was a refreshing change with strong winds almost every day.

Several things happened during the event that I found gratifying. Initially, the nine Olympic classes demanded that each class have its own separate reception in order to demonstrate their independence from one another. These were scheduled for an impressive bodega. The first two were rather dull. Then the members of the Finn Class, the most macho and tough single-handed dinghy, invited all the Europe Class sailors—the women's single-handed dinghy—to their reception at the bodega. The party was a great success, and after that, all classes invited all sailors with the result that the atmosphere was electric. The ISAF always wanted to achieve this sort of interaction between sailors from all classes.

One day a group of Star sailors, the oldest and most intransigent male keelboat class, came to me and said they would support future joint worlds provided that the all-women Ynglings, the three-women keelboat, be placed in the boat park in the order of a Star, Yngling, Star, Yngling and so on. They also demanded that the women wear bikinis. This was obviously a very sensitive negotiation. I called a meeting of the Yngling women and explained the Star sailors' unusual request. This led to intense and serious discussion among the women, after which they proposed a compromise: they would accede to the men's request provided that the Yngling women were permitted to select the Star crew who would wash down nude on the pontoons, because they had found all those who had performed up to that point to be uniformly ugly.

I knew ISAF had won acceptance of the joint worlds as we had wind, the media, and the interaction of the sailing fraternity, especially for the Olympic Class sailors. At the end of Cadiz, several of the most knowledgeable and accomplished sailors in the world asked that the event be held every other year. The media went even further and asked that it be held every year. The last joint worlds were held in 2007 in Cascais, Portugal, because the sailors demanded wind, for which Cascais is renowned. I trust that in the future, ISAF will go to alternative years for what has become essentially the world cup of sailing.

Reflections on Presidential Visits

For an ISAF President the invitations are legion. I accepted as many as I could. Here are my recollections of some that I have not already mentioned:

Yekaterinburg, Russia:

The Russians had developed a match racing regatta in the rather remote venue of Yekaterinburg. Many well known sailors had competed, returning with glowing reports of the hospitality shown in the middle of Russia where there are many interconnected lakes similar to the Muskoka Lakes north of Toronto. (The Tsar and his family had been assassinated there.) I was taken to a walled city to which the USSR had moved all their nuclear scientists in the late 1940s and developed a new town. The lifestyle there was better than anywhere else in the USSR, but I was told that the expected life span was only about 52 years. One encouraging aspect of my visit was that the government had provided grants to the small sailing clubs to spruce up in order to impress me. The sailors there were so enthusiastic and hospitable that I went back again in 2004, just before I retired.

Vladivostok, Russia:

Vladivostok on the Pacific Ocean is ice-free most of the winter. It is the site of a major naval base and a major container port for goods shipped to Moscow. I was invited by the founder of the Seven Feet Yacht Club, who felt that my appearance might induce the governor of the state to sign over the much needed land for the club. The club was named after the Irish maxim, "May the wind always be at your back and there be seven feet of water under your keel."

The club organized a special regatta and named it in my honour. We went for a wonderful sail on the fjord and were served the best seafood and caviar. I was escorted to meet with the governor on his yacht. Amid intense security we posed for the customary photo-ops, and he signed over the land. There was a quiet country hotel and restaurant out in the woods called *Canada Hotel* run by a man from Ottawa. I have never seen more Mercedes and BMWs per capita than in Vladivostok. The residents consider themselves European rather than Asian, even though they are situated just north of Korea.

Novorossiysk, Russia:

Novorossiysk is a Russian port on the Black Sea near the Crimea. It is near Sochi, one of the cities bidding for the 2014 Winter Olympics, in a beautiful region that I am sure will become popular in the future. They had developed a good match racing regatta there, and once again I found the people to be extremely hospitable. They took me to a 100-year-old distillery and winery that had been inaugurated by Catherine the Great and that they say produces the finest champagne. (We opened our souvenir bottle in Toronto on New Year's Eve, 2000, to celebrate the new millennium.)

Bulgaria:

Kamen Fillyov, a member of the ISAF Council, invited me to visit Bulgaria in 2002. Kamen really meant to show me *all* of Bulgaria. We left the capital Sophia and drove along the north border of the country into the mountains, ending up in a remote village with cobblestone streets and perhaps 100 residents. For centuries Bulgaria has been overrun by almost every army intent on invading it, but this town is so remote they had never seen the pillaging hordes. We then drove to the Black Sea with its endless beaches and new hotels. We visited several sailing clubs that rolled out the red carpet for us. Then it was back to Sophia where we toured the National Sport Institute. It is beyond anything we have in Canada, although I saw similar facilities in other former Eastern Bloc countries—a testament to the high regard in which sport is held in those nations.

Dominican Republic:

I first traveled to the Dominican Republic for the Sunfish Worlds in the 1990s. It is another perfect venue for racing sailing. The yacht club is very efficient with a white sand beach protected by a reef, perfect for launching boats. Outside the reef the water is a clear blue, over which the trade winds blow, creating wonderful ocean waves. I never raced there, but I sure wish I had. At Hector Duval's invitation, I visited again during the 2003 Pan

American Games, and participated in opening the event with the minister of sport, Baseball Hall of Famer Juan Marichal. As usual, sailing had the best venue of the Games.

Gdansk, Poland:

I visited Poland on several occasions as a guest of Tomasz Holc. During my first visit in 1997 he introduced me to Lech Walesa, a highlight of the trip. There was a major Offshore Class regatta going on out in the Baltic, but what impressed me most was the Opti kids showing off in the marina. They were playing chicken with the docks, roaring in at full speed in a 20-knot breeze, looking like they were going to crash. At the last minute they would adroitly spin their boats around and sail off. These 10-year-olds would smile and look back to see if I was watching. It took me back about 50 years—that was me, equally as smart-ass a kid from Toronto Island, totally addicted to sailing and dreaming.

Gydnia, Poland:

In 2001, Holc invited ISAF to hold the Youth Worlds in Gydnia. The opening ceremonies were held on their famous training tall ship, *Dar Pomorza*, which I had first seen coming down the Kiel Fjord during the 1972 Olympic Games. Holc took me to the sailing school near Hel, up the coast past some abandoned military installations in the sea. We then went down the coast to a volunteer windsurfing club that had been developed by the local town and was focused on sailing. Polish sailors are emerging as some of the most competitive in the world. He also took me to the Polish National Sports Institute which was as fine a facility as I have ever seen. It demonstrates that if you provide the facilities and coaching, you can motivate young people. It always makes me depressed when I come back to Canada, one of the wealthiest nations in the World, and see public discourse centred on issues like same sex marriage, gun control and government scandals, with a concomitant expenditure of energy, time and money that does almost nothing for sport and delivers precious little to motivate our youth.

Argentina:

It was my great privilege to visit Argentina not once but twice. Argentina has a great sailing tradition. The Yacht Club Argentino in Buenos Aires is well known in sailing circles with its renowned yacht designer German Freres and two old friends and supporters, the late Hugo Warneford-Thomson and Carlos Diehl. My second visit was for the 1995 Pan American Games in Mar de Plata. The administration office was located in a house where Evita Peron summered. Once again, sailing had the best venue and the regatta was well run. I would respectfully submit that the best food in the world can be found in Argentina, including both seafood and its renowned beef.

Cape Town, South Africa:

ISAF was asked to hold its mid-year meeting in Cape Town, South Africa. All the around-the-world races stop there. Mary and I attended with great anticipation, having heard many stories of beautiful Cape Town. The city lived up to all our expectations. Needless to say, we visited the Kruger National Park to see the magnificent animals of the region.

Malta:

The 2003 Games of the Small States of Europe were held in Valetta, Malta. I was excited about going because Toronto has a vibrant Maltese community and the tales I had heard about the knights of Malta made it a place I always wanted to see. My host Peter Valentino and my old friend John Ripard, both well known ISAF judges, squired me around this unique island country. The most impressive sailing club was a small dinghy club that volunteers had converted from a munitions store house. Due to its convenient water access, it had been pressed into use to introduce younger sailors to the sport. After touring the island's historic sites, I decided that being a Knight of Malta was definitely more enjoyable in the later stages of life rather than earlier, since they began as Christian celibates and ended up in the most extreme debauchery.

Warnemunde, Germany:

Warnemunde, a quaint town with beautiful beaches and good accommodations, is the major port for Berlin on the Baltic. My daughter Martha was sailing in the 2004 Yngling Open World Championship there and I went as coach. Because Warnemunde is situated in the former East Germany, it had some bonuses. For one, there was little uncontrolled development over some 50 years, leaving the region unspoiled. The citizens are happy and friendly, proud of their town and unique culture. The sailors loved it, apart from a lack of wind, which can occur anywhere. Each night of the Worlds, the sailing women of a particular region hosted a party where they cooked and served a sumptuous dinner for the other sailors. The North Americans served pancakes—Martha had instructed me to bring lots of good Canadian maple syrup. Seeing the top Olympic sailors having such great fun reassured me that sailing was going in the right direction. If you ever think that Germans do not know how to enjoy themselves, just go to Warnemunde.

Macao and Hainan Island, China:

In 2002 I was invited by the Chinese to attend the Macao-to-Hainan Island race. Since I had never been there and was on my way to Qingdoa to see the 2008 Olympic sailing venue, I readily accepted. Macao had just been turned over to China so the atmosphere was uncertain, but this former Portuguese colony was interesting to see and the sailors, as always, were very helpful. An intense young female interpreter from mainland China gave me an in-depth education on China and its evolving political scene. I flew to Hainan Island which advertises that it is the most remote destination in the world. It is a beautiful place, with white sandy beaches and fine hotels.

Cuba:

Before I became president I attended the 1991 Pan American Games in Havana. None of the other ISAF vice-presidents wanted to go, which shows how foolish they were. Canadian Airlines operated a cheap flight to Cienfuegos, a simple military airport. I had no idea how far it was from Havana but I soon found out. When I got off the plane, I asked the airline attendant how to get to Havana. She laughed and suggested I get back on the plane and go home. She explained that this was a difficult time economically for Cuba and that fuel was in very short supply. There was just no way I could get to Havana by air. Hearing my plight, an elegant Cuban who had been standing in a corner of the room came over and told me his cousin owned a taxi and might take me, but it would be expensive. It seemed I had no choice. His cousin showed up in a Russian Lada so well used that I could see the road through the floorboard. He told me the fare would be 60 dollars plus gas for a trip that should take about three hours.

What a day I had! We first had to go to the cigar rolling factory, then to lunch with his aunt, then to visit his girlfriend, who was a dancer in a hotel revue, then to tea with his grandmother before arriving finally at the famous but now run down Tropicana Hotel. I checked in uneventfully, but the next morning when my phone rang, I was ordered down to the office immediately. Dressed uniformly in drab grey suits, the officials said they could not believe that I had come the way I had and chastised me for being so cavalier. I replied that my driver—now my friend—was going to pick me up a week later to take me back and that I did not need their help.

I was invited to a VIP reception one night for about 200 people. After cocktails, Anita DeFrantz, IOC member in the USA, told me to hang around in the private banquet room. After a few minutes Fidel Castro entered and 20 of us had dinner with him. He gave a speech in English, which he spoke well having spent time in New York. Castro was an avid sports fan and had played minor league baseball.

I found the Cubans to be very friendly and, although the maintenance of the buildings was not as good as it might have been, the young people were well educated and outgoing. The special tourist restaurants were excellent. I found all the old cars intriguing. New cars were simply not available so they kept all the old ones running. It made me feel like I was in a 1958 time warp. It was obvious that several European countries were investing large sums of money in the Cuban tourist industry. It is a beautiful island, much larger than I had imagined. The Cubans have practiced birth control extensively, keeping the population under control. That, together with an excellent education system, bodes well for Cuba's economic future.

Qinhuangdao, China:

In 1992, the Asian Sailing Regatta was held in Qinhuangdao, where the Great Wall meets the Pacific Ocean. It is a strategic military city that, until the late 1980s was not accessible to foreigners. I represented the IYRU and was not sure where I was going. I flew from Beijing in a 50-seat droop-winged Russian airplane to Qinhuangdao's rather primitive airport—primitive in the sense that the runway landing lights were nothing more than lanterns in the hands of soldiers. I found the new marina well designed and the Chinese officials very hospitable. I must have set a new world record eating three Peking duck dinners in the space of 24 hours.

The Russians had donated a boat about 70-feet long to which the Chinese had added a well appointed three-level superstructure. The vessel, however, was a river boat with a shallow draft, and the races were being held in the Pacific Ocean with its ever present swells. This meant that the boat rocked and rolled incessantly. When I showed up to be escorted out to the races, I was surprised to see that the numerous officials and members of the press gallery had brought along their families, and there were about 500 people on board. Out we went to sea and after giving a number of media interviews I went up to the top deck and spoke with the renowned sports writer from *The Times* of London, David Miller. After about half an hour, David asked whether

I had noticed a disaster in the making. He suggested that I go and look over the rail, and when I did I saw a long line of people throwing up over the side. I went to the captain and told him we had better return to shore. At first, he refused to do so—he said there was a special VIP aboard. I convinced him that I was that person and that we should return to dry land. As soon as we arrived, they began carrying passengers off, some of whom were whisked away in ambulances.

There were only two flights each week back to Beijing, so I got up the next morning and boarded the 4:30 a.m. train for the seven-hour ride back to the capital. The sun rose on a solid black cloud of air pollution that hung over the countryside. I could scarcely believe my eyes. Two rows ahead of me, a balding middle-aged American man was seated beside a Chinese girl who could scarcely have been half his age. I finally got up the nerve to start a conversation. He told me that they had just been married the day before—he had met her in person only three days before that. It seems he had selected her from a catalogue and was now taking her back to his potato farm in Idaho.

I arrived in Beijing just before noon and was met by Chinese sport and sailing officials. We had dinner at a revolving restaurant atop the largest hotel there. As the restaurant revolved, my hosts pointed out various tourist sites, such as the Forbidden City and the Great Wall. When Tiananmen Square came into view, the senior official said, *"You Canadians are misinformed and should not listen to the propaganda of the USA."*

"What did we do now?" I asked.

"We did not kill 3,000 students in Tiananmen Square, only 500," he complained.

"In Canada, 500 is still a great number," I gently pointed out.

I have been back to China several times in the last few years and the change is dynamic. My last visits have been to Shanghai to the 2005 World Dragon Boat Championships and to Beijing and Qingdoa for the 2008 Olympic Games. The changes in such a short time are dramatic.

Croatia:

Sailors love Croatia, especially Finn sailors, because the waters are clear, the winds good, the coastline and islands unique, and the young ladies elegant. The Croatian government has built a series of 22 excellent marinas from Umag to Split to Dubrovnik. I first visited Dubrovnik in 1996, a few months after the civil war. The combatants saved the historic part of the city, but greatly damaged other parts. Walking through the parking lot of the expansive marina, I noticed black stains on the concrete at about five-metre intervals. I asked what had caused it and was told that the Serbs had set up mortars on the hills abutting the harbour and lobbed shells into the fibreglass boats stored on the concrete. The boats caught fire and melted, leaving only a small pile of black ash.

The Croatians are fine sailors and hosts.

Estonia:

I visited Estonia twice during my presidency, once during the Finn Gold Cup in Parnu, and once during my brief stay as a member of the World Anti-Doping Agency (WADA) when I traveled to Tallinn. I always say I do not believe the Estonians who say there are so few of them—yet everywhere I go I meet Estonians. Many of the sailors who raced in Parnu fell in love with the gracious Estonian ladies. A bevy of beautiful young Estonian dancers entertained us at the opening ceremonies of the Finn Gold Cup. Sadly, many of them perished a few months later in the tragic sinking of an auto ferry in the Baltic en route to Sweden.

Slovenia:

Slovenia has a very small but beautiful coastline wedged between Trieste, Italy and Umag, Croatia. Although it is only 30 kilometres long, it features an active sailing community with very good facilities. In 1998, Slovenia did a superb job hosting the Star Class World Championship, which suffered only from a lack of wind. I was surprised at the health of the economy in Slovenia and its dynamic business community.

Dubai:

ISAF picked Dubai for the second World Sailing Championships in 1998, after the successful 1994 championships in La Rochelle, France. We had been assured that all countries would be allowed access and when the regatta was awarded in 1995, there were hopes for peace in the Middle East. The United Arab Emirates (UAE) went out of their way to make the regatta a success—the organization was outstanding. They bought new boats and supplied them free to all competitors. Free accommodation was also provided in temporary buildings, with the superb Dubai hotels always available for those who wanted to pay.

I delegated all aspects of the organization to two vice-presidents, Fernando Bolin from Spain and Sadi Claeys from Belgium. One month before the event, conflict broke out between Israel and the Arab world and the Israelis were refused visas. The UAE said they would admit the Israeli sailors provided they did not ask to come through diplomatic channels. The Israelis said they would come only with formal invitations and visas from the UAE government. The Israelis had entered only in the Laser Class, the sole class that was using this event to qualify sailors for the Sydney Olympics. Some 3,000 competitors from 80 different countries were there to compete in ten separate classifications. The Israelis had bought their airline tickets and their boats were already on site. Bolin and Claeys said the regatta must be canceled unless sailors from all countries were allowed to compete. I had to find a compromise because canceling the regatta was not a viable alternative.

Thanks to ISAF Israeli delegates Aaron Botzer and Zvi Ziblat, a solution was worked out. The Israelis did not want the event canceled, thus affecting all sailors, but they wanted to qualify their Laser sailor for the Olympics. I offered that ISAF would give Israel a bye in the Laser Class to the Olympics if they withdrew their entries in Dubai. After much debate in Israel, they accepted. The two ISAF vice-presidents were not happy with the compromise and demanded that their countries get byes as well, citing this as a bad precedent. It was, but the alternative was even worse—canceling the regatta was just not acceptable. Forty-five nations are admitted to the Olympics in the Laser Class and the Israelis were easily ranked in the top ten. They would have qualified without the concession, so it was not that great an imposition. The regatta was superb and the UAE were great hosts. Camel-riding was a wonderful diversion.

Nassau:

The Bahamas have a great tradition in hosting sailing events and also producing excellent sailors. Sir Durward Knowles won Olympic Medals in the Star Class in 1956 and 1964, and Bobby Symonette was a legend in the 5.5 Metre Class. I was asked to race in the annual Bahamas Workboat Regatta. Workboats are sailing boats unique to the region that are still used to deliver goods to the out islands. They have their own racing rules. They usually invite famous sailors to come and race with local crews against the best workboat skippers. The year I was invited the guests included Lowell North (Olympic Gold Medal and founder of North Sails), Tom Blackhaller, and Ted Turner of America's Cup fame. Nassau's accomplished sailor was the semiofficial ambassador of Bahamian goodwill, "King" Eric Gibson, who owns *The Blue Note* night club and fronts his own calypso band, King Eric and His Knights.

After the first day's races, we all went to King Eric's club. The stories and jokes flowed well into the night, with the others sailors unceasingly making derogatory comments about the shiny bald heads of King Eric and myself. To deflect these personal attacks I yelled to King Eric the old line, *"If they put our heads together, we would make a perfect ass."* Everyone broke up and King Eric was beside himself with laughter.

The prize presentation was held in Nassau's main park on a radiant, sunny day, with King Eric officiating as master of ceremonies.

Before the assembled throng of 4000, he asked, *"Where's Henderson?"* I walked forward and he put his arm around my shoulder, leaned his black head against my white one and announced to the world gathered there, *"Henderson if we put our heads together we would make the most unusual ass in the whole world!"*

Several years later I was playing golf at the Toronto Hunt Club with Andy Donato, political cartoonist for *The Toronto Sun,* who refers to himself as the Italian Stallion, and Llewellyn MacIntosh, who works in the pro shop. Llewellyn, a Trinidadian, is black and bald like Eric Gibson, and on the eighth hole I made the King Eric remark to him. A holier-than-thou club member heard the remark and reported me to the board for uttering a racial slur. I asked the accuser why he had interpreted the comment the way he did. His answer was that he grew up in the USA and was therefore more sensitive to the issue than Canadians. I was speechless. Life takes peculiar turns in this politically correct world we have had imposed on us.

Larnaca, Cyprus:

I visited Cyprus many times. It is a marvelous place to sail. I would always rent a car and drive up the small country roads. I could scarcely believe what I found—on that sunny Mediterranean island there is a mountain with ski lifts. One warm year not too long ago, Cyprus was the only place in Europe with snow. Although it was quite warm at the ocean, you could ski the mountain the same day.

The guru of sailing in Cyprus is ship and cargo forwarder Totos Theodosiou, who invited me to Cyprus in the 1990s. Totos had founded a small sailing club geared to dinghies and windsurfers, after acquiring land from the local government. Every two or three years, I would go back to Cyprus on whatever pretext I could think of. On each visit I found that Totos had built an addition to the club and had somehow absconded with more land on the ocean. Over the last twenty years he has built a magnificent facility totally geared to small boat sailing. It reminds me of the Water Rat in Toronto.

Totos well understood the politics of the Middle East,

having been born in Israel during the English period there. Being Cypriot Greek, he understood that culture as well. Cypriots are very industrious and well organized.

Torbole:

I leave Torbole and the Villa Stella, run by the Tonelli family, to the last. Torbole is at the north end of Lago de Garda in Northern Italy. It has an Italian wind, meaning that in the morning it blows quite hard from the south, and then at about 11:00 a.m. it stops for lunch, building again until at about 2:00 p.m., it blows quite hard from the north before stopping for dinner—so you can eat at the many restaurants and pizzerias. Very Italian!

Torbole is the venue for recreational windsurfers. It is also poplar with mountain bikers. ISAF held the trials for the new two-person dinghy class there due to the predictable winds. Torbole was where ISAF selected the 49er skiff for the Sydney Olympics. One of the other entrants was a Mader design from Germany sailed by Raimondo Tonelli. He asked if I wanted to go out on the trapeze, which was rather exciting for a then 65-year-old (see photo). He provided a wet suit for me, as it was obvious that I was not going to stay dry.

After we screamed across Lago de Garda, Raimondo told me to return the wet suit to the Villa Stella up the valley. I was taken on a tour of this wonderful family-run hotel where I met his Italian father Franco, his Dutch mother Anna and his sister Angelica. The walls were covered with pictures of well known sailors, many of them Canadians who had stayed there. I was getting sick of staying in high-powered hotels and decided this would be a great place to hold an ISAF executive meeting. That would also serve to honour the Federazione Italiana Vela under Sergio Gaibisso, who was always helpful. The Tonelli family had been the major promoters of windsurfing and Opti regattas on Lago de Garda.

What a time ISAF had there! I am sure the members of the executive look back on that meeting as the finest ever. A little later, I had the great honor of paying tribute to Anna and Franco in Denmark as I retired. If you want a few days in Lago de Garda, you must book early, as the Villa Stella is the home away from home for sailors and always full.

Kings and I and other Royals

Sailing and equestrian sports attract enthusiasts who run the gamut from royals to plumbers. One story highlights the exposure that I, as ISAF president, had to these people of privilege, most of whom are more down to earth, easier to talk to and less pretentious than those who have come by their positions of influence more recently.

Every year in November, at the IYRU annual general meeting, 250 of the beautiful people of the sailing world would be hosted at a black-tie dinner at the Royal Thames Yacht Club in Knightsbridge, London. One year it was the eightieth birthday of H.M. King Olav V of Norway, and he was duly honoured with the appropriate speeches. I was then an IYRU vice-president and, knowing an excellent model boat builder in Toronto, was able to arrange to present him with a replica of his 5.5 metre sailing vessel. (I had brought it to London strapped in an Air Canada seat at no charge. I was moved to business class to look after it, thanks to an always considerate Air Canada cabin crew.)

The next year at the black-tie dinner, James "Ding" Schoonmaker of the USA found out it was my birthday. He conned IYRU Honorary President H.M. King Constantine of the Hellenes to surprise me with the gift of a peaked hat with a felt faucet dripping water. The King gave an elegant speech before the assembled multitude and presented the hat to his "plumber friend from Toronto." It was my turn to respond. I took the microphone and with due reverence to all present, I began, *"My great friend His Majesty King Olav; my great friend His Majesty King Constantine; my great friend His Royal Highness Crown Prince Harald; my great friend His Royal Highness Prince Philip...."*

With that King Constantine yelled out, *"Name dropper!"*

I had the microphone and without hesitation replied, *"What do you mean 'name dropper'? I know five kings! You know only one plumber!"* I immediately thought, *"What have I said?"* H.M. King Constantine tells that story to this day.

Introduction to International Yacht Racing Union (IYRU)

In 1970, Montreal was designated the host city for the 1976 Olympic Games. Paul Phelan was the only Canadian member of the International Yacht Racing Union (IYRU) at that time. President Beppe Croce from Italy asked the Canadian Yachting Association (CYA) to nominate members to sit on various committees. The important people took the committees they knew, such as Racing Rules, Constitution, Youth, and so on. When they came to a committee called the Class Policy and Organization Committee (CPOC), the Association had no idea what it was, so they asked me to serve since I was the hot-shot sailor of the day.

The first meeting of the CPOC was held in Madrid during the time of Franco's regime. Mary and I were really nervous, since we were there as guests of the then Crown Prince Juan Carlos. We noticed that Queen Sofia's brother King Constantine was also scheduled to attend. It was our first exposure to the world of international sport politics and we found it both exciting and not a little intimidating.

I noticed that, with the exception of King Constantine, I was by far the youngest. The other delegates were surprised that Canada would send me to this group. The CPOC was President Beppe Croce's de facto executive committee and he had personally selected all the other members, most of whom had gravitated to one another as young men after World War II to reorganize the world of sailing. Croce hardly expected to see such a young nobody from Canada, yet he was very gracious to me and we became good friends. He lived life to the fullest. I eventually outlived the others and became ISAF president 25 years later.

The first day was intimidating. At the end of the proceedings, Croce reprimanded me, *"Paul, you have been addressing the King*

inaccurately, calling him 'Your Royal Highness.' He is 'Your Majesty.'"
With my usual glibness I replied, *"That is all right. He has been calling me 'Peter' all day."* That story has often been repeated by those who were within earshot that day.

East Berlin

At a later meeting held in East Berlin, we attended as guests of Herbert Fechner, a CPOC member who also happened to be mayor of East Berlin. During that difficult Cold War era, he was a great help to us all. Because he understood the politics of the Eastern Bloc and the USSR, he was able to act as a bridge between the opposing policies of the USSR and those of the West. We were taken to the Berlin Presidium where King Constantine was seated in the speaker's chair. Looking down at the assembled crowd, he announced that he was probably the first king ever to sit in such a seat.

I immediately removed my shoe and pounded the table, burlesquing Nikita Khrushchev's infamous gesture at the UN General Assembly in 1960.

That night we were bused to a workers' hotel for a formal dinner with the Communist Party hierarchy. It was an extremely dead and stilted affair. You could cut the tension with a knife, much to Mayor Fechner's dismay, as he wanted it to be a friendly party. Croce turned quietly to me and said, *"Do something to liven this up."* So with my bald head gleaming under the lights, I rose to speak.

"Herr Fechner!" I began, *"This is a very prejudiced country."* Croce almost expired but I carried on regardless. *"At lunch time today, I went to the hotel swimming pool in the basement for exercise, instead of eating. There were four Arabs swimming. The pool attendant, a beautiful German woman, sashayed up to all of them and gave each a swimming cap. She did not give one to me. That is prejudice!"* Everyone broke up. As the tension melted melt away, stories began to flow and we had a great evening replete with a good number of the customary vodka toasts.

"Thanks Paul," Fechner said to me as he walked out

smiling into the night.

H.M. King Olav V of Norway

For years, IYRU held its annual general meeting at the Institute of Directors in London. At lunch time on my first day there, I was standing alone at the bar when all of a sudden I felt a forceful slap on the back. Spinning around I found myself face to face with King Olav, who I noticed was also alone. I have observed on more than one occasion that royalty does not appear to appreciate solitude. For reasons I cannot recall, I immediately began to talk sailing, which seemed to please him greatly. He said, *"Come with me. I want to show you something, and let's have lunch."* The King led me to a table in the corner of the dining room. He told me that he had lunched at that very table every day during World War II.

King Olav was a true sportsman. He always sailed his eight-metre royal yacht through the starting line five minutes prior to both the start and the finish of races to make sure the markers were properly set. I asked one of the locals why the King was allowed to do this. He answered affectionately, *"These are his waters and he knows what he is doing."* (Incidentally, the eight-metre classification is another of the ridiculous terms in sailing: it has nothing to do with the length of the boat, which is rather closer to 20 metres.)

In his youth, Olav had been an accomplished ski jumper and had competed frequently at the Holmenkollem. Even at age 80, he would leave the palace in winter with his cross country skis over his shoulder and walk, without security, to the streetcar to go up to the mountains. When asked why he did not travel with security, he answered, *"I have a whole country to protect me."* When the King died, the transit employees commissioned a bronze statue of him sitting with his skis. It now has pride of place sitting in the front seat of one of Oslo's streetcars.

I have fond memories of King Olav from 1973, when the Soling Class World Championship was held in Hanko, Norway. Hanko was the king's summer retreat where he lived on the royal yacht, which he sailed every day except Fridays when he had to get to parliament. Early July in Norway is the time of the midnight sun when the sun never sets. It is during this time that the king's birthday is celebrated.

Many of the competing sailors were invited to the royal yacht along with the beautiful people of Norway. My old crew, Dennis Toews, an ex-RCMP officer from Manitoba, was there sailing with Hans Fogh. Dennis is one of those people who never forgets a joke—the more risqué the better—and who can recite them ad nauseam. The Norwegians had all congregated on the back deck, the sailors in the main cabin. King Olav gravitated to the sailors where Toews had started in on his jokes. The King laughed heartily at all of them with his distinctive loud laugh. After about half-an-hour, his attaché informed him that there were other guests to see. On leaving, he told Toews to stay put and that he would be back. Fifteen minutes later, King Olav returned for another round of jokes. Half an hour later, the attaché again pleaded with the King to spend time with the other guests. This routine was repeated twice more before the jokes ran out. Then we all sang *Happy Birthday* to a great man.

The next night we were guests at Frederick Horn's house. Frederick was a formidable character who sat on the CPOC and owned the renowned Horn men's clothing store in Oslo. During dinner, I noticed him checking his clock. At exactly five minutes to nine, he rose from his seat and hurried out the door into the still bright sunshine. My curiosity got the better of me so I watched out the window as he went first to the flagpole in his yard and lowered the flag, then to the yacht club where he likewise lowered the flag. Next, he rowed out to his boat and lowered the flag there, too, before returning to dinner. I asked him what that exercise had been all about. *"This is Norway and the sun does not go down in the summer,"* he explained. *"King Olav has decreed that sundown is 9:00 p.m. If I hadn't got the flags down, the King would be on the phone tomorrow to dress me down."*

Frederick's three young grandsons, all wide eyed, were also at the dinner. I spent some time speaking with the oldest, who was then nine. I told him that when he turned 16 he should come and visit us in Toronto, and then promptly forgot the matter. Seven years later, on his sixteenth birthday, my telephone rang.

"Mr. Henderson, this is Herman Horn Johanassen, Frederick Horn's grandson, and I am now 16 and looking forward to seeing Canada with you this summer." We had a great time with Herman, traveling across the country to Banff, Gladstone Mountain Ranch, O'Hare Lodge and Vancouver.

Herman turned out to be a great sailor. He won a Bronze Medal in the 2000 Olympics in Sydney. One of his crew, Paul Davis, had married a Norwegian woman and moved there from Toronto. Paul's father Bob had been an old sailing friend from my 14-foot Dinghy days when he sailed with Peter Jarvis, but he died quite young from cancer. The honour fell to me, as president of sailing and an IOC member, to present Herman and Paul with their Olympic medals before 50,000 people in front of the Sydney Opera House.

H.M. King Harald V of Norway

Norway's King Harald also a great sailor, is both a world and a European champion. He was an honorary president of ISAF along with H.M. King Constantine of Greece. I first met the then Crown Prince Harald at the 1968 Mexico City Olympics. He was competing in the 5.5 Metre Class and I was sailing the Finn Dinghy. Prior to the start of the regatta, we all worked to ready our boats. Lee Gentile, a tobacco-chewing Texan who was sailing a 5.5 for Puerto Rico, had just finished sanding and polishing the bottom of his keel on the tarmac there in Acapulco. He took a step back from the boat and bumped into a man who had been watching him work.

"Sorry! My name is Lee Gentile from Puerto Rico. Where are you from?" he said.

"I am from Norway," came back the reply.

"What do you do there?" continued Lee.

"I am the Crown Prince," Harald responded.

"Does it pay well?" was the only response Lee could think of.

(I had met Lee years earlier sailing Finns in San Juan, where he took me down the beach from his home and introduced me to his friend, the great cellist Pablo Casals.)

Recently at the Turino Olympics, I found myself sitting with a group of Norwegian fans at the curling event and turned around to ask, *"Is King Harald here?"* I was informed that he had had to return home on government business.

At the break, a very tall athletic man approached me in the hospitality lounge and said that we had met in Calgary when he was very young. He said he was sorry that his father was not present to talk sailing. It was Crown Prince Haakon. Norway will continue to be in good hands.

Spanish Royal Family

The Spanish royal family is impressive. Most are world class sailors, although some of the women are also equestrians. I met H.M. King Juan Carlos and Queen Sofia in 1970 at my first IYRU meeting that they hosted in Madrid. We met again at the 1972 Olympic regatta in Kiel, Germany. Although he was then the crown prince and subject to intense security, he refused the privilege of special quarters, preferring to stay in the Olympic Village with the other athletes. One day, Mary arrived sporting a nice Spanish Yachting Federation tie. When I asked where she got it, she explained that she was going up in the elevator with this sailor and complimented him on his tie. To her surprise and delight, he immediately took it off and gave it to her. She was embarrassed, however, when she realized it was Crown Prince Juan Carlos.

When I became ISAF president, I flew to Palma for race week. After the regatta, I was invited to breakfast with Spanish Yachting President Arturo Delgado at the king's summer home. During a spirited exchange about some of the current challenges to sailing, I explained how the English were endeavouring to stop an initiative on some small technical point. The King came forward with an observation apropos of many political issues, one that is especially true in Canada (and always with lawyers): *"The problem with the Anglo-Saxon brain,"* the King offered, *"is that they debate the 10 per cent that is wrong with an issue, not the 90 per cent that is right."* I replied that I was a Celt and have no Anglo-Saxon blood, as my ancestors were all Scots and Irish. *"That explains you,"* he concluded. To this day, I still don't know whether that was a compliment.

The rest of the Spanish royal family is equally as strong as the king. HRH. Princess Christina was a member of the 1998 Spanish sailing team and is married to the former captain of their successful handball team. She has been actively involved in sporting for disabled people and led the IYRU Disabled Sailing Committee for several years.

In 1991, during the Canadian Olympic Regatta in Kingston, Ontario (CORK), I was walking through the parking lot and came upon a group of what I later learned were Spaniards. Their car horn was honking incessantly and they had the hood up, trying to determine which wires to disconnect to stop the racket. They had not understood a newfangled North American anti-theft device that caused the horn to honk repeatedly if the locked door was opened improperly. In my forthright way I said, *"You stupid SOBs, give me the keys."* Irritated and distracted by the noise, I took the keys from a rather tall man and unlocked the door. The honking stopped and that's when I finally looked up at his face. Much to my dismay, I had called Crown Prince Philippe an SOB.

Crown Prince Philippe was a member of the 1992 Olympic team. He was picked to be dope-tested and the doctors had to witness the producing of the sample. Everyone was too embarrassed to do so. We were all standing around at the marina debating how to go about the rather delicate procedure. With his customary engaging smile, Philippe approached the nearest official and said, *"Let's just go and get this over with."*

At the ISAF World Championship in 2003 in Cadiz, Andalusia, the crown prince went out with me on my special launch. We sat on the flying bridge, where he spent a good part of his time on his cell phone, laughing and smiling. I figured that he wanted me beside him because he knew I did not speak Spanish and he could chatter away uninhibited. I knew something was up and wasn't surprised when, a few weeks later, he announced his engagement.

I have also come to know and respect King Juan Carlos' sister the Infanta Pilar. She is equally as impressive, inclusive and down-to-earth as her brother. Through her roles as president of the International Equestrian Federation and an IOC member, we have become great friends and respect one another, even though we come from opposite social poles—which is what sport is all about.

A woman with a great sense of humour, she loves a good laugh. In 2001, we were in Prague for an IOC session. At the lunch break, I went down to the cafeteria and found the Infanta Pilar sitting by herself. She beckoned me to come over and sit with her. When the bill came I grabbed it.

"Let me pay! I asked you to sit here," she demanded.

"Try to be a kept woman!" I replied.

She broke up and could hardly contain herself. *"Nobody has ever said that to me before. Wait till I tell the king!"*

British Royal Family

The British royal family is also actively involved in sport. I had met HRH Prince Philip several times at the IYRU annual meetings in London. He often crewed in a Flying Fifteen with the raucous dinghy designer Uffa Fox, who came from the humblest of backgrounds and whose company the prince enjoyed immensely.

In 1981, as honorary patron of the Royal Canadian Yacht Club (RCYC), Prince Philip came to Toronto to lay the cornerstone of the new city club. The RCYC commodore at that time was Bruce MacGowan, a thorough and understanding man from New Brunswick who was as insightful a commodore as the club has ever had. We were asked to go to lunch with Prince Philip, where he was presenting the Duke of Edinburgh Awards. The next stop was to be the RCYC in the city for the cornerstone ceremony, after which we had planned to ferry over to the RCYC on Toronto Island for a walkabout, as it was a beautiful June day. Bruce and I were asked to go to the Royal York Hotel to escort Prince Philip to the luncheon. We arrived at the royal suite dressed in our brass-buttoned blazers, white pants and naval hats. Leaving the hotel, we were met by a phalanx of RCMP officers leading us to the limousines that were waiting to take us away.

Prince Philip turned to me and asked, *"Henderson where are we going?"*

I answered, *"One block right and then two blocks north, sir."*

"Are you with me? Let's walk."

"Do I have a choice?" I asked.

"No!" he said, and the three of us walked away to the horror of the RCMP security detail. The crowds parted and cheered as we went by.

It was late in the afternoon when we departed for the RCYC Island Club. We had organized a sailpast by junior club sailors for His Royal Highness while we ferried across the bay. As the parade of junior clubbers approached, however, the harbour police intervened and blocked them. *"Get those damn police out of the way, Henderson,"* Prince Philip demanded.

I replied, *"If you cannot prevent them, then how did do you expect me to do it?"*

When he disembarked, the club members were lined up to greet him. My 80-year-old mother was there and he stopped to talk to her. Fortunately, somebody snapped a photo of them speaking together (see photo). At 90, my mother was afflicted with dementia and confined to the long-term care ward of Belmont House, where they allow one memorable picture to be displayed outside each patient's room. Of all the photos taken over close to a century, my mother chose that picture of her and Prince Philip at the RCYC.

Princess Anne, The Princess Royal, is chairman of the Royal Yachting Association (RYA). I met her many times at sailing meetings as well as at various IOC sessions. I found her to be an attractive, opinionated and determined sport person. The year that I ran for ISAF president, the meeting was held in London. All delegates were invited to an audience at Buckingham Palace. Canadian Yachting Association President Audrey Davis, the first woman to hold that office, asked if I would introduce her to Princess Anne. As we passed down the receiving line to the dignitaries, Princess Anne shook my hand and said, *"I hear you are causing trouble again, running for president."*

"Just following your example," I replied.

"I have been good lately," she shot back.

After the receiving line, we all filed into a portrait-lined hall to a reception. At these events, a sailing official walks beside Princess Anne and introduces those waiting to meet her.

I stood for about 10 minutes with Audrey, who again asked if I would introduce her to the princess. As they approached us, the official said, *"Ma'am, I would like to introduce the president of the Canadian Yachting Association."*

Princess Anne said, *"I know that guy!"*

"With respect, Your Royal Highness," I butted in, *"the Canadian president is Audrey Davis, the first women ever to hold that position."*

Princess Anne stuck her hand between Audrey and me, declaring, *"I have had enough of this fellow. Let's go over to the side and talk."* The two women went over to the side of the room where they discussed sporting issues for about 15 minutes. Audrey was ecstatic.

Several years later we held the ISAF annual general meeting at the Grand Hotel in Brighton, where the IRA had tried to blow up Margaret Thatcher. Princess Anne flew in by helicopter to host the dinner in the hotel's large ballroom. As ISAF president, it was my turn to take her around and introduce her to all the delegates. I was doing my job when I noticed that everyone had disappeared except The Princess Royal and me, standing together in the middle of the large hall. Two Scotland Yard detectives came up and informed her that they had found a brown bag in the corner.

They suspected it might be a bomb and would she please quickly leave the room. She turned and said, *"Henderson! Do you know how many times this happens? You and I will just stand here and wait, okay?"*

I answered, *"Do I have any choice?"*

"No!" came her immediate reply, which reminded me of the same response from her father back in Toronto.

The two of us stood alone in the middle of the floor. A few minutes later the detectives announced the all clear—the bag contained only a pair of women's shoes.

The delegate from the USA apologized for having left her walking shoes in the corner. We then went into dinner, where Princess Anne asked me to dominate the dinner conversation, making it look as if we were engrossed in a serious one-sided debate—this was perhaps the only time in my life that anyone had asked me to do such a thing. The Princess Royal was suffering from a bad case of laryngitis and said she had only about 15 minutes left in her voice and that if she strained to talk across the table, she would lose it and not be able to deliver her welcoming speech.

Her speech was great. She said that, although she had competed in the Olympics as an equestrian—she had been European champion—she was noted for having an affinity for water. This was a not-so-veiled allusion to an ignominious event during the three-day Olympic equestrian competition when her horse balked at a water jump and she was thrown into the ditch, receiving a concussion in the process.

In November 2000, we were again hosted by the RYA, this time in Edinburgh, Scotland. This was especially significant to Mary and me, because my grandfather had been born there. Henderson was an offshoot of the clan McKendricks; Mary's parents were McLeod and McKenzie. I wrote to the Scottish arm of the RYA asking that they arrange for a Henderson tartan kilt for me and a McLeod sash for Mary.

Since Edinburgh is Princess Anne's ancestral home, she insisted on hosting the annual dinner at the Palace of Holyroodhouse. We were elegant at the reception! The VIPs were in an ante-room waiting for

The Princess Royal to arrive so I could take her into the large hall and introduce the delegates.

I escorted Princess Anne through the crowd where I was the butt of all the usual rude comments about wearing a kilt.

We then went into the formal dinner where I was to act as master of ceremonies. After grace and the usual toasts, I began: *"Her Majesty the Queen! Heads of state of all countries here gathered! Sailors everywhere..."* I stood on the stage in my kilt and sporran, asking for five minutes from the 400 attendees, and delivered my address with no little emotion.

> *"Please put your mind into 1880 and the situation that was facing both Scotland and Canada at that time. Scotland was destitute and the future bleak.Canada was the new world. My grandfather, age 9, was an orphan as his mother had died in the Edinburgh workhouse. The Scots emptied the orphanages and sent the young waifs alone to Canada.*

> *"In Quebec City my grandfather was taken in by the local community and then shipped to the frontier of Canada just north of Toronto where he was apprenticed as a "tinker." Toronto was called "Muddy York" in those days.*

> *"In 1896 he walked to the outskirts of Toronto and started the famous plumbing company that bears his name. He educated himself by reading every non-fiction book in the local library and never missing a Wednesday afternoon matinee at the Royal Alexander Theatre.*

> *He became the Company Sergeant Major of the most famous highland regiment in Canada, The 48th Highlanders and although 46 years old served in the First World War. My great-grandmother is buried 100*

metres from where we are having dinner tonight, in Grey Friars Cemetery.

"It is great honour for Mary and me to return to Edinburgh as president of the International Sailing Federation."

When I returned to the head table, King Harald reached across the table and said, *"You have the complete right to wear the kilt, me boy."*

A sad thing happened there. Bob Kim always came to the meetings to support "his president." He had told me how much he wanted to be with me when I returned to my roots, because he had not been able to do this himself, having walked south from North Korea in his youth, never to return. He had been ill for about two years, but always demanded that he be there to help. Sadly, he died in his room there one night. I lost a real friend and a supremely dedicated servant of sailing. When his wife and children came to Edinburgh in their grief, I was able to meet them for the first time and tell them how much we had all respected Kim Bong-Sik.

Sailing Innovations

During the time I spent at the IYRU and later ISAF, sailing benefited from more than a few innovations. Here are five that come to mind:

1. Containers: The practice of shipping containers around the world has completely altered the requirements for regatta organizers, saving them a tremendous amount of money. Containers were used first in Los Angeles in 1984 to avoid building a large permanent structure to house and secure the teams' equipment and to provide for sail making, boat repair, food services and even tool shops and changing rooms. The wealthier teams who have all these facilities are quite generous and look after less affluent competitors. We saw Carl Eichenlaub from the USA fixing a damaged windsurfer from Sri Lanka, Italians giving

an Icelander a bottle of San Pellegrino, and Brits repairing the sail of a Venezuelan. The use of containers has really had a major impact on sailing. All that is required now is a parking lot to house them.

2. Laser Class and Windsurfers: Both boats came out of an unusual regatta held at the Playboy Club on Lake Geneva, Wisconsin, in 1971. It was called "the Little America's Tea Cup" for boats under 14 feet. The Laser was the idea of two Canadian Olympic sailors, Ian Bruce and Bruce Kirby, both originally from Ottawa. At first it was thought to be a toy but the best sailors in the world took to it. A sailor cannot customize anything on a Laser, so the equipment is all standard. The emphasis is completely on talent, not technology. It is the most popular sailboat in the world. The Laser Class was introduced as an Olympic event for men in 1996 and for women in 2008. Best yet, the Laser's price is half that of a Lance Armstrong bicycle.

The Windsurfer came out of the same event to sweep the world. It has not been kept under control like the Laser; windsurfing has become more of an extreme sport, being included in the Olympics for the first time in 1984. There are both men's and women's events in the Games, for which the boats are supplied. Technology is therefore de-emphasized in four of the 11 sailing events in the Olympics—the equipment is supplied standard and every country in the world has the same opportunity.

When windsurfing was proposed as an Olympic discipline, it created great debate. Traditionalists argued that it was not sailing; I rebutted that it did not matter whether it was sailing or not. What mattered was whether young people thought it was sailing.

3. 49er skiff: Evolved from the Australian 18-footers, the 49er skiff was first selected as an Olympic class for the 2000 Games in Sydney. Its designer, Julian Bethwaite, decided that all the equipment should be the same and not subject to an expensive "armaments race." All the boats are true one-designs. They are very fast, requiring great skill to sail well. One of the major problems in sailing that is especially bad for windsurfing is what I call

"kinetics"—sailors do not use the natural action of the wind on the sails or the waves on the boat, but rapidly pump their sails continuously and rock and scull their boat around the race course. I call this "air rowing" and it is bad for the sport. Skiffs and catamarans minimize kinetics. I hope ISAF will include a skiff in the Games for women.

4. Catamarans: Due to their twin hulls, "Cats" must be sailed, not fanned around the course. The Tornado is a sophisticated and high-tech multi-hull. I tried to get an off-the-beach simple catamaran into the Games, such as the Hobie 16, because they enjoy an outstanding fraternity. If ISAF could manage to include the 49er skiff, Laser, Windsurfer and the Hobie 16, all supplied standard for both men's and women's competition, it would open seven events for all nations. The focus of the Games would be on talent, leaving the remaining events for those who like to play with technology.

5. Lunenburg wash: Sailing runs more than 100 world championships every year and thousands of other regattas. Once in a while a new concept appears to solve an old problem; the "Lunenburg wash" was one of them. ISAF accepted the bid of Lunenburg, Nova Scotia, to host the ISAF 2003 Youth World Championship. With its whaling and yachting traditions, Lunenburg was a magnificent venue. Its designation as a world heritage site exposed the young sailors to a unique part of Canada. Sea salt poses a particular challenge to both sailors and organizers. When sailors return to the marina after a long day of racing out at sea, their boats are covered with salt, which must be washed off. All the boats return at around the same time and there are usually only one or two small garden hoses for dozens of boats. Washing off the salt is a trying and time consuming experience.

When I arrived at the efficient and modest Lunenburg Yacht Club for the superb volunteer-run regatta, I noticed that at the top of the ramp where some 100 boats were about to be hauled out, four burly firemen were standing beside a magnificent fire truck, their hoses uncoiled. I asked them what they were doing there. *"We wash boats,"* one of them proudly replied. As the boats came up the ramp, the firemen turned on their hoses, washing the salt from each boat. The sailors loved it and asked to be sprayed themselves. Instead of the hours it would usually take at most regattas, it took only 20 minutes to wash all the boats. It was extremely cost-efficient and required no capital installation. The firemen had a great time, too. The Lunenburg wash is an innovative solution to a vexing problem.

Memorable Sailors

Tom Hsueh:

Tom was born in Taiwan but received most of his formal education in California. He was the major promoter of sailing in Taiwan, always working to get his sailors into the Olympics. At his invitation I visited Taipei on several occasions, each one memorable in its own way. I could always count on Tom for support and advice, especially on issues relating to mainland China. He was a bridge between the two Chinese cultures. A few years ago, Tom retired to Bellingham Bay in Washington, where his house overlooks a marina. He wrote me a short time ago that some developers were trying to build houses on a hill opposite the marina overlooking the Pacific Ocean. Tom bought out the developers and deeded the property to the State of Washington as an unspoiled park in memory of his father.

Peter Harken:

I was feeling quite patriotic on Canada Day, 2002, and wrote out 20 reasons that I was proud to be a Canadian and why we are different in the true north strong and free. One of the reasons I gave was that in Canada, there is no constitutional right for citizens to carry guns. In response, Peter Harken wrote me a wonderful letter from his home in Pewaukee, Wisconsin, which he refers to as "Peeville." Peter and his brother Olav, who were born in Indonesia to a Dutch father and Swedish mother, have developed the best known and most successful line of sailing hardware in the world. The mayor of Pewaukee announced the construction of a war memorial. Peter, whose father was interned in a Japanese prisoner of war camp during World War II and emerged in bad shape, decided that the design was not up to standard; in fact, it was downright chintzy. He berated the mayor and offered to take over the project and pay for it. He always says he should keep his mouth shut, because he really did it up right. *"The old man would be proud of it,"* he wrote me.

Takao Otani:

Takao Otani is a graduate of Waseda University in Tokyo, and a unique man. He usually wears a coolie's straw hat but seldom wears shoes. I first met him when he sailed the 470 Class Dinghy for Japan. He then became a coach and a respected Laser umpire. Takao was involved in the design of the now popular youth skiff, the 29er.

We had many talks about his family and his son, who has Down's syndrome. Takao moved into his family home near Enoshima and started a business to employ young people with autism and Down's syndrome in making stained glass sailing trophies. He now has about 20 employees. One was raped when she was 18 and did not speak for years until she was placed with Takao. A boy who had never spoken at all also started to speak after joining the group. It was soon discovered that he had learned five languages by watching television. Another boy loves trains and knows all the schedules by heart, but this poses a problem for him—if he sees a train go by, he stops and watches it, which sometimes makes him late for work. Yet another is very skilled with his hands and does all the fine lead work. Some travel over three hours one-way to get to Takao's factory, which he had built over the garage at his home.

I went to visit him and found it to be a heart-warming experience. As I left, his son presented me with a mobile from which dangled coloured glass replicas of all the boats I had sailed, and which now hangs proudly over my desk. As I left, I gave the two volunteer ladies a big hug and kiss. This did not go down well with the boys, as they considered the ladies to be their girlfriends, not mine!

Commodore Henry "Harry" Anderson:

Harry Anderson has been around sailing in various forms for as long as anyone can remember. He has served as commodore of the New York Yacht Club and vice-president of IYRU, and was most recently involved in the Tall Ships Festival and Marine Museum in Newport, Rhode Island, where he lives at the age of 90. Harry and a few friends from Yale loved to cruise the Bras d'Or Lakes in Cape Breton, Nova Scotia, and bought a farm there.

In 2003, during the World Youth Sailing Championship in Lunenburg, we drove north to Bedeck. Harry met us there and drove us to the pristine peninsula sticking out into the Bras d'Or Lakes to a 100- acre spread of farmland with a traditional, simple farmhouse. His associates all loved their Canadian land and never wanted it to fall into a developer's hands. They were afraid of leaving it to their heirs, who might not value it the way they had, and spent years dividing the land into very small legal parcels so that nobody would be able to put it all back together and sell it to developers. These men epitomize the American neighbors that Canadians appreciate.

James "Ding" Schoonmaker and Herman Whitton, Jr.:

James "Ding" Schoonmaker, his mother Greta and the Whitton family have left a great legacy to all sailors in Coconut Grove, Miami. One of the most famous sailors in the world, Ding is a Star World Champion and ISAF vice-president. He owned a wonderful estate bordering on Biscayne Bay, where he loved to have sailors come in the winter to race, but found launching boats to be expensive and difficult. Ding, Herman Whitton and a few others acquired a piece of land from the City of Miami and built a small-boat regatta centre. They turned it over to US Sailing, and sailors from all over the world now come there to race.

Conclusion:

No doubt I have failed to mention other wonderful places we visited and people we met as we traveled to more than 50 countries during my tenure as ISAF president, and enjoyed the great hospitality shown by sailors the world over. On behalf of my wife Mary and myself, I cannot thank them enough for the kindness they showed us.

Chapter 12:
1996 Olympic Games in Atlanta

The Olympic Games in Atlanta were by far the most interesting to me for at least three reasons:

- I had led the bid for Toronto against Atlanta. Toronto had the best technical bid, but technical bids do not win. Political ones do.
- I had traveled the world with Atlanta's leading lobbyists Billy Payne and Charlie Battle, and I knew all the promises they had made to influence voters.
- Eighteen months before the Opening Ceremonies, I was elected president of the International Sailing Federation (ISAF). I was responsible for ensuring the success of the Olympic Sailing Regatta and that the sailors' Olympic experience would be to an acceptable level.

Located in the middle of the State of Georgia, Atlanta itself has no water to host any sailing event. More for political reasons than geographical ones, however, the event was scheduled for Savannah. If you are unfamiliar with Savannah, its culture is clearly defined in the bestselling novel *Midnight in the Garden of Good and Evil*. It was a very unusual venue in that there were no proper shore facilities near the ocean. Everything had to be situated up the Wilmington River. It is a beautiful region, but one with unique challenges. There was the added problem of the animosity between Savannah's good old boys and Atlanta's nouveau riche, a hatred with deep roots in the American Civil War. The two cities did not like each other—both sides made that very clear right from the outset. Sailing was caught in the middle of these two diverse cultures. And I knew that the Atlanta Committee for the Olympic Games (ACOG) was not overjoyed that I had been elected ISAF president.

My daughter Martha had started to sail a J-24 keelboat with a five-person, all-female crew. The boat was named *Lady Chablis*. Most people had no idea what it meant and thought it was a lovely name. Those who had read *Midnight in the Garden of Good and Evil* were amused, however; the Lady Chablis was the novel's bizarre black transvestite who entertained at a risqué cabaret in downtown Savannah. Martha and her crew followed up by naming their new Olympic Class Yngling *Frank*, the real name of the Lady Chablis.

As newly elected ISAF president, my immediate priority was to focus on what was happening in Savannah. I was shocked to discover that nothing was happening at all. The land to be used for the marina proposed in the Atlanta bid documents was owned by the University of Georgia, ACOG President and CEO Billy Payne's alma mater, and was said to be secured and guaranteed. This was completely untrue. One so-called environmentalist who owned adjacent land did not want his property near a marina. He stopped the use of the land, saying it was the natural mating ground of the wood stork. The old Sheraton Hotel on the river was proposed to serve as the Olympic Village with the addition of new condominiums and other upgrades. It was also said to be secured and ready for construction to begin. This was pure fantasy, as the hotel was in bankruptcy. In fact, it had been condemned and was scheduled to be torn down. ISAF was faced with the dilemma that, with only 18 months left to the Opening Ceremonies, Olympic sailing had neither a marina nor an Olympic Village. Richard Pound has quipped, *"Bid books are the greatest pieces of fiction ever written,"* and Atlanta confirmed that. So it is obvious why I moved into the administration of the Olympic Sailing Regatta in Savannah with my customary bulldog approach.

I announced that I would not delegate the position of ISAF technical delegate, taking on that responsibility myself. I had done it for three of the previous four Olympics and it was established practice that the closest ISAF executive member who was not a national of the host country take on the job. When Billy Payne was informed that I was now in charge, he said that I was to work everything out with

Chief Operating Officer A.D. Frazier and Director of Sport Dave Maggard. Neither of them had been around during the bid process so I did not know them. One of the shots I fired across their bow when trying to make a point or get a laugh was that I wanted to know when they had scheduled to fulfill the most outrageous promise in the Atlanta bid book—that all athletes would be flown to Disney World in Orlando, Florida, for a three-day, all expenses paid holiday. The first time I met Maggard I brought this up, knowing full well that none of the 440 sailors would ever want to go, but it was my way of counter-punching ACOG.

I went to Atlanta in early 1995. Charlie Battle, the number-one Atlanta bid schmoozer, met me at the airport. He was his usual gracious self. Charlie took me to the ACOG offices in a prestigious office building with plush rugs and palatial boardrooms, which were almost exactly opposite to the style of Peter Ueberroth's warehouse in Los Angeles. When we went into the meeting with Dave Maggard and A.D. Frazier, they quickly got down to the key issue. A.D. began, *"Paul, we know that you are apprehensive about the Atlanta Organizing Committee, especially since you led the Toronto bid. ACOG has a policy that nobody talks to the media unless authorized by Billy Payne. I am sure you understand and that you will live by that decree."*

I plastered a smirk across my face and said, *"A.D., I really am not afraid of the press, and when it serves the purpose of forwarding the needs of the Olympic Sailing Regatta in Savannah, I will use the press to focus on what is required. I do not subscribe to the ACOG decree."*

They knew full well what I meant. I had taken Spain's ISAF Vice-president Fernando Bolin to the first meeting in Atlanta, and he too was shocked that nothing had been done. Dealing with A.D. Frazier was quite straightforward, considering that he was under great pressure. I think I got along with him reasonably well, especially when he realized that ISAF's requests were not unreasonable.

Maggard was a different story. A large bear of a man who hailed from the University of Miami's athletics department, he was quite unlike Ted Hinshaw in Los Angeles or, later, Bob Elphinston in Sydney. If he told you one thing, he would quite often do exactly the opposite. He preferred to be evasive on almost every issue. Organizers of other sports had exactly the same problem with him. Maggard was the person I had to deal with, and often the only way I could get his attention was to determine the facts pertinent to a situation and release them to the Savannah press. ACOG was paranoid about bad press. James Pilcher of *Savannah Morning News* was assigned to the Olympic sailing portfolio and covered all issues fairly and openly.

On this first visit, I traveled from Atlanta to Savannah and was well received by the citizens there. In fact, they briefed me on how to handle Atlanta. They had heard of my reputation for being straight, blunt and experienced. They advised me not to change, saying that straight and blunt was all ACOG would understand. Since Savannah wasn't even on ACOG's radar, the Savannah leaders confirmed that nothing had been done to prepare for sailing.

I reported back to the ISAF executive that Savannah was a disaster and that I would put most of my energies into preparations for the next few months. ISAF's US Vice-president Ding Schoonmaker suggested that I get Tom Webster actively involved. Webster had sailed with Ted Turner and was deeply involved in the development of Hilton Head Island. Tom is the most outgoing, gung-ho new friend I have. He was my eyes and ears in both Atlanta and Savannah. Maggard and A.D. could never understand how I knew so much. It was all due to Tom, who had close friends and relatives inside ACOG, including one of Ted Turner's Atlanta Braves advisors.

When Tom heard that ACOG refused to hold a practice regatta anywhere near Atlanta in the months before the Games, as is established practice, he personally organized and secured sponsors for an Olympic Classes regatta off the beach in Hilton Head. Tom conscripted all his triathlon friends to help run it as volunteers. Without Tom Webster's actions and advice, the Savannah Olympics would never have worked.

The Day Marina

Since there was no practical place to launch boats, Andy Kostanecki, a US Sailing delegate to ISAF, came up with the idea of building a floating marina. The plan was to use Mississippi River barges tied together and floating inside the barrier islands at the mouth of the Wilmington River. The installation was christened the Day Marina. Andy and his good friend Mike Jackson from the UK figured out the sizes and logistics required, and submitted their drawings to Maggard, who passed them on to the ACOG engineering department.

We heard nothing from ACOG for about two months. Without discussing the plans with ISAF, Maggard asked for construction firms to bid on the installation, and five did. Two were Canadian firms that I knew through my plumbing business. They reported to me what was going on. I never did see the ACOG drawings, because ACOG members were instructed not to show them to us. Finally, I demanded that ISAF see the drawings and vet the proposals before the contracts were let. Maggard agreed and a meeting was scheduled. I was aware that, in the IOC host city agreement signed by Atlanta, ACOG had accepted that all technical aspects of each event at the Olympic Games were the responsibility of the relevant international sport federation, which in our case was ISAF.

A date was set for ISAF to meet with the ACOG engineering department in Atlanta. I asked Andy Kostanecki and Mike Jackson to accompany me. ISAF paid for them to fly in from Connecticut and London, respectively. I always took somebody with me to meetings because I never like to be alone—I get so focused on the issues that I need others to debrief the concepts, what was discussed and, perhaps most important, the tone of the presentations.

Before the meeting, Maggard had met with John McIntosh and Rich Jeffries, Atlanta employees who had been charged with delivering the Olympic Regatta in Savannah. They were both well known sailors in the USA and at ISAF. In a recent statement, John McIntosh confirmed what we had to deal with: *"Paul, I can tell you now that I came very close to walking out the day our*

[ACOG's] construction department presented the first Day Marina drawings. But Rich and I were threatened before the meeting to toe the party line." This confirmed where they stood on any conflict, and it meant that it was ISAF's responsibility to fight ACOG for an adequate regatta because no one else was going to do it, not even the IOC.

Our meeting was scheduled for 11:00 a.m. on a Thursday in May, 1995. At 7:00 a.m., one of the Canadian bidders phoned me and told me that an Alabama barge company had been chosen to construct the Day Marina and that the contract was to be signed by Maggard at 10:00 a.m., one hour before our meeting. My informant gave me the name of the barge company along with the telephone number and the names of the father and son who were its principals. As soon as I arrived in Atlanta, I phoned the barge company in Alabama and got through to the father. He confirmed that his son was in Atlanta to sign the contract with Maggard at 10:00 a.m. that day. Being lied to is not something I handle well and my temper was about to explode—my mother was Irish, after all.

Andy, Mike and I walked into the 11:00 a.m. meeting in a domed board room that I believed was bugged. Initially, I was under control when I asked Maggard to confirm that he had already signed the documents for the delivery of the Day Marina without ISAF having vetted it. He denied it shamelessly. I then told him everything I knew, including the name of the Alabama barge company that had been chosen, and that I had spoken to the father that morning. Maggard clenched his fist. If he had chosen to deliver it in a punch it would have flattened me. I called time and Maggard left, leaving the three of us alone.

I immediately wrote a note to Mike and Andy that I believed the room to be bugged and we should act accordingly. We talked, but in gracious platitudes; the oozing venom was conveyed only in the notes we passed to one another. We set out a plan: I would say nothing, but Mike and Andy would ask to check the plans. We announced this loudly so the eavesdroppers would hear. Maggard returned after lunch with the plans under his arm.

Andy and Mike, both experienced engineers, were taken aback at the measurements on the drawings. They were too small, being only two-thirds of what was required. Maggard and the ACOG engineer said they knew what they were talking about, concluding that Andy and Mike had, as in all Olympic sports, oversized the requirements. The meeting deteriorated again and I realized that we were at an impasse. Maggard called the meeting over. By this time I was fairly well under control, considering the situation we faced. Before Maggard left, we suggested that Mike be flown in from London two weeks later, again at ISAF expense, to meet with the ACOG engineers and work out a compromise.

When he met with the ACOG engineering department two weeks later, he could scarcely believe what he discovered. That night he phoned me in Toronto and begged me not to make an issue of it, but he had solved the problem. A three-sided engineering scale ruler has a triangular cross-section and six long edges, each engraved with a different scale. The Atlanta engineers had used the wrong edge with the wrong scale in determining their projection for the number of barges required for the Day Marina. The Alabama barge company's bid was for only two-thirds of the total number required, just as Andy and Mike had pointed out at our meeting with Maggard. Maggard refused to order the extra barges on the grounds that they would come only at a substantial premium, being outside the scope of the original signed contract. Fortunately, fate stepped in and solved the problem.

The on-shore facilities required to allow launching into the river to get to the Day Marina 10 kilometres downstream were impractical. The problem was solved with a short-term lease on the shoreline at the bankrupt Sheraton. The Olympic Village became instead the Marriott in downtown Savannah, and although it was a 30-kilometre trip to the race course, this was much more acceptable overall. Maggard was still stonewalling on the Day Marina's platform size, however.

For the competitions, the sailors would have to leave the Marriott in downtown Savannah every morning, and board a bus for the 20-kilometre ride to the Sheraton where the team tents and containers were stored. There they would get on a catamaran motorboat for a 10-kilometre ride out to the Day Marina where their equipment was stored, rig their boats and head out into the Atlantic Ocean to race. The trip from the Marriott to the Sheraton and then out to the Day Marina by catamaran took about 90 minutes. It was not a bad experience, since it was a unique and beautiful wilderness trip. As it turned out, the sailors liked it. That alone should have demonstrated to ACOG that sailors are quite flexible. No other athletes would have accepted a venue with such complicated logistics. ISAF did, and we made it work against even more challenges and roadblocks thrown up by ACOG.

The year before the customary test event was to be held, ACOG had ordered a few barges to see how they would work, pulling up most of the centreboard dinghies on the nearest sand spit. The day of the first race, A.D. Frazier and Dave Maggard showed up with the ever present TV cameras. It was a hot and sunny summer day in Savannah. A.D. was being interviewed out on the Day Marina. Live on television, he chastised ISAF for wanting to escalate the cost of the sailing regatta by demanding more barges than the original contract had specified. Maggard had decided that a better and more cost-effective solution would be to use the barrier island sand spit instead of ordering the right number of barges. As I walked by with the ever present Tom Webster, A.D. said—on tape, no less—*"Henderson! The sand spit works well! Maggard was right! We don't need more barges!"*

As usual, fate intervened. Tom Webster, a thoroughly experienced fisherman, had warned me that, due to the alignment of the moon and Earth during the following year's Olympic Regatta, the charts were predicting the highest tides in 100 years. The sand spit would be completely flooded. Tom also said that I should not react to A.D.'s comment. He predicted that in two days the point would be made. Tom had been tracking Hurricane Bertha coming up the Atlantic seaboard and, although there would be no direct hit, it would rain and blow enough to raise the sea to the level to it would be the following year during the Olympic Games.

Tom was right. When the storm hit, we went down to the Sheraton to go out to where the boats were and found that Maggard had instructed ACOG Venue Manager John McIntosh that under no circumstances was I to be allowed to see what was happening. Tom knew all the fishermen around, so it was easy for us to find a boat to take us out into the deluge and the gale. The sand spit was totally under water. A deck chair floated by and I sat in it, up to my chest in water (see photo). The boats were banging around and floating out to sea, and volunteers were out there trying to save them. A number of volunteers were seriously hurt. The pictures were all over TV and the newspapers, because the press had somehow also managed to get out there. The Day Marina was rocking and rolling, but it held together—which proved that Andy Kostanecki's design would work. When I returned to the Hyatt, there were several messages from A.D., who had gone back to Atlanta, asking that I phone him immediately. When I did, he said, *"OK! You got your extra barges. What do we do now with the chaos on the sand spit?"*

"Pray to whatever god you think might listen," was my curt reply.

I thought that by now Maggard might have become less strident and a little more forthright, but it was not to be. The reason most Olympic Games succeed in the end is that the 28 international sport federations bring in their best and most experienced experts from around the world. As long as the physical plant is acceptable, they make the Games work, with the support of some 2,000 local volunteers. In the case of sailing, it is usually about 60 such experts who roll up their sleeves and deliver the event. They are usually at the venue by 8:00 a.m. and are lucky to get to bed before midnight every day for almost three weeks. Most of them are over 50 years old and their competitive days are over. Adequate three-star accommodations are the minimum acceptable. When Tom Webster told me that he had it on good authority that Maggard had rented a sleazy motel in the worst part of town for ISAF officials, I immediately phoned Maggard. He denied it, saying that nothing had been finalized. The next day, both the Atlanta and Savannah newspapers announced that ACOG had rented this motel. I phoned A.D. Frazier and blasted. He agreed to rent the Hyatt on the river in Savannah, an excellent hotel with a surprisingly reasonable room rate.

Shortly after this, Richard Pound phoned me and said that Billy Payne and A.D. Frazier had asked him to speak to me as a friend. A successful Montreal lawyer, Pound advised me that I must stop lashing out at ACOG. He said they would sue me for slander if I continued my public harangues. I told him that I had not survived in a downtown Toronto plumbing business by being intimidated by lawyers' threats of litigation. *"Please inform ACOG that you can sue people for slander only when the allegations are wrong,"* I added. He said he would deliver the message, and I was never threatened again.

I was extremely concerned about the organization in Savannah and the demonstrated lack of understanding of what was required. I was further vexed by ACOG's refusal to acknowledge the gargantuan proportions of an Olympic Regatta. A number of influential and concerned citizens of Savannah, many of whom could have helped, told me that they had been marginalized by Atlanta. I convinced the ISAF executive that we needed to have our own person on the ground in Savannah for the months leading up to the Olympics. This was an unprecedented move, but ISAF had to act. We hired Phil Jones from the UK, and he took up residence in Savannah for almost a year. Calm and collected in his manner, Phil worked with the ACOG team of John McIntosh and Rich Jeffries to resolve many issues.

Computer Bugs and Racing Results in Savannah

At earlier Games, the mark-by-mark roundings of all the sailing races were transmitted live from the race course to the shore and around the world. ACOG refused to do this even though they had made a commitment in their bid book to do so. ISAF wanted the race results to be transmitted worldwide using its new Internet capabilities. Sailing may not be one of the most highly rated Olympic TV sports, but it is in the top few with regard to Internet usage. It was imperative that we get this feed.

Fate stepped in again. I received an email from Paul Pascoe, president of the Hobie 16 Catamaran Class and a computer genius consulting to a firm doing work with IBM in the UK. Paul wanted the Hobie 16 to be considered for inclusion in the Sydney 2000 Olympics. I agreed to meet with him at Heathrow Airport the next time I was flying through, which happened to be in March 1996. A joy to be with, Pascoe is an Aussie with a unique, if not risqué, sense of humour.

As usual, I dominated the conversation at Heathrow, easily changing the subject from Hobie 16s to live Internet dispatching of mark-by-mark roundings. I explained the problem and the refusal of IBM and ACOG to address the issue. Pascoe, with his usual glibness, said he could solve the problem, but it would take two weeks to write the required program.

In April, he sent me an email saying that the program was written and that, while it worked on his system, he had to go to Atlanta and Savannah to try it out on the IBM Olympic system. I had accumulated a lot of air miles, so I was able to get him a free ticket. When he got to Atlanta, he phoned me to say that, in his opinion, the IBM results system for the Games was in chaos. He was also worried about what would happen to the results system for all sports during the Games. How right he proved to be! Next day, he went to Savannah. Pascoe was sure his mark-by-mark rounding program would work. He had also written his own accumulated results program and did not need the IBM system. It had taken him less than two weeks to do this in his spare time. He phoned me the next day and announced, *"Eureka, boss! Everything works as planned."* He said that he had met the IBM manager in Savannah, and found him to be very cooperative. The manager had given Pascoe the two-by-three foot washroom in the big IBM trailer as an office, having removed the toilet and basin, and Pascoe was in business.

I asked him what he wanted as reimbursement for his work. He replied that, in addition to a nominal fee for his time away from his real job, he would love it if he could bring his daughter and wife to the Games. IBM's budget for the complete Games results—which didn't work—was over 100 million dollars. The rest of the story is even more scandalous.

During the Games, there were 500 accredited sailing journalists and many TV networks from around the world covering the regatta in Savannah. After the first practice race, I returned exhausted to the Hyatt in Savannah. Most of the media were staying there as well. I walked into the bar for a drink and all hell broke loose. Bob Fisher and Malcolm McKeag, two of the best known yachting journalists from the UK, started screaming at me. There were no results in the journalists' tent and they were doing live TV back to the UK. They had paid a lot of money to ACOG for the rights. Fisher lashed out, *"You are the pope of sailing! Do something before tomorrow's race!"*

I had no idea what to do. Sitting in the lobby with his wife and daughter was Paul Pascoe, enjoying the whole tirade. *"Hey boss! That was fun to watch. I think I can solve the problem, at a cost though."* Immediately, huge dollar signs flashed through my head. *"How much do you think it will cost?"*

"About 800 dollars to buy two modems to plug into the computers and make the TV screens display the mark-by-mark roundings and final results in the journalists' tent," he replied.

"Get it done now!" I ordered.

I have no idea what Pascoe did, the technical aspects being beyond my comprehension, but he came through—and he didn't have to buy a drink for the rest of the Games. Fisher, McKeag and the rest of the press were very appreciative, but that is still not the end of the story.

The 100-million-dollar IBM results system crashed in Atlanta on the first day of the Games. IBM brought all the technicians they could find to the command centre in Atlanta to repair their systems, including Pascoe's IBM friend from Savannah. Pascoe was left alone in his little washroom in the trailer in Savannah. Early in the morning, I got a telephone call from the IBM project manager in Atlanta, explaining how their system had crashed and would ISAF mind if they just plugged into Pascoe's system, solving the problem for at least one of the 28 sports. Naturally I agreed, but I made a mistake in not insisting on a contract from IBM to pay Pascoe and ISAF for what we delivered.

After the third race, the IBM manager in Atlanta called me to say they had fixed all the problems and no longer needed Pascoe's system. He thanked ISAF for our help and hung up. I told Pascoe, who just smiled as usual and said, *"Boss, just wait till tomorrow."* Then he walked away. For the Atlanta Olympic Regatta, the teams counted only their best eight results out of the 10 races, dropping their worst two. IBM had not programmed for the drop races, but being an accomplished sailor, Pascoe knew this and had written his program properly. The IBM manager phoned back and sheepishly asked if he could once again plug into our system. Pascoe's program was used for the rest of the Games for all the sailing results worldwide.

ACOG had originally agreed to have TV cameras installed on the Day Marina out on the barrier islands, so that the support crews and those not racing could follow what was going on. Just prior to the start of the Games, however, Maggard refused to provide the dish, saying it was not in his budget. There was no way to get the Internet feed on the Day Marina without a satellite dish. Atlanta had a two-billion-dollar budget but apparently could not afford one satellite dish.

During the first race, I went out to the Day Marina myself and found the ingenuity of the sailors to be absolutely incredible. The Danish team members were using their cell phones to call their friends back home in Denmark, who were receiving Pascoe's mark-by-mark roundings on the Internet at *www.sailing.org* and then relaying the results back over the phone to them at the Day Marina. They would then announce the results to the gathered throng floating at the mouth of the river. (In those days, cell phones could not connect to the Internet.) The next day, ISAF got more sophisticated and bought large blackboards and chalk. We commandeered some volunteers and, as the roundings were received by cell phone from Denmark, they would chalk up the results on the blackboards outside the trailers on the floating Day Marina—a prime example of modern technology at work in ostensibly the most sophisticated country in the world!

After the Games, I sent a bill for Pascoe's services to IBM in Armonk, New York. As I expected, they refused to pay. In fact, Pascoe received not so much as a thank-you from IBM. ISAF honoured him for his great job at its November annual general meeting, however, and took the opportunity to express its appreciation to Tom Webster for his hard work as well.

Toronto gets vicious thunderstorms, but the ones in Georgia are really something. IOC Director of Sport Gilbert Felli arrived at the Day Marina at about 3:00 p.m. one day when the sky turned pitch black and the worst storm of the Games hit. The sailors were out at sea at the mercy of the thunder, lightning, wind and driving rain. I was supposed to pick up Felli and take him out to see the last race of the day. I arrived back at the Day Marina at the height of the storm to find Felli, like a wet rat, giggling in complete amazement at what sailors have to cope with.

Opening Ceremonies

To get to the Opening Ceremonies in Atlanta, we boarded a bus at the hotel, but the driver started off in the wrong direction, heading away from the Olympic Stadium. I told him that if he did not turn around we would end up in Savannah. He said it was his first time in Atlanta, having driven his bus in from St. Louis that morning. He turned the bus around and drove toward the stadium. As he was making a wide turn, a Mercedes with a large Coca-Cola sign on its side tried to sneak inside. The bus took the front right off it. We had to get out and walk about a mile to the ceremonies.

I still smile when I remember the Parade of Athletes. My wife Mary and I were sitting with a group of local people from the State of Georgia. They cheered loudly for only two countries that entered. Naturally, they were rambunctious over the entrance of Team USA, but they were also jubilant when the announcer introduced the team from Georgia. The locals around me went wild. The woman beside me said she had been unaware that their state had a team. I did not disillusion her that Georgia is a country in Eastern Europe.

Being so far from Atlanta, Savannah had its own Opening Ceremonies. IOC President Juan Antonio Samaranch flew into Savannah to preside and officially open the sailing competitions at 7:00 p.m. The ceremony was held in a park in the centre of town that had been outfitted with grandstands and an amphitheatre to house musical groups and other entertainment. The tented stage was filled with audio equipment, amplifiers and loudspeakers.

The mayor spoke first, then the organizers. As ISAF president, I was to speak next, after which Samaranch was to declare the Sailing Games open. The finale was to be the lighting of the Olympic Flame. The sky turned pitch black as thunder clouds rolled in. As I opened my mouth to address the crowd, a terrific thunderstorm hit with lightning strikes and a downpour unique to Savannah. You could swim upwards. We were all huddled in the tent, getting thoroughly soaked. Sparks flew everywhere from the amplifiers. It was scary, to say the least. Gerardo Seeliger, one of Samaranch's protégés and a sailor, picked up a saxophone and played *Georgia on My Mind*. Samaranch sat there calm but very wet.

After what seemed an eternity, the storm abated, but the ceremony was ruined. The VIP entourage slogged through the park, now a sea of mud, onto the bus to return to Atlanta. After we were all on the bus, I decided I should thank them for coming and see what I could do to remedy the situation. I walked down the aisle to my seat only to see Samaranch standing in the back of the bus looking like a drowned rat. Addressing everyone on the bus, he said, *"As president of the International Olympic Committee, I declare the Sailing Games of the Twenty-sixth Olympiad officially open!"* What a man!

Olympic Sailing Regatta

On one of my many visits to Savannah, I had been invited to play golf at the Savannah Golf Club, alleged to be the oldest in the USA. I was playing with two 30-year-old local lawyers.

When we got to the fourteenth hole, they decided to brief me, opening the conversation by confiding that they thought they could trust me. They proceeded to inform me that both the Savannah Golf Club and the Savannah Yacht Club were effectively racially segregated, and that the local press was just waiting to make an issue of it during the Games if any of the ISAF executive went near either club. I instructed ISAF executive members that both clubs were out of bounds.

During the Games, ISAF always hosts a reception for our officials from around the world, several of whom, naturally, are people of colour. I delegated the organization of the reception to the vice-president from Belgium, with strict instructions not to book the Savannah Yacht Club. I was shocked when, two days before the event, the local newspaper ran a scathing editorial about ISAF holding their party at the segregated Savannah Yacht Club. I had no idea that he had scheduled the party there as I had been consumed with other issues. He said that he had not believed my instructions, because the English team was sequestered there. The damage was done. We could not cancel the party because many of our volunteers were members of the club and, if we did, they would no doubt withdraw their services and we would be unable to finish the regatta. The sailors would be the losers. I was between a rock and hard place.

Mary came up with a solution. The new mayor of Savannah, Floyd Adams, Jr., was a very upbeat, large black man. ISAF would invite him and, if he came, it would defuse the situation. The mayor accepted. I arrived at the Savannah Yacht Club early to ensure that there were no picketers or other protesters—thankfully there were none—but state troopers were everywhere. I was shocked at what I found. The Savannah Yacht Club had situated our distinguished group not in the formal main clubhouse, but in the smelly, unpainted old junior club, complete with holes in the floor. I went to the clubhouse and demanded to meet the manager and commodore. I can be rather brutal, but nobody has ever seen me like I was that night. I reamed them both a new "after porthole." They were in shock and said they would try to accommodate us a little later.

The mayor arrived at the dilapidated junior club driving his own Cadillac. He was brilliant, shaking hands with everyone before delivering an insightful and complimentary address. At the end of his speech, he announced that he had to leave to attend a Ray Charles concert. ISAF Vice-president Jean-Louis Monneron from France was there with his elegant and engaging wife Danielle. She stepped up to her husband and announced, *"Jean-Louis, you know how I enjoy jazz. You do not mind if I go with the mayor?"* Floyd and Danielle left the room arm in arm and went to see Ray Charles. Shortly after that, the Savannah Yacht Club moved us all into the main clubhouse. When all the ISAF officials were seated and served, I left. I will never return. To this day, the vice-president from Belgium apologizes for not listening; he was deeply and truly embarrassed that day.

A tabloid newspaper personally attacked me for using the Savannah Yacht Club, labeling me a "Canuck." I wrote the editor that I was very disturbed about this racial slur, pointing out that to call Canadian a "Canuck" was analogous to calling an Afro-American a "nigger." The editor wrote back a sincere apology. It was really a gotcha, because "Canuck" is not pejorative or demeaning at all, although he didn't know that. It is like calling a New Yorker a "Yankee"; indeed, Canada's Vancouver NHL hockey team is called the Canucks. Still, it was fun to watch the "Cracker" squirm.

The press really hammered Atlanta and ACOG. Samaranch was very upset with the Games. The reason, I believe, was the stubbornness of Atlanta's mayor, who had evidently decided to take on the press. You would think a politician would know better than to have a "pissing contest" with someone who has more ink, let alone 20,000 journalists from around the world. Coupled with the inexperience of the bus drivers who were continually getting lost, this ensured bad press. If you asked the members of the media, they would tell you that when they got to any Atlanta venue, the events went off very well. This is due the international federations' bringing in their best officials from all over the world; it is they who really make the Games work.

Richard Pound personally suffered a very unfortunate episode during the Games. He had tried to make ACOG listen to reason, based on his broad experience with running Games and other aspects of the Olympic movement. I was told the schism between the two camps was deepened by Atlanta's belief that the television contract that Pound had negotiated was inadequate. The revenue accruing to Atlanta was much lower than Billy Payne and A.D. Frazier believed they could have received if ACOG had been left to their own devices.

Pound's vivacious wife Julie, a successful author in her own right who has been nominated for several Canadian Governor General's Literary Awards, is not at all awed by the IOC. At the conclusion of each day's events in Atlanta, they usually went out for dinner with a few friends. The Pounds do not seem to enjoy the usual cast of thousands, buffets and sponsors' parties as much as the amenities of a good restaurant. I can confirm that you could fire a gun down any street in Atlanta at midnight and not hit anyone. One night, they were walking home at about midnight after a nice dinner. Arm in arm, they were strolling across an intersection when a rather robust police woman grabbed Julie by the upper arm from behind. Julie is quite athletic and did not know who was assaulting her. She reeled around and kicked her assailant in the groin. The police woman charged her with jaywalking and hauled her off to jail.

The Atlanta officials did nothing and—perhaps on account of their rather cool relationship with Richard—let the case proceed. Two days later, I was in Atlanta for the Closing Ceremonies and sat beside Julie. She was still visibly shaken. She rolled up her sleeve and showed me her upper arm, black and blue with bruises. Atlanta should be ashamed. Pound now openly states that the 1996 Games should have come to Toronto.

The sailing regatta came to a successful conclusion in Savannah. The sailors thought it was a great experience and the best sailors won which, at the end of the day, is all that mattered. The more than 2,000 volunteers in Savannah were extremely dedicated and competent. Every morning and after each day's racing, I would walk through the operational tents to thank them for their great work. Each volunteer team hosted a party during the Games, and they invited Mary and me to attend. I have many pictures of the friends we made in Savannah. Two weeks after the last race, the Day Marina was towed to Mexico. If you go back to Savannah today, you will see little to show that, in 1996, Savannah was the centre of the sailing world.

Mary and I had two days left after the end of the Olympic Sailing Regatta to see the final events in Atlanta. We went to the finals of athletics to see Canada win the 4 x 100 relay with Robert Esmie, Glenroy Gilbert, Bruny Surin and Donovan Bailey anchoring the team, beating the USA for the first time in history. I was standing in the IOC hospitality suite waiting for the event to start when I saw Olympic boycott perpetrator Jimmy Carter in the corner. I was trying to get up enough nerve to tell him what I thought of him when Samaranch came in just before the races started. He saw me for the first time in Atlanta, as I had been consumed with the challenges in Savannah. Samaranch walked over to me, shook my hand and paid me what I considered a great compliment: *"I wish we had all been as tough with ACOG as you were, Paul."* I was so proud that I forgot about Jimmy Carter, and left him alone to his fantasies.

Tom Webster recently took me to see the Masters Golf Tournament in Augusta, Georgia. The three most prestigious and outstanding premier sports events in the world are Wimbledon Tennis, the Masters Golf Tournament and the America's Cup sailing. The Masters is one of the few events I have ever attended where the reality of being there is bigger than the hype. Tom took Mary and me into the press area where I was met by Billy Payne. He was his usual gracious self and took me on a tour, which was great. Billy had just been appointed chairman of the Augusta National Golf Club. He will do a great job. I am sure he is much happier there than he was dealing with the Olympic family.

Chapter 13:
2000 Olympic Games in Sydney

In 1993, I was invited to Monaco as a guest of the IOC to be awarded my first Olympic Order. I am the only person in history to receive two silver Olympic Orders, not because of excellence, but because the IOC forgot I already had one when it awarded the second in 2004 on my retirement from the IOC. In 1993, I was an ISAF vice-president and not nominated for the presidency. The IOC presumed I was leaving the international stage. In 1994, however, I was elected ISAF president and stayed around for another decade, much to my enjoyment.

The 1993 Olympic Order citation was read by President Samaranch in Monaco:

Paul HENDERSON, Your commitment to the service of Olympism began with your passion for sailing. Since then, within the IYRU, you have been at all the sailing competitions. Your support for the Olympic Movement has come through the hazards of the bid by your city, Toronto, for the Games. Throughout these many years, you have made a most significant contribution to promoting the Olympic ideals, and it is this which the IOC is honouring today.

Selection of Sydney, 2000

The Monaco IOC session was also where the vote for the 2000 Olympic host city was held. It was great to be a spectator and watch the bid cities courting favour, especially since Mary and I were guests of the IOC. Most of the power brokers in the IOC were pushing for Beijing. Two days before the vote, I went to see Aussies John Coates and Phil Coles in the Sydney hospitality suite. They were in a deep depression, convinced that they had lost. When the results were about to be announced, the atmosphere was electric. When Samaranch pronounced *"Sydney!"* the reaction was dramatic. Sydney had won by two votes; needless to say, the Chinese were very upset.

That night I went to the Aussie celebration, which was wild. Coates and Coles were getting quietly drunk, walking arm in arm holding each other up. The only thing they could say was, *"Two votes! We won by only two votes!"* I reminded them that in sport, the scores are never engraved on the trophy, just the names of the winners. The losers make excuses and the winners smile. They continued on their rounds of the attendees, smiling a lot. Sydney was to prove that the IOC needed Sydney more than Sydney needed the IOC. The 2000 Games were to a standard of quality never seen before.

Bob Elphinston

The Sydney Organizing Committee for the Olympic Games (SOCOG) engaged Bob Elphinston as director of sport. He was always open and fair, a welcome contrast to what we had experienced in Atlanta. All international sport federations heard Bob's challenges directly, including what could be done and not be done. He worked 24-7 for four years. Bob hosted a dinner in a modest restaurant for all 28 international federation presidents and secretaries general who had worked with him over the years. The greatest tribute that Bob received was that everyone, without exception, showed up to thank him. He now knows what all international federations go through. Later, he crossed the bridge over to the other side, becoming president of the International Basketball Federation. They could not have chosen a better leader.

Sydney Harbour Marina

There were controversies in Sydney over where the sailing marina would be situated. Any installation on any waterfront these days arouses much concern. Peter Tallberg and Mike Evans were in control of ISAF when the venue was selected and they had said the event must be in Sydney Harbour to give sailing a dramatic regatta with the Sydney Bridge and Opera House as a backdrop. Two sites were proposed, one at Rushcutter's Bay in an old navy yard and the other across the bay in a more remote naval site. In many ways the remote venue would have been a better choice because it would have left a legacy to sailing. Sydney was in need of a national training facility for sailing as a legacy from the Games.

Coates asked me to fly to Sydney to try to secure a commitment that the sailing venue would be left after the Games and not just be temporary. He was a sportsman and wanted legacies left for all sports, which he was able to achieve for his focus, rowing. I pushed for a permanent site. SOCOG insisted on Rushcutter's Bay, agreeing that some of the venue would be left to launch boats and for sailing for disabled people.

The area had consisted of a collection of derelict, ugly naval buildings that were demolished to make way for the new Olympic Marina, giving local residents an uncluttered view of the harbour. A somewhat self-interested member of the state parliament who sat as an independent lived near the venue. The government needed her vote to stay in power so she effectively held a trump card, one she did not hesitate to play. She had all the docks and facilities removed after the Games, leaving little legacy to sailing, all for the sake of an unobstructed view of Sydney's magnificent harbour. There was nothing ISAF could do about it and John Coates was very apologetic.

Australia has a history in sailing. Competition Manager Glenn Bourke was a three-time world champion in the Laser Class. He certainly understood our needs. The challenges to run the regatta successfully—a narrow harbour coupled with a variable wind—were made more acute by the multitude of ferry boats plying the waters. It turned out to be a great regatta, however; the narrow marina venue was all that was needed to run successful Games, and the sailors and media loved the compactness.

Each day, some 100,000 people lined the shores of Sydney Harbour. They could watch the races from the shore as the turning marks were very close in and with the large flags on the sails, the spectators could easily tell who was winning (see photo). I was allocated a 50-foot motor launch, manned by the owner's friends who made our long days very enjoyable. Patrick deBarros, the ocean rescue hero from Busan, had brought his elegant sailing yacht *SELJM* all the way from Portugal to be a host yacht for the IOC at the Games. HRH Princess Anne was aboard many days, watching the very good British team compete.

Sailing became a popular event, being in the centre of everything in Sydney. Mary and Martha were responsible for allocating the VIP spectators to the various boats. The Aussies were very complimentary about their work, being overwhelmed themselves by the influx of VIPs.

A major problem with being so close to shore was that the wealthy teams had set up special weather stations on the cliffs and were using modern telecommunications to relay information to their coaches which was then passed on to the sailors. After this, ISAF outlawed all modern communications equipment on coach boats. It is in the tradition of sailing that the responsibility for what goes on during the race must rest entirely with the sailors with no outside influence.

The sailing medal ceremonies were dramatic, held in front of the marvelous Sydney Opera House with more than 50,000 spectators cheering the medal winners.

Aussie 49er Skiff

This was the first Olympics where the Australian-designed 49er skiff was an Olympic Class (see photo). ISAF had tried to get the sailing classes to put large letters and flags on the sails to enable the spectators to see them from a distance, but that was like pulling teeth with the traditionalists. President Gerardo Seeliger of the 49er Class was a real promoter. He wanted to have a high profile for the 49er; together with 49er designer Julian Bethwaite, he figured out a way to have all the spinnakers dyed with representative flags and the Olympic Rings. ISAF supplied the sails, which were spectacular. As happens with first time trials, however, there were problems. The process used to apply the colours made the material brittle, causing the sails to rip in the wind. ISAF had to make the very difficult decision to replace the sails, even though the 49er sailors wanted to take a chance on them. They loved the exposure, but ISAF could not risk failures.

At the end of the last race, the medal winners from Finland, UK and USA had planned a spectacular show. Dousing their bland replacement spinnakers and raising the national flag sails, they screamed together down Sydney Harbour in a wonderful sail past (see photo). Now every class wants to show off the nations they represent, and at each subsequent Olympics, the sails that were once plain white get more and more colourful with larger and larger national flags and letters. Another innovation has been the addition of the names of the crews on the sails. Athletes in other sports, such as triathlon and athletics, have copied this and are putting their competitor names down the legs of their track suits.

Sydney Aggravation

The biggest crisis I had to deal with was caused by the Canadian Olympic Committee (COC) and Sport Canada. The incident is indicative of the lack of respect and understanding on the part of both bodies for the manner in which sport operates at the international level.

The IOC puts a quota on the number of athletes each sport can enter in the Games. Sailing was allocated 400 entries for Sydney. This requires an elimination process that the IOC delegates to the relevant international sport federation. The national Olympic committees, including the COC, have nothing at all to do with developing these criteria. I was able to ensure that Canadians got all the legal breaks they deserved, but I could not break the rules.

To be asked to do so by the COC and Sport Canada was unfortunate and regrettable.

Trevor and Tina Baylis, a husband-and-wife team, wanted to compete for Canada in the 49er Class and they were quite good. The problem was that Tina was Canadian but Trevor an American. They lived in Oregon. They needed dispensation from both USA and

Canada to enter, plus ratification from the IOC. This is the IOC requirement.

In January 2000, the couple finally realized that they needed to do something, having left it to the last minute. The COC's Carol Anne Letheren orchestrated a fast track citizenship for Trevor, a process that can take several years. Canada's minister of immigration became actively involved as well. Just two months before the start of the Games, Trevor received his Canadian citizenship and all the required waivers, but only after all the slots had been allocated and all boats shipped to Sydney.

Trevor and Tina Baylis, the COC, Sport Canada and the Government of Canada harassed me, demanding that I circumvent the ISAF/IOC rules. I was chastised in the Canadian press for being anti-Canadian. It was clearly stated that if the number of entries fell below 400, ISAF could award them a wild card legally. One week before the Opening Ceremonies our number stood at 403. The Chinese said that two of their sailors had missed their flights. I told the COC that sailing was now at 401—still over the limit—but I would quietly ask IOC Director of Sport Gilbert Felli if ISAF could fill back to 403. My responsibility was to get as many sailors sailing, not to prevent them from sailing. Felli responded, *"No way! You are out of line even asking."*

The COC did not accept this, went to the Court of Arbitration for Sport and were turned down. I was painted as the bad guy and anti-Canadian. Trevor and Tina Baylis still live in the USA.

The volunteers in Sydney made the Games. They were always open and friendly, welcoming us wherever we went with a friendly *"G'day, mate."* Rob Ashburn, our driver, was excellent and took us everywhere. His hobby was running an amateur opera company in one of Sydney's suburbs. The SOCOG regulations said he must take days off but he refused to do so. Volunteers were not allowed to sit in the VIP stands at events in their SOCOG uniforms. In typical Aussie fashion, Rob kept spare clothes in the car so he could go with us to all the events. I was able to get tickets to the Closing Ceremonies for his entire family. When we were going home after the Games, Rob showed up at the airport with them all. Eyes brimming with tears, he presented us with a colourful aboriginal boomerang as a souvenir. We keep it in a place of honour in our home to remember the great experience we had in Sydney.

Sydney Closing Ceremonies

The Closing Ceremonies at the 110,000 seat Olympic Stadium were brilliant. The Aussies had been great hosts and were determined to have fun at their Closing Ceremonies in the Aussie way.

At the beginning, a master of ceremonies appeared on a tiny stage in a grey suit and tie. He started to read a list of rules that all spectators had to follow that night. Just then, a dune buggy came out of the stands and hit the small stage, disintegrating it on impact and setting the atmosphere for the evening. The Aussies made fun of themselves and the IOC, but respectfully. They had two comedians named "The Dream" to warm up the crowd. The Dream had their own late night TV show on which they spoofed the Games every night. They were riotous with their own Olympic mascot, Fatso the Fat Arse Wombat, who had a diving competition one night with other mascots and almost drowned, having to be resuscitated. They also made fun of several IOC members, including "Dickie the Pound." One night, a very tall RCMP officer appeared in their audience. The comedians asked who he was and as he towered over them he said he was Richard Pound's son. They called him "Sir Dickie the Pound" after that.

Next they brought in very big floats with an Australian star atop each one. Greg "The Shark" Norman hit plastic golf balls off one into the crowd, Crocodile Dundee stood atop an outback float, a bevy of drag queens strutting along seductively. There arrived a float which looked like a movie set with a tall and elegant woman as the focus. It was model and actress Elle McPherson, whose name I had missed a few nights earlier when she was introduced by her date that evening, King Constantine's son Nicholas.

The finale was the most memorable scene I can remember from

any Closing Ceremonies I have attended or watched on TV. The lights dimmed and Aussie icon Slim Dusty strode alone out of the stands, dressed all in black, strumming a guitar and singing *Waltzing Matilda*. We all joined in with tears in our eyes—none of us wanted the 2000 Sydney Games to be over. The only mistake he made was in not singing it twice.

Chapter 14:
Member of the International Olympic Committee

The IOC instituted several changes arising from the 1998 Salt Lake City scandals. New rules for membership stipulated that 15 members be appointed from international sport federations and 15 former athletes be elected by their peers at the Games. Canada had two IOC members up to 2000, Richard Pound and Carol Anne Letheren. Their paths had both been through the Canadian Olympic Committee, not through sport federations. There was no way I could become a member of the IOC until the new rules came into effect.

There are 35 Olympic international federations, seven Winter and 28 Summer. I was gratified when Samaranch nominated me to be one of the first group inducted in Sydney in 2000. Two other Canadians were also appointed to the IOC: Bob Steadward, president of the Paralympics, and Charmaine Crooks, elected by the athletes. This brought the number of Canadians to five for a short time in 2000. By 2005, however, Canada was down to only one, Richard Pound, but with the election of Becky Scott as an athlete representative, Canada is back up to two IOC members. Several European countries have five members each, which means that each of these countries has more IOC members than the USA and Canada combined.

One of the new rules is that if your country or a citizen of your country is to be voted on, you cannot vote. This meant that, while I was an IOC member, I was involved only as a spectator for most of the major political decisions, such as the votes for Toronto 2008 and Vancouver 2010, and the vote for the new IOC president. Those elected from international federations were members only as long as they held their federation positions or until they reached the age of 70; both conditions applied to me within the space of two days in November 2004, when I retired.

The seating at the IOC sessions is very interesting. A new

member sits in the back row; as members retire due to age or die, other members move forward. The front row, affectionately called "death row," is occupied by members who have been there seemingly forever and who have been "grandfathered" (apropos because they are all men) and do not have to retire when they reach 70. Richard Pound and Peter Tallberg, my sailing friend from Helsinki, have reached these exalted front row seats. At the beginning, I sat at the back; I moved one-third of the way to the front before I retired. Members always sit in the same order no matter the event, with the result that you really get to know those near you and have little contact with the others. Here are the IOC members with whom I sat at most sessions:

Kipchoge (Kip) Keino (Kenya):

Kip is a great athlete, having won Gold in both Mexico (1500 metres) and Munich (3,000 metres). He was revered in Toronto, where he ran many times at our indoor track meets. Kip comes from a mountain village in Kenya and has never really left his roots. He started an orphanage there and has adopted more than 70 children. Two years ago, he was so proud when two of his brood were accepted into university.

Many Africans love ice hockey. They feel it is soccer on ice and, as it is played indoors, they do not freeze at the Winter Games. I would always take an entourage with me to most hockey games, much of the time including Kip and Egypt's handball team President Dr. Hassan Moustafa. I would explain the various whistles. Kip would get very excited and start hitting anyone sitting beside him yelling, "*Shoot the ball! Shoot the ball!*"

"*Kip, it is a puck!*" I would try to explain, but his excitement would invariably turn it back into a ball. To this day, when he sees me he always starts with, "*It's a puck! It's a puck!*"

Bill Hybl (USA):

Bill Hybl was a much respected member of the IOC for the short time he was there. As chairman of the well known

Broadmore Hotel in Colorado Springs, he hosted the Olympic family in 2002. Bill sat beside me for only two years because the United States Olympic Committee (USOC) elected a new president in 2002 and demanded that Bill resign to permit her to sit as an IOC member in the USA. He did so against my strong advice that he stay. It takes years for someone to become accepted at the top level of international sport, and the USA was throwing away a real strength. He resigned, but before the new USOC president could be inducted into the IOC, she was accused of misrepresenting her academic background and replaced. The next USOC president lasted only a short time because of internal USOC problems. Bill Hybl should never have left. I remind him of it every time I see him. The little influence held by the USA and the Americas continues to diminish as the IOC becomes more and more Eurocentric, centred in Lausanne, Switzerland.

Mostafa Taba (Iran):

Mostafa Taba had spent several years in Vancouver and loves Canada, so we got along well. Whenever IOC debates dragged on, he would take the opportunity to educate me on the situation in the Middle East from a Muslim perspective. His penetrating insights showed me that there are at least two sides to every issue. In turn, I tried to demystify things that lay outside his area of expertise, such as ice hockey. When he decided to run for the IOC executive board, I signed his nomination papers. We sat beside each other at the Closing Ceremonies in Sydney. When the lights dimmed at the finale and Slim Dusty strolled in alone singing *Waltzing Matilda,* Mostafa turned to me and asked, *"Who is Matilda?"*

Explicating the meaning of that phrase was just another of my IOC responsibilities.

Bruno Grandi (Italy, President Gymnastics):

As president of the Federation Internationale Gymnastique, Italy's Bruno Grandi joined the IOC in 2000 along with Tamás Aján (Hungary, weightlifting), Ruben Acosta (Mexico, volleyball) and Gian-

Franco Kasper (Switzerland, skiing). Gymnastics is one of the five most important TV sports in the Summer Games. Grandi was the same age as me and had to leave the IOC at the same time. This left one of the major sports without a voice at the top level, which is just not right. Juan Antonio Samaranch has gone on record saying that the Olympic Games could be run without the national Olympic committees, but never without the international sport federations. The IOC must address this exclusion of important international federation presidents.

Presidents of the IOC

The first IOC president I met was Avery Brundage, but that was only to shake his hand at the 1980 Lake Placid Winter Olympics where Jim Worrall, IOC member in Canada, introduced me to him.

I never met Michael Morris (Lord Killanin) during his IOC presidency, but during the Toronto 1996 bid process I visited him in his townhouse in the centre of Dublin where we talked for an hour. Content to be out of the firing line when he retired, he was most gracious and deeply appreciative of the respect he received from his successor.

Juan Antonio Samaranch:

To me, the one thing that explains Juan Antonio Samaranch was an observation he made on the death of President Primo Nebiolo of the International Amateur Athletic Federation (IAAF). Primo led the IAAF successfully during the 1980s and 1990s with dictatorial aggressiveness. Primo made not only his federation strong, but took all the international federations along for the ride as well. If he negotiated something for the IAAF, he included the rest of us. When Primo died at age 75, the executive of the Association of International Sport Federations, of which I was a member, met at Chateau de Vidy in Lausanne to decide what to do without our strong leader. In truth, he was impossible to replace. Primo and President Samaranch had many disagreements, but they held each other in great regard. Samaranch arrived at the meeting to show respect for his old friend and, demonstrating great insight, commented, *"Primo was a lucky man—he died in office."*

If you ask any member of the Olympic family who had the honour of serving with Samaranch, I am sure you would hear great reverence for the man. Was he perfect? No! But he was right 95 per cent of the time and for the other five per cent, the press was thoroughly unfair. He brought Olympic sports kicking and screaming into the modern world and was a much more open man than anyone would think, with a great sense of humor.

Whenever there was a problem in sailing my telephone would ring at 8:00 a.m. in Toronto, it would invariably be Samaranch on the line, never an assistant. *"Paul, Juan Antonio—what do you think of ...?"*

I would give him my opinion. Sometimes he agreed and sometimes he did not, but at least he asked. He answered all his correspondence, even if it was just a short handwritten note indicating that he had noted the writer's observation. During the seven years that I was sailing president under his leadership, I could always get a one-on-one meeting with him. He would sit at his table with his little notebook as we talked. I was always surprised at how much he knew about our sport—about every sport, for that matter. I would leave our meeting thinking I was part of his team and that he had given me good advice salted with compassion.

Juan Antonio Samaranch slowly opened up the IOC, endeavouring to make it a more liberal family rather than a club. In no way was it bureaucratic. He appointed more than 125 IOC members from all corners of the world. When you have 125 of anything, be they priests, rabbis, lawyers, journalists or figure skating judges, there are bound to be a few unethical ones among their number.

The Salt Lake City Olympic scandals found eight bad apples, certainly enough to kick start the media frenzy. The press tried to tar all IOC members with the brush of scandal, and that was unethical on their part. It was the cross Samaranch had to bear in his remaining years. He did not hide from the problems but met them head on, personally taking responsibility for ensuring the Olympic movement came out of this period strong—and it did.

During Toronto's 1996 Olympic bid process, I got to observe President Samaranch up close when he visited Toronto in the summer of 1988. I took him sailing around Toronto Island and he loved it. He was in no hurry to attend the formal receptions we had planned. TOOC had researched his preferences and most were very simple. He liked to have stamped postcards at his bedside; a stamp collector since his youth, he would write notes to his children and grandchildren from wherever he was in the world, giving them a wonderful collection of stamps. He preferred rather bland food, we were told, such as consommé, white fish, and vanilla ice cream. The first night of his visit, TOOC hosted an impressive dinner for 20, including the mayor and other dignitaries at the upscale and historic Toronto Club. TOOC sat him between our renowned athletes Sue Holloway and John Wood. John had won a Silver Medal in Montreal in canoeing, having been beaten for the Gold by an East German who was later disgraced as a dope cheat. John is now a successful businessman whom I see regularly at various functions in Toronto. Sue was the first Canadian to compete in both the Summer and Winter Games and is married to Olympic Silver Medalist, high jumper Greg Joy. Sue is a red-haired pistol and great fun. Samaranch really felt at home with these two on either side, leaving the politicians out of the dinner dialogue, which I am sure he enjoyed immensely.

When dessert was served, Sue really did it. It was the berry season in Ontario; the Toronto Club served a combination of raspberries, strawberries, blueberries and peaches to all of us except Samaranch, who got a dish of vanilla ice cream. In a loud voice, Sue blurted out, *"This is unfair—you get vanilla ice cream and I get berries!"*

Samaranch immediately took his spoon and put half his ice cream in Sue's dish in return for half her berries.

At the end of his visit, TOOC held a press conference

in the beautiful Sir Edmund Walker Memorial Court at the Art Gallery of Ontario. Walking in, I told Samaranch that I would be the master of ceremonies and, expecting our press to be rather aggressive, I would filter the questions to ensure he would not be embarrassed. He curtly replied that he conducted his own press conferences and did not need to be protected. As it transpired, he handled the press with flair and uncommon diplomatic acumen.

Mary took him on a tour of the famous Henry Moore Sculpture Centre at the gallery. He stopped, looked down at the marble floor and said, *"Chateau de Vidy [headquarters of the IOC] has a new building with marble floors and we cannot keep them clean. Paul, I want you to find out how the Art Gallery of Ontario does it and report back to me."*

I reflected on this request, thinking how strange it was that the IOC president even worried about keeping the floors clean at head office. Because Mary was very involved in the Art Gallery of Ontario, she easily learned the name of the cleaning company in Mississauga, and that it was run by knowledgeable Portuguese Canadians. When I met with them they laughed, delighted by my story and proud to have had their work recognized by such a distinguished visitor. They gave me bottles of cleaners, buffers, waxes and an instruction sheet on how to use them. The supplies filled a large hockey equipment bag. As I left, the owner said the real secret to cleaning marble floors is to wash them with cold water, not hot. I guess the Swiss needed some Portuguese to teach them about marble floors.

Off I flew to Lausanne, my cache of marble reconditioners packed in a hockey bag. I walked into the IOC headquarters at about 10:00 a.m. and found the lobby full of journalists. Unbeknownst to me, this was the day on which the IOC was sending out the invitations for national Olympic committees and athletes to attend the 1992 Lillehammer Games. I was standing just inside the doorway with my large hockey bag when Samaranch entered.

With his quick eyes, Samaranch looked over the crowd and, noticing my bald head, strode over and asked, *"What are you doing in Lausanne?"* I pointed to the hockey bag. *"I brought all the material to clean the marble floors."* Ignoring the news conference, he proceeded to inspect the contents of the bag, taking his time reading the instructions given by our marble experts while everyone was kept waiting.

"Well done, Paul!" he said, and took the bag up to the podium where he proceeded with the news conference. The press was all over me asking what it was about.

I have told this story on more than one occasion; George Gross even wrote about it in *The Toronto Sun.* One pompous IOC member chastised me for making public this type of personal anecdote, which upset me greatly. A few months later, I apologized to President Samaranch, adding that I had not done it with any malice aforethought. He replied, *"I loved the stories. They made me look human."*

I have always believed that in organizations such as the IOC, the president should receive an honorarium for the sake of transparency, if nothing else. At Jacques Rogge's first session, I put a motion on the floor for the IOC to address the issue. It was dismissed out of order. As we left the meeting, Samaranch, walking with my good friend Juan Antonio Jr., said to me with that wonderful smile of his, *"Can you make the honorarium retroactive?"*

He was very inclusive. Whenever he came to Canada on any mission, even to meet the Prime Minister, he always asked that the members of the Olympic family in Canada be invited to all receptions. He kept his friends close and his enemies even closer. It is a good lesson for those who follow. I was proud and honoured to serve the Olympic movement under Juan Antonio Samaranch.

IOC Presidential Election

I feel that if Samaranch had retired after the 1992 Barcelona Games or even after the 1996 Atlanta Games, he would have gone down as one of the greatest leaders of the century. But he did not and thereby left himself open to the opprobrium of the Salt Lake City scandals. He loved the president's job; it was his whole life. Unless you knew him personally, you could not imagine how hard he worked to ensure the success of the IOC. He finally decided to retire in 2001 with the vote at the Moscow session. The campaign to replace him was intense. There were several presidents-in-waiting:

> **Jacques Rogge:** Belgian orthopedic surgeon, European Olympic Committee president, Olympic sailor and captain of Belgium's rugby team;
>
> **Richard Pound:** Canadian lawyer from Montreal, Olympic swimmer and squash player. Pound was responsible for IOC revenue-producing initiatives and a good number of other tough jobs.
>
> **Un Yong Kim:** Korean diplomat and politician, president of the World Taekwondo Federation and influential leader of the Asian Olympic Committee;
>
> **Anita DeFrantz:** American lawyer from Los Angeles, Olympic rower, champion of IOC women's issues and opponent of the 1980 Olympic boycott.

Pound was the front-runner to replace Samaranch during the 1990s. He believed that IOC members would respect his contribution and vote him into the presidency as the person who had put the IOC on a sound financial footing, and headed such important matters as anti-doping in sport, the investigation into the Salt Lake City bribery scandal, and the creation of the Olympic Marketing Commission. As time went by, however, the IOC became more and more Eurocentric. The Europeans were not going to let the IOC presidency out of their hands. They centred more and more power in the shadow of Lausanne—more than half the IOC voting members live in countries bordering on Switzerland. The campaign was fierce, but in the end it was no contest. With their overwhelming voting plurality, the Europeans made sure that Jacque Rogge won handily.

Pound and I have had our battles over the years, as Canadians tend to be this way, but I respect him and I believe that respect is mutual.

Dr. Jacques Rogge

Jacques and I raced against each other in the 1968 Mexico Olympics and knew each other very well. I have had dinner at his house on several occasions. Mary and Anne, Jacques' impressive wife who also is a physician, would sometimes find a way to escape the boring IOC sessions and tour the art galleries in whatever city they were in. When Rogge was elected IOC president, I wrote him several long epistles stating my views from the perspective of a North American international sport federation president and an entrepreneurial businessman. I realize that my opinions are different from most, but feel they were useful input to a man who had assumed one of the most demanding jobs in the world.

One example of the new regime under Rogge bears recounting. The IOC program commission was charged with studying the events and sports of the Games, a fact that in itself reflected the direction and wishes of the new president. In 2003, I was in Lausanne attending the annual general meeting of the Association of Summer International Sport Federations (ASOIF). During the day, I had paid Jacques the customary courtesy call. While I found him to be gracious and pleasant, he never mentioned a word about how he had planned to reshape the Olympic Sailing Regatta—without consulting ISAF and, therefore, me, even though we had known each other long before either of us began to climb the sports ladder.

About midnight that night, I was in my room at the Palace Hotel preparing to retire when an envelope was slipped under my door. Over the signature of President Jacques Rogge, the note told of his decision to release to the press the next morning the news that the IOC would delete all keelboats from the Olympic Regatta and reduce the number of competitors from 400 to 360.

I was furious. Right then and there I called a meeting with ISAF Australian Vice-president David Kellett, and ISAF Secretary General Arve Sundheim, both of whom were in Lausanne. I was deeply distressed. The press release went out and, sure enough, the sailing world was up in arms, accusing me, ISAF president and friend of Jacques Rogge, of not making them aware of this drastic change in Olympic sailing. No one believed that I myself had been blindsided by Rogge's decision.

That night as I lay awake unable to sleep, a solution occurred to me. I got up and wrote Jacques a tightly constructed letter. I began by expressing my extreme disagreement and frustration with his directive and the style in which it had been delivered. I then put forward the case that he was out of line and should reconsider his decision. I forcefully pointed out the impact this unilateral decision would have on the Paralympic Sailing Regatta: sailing is one of the major sports in which disabled athletes can compete, but only in keelboats, and if the Olympics do not admit keelboats then the installations would not be available for the Paralympics.

In that state of mind, I recalled that at an America's Cup Regatta in San Diego back in 1994, a regatta for disabled sailors was promoted as one of the events. I never like calling these sailors "disabled." US Sailing calls their disabled division "Shake-a-Leg," a great name. These regattas are fun and these sailors sure know how to sail, as well as laugh, enjoy themselves and drink beer. As I went up to give my congratulatory speech, one of the sailors took off his artificial leg and tripped me, much to the delight of the assembled throng. After the formalities, I spoke with Paul Callaghan, a former Harvard basketball player who, running to a practice when he was 18, slipped and hit his head, breaking his neck. Now a quadriplegic Paul is married with twin boys. I asked him, *"Why do you sail?"* *"Freedom,"* he replied without missing a beat. Some time later, our family donated a sailboat to the disabled sailing facilities at Toronto Harbour. Recalling that conversation, we named the boat *Freedom*.

With all this in mind, I continued my letter to Rogge, tersely pointing out the destruction he was about to cause. I asked him how he was going to explain to disabled sailors in the Paralympics that their orthopedic surgeon from Gent, who was now IOC president, had taken away their ability to race at the Olympics. Fortunately, the message eventually got through and Jacques withdrew the directive.

The move by the IOC to delete baseball and softball from the Olympic program is, in my opinion, another example of the Eurocentricity now prevalent at the IOC. These sports are nowhere near as popular in Europe as they are in the Americas and Asia. The IOC wanted to include rugby and squash instead, which it could easily have done had it not stuck intransigently to its position of limiting the Summer Games to 28 sports, 300 events and 10,500 athletes. The solution I suggested was to go to 30 sports while maintaining the 300 events and 10,500 athletes, and thus achieve the desired objective almost painlessly.

Because of its fixation on 28 sports, the IOC had to delete two in order to get the two new sports included. Baseball and softball were sacrificed in what was a rather questionable procedure, but the gambit backfired. Baseball and softball were gone but the IOC members, in their wisdom, turned down both rugby and golf, resulting in there being only 26 sports on the slate for London in 2012.

Although I did not realize it was happening and had not previously given notice, I did get my second Olympic Order during the IOC session in Athens in August, 2004. My term was not officially over for another three months, however. Jacques Rogge called me to the stage and asked me to say a few words to my colleagues. Never at a loss for words, I managed to say something, but I was taken off guard and unprepared. After being involved with the Olympic movement all my adult life, I would have preferred to have prepared something to thank them properly for what had been a great experience. As I mentioned earlier, I am the only IOC member ever to have been awarded two of the IOC silver necklaces. I suggested to Jacques that I trade the two silver for a gold, but I never heard back. (Even though I retired in 2004, ASOIF subsequently appointed me for 2005 to the 2012 evaluation commission, which was a great experience.)

Jacques Rogge is a dedicated Olympian. He has spent most of his adult life in the Olympic movement. He has my complete support and best wishes for a successful presidency in what has to be one of the most onerous challenges in the world today.

Toronto 2008

Immediately after TOOC lost the '96 designation in Tokyo in September 1990, the city's 2008 bid was initiated by a consortium consisting of Carol Anne Letheren, CEO of the Canadian Olympic Committee, Joe Halstead from the City of Toronto, and entrepreneur John Bitove, Jr. Letheren demanded that the major players from Toronto's 1996 bid be excluded. Richard Pound and I both advised the new group that bidding for the 2008 Games was a waste of time and money because 2008 was a slam dunk for Beijing. Toronto went ahead anyway with John Bitove Jr. designated to lead the bid.

When we returned home after the loss in Tokyo, Blair Tully from the Government of Ontario hosted a dinner for me at La Scala Restaurant to see how Toronto could exploit the contacts we had made in order to secure major events for the city.

I had heard through my IOC colleague Boris Stankovic, secretary general of the International Basketball Association (FIBA), that the 1992 World Basketball Championship originally scheduled for Yugoslavia had to be moved due to the political unrest there. He suggested that Toronto would be a good alternative and we should come and see him at the one hundredth anniversary celebration of Canadian James Naismith's founding of basketball in Springfield, Massachusetts, so I set up the meeting. Joe Halstead, John Bitove Jr., Rick Traier of Basketball Canada and I met with Stankovic in Springfield and we had a very positive meeting. I was quite taken aback when he told the group that if I was involved, he was sure Toronto could get the Championship because Toronto's 1996 Olympic bid was technically superior to Atlanta's.

Stankovic took us to a reception where he introduced us to National Basketball Association (NBA) Commissioner David Stern. I did what I could to promote Toronto with Stankovic and our efforts proved successful. Bitove organized the World Championship, then used his introduction to David Stern as a lever to help win his bid for a new NBA franchise, the Toronto Raptors. This meant that he had to step down from the leadership of Toronto's 2008 Olympic bid because organizing the Raptors and building the new Air Canada Centre took all his time and energy. The consortium asked Toronto's former "Tiny Perfect Mayor" David Crombie to lead the 2008 bid in his stead.

I had known Crombie since our unlikely meeting at a children's magic show back in 1972. When I lived on Summerhill Avenue, our next-door neighbour was the artist Heather Cooper, whose young daughter was about Martha's age. Heather invited us to her daughter's sixth birthday party. She told us she had hired a magician to entertain the kids and that we should come at 7:00 p.m. The magician happened to be the amazing Doug Henning, who was spectacular. Sitting next to me on the floor with the children was a small man who said, *"I am David Crombie and I want to be mayor of Toronto."*

"I am Paul Henderson, plumber," I replied. Hearing this, Crombie asked if I might have an old truck to lend him, because he needed one to transport lawn signs for his campaign. I lent him one of my plumbing trucks and paid for the insurance and gas, as well as the repairs because his volunteer drivers did not take very good care of them. In fact, I supplied a truck for every campaign Crombie was involved in, and lent him two when he ran for a seat in the federal government in the riding of Rosedale where I live.

At about 10:00 a.m. one morning in the summer of 1999, I received a call from Crombie who was out of town at his cottage. He said that at 11:00 a.m. that day they were going to announce the board of directors for the 2008 bid and that he would like to appoint me an honorary patron. I told him that I never had been asked to serve in such a position before and asked who the other honorary patrons were. When he told me they were all former Premiers and Lieutenant Governors of the Province of Ontario, among other dignitaries, I replied that I did not appear to fit into that exalted group and declined the appointment.

John Bitove, Jr. became available to resume the leadership of the 2008 bid for its remaining two years when he hired Olympic sailor Jay Cross to build the new Air Canada Centre for his NBA franchise and then sold his interest in the Raptors to Alan Slaight. Crombie moved quietly into the background but stayed on the committee because his involvement ensured political peace in the city. Bitove and his old friend James Villeneuve of Labatt Brewery were the face of the bid; in my opinion and that of the IOC, they did an excellent job. Toronto was again considered to have the best technical bid, but as usual, technical bids do not win.

On February 2, 2001, Carol Anne Letheren died of a brain hemorrhage at age 58. Bob Richardson took the helm as CEO of the bid.

George Gross

I had been helping Bob on the final pitch to the IOC when George Gross asked me to accompany him on a tour of Eastern Europe to lobby his old friends. George was an incurable worry wart when he traveled. I am exactly the opposite, believing that if one way doesn't work to get you where you're going, you can always find another. The trip was great as long as I ignored George's paranoia. Our first visit was to my IOC colleague and George's friend Boris Stankovic in Munich. After a rambling, affectionate conversation over dinner at a local restaurant, these three old men concluded that we had indeed lived through the "golden age of sport."

We drove from Munich to Bern, Switzerland, to meet Hungarian Ambassador to Switzerland Pál Schmitt, multiple Olympic Gold medalist in fencing. George was worried that were going to miss our plane to Zurich, but as it happened, we rented a car and drove there; still, he worried all the way. We then traveled to Vienna to meet the inscrutable Austrian IOC member Philipp Von Schoeller.

As we were driving beside the Danube from Vienna to Budapest, George told me to stop the car. We got out and walked to the river edge where George was overcome with emotion as he recounted the story of his escape as a young man from the Communist regime of Slovakia. Austria's Vienna region had been divided into four zones: American, French, English and Soviet. The Austrian shore where we were then standing had been in the Soviet zone.

One of his friends at the time was a rower and had a special permit to train on the Danube. Dressed only in a track top and shorts and with none of their possessions save for two gold rings to use as a bribe for help, the two of them rowed a shell across the Danube to Austria. They were stopped three times by border guards, on each occasion explaining that they were training for the Slovakian national championships. They hid in a farmer's field until it turned cold at dusk. When a farmer and his wife walked by, they showed themselves and asked for help. Fortunately, George spoke German with an Austrian accent. He asked the farmer if he was a communist. The farmer replied that he was an old Nazi supporter. While he could not help them personally, he told them what to do, refusing the offer of one of the gold rings for his assistance. His instructions were that they should wait until dark, then stop the first car that came along. If the driver was American they were safe. If Soviet, they were to say they were training for a marathon and had missed the last bus, then ask for a lift to the next village, Heinburg. They were never to mention Vienna. If the driver was a civilian, they were to play it by ear. George was to do all the talking, as his friend spoke only Slovak.

As it turned out, they were lucky. They stopped a helpful civilian en route to Vienna, exactly 42 kilometres away—the length of a marathon. When they could see the lights of Vienna, George's friend blurted out, in perfect Slovak, that they were almost safe. The driver immediately said, *"Do not worry. I knew you were Slovak escapees."* He then explained that they now had a decision to make because the Soviets had their checkpoint and offices in a brewery at the next village, Schwechat. The safest course of action was for the driver to let them out so they could walk by the brewery as if they were locals. They were not to run or react when the searchlights were turned on them. This is exactly what they did. The driver waited on the other side, then drove them to the American zone in Vienna. George was in quite a state by the time he came to the end of the story, closing with, *"And the rest is history."*

We got back in the car and drove to Budapest, where Tamas Ayan entertained us in his lovely house. We traveled to George's hometown Bratislava to meet Vladimir Cernusak, IOC member in Slovakia. George met with his brother, who was also a well known sports journalist. It was a joy to see them reunited. Finally, we went to Warsaw to meet the all-time top athlete in Olympic women's track and field, IOC member in Poland Irene Szewinska. She and her husband entertained us in an impressive, traditional restaurant in the heart of the city.

It was a wonderful trip. I say of George "the Baron" Gross that it was very hard to become his friend, but having once achieved that status, it was impossible to get rid of him. If I did not phone him every week he would get mad. We would always reminisce about the great experiences we had on that trip. I am sad to relate that while I was writing this book, George Gross died in his sleep at age 85. He remained to the end a vital contributor to the *Toronto Sun* and a champion for all sports. He himself edited the account detailed above of the manner in which he left the country of his birth before adopting Canada as his new home. I miss him very much.

IOC 2008 Evaluation Commission

In May 2001, the IOC Evaluation Commission was slated to come to assess Toronto's bid. Bitove and consultant Karen Pitre scheduled a dress rehearsal a week ahead of time.

Canadian Olympic rowing medalist Doug Hamilton, who had prepared the technical bid, asked if I would attend to assess his presentation. Toronto had decided to host the Evaluation Commission at the Four Seasons Hotel in mid-town Toronto. I thought this was inappropriate because the bid's focus was on the waterfront five kilometres to the south. Furthermore, the room they had booked for the four-day presentation could barely accommodate 20 people, let alone all the audio-visual equipment required for the meeting. Sitting around the table vetting the trial presentations were people who had been flown in from all over the world, expensive consultants who feed at the trough of bid cities purporting to be experts on what the IOC requires. I believe they had charged well over 250 thousand dollars, a completely unnecessary expense.

Later in the day, I attended the presentation of the sport logistics and overview of the bid at the Toronto Design Exchange. Again I was shocked, this time at the committee's choice of principal presenter Walter Sieber. Originally from Switzerland and very connected in the IOC, Walter was at that time a community college professor from outside Montreal and knew nothing about Toronto. His presentation was inaccurate and bland. I phoned Bitove and offered to take Sieber and others on a tour of Toronto to educate them about Toronto's waterfront, my part of the city. Bitove was most receptive to the idea. Why does Toronto—or for that matter, all bidding cities—do this, always looking to outside gurus?

I told Karen Pitre that the Four Seasons Hotel would not work for the presentation to the Evaluation Commission, and that they should instead book the Harbour Castle Westin on the waterfront. Within walking distance of all the proposed Olympic venues, the Westin also has excellent access to the Gardiner Expressway that links to all the other highways around Toronto. It has 1,100 rooms and 12 elevators in the south tower alone, a feature that is of significant interest to any IOC person.

Bitove decided against this, but did move across the street from the Four Seasons to the Hyatt, which was being renovated. My firm did the plumbing and restaurant service there, so I knew the facilities well. I told Pitre and Bitove it was all wrong, but to no avail. There are only two elevators in the south tower where the IOC visitors were housed and one was out of service. Coming down just before the final press conference, the Evaluation Commission members overloaded the only working elevator. It got stuck between floors and 10 of our distinguished guests were stranded for an hour and a half. To this day, they make fun of Toronto because of this. I take no comfort in saying, "I told you so." I prefer instead to operate by the maxim that if you do something right the first time, nobody realizes how hard it was to accomplish.

Jordan Bitove produced the excellent cultural show on the final evening. He also produced the final 50-minute presentation to the IOC Session in Moscow. I was asked to help in Moscow, and for that event his sister's company attired me in the finest Hugo Boss suit I have ever worn. That Session saw the retirement of Juan Antonio Samaranch, the election of the new IOC president and the designation of the 2008 host city, so all in all it was an exciting time. The receptions held almost nightly to honour Samaranch were over the top, showing great respect for the 17 years he had led the IOC.

Bitove asked me to help squire the Canadian VIPs around and introduce them to IOC members and international federation presidents, which I did throughout the Session. I had the responsibility of escorting Prime Minister Chrétien and Ontario Premier Mike Harris through the lobbies. They sure knew how to work a crowd. I think they shook hands with all 28 international federation presidents and at least half the IOC. Julie Osborne, who had worked so hard on Toronto's 1996 bid, came up with the brilliant (and inexpensive) idea to paint sets of Russian matryoshka nesting dolls with the Olympic mascots from Moscow 1980 to—optimistically—Toronto 2008. The IOC Ethics Commission outlawed them, but by the time they found out, the dolls were already circulating. Many IOC members asked for extra sets for their numerous grandchildren after they saw them, and Toronto was only too happy to oblige.

As predicted, however, Beijing won easily. Toronto received about the same level of support as we had for 1996, but at a significantly higher cost. The cost of the 2008 bid was reported to be in excess of 60 million dollars, but it was not wasted money. The promotion and worldwide publicity were worth the time and effort in both instances. If Toronto had won, however, the benefits would have been immeasurable.

The TV frenzy after the vote in Moscow was intense. I was in the meetings and knew the results of the vote, which had been kept from the media. I had promised the CBC's Brian Williams (who later moved to the rival CTV network), that he would be granted the first interview after the announcement. I was the first person to leave the session and went immediately downstairs into the sea of TV cameras. I was grabbed by all the Canadian media but fought my way to Williams. He was in a panic because the CBC satellite was down and he was screaming at his producer to do something. Finally, CBC got back online and Williams, with his controlled style, started the interview live on television.

Just as we got underway, a group of Chinese journalists came downstairs and saw what they thought were the Chinese bidders over in a corner. One of their cameramen climbed over me to get to them. They realized it was the wrong group when they saw the real Beijing team coming down the stairs. When the cameraman tried to crawl back over me, his camera struck me and I reverted to the Gordie Howe school of "Canadian strategic elbow placement." Without interrupting my report to Williams, I cupped my right fist in my left palm and drove my right elbow into the intruder's gut, laying him out. The incident was captured live on national TV. The look on the Chinese cameraman's face was something to behold. Brian Williams carried on the interview as though nothing had happened. I never knew what impact this would have back home, but to this day I still get people laughing at what I had done. It was a reflex action known to most Canadian youth, a skill honed on every Canadian backyard hockey rink. I play golf with Brian Williams and Dave Perkins of *The Toronto Star* and they bring it up whenever we get together. The story gets more and more embellished, of course, as tends to happen with journalists.

John Bitove, Jr. later moved to Florida with his family, where he runs his successful KFC franchises and satellite radio network. Crombie is still the most respected ex-mayor of Toronto. Karen Pitre seems to be everywhere, working as the prime technical sports consultant to all levels of government. Among other members of the 2008 bid committee, James Villeneuve is a vice-president of Labatt Brewery, which recently moved to Belgium. Gordon Ashworth and Bob Richardson run a respected political consulting firm in Toronto. Doug Hamilton continues his legal practice and has developed an obsession to deliver a national sport institute for Toronto.

Chapter 15:
Vancouver Wins 2010 Bid for Winter Games

The Canadian Olympic Committee (COC) allowed Vancouver to bid for the 2010 Winter Games at the same time that Toronto was bidding for the 2008 Summer Games. Vancouver is a spectacular city; it had a great chance and should have won easily. The commitment the COC and the bidders made was that Vancouver would do nothing until Toronto's bid for 2008 wound up in 2001. Only then would Vancouver emerge with its bid for 2010—which would be decided in 2003, a scant two years later. What a ludicrous way to try to box Vancouver in!

The IOC knew that Vancouver was waiting in the wings and thought Canada was being greedy. I am a supporter of all Canadian bids because the process puts an intense focus on sport. Canada already has good winter facilities in Calgary, but our summer sports are badly hurting for facilities, coaching and funding for athletes, which I continue to champion. Canadian summer sports are in need of major facilities, which it seems can be obtained only by hosting the Olympic Games or Pan American Games. Canada is a small country and must put its bids forward astutely and with care. We should not put two competing Canadian bid cities on the international stage at the same time. Moreover, bidding for the Winter Olympics is much less competitive than for the Summer Games.

Vancouver 2010 Bidding

Vancouver lobbyists attended all IOC Sessions and the various regional games. As an IOC member, I was able to get the Vancouver bidders into events at which they did not have access. I was able to secure additional tickets for them to many events, as well as access to hotels and rooms that would otherwise have been off limits to them. At the regional games, the number one lobbyist was Crazy Canuck Skier Steve Podborski, who worked very hard and invariably asked for my help. I also became good friends with Jack Poole and his enthusiastic wife Darlene, and looked after them whenever I could. Premier Gordon Campbell was also quite receptive to any help I could offer, particularly with regard to speaking with my IOC colleagues.

I was able to work on involving them at the Salt Lake Games and was proud of myself at the men's hockey final between Canada and the USA. Tickets were going for thousands of dollars each and were virtually impossible to come by. Furlong was looking like a "forlorn Furlong puppy" since he wanted to go and cheer for Canada, but didn't have a ticket. Two hours before the game, however, I was able to get three free additional tickets from the IOC cache so that he and two others from Vancouver could attend the game.

In 2003, I was invited by a number of my good friends on the IOC Evaluation Commission to attend their assessment of the Vancouver bid. Vancouver's presentation was excellent. On one of the four days, we all went by bus to Whistler via the spectacular Sea to Sky Highway, which deeply impressed the IOC. I must admit that I support the protestors who want the new highway to go through a tunnel in one section, instead of scarring the beautiful countryside. The Sea to Sky Highway will be a great legacy for generations to come and it should be built in such a way that it has as little impact on the environment as possible.

When we arrived in Whistler, we were asked if we wanted to go skiing A few of us said yes, including Swedish skiing medalist Penilla Wiberg, who was six months pregnant, Steve Podborski and fellow Crazy Canuck Ken Read, Swiss national ski team member and IOC Director of Sport Gilbert Felli, former president of the Lillehammer Games Gerhard Heiberg, the Prince of Orange of the Netherlands, and myself. It was a brilliant sunny day in the mountains. They furnished us with all the necessary gear and we went up to the top of the proposed women's downhill course. At the top of the hill, Heiberg and I were still adjusting our skis when the others disappeared down the slope. I could not believe the speed at which they joyfully departed. I think they reached the bottom before we made our first turn.

The final presentation and IOC vote for 2010 was held in July, 2003 in Prague, certainly one of the most beautiful cities in Europe. Competing against Vancouver were Pyeongchang, Republic of Korea, and Salzburg, Austria. I thought that Salzburg was the threat, but knew never to underestimate the Koreans.

Presentations in Prague

Two days before the vote, a friend on the Salzburg committee told me that they had 60 per cent of the IOC members locked up. The Austrian presentation was the worst I have ever seen, featuring as their master of ceremonies an Estonian opera singer who dwelled on their culture, forgetting who their audience was. Salzburg received 16 votes out of 107 in the first round and was dropped.

Vancouver's presentation was quite good, but they made a mistake that may have cost them a few votes by misreading their audience. IOC members are acutely aware of their own IOC colleagues' involvement in and support of their country's bid. Neither I nor Richard Pound, who had run for the IOC presidency two years earlier and had been the face of Canada at the IOC for 30 years, was included in the Vancouver entourage marching into the presentation. In fact, we were not even seated at the presentation table at the front of the room, as is customary for IOC members during their country's presentation. Pound and I both left our seats and went to the back of the hall to applaud the Vancouver team as they entered, encouraging them to "knock 'em dead." We then went back and sat in our normal seats. Several other members came to us before the final vote to comment pointedly on this, but we both gave strong reassurances that they should read nothing into it because we supported Vancouver unconditionally. Vancouver received 40 votes in the first round.

Pyeongchang had more than 300 supporters flown in and they were everywhere. They had mobilized the Samsung offices worldwide and put a full court press on each voter individually. They received 51 out of 107 votes in the first round, just three short of a clear win.

When Salzburg was dropped, its 16 votes were freed up, and the Austrian IOC member was now eligible to vote, meaning 17 votes were available. In addition, another member who did not vote in the first round was added, so the total was 109 in the last round. Korea needed only five of the 18 newly available votes to win, provided they could hold on to their existing support. My sources, and they are good, reported that at least five of the Salzburg bloc went with Korea, including two of the three American IOC members. The USA seems to believe that if Canada is awarded the Games, it will preclude the USA from hosting future Games. The USA wanted the 2012 Summer Games, so to them Vancouver 2010 was a negative, and they supported Korea, although USA athlete representative Bob Ctvrtlik voted for Vancouver. In the last round Vancouver received 56 votes versus Pyeongchang's 53. This means that some IOC members changed their first-round vote from Korea to Vancouver, but that will never be verified because the vote is secret. I believe it should remain so.

So much for a slam dunk, but Vancouver won and that is all that mattered. The Koreans accused Un Yong Kim of siphoning away votes from Pyeongchang because of his running for the IOC Executive Board at the same session. Nothing could be further from the truth. Kim's substantial presence at the IOC brought votes to his country, but in the strange political atmosphere of Korea, he was tried and imprisoned for two years, and forced to resign from the IOC. He remains a major force in the Olympic movement, however, especially in Asia and Africa.

After the vote, IOC members were not permitted to leave the room until the winner was announced. I had promised Lisa LaFlamme of CTV an interview following the vote. Leaving the room, I bumped into one of the scrutineers who told me the breakdown of the votes. I went immediately to Lisa, who was interviewing Wayne Gretzky at the time. Everyone was after him and he was trying to hide from the media frenzy. Gretzky stepped aside while I told Canada the results.

Television networks covet scoops, and Lisa scooped the world. As soon as I was through, Gretzky asked if I could get him away from the media, so I took him across the hall to an IOC hospitality suite where I conversed with this humble Canadian icon for about an hour until everything settled down.

That night Vancouver hosted a victory party in the impressive Prague Concert Hall. I was invited onstage to speak. Having been through the agony of two Toronto defeats, it was heartwarming to have a Canadian victory at last. It was very emotional for me; my voice cracked during my brief address to the gathered throng. When I left the stage to return to the back of the long room, a tall man, obviously from the USA, yelled at me to come and talk to him. It was Dick Ebersol, president of NBC Sports, who had paid millions for the television rights to the Olympics. (NBC's parent company General Electric had also paid a handsome sum as an IOC sponsor.) Ebersol was in shock. He could not believe that the IOC could be so blind to the reasons they had paid so much for the rights and sponsorship—NBC wanted Vancouver because it would be one of the most spectacular host cities possible, and the corporate networking opportunities would be outstanding.

VANOC 2010

The IOC Charter demanded that as an IOC member I sit on the board of directors of the Vancouver Organizing Committee for the 2010 Olympic and Paralympic Winter Games (VANOC). I was slotted in the structure as one of eight COC members, along with five-time Olympian Charmaine Crooks and Richard Pound, the other IOC members in Canada. British Columbia had three members and the federal government another three. Whistler and Vancouver each had two members, and the First Nations one. This made a total of 19, in addition to the chairman.

The first VANOC meeting was quite constructive. I sat there for three hours listening to all the niceties and was chagrined to note an important subject absent from the agenda—not once during the whole dialogue was there a mention of the athletes. At the end of the meeting, under "Other Business," I went into a long harangue on the need to focus on the athletes, especially the needs of Canadian athletes, both summer and winter. I also lectured them with my observations on Olympic organizing committees, pointing out that since the Games are awarded seven years before they are held, one of the keys to a financially successful Olympics is to ensure that work on new facilities is initiated immediately because crisis management does not work in the construction business. Montreal and Calgary proved this. Montreal did not address this issue until two-and-a-half years before the Games, and subsequently took a financial bath. Calgary, on the other hand, had all the facilities finished a year before the Games due to the policy of Canada's Minister of Sport Otto Jelinek, who understood sport and business. The Calgary Games were financially solid.

The representative of the mayor of Vancouver then said, *"Vancouver has organized larger events than the Olympics and there is plenty of time."*

"With all due respect, Madam," I replied, *"Vancouver is already behind and you have never held anything with the intensity and demands of the Olympic Games."*

The second meeting was held three months later and was equally as interesting. My friend Jack Poole, who was appointed VANOC chairman, announced the names of the appointments to the numerous committees. As the names were read out, I noticed that all members were appointed to several sub-committees of the board except me. Prying I asked, *"Who selected these names?"* Jack responded, *"The various stakeholders. You are considered a COC appointee."*

With that, COC CEO Chris Rudge retorted, *"Paul, the COC considers you an independent voice representing sport federations."* *"Thank you, Chris,"* I replied. *"I consider that a great compliment."* With that Gibby Jacobs, Chief of the Squamish First Nations, interjected, *"I would like to be considered an independent with Henderson."* What a great guy!

The next most pressing issue was selection of the CEO for VANOC. The Province of British Columbia wanted John Furlong. The COC, led by Pound and the federal government, wanted someone independent from outside the province at the helm because they feared they would otherwise not be able to control VANOC. Two days before the decision, I was involved in a conference call with the COC representatives. I was lobbied to vote for a well qualified hotel executive from Toronto who was then living in Atlanta. I showed my independence by announcing that I did not agree with what they were trying to do. Proposing a person from Toronto was like waving a red flag in front of a Western beaver.

Although it was the party line that Vancouver 2010 was to be a Canadian-hosted Games, I believed that it would be and should be mostly a British Columbian organization with a BC flavour, and that is what has evolved. British Columbia is the major player, as New South Wales had been with Sydney, and Alberta with Calgary. The COC and the feds wanted to delay the appointment and stymie the vote. By voting together they could carry the day. I told them clearly that I would vote for Furlong, which also shows I do not harbour a grudge. I believed that VANOC was already behind schedule and had to move forward. I also said that Furlong would either tie the knots or hang himself, but that a firm administration was required immediately. He was the obvious candidate.

Pound hung up from the conference call and immediately called a press conference where he announced that it was a mistake to appoint Furlong. My phone rang off the hook from the Vancouver media. I stated my position supporting Furlong. The whole controversy was now public and both of us were splashed across the front pages of all the Vancouver daily newspapers. We were to make the decision by teleconferencing that afternoon. I got a second, frantic call from the press saying that Jack Poole was thinking of canceling the decision on the advice of Mike Phelps, a COC appointee. Neither wanted to lose the vote. I phoned Jack, as did Bob Storey, and convinced him to move forward, reassuring him that he could carry the day. As it turned out, he did go forward and Furlong was appointed.

My days on the VANOC board came to an end in 2004 after I retired from the IOC. I had traveled to Vancouver and Whistler every three months from 2001 to the end of 2004 and had enjoyed every minute of it, especially spending time at the Royal Vancouver Yacht Club in conversation with my old sailing friends. Vancouver-Whistler 2010 will be the most spectacular venue ever for any Olympic Games. The IOC will thank their "lucky Loonies" that they decided to go there.

A most amazing thing happened that again made we wonder who is looking out for me. In June 2009 I received a call from John Furlong, Vancouver 2010 Olympic Games CEO, who asked if I would like to run the Olympic Torch as I had been a VANOC board member. I was very honoured to do so. A few weeks later I received a letter from the Torch Relay organizers advising me that I had been selected to run the Olympic Flame and they would let me know where. I assumed it would be in Moosenee or Napanee or some other venue. In October I was informed that on Dec. 17, 2009 at 5:55 P.M. I would run the flame down Yonge St in Toronto from McPherson Ave to Ramsden Pk. In 1896 my grandfather had run the plumbing company and lived on McPherson Ave and my father had played Junior "A" hockey for the Aura Lee team at Ramsden Pk. VANOC had no idea of my family history and I had no input whatsoever where I would run. It was a great evening and it was humbling to see how many of my old friends especially from the Toronto '96 Olympic Bid showed up to cheer.

Chapter 16:
2004 Olympics in Athens

Athens 2004 was the only Games in which I was totally responsible for the sailing event. As president of the International Sailing Federation, I had oversight of the Olympic Sailing Regatta, from choosing the venue during the bid procedures through to the end of the competitions.

The excellent Athens 2004 Games were a great tribute to the ordinary people of Greece who made them work, and to the experts from the international sport federations. The historical aspects of Athens and the traditions of the Olympic Games arising from ancient Greek culture made the 2004 Games unique. I really enjoyed my many visits to the great city of Athens.

Three looming concerns were expressed in the press before the Games: first, that the venues would not be finished; second, that the traffic would make getting to events impossible; and third, that providing security would be very difficult, if not impossible. These concerns proved to be unfounded, however. All venues were finished, albeit some at the last minute, and all were good. Sailing had no installation problems because 30 years earlier, Greece's military junta had begun construction of a very large marina. It was left unfinished with only the seawalls in place and had long been an eyesore on the Glyfada waterfront. When I first went there, it was an area frequented by homeless people and drug dealers. Renowned sailor George Andreadis and his sailing friend Elias Caronis were actively involved in the design and completion of the marina.

Athens' municipal engineering department developed a working transit system for the Games and the traffic snarls did not materialize as feared. Furthermore, the local volunteers were as friendly and helpful as they had been in Sydney.

Security was tight but there were no serious disruptions.

Constant surveillance is a fact of life at any major event these days. Since I was both president of a sport and an IOC member, I had the highest level of protection. I was allocated a nine-passenger van with a driver, Elias Nellas, who was a graduate of Harvard University and ran a high school in Athens. A police officer always sat beside him while another police officer on a motorcycle rode as an out-rider everywhere we went. Driving behind in an unmarked car were two more police officers with machine guns. All four officers came from the Athens anti-drug squad. This was my team and they were great ambassadors for Greece, always there doing their job efficiently. I had the great privilege to take them out in my private boat to see a race (see photo). I cannot sing their praises highly enough. We also developed a great friendship, and our driver came to visit Mary and me in Toronto the following year.

The Olympic family hotel was the Hilton, the best hotel I had stayed in as an IOC member at any Games. When you stay in a hotel for four weeks under strict security, there has to be room to move around and to relax. The Hilton had everything we needed. The food was great throughout Athens; some of the small owner-operated restaurants are the finest anywhere.

Venue Challenges

We had a very difficult situation with Athens Olympic Committee (ATHOC) General Manager of Sports Makis Assimakopoulos. With no experience at all in running the Games, he announced—for domestic political reasons—that the Greek National Sport Governing Bodies (GNSGB) would run and control the Games. This ran contrary to the Olympic Charter, which provides that all technical aspects are the responsibility of the international sport federations, which have the expertise to ensure a level playing field. The priority of any national sport organization in any country, on the other hand, is to win medals for the home country, not to level the playing field for all nations. Giving the GNSGB control of the Games was irresponsible, especially in sports where the Greeks expected to win medals, such as sailing.

The Hellenic Yachting Federation wanted to appoint one of their employees, Takis Nikiforides, to head the sailing organization and be venue manager. ISAF wanted Elias Caronis and originally won the day. Sadly, Elias died two years before the Games. ATHOC then appointed Takis venue manager. He and the sports director were both supporters of Greece's socialist political agenda and had little use for George Andreadis, H.M. King Constantine or me, for that matter. Every morning during the Games, I would tell Mary that I was not going to fight with Takis that day. My resolve lasted about 15 minutes and then I would be at him again for some obstructionist decision he had made.

When I arrived at the sailing venue about six days before the Opening Ceremonies, a group of national sailing team leaders announced there was a serious problem and demanded that I solve it. They had already complained to Takis, but he had stonewalled them. Back at the Olympic Village, the various team leaders from each country's various sports would get together and talk about what was happening at their venues. The sailors complained that not only was the food at their venue terrible, but that the athletes had to pay for it as well. They had been told by their team leaders that at the rowing venue the food was both excellent and free to the rowers and team officials. I immediately went to Takis and complained, but he denied it, assuring me that athletes had to pay at all venues and the food was the same everywhere. I never believed him so I phoned IOC Sports Director Kelly Fairweather and asked him to check it out with ATHOC's Makis Assimakopoulos. I said I would meet with him back at the hotel in two hours.

One of my annoying traits is that I tend to check out both sides of an issue before accepting what I am told, so I got in my car with my police escort and drove to the rowing venue an hour away. Since I had IOC accreditation, I could go anywhere, so I went immediately to the cafeteria. I found the food to be much superior to that at the sailing venue. I then asked the rowing catering manager about the prices. He told me it was free for all athletes and coaches, and had been from the opening of the Olympic

Village weeks earlier.

I was furious because I was being accused of not looking after the sailors. I drove back to the IOC offices in the Hilton and met with Kelly Fairweather. He said Assimakopoulos had assured him that the policy was the same at all venues: athletes must pay at the venues; food was free only at the Olympic Village. I told him this was a lie and that I had just come from rowing where the food was free and of a higher quality. Kelly is a very straight and a concerned supporter of IOC sports. He phoned Assimakopoulos, and as I listened in, he explained that I had gone to rowing and found that the food was free. Assimakopoulos again was not forthright, replying that this was the first day for free food at the rowing venue. When I informed him that it had been free there for two weeks, he was caught. The next day food was free for all athletes at every venue. I could not believe that ATHOC would charge athletes when politicians, government officials and VIPs got everything free, including food and wine. And this was just one of the challenges we had to face.

Medal ceremonies for sailing were scheduled for 8:00 p.m. on three specific evenings. At noon on the day of the first medal ceremony, I went to Takis and asked to be briefed on the logistics of the ceremony, making sure it was proper so I could brief the ISAF officials. ISAF was responsible for coordinating with the IOC who would award the medals, and delegating which ISAF officials would present the flowers.

In his arrogant and supercilious manner, Takis dismissed my queries saying, *"Just show up and present the flowers."*

I explained that as president of sailing, I was responsible for all such functions according to the Olympic Charter. I then asked for the complimentary tickets that ISAF was entitled to allocate to the officials and families of medal winners. He answered that the tickets had not been printed yet. I put my hand into my pocket and showed him a printed ticket given to me by a member of the French federation. He said that ISAF would get only 10 tickets—when there was seating for over 2000! ISAF had to look after the families of the non-Greek medal winners, plus our 60 volunteer officials. By this time, I was sick and tired of dealing with ATHOC. I reverted to beating the system, which has always been my way when faced with bureaucratic obstructionism and incompetence.

Each night of the medal ceremonies, all 2,000 seats were rush seats, but they were never completely filled. I would arrive early with my IOC accreditation that allowed me to move in and out. I would stand outside the entrance and take 10 competitors' family members from their various countries inside with me using the 10 tickets Takis gave us. I would sit them down, retrieve the tickets, go back outside to get another 10, and repeat this over and over. I was able to get more than 100 people into the ceremony each night. I had the same problem with day passes into the venue as well, so I worked out a plan to circumvent the obstructionism and get family members in to see the races. I took them out on my boat or on one or another of George Andreadis' wonderful crafts. It was better to ask forgiveness because getting permission for what was our right was impossible. The brother of one of the competitors got caught illegally inside the venue going home from my boat and Takis caused a real problem, but not one that was beyond the ability of my Greek police escort to finesse for me.

Another incident was brought to my attention by my daughter Martha, who was a good friend of the Spanish sailors. The skipper of the Spanish 470 was expected to win a Silver Medal, being the main competitor to the excellent Greek team. Her sister, a volunteer at the sailing venue who spoke many languages and was herself an experienced sailor, attended a basketball game where Spain beat Greece and came back to the volunteer tent that night waving a Spanish flag. For this innocent act of patriotism, Takis lifted her accreditation. When I confronted him, he refused to do anything, so I used my system to get her out to see the races and watch her sister win the Silver Medal.

H.M. King Constantine
King Constantine had been an IOC member and ISAF

honorary president since he won a Gold Medal in 1960 in the Dragon Class. He had lived in exile in London for years, and it was uncertain what effect his return to Greece would have on the Games. The King has a large and dynamic immediate family, including the attractive Queen Anna Marie who also happens to be a Danish princess. We talked many times about what was going to happen during the Games. He wanted to attend, as was his right, but he was intent on not making a spectacle of it. Two years before the Games, he told me his plan: he intended to return quietly to Greece several times in the years before the Games to allow the Greeks to become accustomed to his presence. One of the first such trips coincided with an ISAF meeting in Cyprus in 2002, when the outpouring of respect for him was very impressive.

Family Andreadis

George Andreadis and his family Anna and Stratis are well known and very successful competitive sailors at the highest level. George's whole life is racing sailboats, from the smallest to the largest. Nobody knows more about the sport and its history than he does. Anna is vice-chairman of the ISAF Women's Committee and also very knowledgeable. I have never seen her happier than she was during the Athens Games, being involved as a volunteer in all the major protocol issues for ATHOC. Stratis is very good sailor and boatman whose conversation I really enjoy.

George supplied at least five VIP boats along with their drivers and crew at his cost. He knew what spectator boats were best for watching sailing, ranging from his large 100-foot yacht to fast, open inflatables. He also provided a special modest boat for the King and his family. The ISAF president always has his own private boat. I like a small, fast open boat to get from course to course and right onto the field of play without disturbing the sailors. The boat ATHOC had designated for me was not suited to the Mediterranean; furthermore, the driver was inexperienced. George lent me one of his open inflatables that accommodated about 12 people, along with his experienced driver Anthony.

ISAF should have had day passes, but Takis had made them difficult to come by, so I had to sneak sailors' relatives and foreign national authority officials into the venue. I would then take them out to the races. The VIPs and IOC members all had magnificent days on George's various yachts watching the sailors compete. Thanks, George!

I had invited all the board members from Vancouver 2010 to come and watch the sailing races. About two weeks before leaving for Athens, I got a call from First Nations Squamish Chief Gibby Jacobs, who asked if he could come down one day and watch the races with his wife. I was so glad he wanted to come and agreed to look after him in George's best boat. He loved golf and told me he had just won a tournament with three other Squamish chiefs. I asked him if it was a handicap event. He confirmed that it was and I said he must have kited his handicap. Without missing a beat, he retorted, *"We are Honest Injuns!"* What a guy! He too enjoyed watching the races on George's wonderful yacht.

Athens Regatta

I must state clearly at the outset that all 33 sailing medal winners deserved the place they achieved in Athens, but there were a number of problems on the race course. ISAF selected the experienced and respected Tony Lockett from the UK as the chief race officer. A teacher, he took the training of the Greek volunteers seriously. I tried to tell him that under no circumstances should he delegate responsibility to the Greek volunteer race officials, but that he must be militant in ensuring that the ISAF race officers remained in control. The Greeks must not be permitted to overrule ISAF decisions. Unfortunately, Tony did not believe me. He was sure his rigorous training would stand him in good stead. Halfway through the regatta, I went into the ISAF marina office to see Tony holding his head in his hands. He looked up at me and said simply, *"Hey Boss, I wish I had listened."*

That same day, I had taken Russell Coutts and Peter Harken out on my boat, and they witnessed what happened. Among the most respected and knowledgeable sailors in the world, Russell gained fame in both the Olympics and America's Cup, while Peter made his name establishing his advanced marine hardware company. The winds were most often offshore, funneling down the valleys of Athens. When this happens anywhere in the world, the wind can shift up to 30 degrees, flicking back and forth and making sailing difficult, but the good sailors usually win anyway. In fact, on small lakes the wind is always offshore. Tony Lockett had set a rule that once one sailor had passed the first mark, the race must continue no matter what shifts occur in the wind. The skilled Race Committee was trained to reconfigure the course.

That day our anometer showed wind shifts of about 25 degrees with a strength of about 15 knots—excellent sailing conditions! On Course "D" the Finn Dinghies were at the third mark and the Ynglings had rounded the first mark, with the Greek sailors running almost last in both classes. Without consulting with the ISAF official on the Race Committee, the Greek official ordered, in Greek, that the marks be pulled, nullifying the race. New Zealand's Dean Barker (of America's Cup fame) was first in the Finn and could not believe what had happened. The French ISAF official on the committee boat was beside himself. As it transpired, the Greeks won no medals at all on this course, so any influence that may have been exercised on their behalf was ultimately fruitless.

The Greeks had several potential medal winners, of whom two were icons in Greece. Their women's 470 sailors, Sofia Bekatorou and Emilia Tsoulfa, were in a league by themselves and easily won Gold, requiring no help from partisan race officials to do so. They were so far ahead they didn't even have to sail the last race.

The men's windsurfing event, however, was a different story, and the interference of Hellenic Olympic Committee President Lambis Nikolaou here was disturbing. IOC member in Greece and a member of the IOC Executive Board, Nikolaou should have known better. The Greek men's windsurfer Nikolaos Kaklamanakis is a legend in the sport. He had won a Gold Medal in Savannah and had just barely missed a trip to the podium in Sydney. Kaklamanakis was at the end of his career in 2004 and winning any medal would have been a great achievement. He had been singularly honoured in being chosen to light the flame at the Opening Ceremonies, which was also a great tribute to the sport of sailing.

The men's windsurfing medal, however, was one the Greeks were counting on and they wanted Gold. Nikolaos' main competition was Israel's Gal Fridman. Alex Gilady, IOC member from Israel is very powerful, being the chief liaison for NBC. It seemed to many of us that the stage was set for something to happen.

In the first race, disaster struck. All 40 men's windsurfers had sailed the Olympic course many times and knew the race required three circuits around the windward and leeward legs to be completed. Kaklamanakis was leading but got confused; after only two rounds, he saw the committee boat set up for the finish of the women's event and sailed to that finish line. Horns blared and everyone thought he had won the race. All the other competitors followed him like lemmings. The race was declared not completed. All competitors were marked "Did Not Finish," which meant no points were awarded.

The Greeks went through the roof and protested to the Race Committee, declaring that their sailor got a horn going through the line, which meant the Greek finished first. To put this in perspective, consider a downhill ski race: when the skier goes through the finish line, the time is posted and the spectators cheer the perceived winner. A few minutes later, a gatekeeper up the course reports that the competitor missed a gate and therefore did not complete the course and is disqualified. In this case, no sailor legally completed the course.

ISAF convened an international jury of the most experienced in the sport to hear the Greek protest the same day at about 8:00 p.m. As ISAF president I had nothing to do with this process because decisions that influence individual regatta results were beyond my jurisdiction.

I was shocked to learn that Lambis Nikolaou had arrived at the sailing venue at 8:00 p.m. in his black limousine, demanding that he be allowed to intervene as an advocate on behalf of the Greek sailor. He had no right to be there and was out of order. The ISAF jury rightfully excluded him from the hearing, heard the protest and decided fairly that, because no one had completed the course properly, the race would be resailed. They could just as easily have counted the race and disqualified all 40 competitors. Mary and I had gone to the swimming competitions, returning to the hotel about midnight. Lambis Nikolaou was in the lobby waiting for me. As soon as he saw me, he came to me with fire in his eyes. He demeaned sailing and called me incompetent, declaring that the Greek had won the race because of the horn. He just kept on at me so I told him to go to hell and went to bed exhausted.

The next day, ISAF resailed the race and Kaklamanakis won. The Israeli finished eighth, and any sensible person would have considered the matter closed, but not Lambis Nikolaou! He demanded that the improperly sailed race and the replacement race both be counted and his Greek sailor awarded two first places. The Greek Olympic Committee took the case to the Court of Arbitration for Sport (CAS). I do not believe they had the right to do this because the matter was a technical decision of ISAF that was not open to challenge. ISAF went along with the process simply because we knew we were right and believed that any reasonable court would see it in the same light, so we let the Greek protest go forward.

Sailing had many top flight "sea lawyers" in Athens, some of the best in fact, led by John Tinker (Canada), Charley Cook (USA) and David Tillett (Australia). They stayed up all night preparing the ISAF case. The Greek Olympic officials showed up with their lawyers. CAS literally laughed at the idiocy and dismissed the case.

Two days later, I went to the Olympic International Broadcast Centre to inspect the installation, in my capacity as a member of the IOC 2012 Evaluation Commission. Alex Gilady, IOC member in Israel, was walking down the hall and told me that there better be no more tricks, as all of Israel was watching. Alex is an old friend but can be quite difficult. I told him it was an insult to sailing even to bring it up, and that everything would be fair.

During the last race, we were all very tense. Israel's Fridman was leading by a few points, which meant that Kaklamanakis had to win and push Fridman back a few places. There was hardly any wind, but it usually builds as the day goes on, and Kaklamanakis was much more competitive in strong winds. The Race Committee waited and waited for the wind to strengthen and, with time running out, had no choice but to start the race. At the first mark, Fridman was among the leaders and Kaklamanakis was well back, out of medal contention. Kalamankis then showed what a superb competitor he was, pulling up through the fleet with superhuman effort to win the Silver Medal.

Gal Fridman came in first, becoming the first Israeli ever to win a Gold Medal in any Olympics, in any sport. What a celebration followed!

Manolo Romero

During my visit to the International Broadcast Centre, I met with the talented and thorough Managing Director of Olympic Broadcasting Services Manolo Romero, who told me the story of a disaster that had struck two weeks before the Games. The Olympic Stadium was a unique structure designed by the celebrated Spanish architect Santiago Calatrava. (I had met Calatrava years before, when he invited Mary and me to dinner with him in his home in Zurich.)

In their wisdom, ATHOC had decided to let the various Olympic Stadium contracts to three different firms. One did the seating, another the roof, and the third the broadcast cable trenches. There were two trenches, mirror images of each other, one around one side of the stadium and a redundant trench around the other side for backup in case of failure. Housing every cable necessary, both trenches masses of spaghetti. The lights and other electrical units that were installed in the roofs were fed from the trenches. Three weeks before the Opening Ceremonies, the two sections of the roof were slowly moved on wheels along rails from each side to meet in the middle. As they moved the roof sections, all the cables were severed. Twenty-four hours before the Opening Ceremonies,

Manolo was not sure there would be any TV feed at all. The damage was repaired just in time, however; the world had no idea how difficult that was.

Manolo then told me what had happened at the equestrian venue. A major road runs between the venue proper and the parking lot where they had installed several large trailers that transmitted the television feeds. A temporary bridge was built over the road and the cables were laid across it. Shortly thereafter, the technicians noticed severe interference in the signal and had trouble tracking it down. Then they noticed that the telephone company had come and laid their cables over the TV cables. The interference was being caused by the magnetic field generated around telephone cables. That wasn't the end of their troubles, however; a few days before the Games, a large tractor trailer with a crane on top came down the road and wiped out the bridge along with all the cables. Again Manolo's team had to work feverishly to restore the feed for the equestrian events.

I recount these episodes not to be critical of Athens, but as examples of the kinds of crises that plague major events like the Olympic Games that are never conveyed to viewers around the world. It is essential to have experts like the team Manolo Romero assembled to ensure that everything runs smoothly and is tested before the Games begin.

Ghianna Angelopoulou-Daskalaki

I would be remiss if I did not mention the competent and elegant Ghianna Angelopoulou-Daskalaki, who chaired the Athens 2004 Olympics Organizing Committee. I had met her at a press conference in 2002 during the first of two sailing test events prior to the Games. Reporters were asking very pointed questions. After half an hour, as we were trying to draw the interviews to a close, a journalist asked her, *"What do you think of the visitors who come to Greece from all over the world?"*

I immediately butted in, *"We are all nice and easy to get along with."* With that, we were both able to leave and it was the start of a good friendship.

She proved that if you want a successful job done, you should let a competent women do it. Ghianna was a great leader; without her the Athens Games would not have been such a great success. The political and logistical challenges were enormous. In my opinion, she won the Gold Medal for the Athens 2004 Olympic Games.

Ross Macdonald (Vancouver) and Mike Wolfs (Toronto)

I believe that Sport Canada, led by the Canadian Olympic Committee (COC), has lost sight of its fundamental responsibility to our athletes. Athletes no longer appear to be its top priority. Nowhere is this more apparent than in the case of sailors Ross Macdonald and Mike Wolfs. Ross, who runs a sail loft in Vancouver with his talented Brazilian wife Marcia Pellichano, is a world champion in the Star Class, the toughest and most prestigious sailing event in the Olympics. With his crew Eric Jespersen, Ross won a Bronze Medal in Barcelona in 1992.

In sailing, it is essential to put together a team that gets along and that augments the skipper's talents, a combination that is sometimes difficult to find. Ross was struggling to find the right crew. Finally, only seven months before the start of the Athens Games, he teamed up with Mike Wolfs from Toronto. They immediately clicked, but it was an enormous challenge for them to get to the top. It's the same in other sports, such as rowing—Olympic Gold Medal rowers Kathleen Heddle and Marnie McBean were put together in the last days before the Games and were a perfect team. This also happened with Hungerford and Jackson years earlier in Tokyo.

Ross and Mike first had to qualify by ISAF standards, which meant they had to be ranked in the top 16 countries in the world. Then they had to get an even higher ranking among the top 12 to meet the more restrictive COC standards. They accomplished this in March 2004, only months before Athens, but the COC does not fund athletes unless they make it into the top eight. Unfortunately, Ross and Mike were off the COC and Sport Canada's radar screen for funding. Ross had a proven track record, but that was not enough to satisfy the COC and Sport Canada's bureaucratic funding criteria.

Most top athletes start slowly and get better as the pressure is applied, and Ross is no exception. Why, for example, do Stanley Cup goalies excel as the pressure intensifies? I believe they have a reserve of deep inner strength and resourcefulness that gets tapped in the heat of competition. While some athletes who perform well in training die under pressure, others reach their full potential when they are challenged directly in competition. Ross is one of these.

All other top Olympic sailing teams were in Europe training as early as March, 2004. Many were in the Mediterranean, such as the Brits, who had a special training camp in Cyprus where they were able to become acclimatized to the Greek weather, food and culture. Ross and Mike had no money and had to go home to raise the cash for new equipment and travel to Athens. They also needed a good coach, which costs money in any sport. Rather than help them out, the COC almost did not send them. The boys hit up everyone they knew, especially their clubs, and went off to Athens where they sailed superbly.

After the fourth of 11 races, Ross was fighting for a medal. I was interviewed by Brian Williams and Terry Leibel of CBC who asked whether I thought Ross could hang in for a medal.

"Hang in? He gets better as the pressure builds," I said. And he did.

Going into the last race, the Gold Medal in the Star Class had been decided in favour of Brazil's Torben Grael, one of the superstars of sailing who just happens to be Ross' uncle-in-law. Silver and Bronze Medals, however, were up for grabs between Canada, USA and France. Paul Cayard, one of the most recognized names in sailing, was sailing for USA, and France's Xavier Rohart was the reigning world champion.

I took Mike's family and US Sailing President Janet Baxter out to sea in my boat to watch the final race. Ross and Mike got off to a spectacular start, leaving Cayard and Rohart well behind and winning the Silver Medal for Canada.

Canada had an overwhelming number of officials from the federal government, the COC and Sport Canada in Athens, but not one of them showed up to honour our Silver Medal winners at the medal ceremony five hours after the last race. I would hate to think they considered some cocktail party or diplomatic dinner more important, but I am at a loss to explain their absence any other way. Canada won only 12 medals in Athens, and this was one of them. Well done, Ross and Mike! The Canadian sailing fraternity is in awe of your accomplishment.

Chapter 17:
Sitting on the IOC 2012 Evaluation Commission

In the wake of the Salt Lake City scandals, the IOC established the Evaluation Commission (EC) to assess the merits of all cities bidding for the Olympics according to set criteria. This commission does not rank applicants, but evaluates each city's proposal in absolute terms to provide an expert critique and determine whether it meets the requirements of the IOC. There is little need for expensive outside consultants or lobbyists now that the IOC exercises its own technical expertise through the Evaluation Commission, but bidders are so intent on outdoing each other that they spend a lot of money hiring these so-called experts themselves.

The EC documents and amendments that are required of bidding cities are essential commitments to the IOC during the organization phase of the Games. After the designation of the host city, the IOC's Coordination Commission oversees the local organizing committee. The Coordination Commission uses the EC documents to ensure that the host city keeps the promises it made during the bidding process.

Our job was to evaluate the proposals of five of the most impressive cities in the world bidding to host the Olympic Games of 2012: Madrid, Paris, London, New York and Moscow. The EC spent four days in each city, scrutinizing the bids under 16 different headings: concept and legacy; political and economic climate; legal and guarantees; customs and immigration; environment; finance; marketing; sports and venues; Olympic Village; medical services; security; accommodation; transportation; Olympism and culture; Paralympics; and media.

The Association of Summer Olympic International Federations (ASOIF) appointed me to the EC along with International [Field] Hockey Federation President Els van Breda Vriesman of the

Netherlands, and Fédération International de Natation [Aquatics] President Mustapha Larfaoui from Algeria. I was responsible for the area of sports and venues under the leadership of Bob Elphinston, who is the most knowledgeable expert on Games installations and sports logistics. We worked every day from 7:00 a.m. and usually did not get to bed until after midnight, having spent the day listening to seemingly endless presentations and then writing reports—exhausting but invigorating work. The commission was chaired by Mrs. Nawal El Moutawakel, IOC member in Morocco. A mother of two children, Nawal is a very attractive person in all ways. I have met many people during my long involvement in sport, but none has impressed me more than Nawal. She is the first woman from an Islamic nation ever to win a medal in the Olympic Games, and the first Moroccan to win a Gold Medal when she competed in the inaugural women's 400-metre hurdles event at the 1984 Los Angeles Games.

If you met her, you would hardly believe her capable of a medal-winning performance because she is only five feet, four inches tall. I asked her how she ever accomplished this feat. She said she had been a good athlete in Morocco, especially at football, and had a coach who got her a track scholarship at Iowa State University. She arrived in Iowa when she was 18, speaking almost no English. The assistant track coach was waiting for her at the airport, holding a sign over his head that read, "Welcome Nawal." A very tall man himself, he was expecting a tall, gangly African, not a petite, attractive one. Nawal walked right past the sign, which was well over her head, and kept going. They didn't connect until she returned to the terminal and sought him out. He could not believe his eyes and immediately phoned the head coach. They both believed they had wasted one of their valuable scholarships recruiting this athlete sight unseen. A few hours later, the coach phoned Nawal in her hotel room to ask whether she had brought along a track suit. She said she had, so he asked her to go down to the track and show them what she could do. They got out their stop watches and timed her. They refused to believe what the stop watches confirmed so they made her run twice more, each time with the same result. She went on to win many NCAA sprint championships as well as her Olympic Gold Medal.

Nawal now speaks five languages fluently. She handled the difficult London and New York press with great aplomb. They tried to catch her out, but she was up to the challenge. I laughed as she manipulated reporters at each press conference with a great sense of humour. Nawal always dressed like a star. We affectionately called her "our beloved leader."

I considered it possible that the staff of the IOC might reveal a bias toward one bidding city or another, but in fact, Gilbert Felli, Jacqueline Barrett and their assistants Helen Stewart and Sophie Willatts acted exactly the opposite—whenever any member of the EC appeared to slant the discussions, they brought everyone back to objectivity. As befits one from the North of England, Helen was always quick with a quip. She also played the trombone in an orchestra in Lausanne. At one of our many dinners together, Mustapha Larfaoui and Sam Ramsamy said they wished they were 20 years younger so they could date her. Without missing a beat, she shot back, *"Try 40 years!"* We all broke up.

Also on the Evaluation Commission were: Simon Balderstone (Australia, head of the Sydney 2000 environment department), Philippe Bovy (Switzerland, transportation expert), Bob Elphinston (Australia, SOCOG Director of Sport), Frankie Fredericks (Namibia, Silver Medal sprinter and Athletes Commission member), Patrick Jarvis (Canadian Paralympics president), Jose Luis Marco (Argentina, lawyer and member of Argentinean Olympic Committee), Ng Ser Miang (Singapore, IOC Executive Board member), and Sam Ramsamy (South Africa, member of the IOC Executive Board and anti-apartheid campaigner).

I had not known Namibia's great Olympic sprinter Frankie Fredericks before we met on the EC. He was a superstar wherever we went. Sometimes when I was tired I would call him Freddie Frankicks but he would answer anyway. In fact, all the great athletes we met on the tour were extremely impressive and made me proud to be an Olympian. Frankie had what should be considered the most important responsibility of the EC, the Olympic Village, because it is the most important part of an athlete's Olympic experience. Only 12 per cent of Olympic athletes ever win a medal; a very large percentage of them will never leave their country again. It is imperative that the Village be right. Frankie took his responsibility very seriously, being quite difficult at times with the presenters, because he would not let them gloss over any details that he considered important. They all knew that he knew what he was talking about. The athletes should be proud of Frankie Fredericks. It was an honour to serve on the EC with both him and Nawal.

Every city was allotted one night to take EC members to a reception to take in the local culture. The Olympic movement views sport as intertwined with the cultural and scientific aspects of human endeavour. The performing and visual arts of a nation are an integral part of the Games, as can be seen in the Opening and Closing Ceremonies and at the Olympic Medal Square, along with the concerts and art exhibitions that are part of the Olympic experience.

The IOC has also established an Ethics Commission to ensure that everything is done properly—according to their view of the world. Like other groups charged with policing the actions of others, however, they can occasionally become over zealous in carrying out their mandate. The EC was sensitive to the great pressure on the bid cities and their desire to put their best foot forward, both to the IOC voters and to their citizens. We were deeply concerned about promoting the Olympic movement positively. I have never been with a group of people who worked so effectively, professionally and diligently.

The EC was very respectful of the challenge we had accepted and acted appropriately, even if that meant ignoring the occasional unwarranted decree from Lausanne. For example, as decreed by the IOC Ethics Commission, we were not supposed to attend any sporting event in a city. As active and involved sports people, however, we recognized that the Olympic movement has its very foundation in sport; consequently, we voted on more than one occasion to overrule this somewhat misguided regulation.

One decree of which I was particularly critical was that I was forbidden to visit the remote venues for sailing. Palma (Majorca), Weymouth (UK) and La Rochelle (France) are great sailing venues, and the citizens there were proud to have been selected as part of their countries' bids.

Madrid

Our first visit was to Madrid, which in my mind was not a frontrunner to host the Games. I had visited the Spanish capital before but only for meetings, and on those trips I seldom left the hotel. Visiting Madrid with the Evaluation Commission, however, I was pleasantly surprised. Their public transit system is so advanced that Toronto would do well to learn from it. Madrid's bid was technically excellent and at least as good as the others. Their presentations were first class and their concepts well developed. The meeting rooms were properly set up and our working area was excellent.

The tours of the venues were all impressive. I felt very proud when the marina engineer thanked me for having initiated construction of the world renowned Olympic Harbour in Barcelona, a project that led to the revitalization of a derelict piece of Mediterranean coastline. I did not see many high priced foreign consultants; rather, it appeared to me that the Spanish had relied on home-grown talent. I am sure other cities learned how Madrid had prepared its bid, because each succeeding presentation became more elaborate.

On our night out, we were taken to the royal palace to meet the royal family over an impressive dinner of the sort usually reserved for visiting heads of state. I felt comfortably at home there, because H.M. King Juan Carlos and his family are all sailors and we spent a good deal of time talking about his new racing sloop. His sister Queen Sofia almost always attends the Olympic Games as a spectator—I believe she is the number one Olympic pin collector.

The Evaluation Commission had our first serious decision to

make in Madrid: would we ignore the Ethics Commission decree and attend a football game between Real Madrid and Barcelona? The stadium was just 100 metres down the street from our hotel, and the game started at 10:00 p.m. We had been working since seven o'clock that morning. I am sometimes accused of being blunt, but Frankie Fredericks was even more to the point. Frankie started the debate by stating simply that he was going. Sam Ramsamy said he would go with Frankie. The vote was unanimous and we all went. I have visited many sporting venues in my life, but to me the Real Madrid home field was incredible. The VIP lounge was expansive and the hospitality first class. North American baseball fans would be amazed—this was no hot-dogs-and-beer affair. After the game, we all went down onto the field and met Zidane, Beckham, Carlos, Owen, Ronaldinho, Ronaldo and other stars of the game. Nawal kicked the soccer ball with the best of them. I left Madrid supportive of their bid.

London

In London we stayed at the Four Seasons, Canary Wharf. The Four Seasons Hotel chain was founded by my old Toronto friend Izzy Sharp, while Canary Wharf was developed by Toronto's Reichman brothers, who named the streets after Canadian places and provinces. The London organizers even arranged for Ellen McArthur to arrive home from her around-the-world race during our stay, and she sailed up the Thames right outside my hotel room window.

London's bid was led by Sebastian Coe and his sailing friend Keith Mills. London kept the politicians somewhat at arm's length, arranging for athletes to deliver the presentations, which they did in a very professional manner. Coe maintained complete control. Having won a Gold Medal in Los Angeles in 1984, he enjoyed a great rapport with Nawal and Frankie, and they in turn did not let him get away with anything.

London's concept was to revitalize the Lower Lea Valley, a depressed industrial section of East London. It was an expensive proposition, but one that would leave a tremendous legacy to the region, accomplishing 30 years of urban renewal in seven—an impossible feat without the Games. I found myself wishing that the so-called socialists in Toronto had listened to us instead of destroying Toronto's 1996 bid; our Portlands industrial wasteland needed the Games for the same reason. That Coe was able to keep the politicians in the background was a good move. That is never an easy thing to do.

We ate dinner each evening in the hotel, except on the cultural night out. At the end of each exhausting workday, we would have preferred to eat in a different room from the one in which we worked all day. Moreover, most of us ate simply, and would have chosen simple meals over the chic nouvelle cuisine prepared by flamboyant executive chefs. If I appear ungracious, please keep in mind that when you have only 15 minutes to get through dinner, simple meals are much more appropriate.

The presentation room in London was well set up with separate doors for the EC and the bidders. This allowed us to be alone during breaks without being berated by bidders. Our table was positioned close to our door so we could sneak out to the washrooms whenever necessary.

The cultural night was impressive. We walked the few steps from the hotel to a launch that motored us up the River Thames, and from that vantage point we could clearly see the many buildings illuminated with signs promoting London 2012. They even lifted the roadway on Tower Bridge for us to pass under. When the launch docked, a bus took us to Buckingham Palace where we were greeted by the Queen, Prince Philip and the Princess Royal, IOC member in the UK. Some 25 people were seated for a dinner that was truly memorable.

Menu

    Roast Fillet of Sea Bass with Wild Mushrooms
    Breast of Duck with Bigarade Sauce Braised Chicory
    Snow Peas
    Rosti Potatoes

Salads

Caramelised Pear Tart

Wines

Sauvignon, Cloudy Bay, Marlborough 2003

Pinot Noir, Mount Edward, Central Otago 2001

Orange Muscat and Flora, Brown Brothers 2003

Royal Vintage 1960

Music

On arrival

The String Quartet of the Band of the Coldstream Guards

In the Blue Drawing Room

Jemima Phillips, *Harp*

In the State Dining Room during Dinner

The String Quartet of the Band of the Coldstream Guards

Sgt. T. Wilson - *Violin*

LSgt. P. Wedge - *Violin*

Musician W. Casson-Smith - *Viola*

LCpl. K. Benham - *Cello*

The Pipers

W.O. 1 (Pipe Major) Jim Stout *The Queen's Piper*

Colour Sergeant (Pipe Major) Callum MacKenzie

The Highlanders (Seaforth, Gordons and Camerons)

Colour Sergeant (Pipe Major) Gordon Rowan

The Argyll and Sutherland Highlanders (Princess Louise's Own)

On departure

Pipers of the 1st Battalion Irish Guards

As I walked in to dinner, I stopped to chat briefly with Prince Philip. Because our entrance was telecast around the world, a number of people have asked me what I said to him. When he visited Toronto as patron of the Royal Canadian Yacht Club, he had laid the cornerstone for the new City Club. He has come to dislike turning sod and laying cornerstones because so many projects over the years have never been completed. In our case, Prince

Philip had demanded that we complete the building. That evening, I was merely telling him that the Club was completed as planned and he must come and visit his cornerstone. Frankie was nervous, as he is uncomfortable amid pomp and circumstance, but the seating arrangement helped put him at ease. Princess Anne was seated between Frankie and me. I knew her well, but was not happy that she spent most of the dinner talking to him.

It was patently obvious that London had its act together and was on a winning wicket. London kept the pressure on right to the finish line.

New York

New York's bid was led by Dan Doctoroff. Its presentation was impressive and included many simple but effective concepts, such as a ViewMaster presentation of their venues. The tours of the venues themselves were understated affairs hosted by American Olympic athletes. I really liked some of their concepts, especially the legacy to be left by refurbishing the old 369th Regiment armories in Harlem as a recreational centre for the area's youth.

The Plaza Hotel where we stayed had seen better days, and was soon to be converted to a condominium project. Perhaps in response to our raised eyebrows, we were informed that the hotel had been selected by IOC staffers; if this was due to established practice, then it is one that should be changed. No one knows a city and its amenities as well as the bidders who live there, and they should be responsible for choosing the most appropriate accommodation for the Evaluation Commission.

An argument had raged in New York over the redevelopment on the East River that was focused on the spectacular Olympic Stadium, and this did nothing to help their bid. One politician was able to stop the entire project. It brought back memories of how Jack Layton had killed Toronto's 1996 bid, so I was sympathetic to their plight. The much needed legacies left to Olympic sport were a major priority for New York. In this regard, New York's bid was better than any of the others.

Although transit was a major issue for the EC, I did not consider New York's traffic worse than that of any of the other bidding cities, with the sole exception of Madrid. In fact, New York moves millions of people every day, and the Olympics would have had little impact on its transit system.

Our night out was spectacular. First, we first went by bus to hear Jazz at Lincoln Center. Among the more than 500 in attendance, I found several of my sailing acquaintances, including Canadian Olympic sailor Jay Cross, who had become president of the New York Jets NFL football team, George Hinman, Commodore of the New York Yacht Club, and Tom Webster from Savannah, who snuck my wife into the show. Mary had come to New York without anyone knowing because she wanted to see the stunning *Gates* of Christo and Jeanne Claude then on exhibit in Central Park.

One hundred of the 500 guests were ushered into a special concert hall. Mayor Bloomberg welcomed us, promising he would not sing that night. Nadia Comaneci then introduced a modern dance performance by a man with a physique we all wish we had. Meryl Streep was next, introducing a collage of well known movie clips of New York. Barbara Walters introduced a wonderful video depicting a day in the life of New York City, and Whoopi Goldberg delivered a heartwarming and funny monologue before introducing the great jazz and classical trumpeter Wynton Marsalis, who performed for us. Barbara Walters then introduced a Broadway cast who sang a few numbers, including *New York, New York!* and *Give My Regards to Broadway.* As they started to sing, the screen covering a window behind the stage lowered and we found ourselves looking right down Broadway at a spectacular display of fireworks. All the electronic signs on Broadway were programmed to welcome us with the kind of spectacle that only New York can put on.

As we boarded our bus at the end of the performance, we passed a line of limos waiting to whisk the beautiful people off to dinner at Mayor Bloomberg's house. Meryl Streep came on the bus with us, however, which put our environmental guru Simon Balderstone into a tizzy. Acting like a flustered teenager, he asked me whether he should go and sit beside her, as he was a big fan of hers. I told him that if he didn't, I would. Simon was in ecstasy as he rode beside her all the way to dinner.

As we drove through the *Gates* installation in Central Park, Christo and Jeanne-Claude told us about their concept. Arriving at Mayor Bloomberg's house, we were ushered to the second floor for a private audience with a group of about 40 dignitaries and celebrities, including Henry Kissinger, Koffi Annan, Vera Wang, actor Matt Damon, architect Santiago Calatrava, TV producer Lorne Michaels, NBA Commissioner David Stern, and World Bank Chairman James Wolfensohn.

At dinner, we were seated about seven to each round table. As I walked in, Jay Cross looked over at me and yelled, *"What a helluva waste of a seating arrangement!"* I sat in my designated seat beside Meryl Streep. Beside her sat New York Jets owner Woody Johnson, then Peter Ueberroth, Frankie Fredericks and Patrick Jarvis. On my other side sat a Southern Baptist minister. Needless to say, I talked to Meryl Streep as much as possible, and she was terrific. People ask me what we talked about, but it was just about anything I could think of.

I remember starting off rather aggressively with a discussion about the Iraq War. Being a Canadian and not knowing her politics, I blurted out, *"I do not personally have enough information to decide whether it was right or wrong to go to Iraq, but I will strongly defend Canada's right as a sovereign nation to say no and not blindly follow the leadership of the USA. If Canada does engage our troops in any campaign, then we should support them completely."*

She replied, *"We are going to get along."* Meryl Streep was all I had imagined, a truly elegant and impressive person.

At the end of dinner, three more people entered: a drummer, a bass player, and a guitarist who sang, *Hello, Mrs. Robinson*. It was Paul Simon. He entertained us with five of his best known hits, then stayed to speak with all of us.

After the magnificent presentations we had witnessed so far, I was taken aback by their formal presentation on the theme of culture. They had brought in a political ambassador from Washington whose major cultural concept was how he was going to solve the AIDS epidemic in Africa. He delivered his presentation like a sermon, giving the impression that Washington could and would solve all the world's problems. It is customary at the end of each presentation for EC members to ask questions. Figuring he had all the answers, I said, *"Canada is in a depression these days. Can you solve the National Hockey League strike?"* It went right over his head like a flock of Canada geese.

On our way to inspect the proposed sailing venue off Coney Island, New York's knowledgeable young venue consultant Scott Schiamberg told me that he written his master's thesis on the major league baseball stadiums after visiting every stadium in both the National League and the American League. I was surprised that he had placed Toronto's Rogers Centre at the top of the list. In typically Canadian fashion, Toronto's journalists always slag the stadium. He confirmed my assessment that, with its completely retractable roof, it is an outstanding facility.

As we did in every city, we reserved the last night in New York to go out by ourselves. Helen picked the restaurant from among several that had been suggested by our hosts. We went to an Italian restaurant in the middle of the city where the waiters all sing opera— or anything else requested of them.

They knew who we were, since our pictures had been all over the newspapers and TV. Our waiter sang *New York, New York!* Everyone joined in and we were instructed to wave both our hands over our heads. Pat Jarvis put up only his right hand. The waiter said, *"Both hands!"* and grabbed his left sleeve, only to find it empty. Patrick, who had lost his arm in an accident when he was eight years old, yelled, *"You stole my arm!"*

The waiter was beside himself with embarrassment, but Pat laughed it off.

Paris

I must admit, I love traveling to Paris more than any other city in the world, especially walking through the small enclaves with their open markets and restaurants that make up this wonderful capital. I had visited Paris many times as a guest of the Fédération Française de Voile, one of the most supportive of the European sailing federations and one I could always count on to help. I considered it unfortunate that the IOC would not allow me to go to La Rochelle. They had prepared a great concept for the sailing regatta and the locals wanted to strut their stuff.

Paris' bid was mostly a political one, and it was led by the mayor. Paris was definitely the frontrunner. Most of the press and other experts thought it was a slam dunk; indeed, the technical side of the bid was very good. I was honored to be allowed into Roland Garros Stadium, where we had lunch and met many well known French athletes. It looked like the entire Paris police force had been conscripted to ensure that everything ran smoothly. As we were whisked through Paris, it seemed that the traffic lights had all been synchronized for our smooth passage.

The Paris presentation room, however, was another story. It just did not work well for us. There was only one entrance and it was usually blocked by the presenters, who smoked incessantly, spewing out copious clouds of smoke that we all had to fight through to get to the washrooms way down the hall.

Our night out was marvelous, however, as we were the guests of President Jacques Chirac at the Palais de l'Elysée. Skiing icon Jean-Claude Killy, an Olympic multiple Gold medalist and IOC member in France, said it was the first time he had ever been there. Killy is a superb ambassador for sport who represents the best of the IOC. President Chirac is an amazing speaker. Like most politicians, he usually leaves dinners as soon as he can, but not this night. He lingered on for at least an hour after we were scheduled to leave, conversing with all the athletes. He seemed to enjoy himself as much as we did him. Nawal just wrapped him around her finger, and he was enamored of her.

As one would expect in Paris, the menu was brilliant:

Ecrevisses et langoustines en mariniere
Pigeonneau roti aux olives et figues
Pates fraiches
Fromages
Entrements coco caramel
Jus de Fruits

As I left my beloved Paris, I was sure its bid would be difficult to beat.

Moscow

I had been to Moscow several times, and had found the Russian sailing federation very supportive in hosting several major sailing championships. We were housed in the recently renovated Royal Meridien National Hotel, our rooms overlooking the Kremlin and St. Basil's Cathedral. The hospitality and layout for our work was by far the best. We had a separate dining room where we were served food that was far superior to any other we had been offered. The Russians went out of their way to be good hosts.

Moscow is a dynamic city in transition. The move from the previous regime into the Western world is inspiring, but can be confusing at times. It is still bureaucratic and politically dominated, but the private enterprise system is coming quickly to the fore. Facilities for sport in Moscow are a government priority and those used for the 1980 Games have been well maintained and upgraded. From a technical perspective, there was no question that Moscow could run excellent Games.

The EC had another major decision to make against the edict of the Ethics Commission. The World Figure Skating Championships were being held in Moscow during our stay and we had been told that we should not attend. By unanimous vote, however, we again overruled the Ethics Commission and went to the event. How could we not? I think I led the revolt that time.

The cultural evening was again spectacular. We were taken to the Kremlin and escorted through its beautiful, formal rooms, some of which are seen only by a few heads of state. Under Stalin's regime, the Kremlin had become a gathering place for the Communist Party and the beautiful paintings and gilt walls had been painted over. Under President Mikhail Gorbachev, however, the marvelous tradesmen of Russia restored the rooms to their previous grandeur and they were breathtaking.

We were then marshaled into the domed cabinet hall, a square room 100 feet on each side dominated by a large donut-shaped table with seating for about 50. In front of at least 100 journalists and 10 television cameras, we sat down and waited for President Vladimir Putin to arrive with his senior cabinet members. Putin is a compact, steely-eyed man whose piercing eyes remind me of Wayne Gretzky. After dismissing the media, he spoke with us for about half an hour in a friendly and humorous way. Like most important people I have met, he was personable and interesting to talk to once he was offstage and out of the media spotlight. Such people did not get to where they were going by being stupid.

We left this meeting at about 7:00 p.m. and walked outside in the pitch dark. My God, was it cold!—minus 18 degrees Celsius, or zero Fahrenheit. We stood outside on a small grandstand to watch a precision army brigade marching with rifles. If I, a Canadian, thought it was cold, what did Frankie Fredericks from Namibia think? He was in pain. I told him I had foreseen this and had worn a thermal undershirt. With his great sense of humor, Frankie confided, *"Paully, I am turning white!"*

I coaxed, urged and finally convinced him to walk, as inconspicuously as possible, across the square to a door where I had noticed a number of Russian officials entering, obviously for a reception to honor the EC. After he was safely inside warming up, Frankie said I had saved his life.

At last we were ushered into the reception where the vodka and caviar were in seemingly endless supply. We were introduced to a large bear of a man who turned out to be Boris Yeltsin. He was not drinking at all and delivered a humorous address. By the time all the speeches were over, we were distressed to find that there was no food left for the Evaluation Commission. Ng Ser Miang from Singapore, a former ISAF vice-president who was an old friend and mentor of mine, commandeered a taxi to take us to a fine Chinese restaurant in the heart of Moscow. (I used to call Ser Miang a taxi driver because he owns 3,000 cabs in Singapore as well as a fair number of buses.) He is one associate who always gave me straight and honest advice, and will be a great addition to the IOC Executive Board.

One day at lunch, a large athletic man came and sat down beside me. I did not catch his name, but he said he was the minister of sport. I assumed he was just another bureaucrat or politician like those we are saddled with in Canada. I noticed that he had several scars around his mouth, but deemed it impolite to ask how he got them. He spoke excellent English and began the conversation by saying he had played in the National Hockey League. It was then that, as nicely as possible, I asked his name. He replied, *"Vyacheslav Fetisov."*

I apologized. *"You're Slava Fetisov?"* I was embarrassed because he is an icon in Canada where ice hockey is almost a cult and Slava Fetisov ranks beside Gordie Howe, Bobby Orr and Wayne Gretzky as one of the greatest players ever to play Canada's national game.

He told me a story about Gordie Howe. While he was still a teenager, Fetisov had been chosen to represent the USSR when they came to North America for the first time to play the World Hockey Association. Their first game was against the New England Whalers, who had Gordie Howe playing at age 47 with his two sons Mark and Marty. On his first shift in the first period, Fetisov saw this old, grey-haired, blinking man going into the corner with the puck. Slava immediately thought this would be easy, so he went into the corner to relieve Gordie of the puck. The next thing Slava remembers is that it was the second period. He had run into the famous Gordie Howe elbows and was sent flat on his pants, head spinning.

Slava finally got the cobwebs out and was sent out again in the second period against the Howe line. He had a very developed hip check that later became famous in hockey circles. As Gordie carried the puck out of his own end, Slava caught him cleanly with his hip and laid Gordie out. Marty and Mark Howe immediately jumped Fetisov, leading to the now famous 45-minute bench-clearing brawl. When Fetisov got back to the dressing room, the other Soviet players laughed at him for not knowing who Gordie Howe was. Slava said to me, *"How was I to know who Gordie Howe was? I was only 19 and had never been out of the Soviet Union before."*

Twelve years later in 1989, Fetisov was legally allowed to leave the USSR and emigrate to the USA. He played defense for the New Jersey Devils in the NHL. In 1995, he was traded to the Detroit Red Wings, where he won two Stanley Cups. Detroit was where Gordie Howe had played for 25 years as a superstar. Soon after arriving in Detroit at age 37, Fetisov was sitting in the Red Wings' dressing room when Gordie Howe, now 67, walked in. Seeing Slava, he quipped, *"Nice hip check, kid!"*

Leaving Moscow, I knew they were a dark horse to host the 2012 Games. I am sure the IOC will at some point in the future award Moscow the Olympics and I sincerely hope there will be no boycott then. Moscow deserves to host the Games free and clear of self-serving international politics.

Singapore: The 2012 Vote

I attended the IOC Session in Singapore as a member of the Evaluation Commission to award the 2012 Olympic Games. The lobbying was fierce, to a degree I had never seen before. Every well known politician and athlete was flown in to influence the voters. I did not have a vote, so I was able to observe the entire charade at close hand. EC members who were not IOC members sat at a special table on the left side of the room beside the IOC executive. Each of the five cities was given 50 minutes to present in an order determined by draw. The order was Paris, New York, Moscow, London and Madrid. The frontrunner was Paris, according to the press handicap.

I was very interested in the presentations. I sat beside Bob

Elphinston and Philippe Bovy, editorializing quietly as each city made its presentation. Paris' presentation was terrible, focusing on the tourist sites. During the very long video, I told Bob that if any voters were sitting on the fence, Paris had just lost them. New York gave a creditable presentation second only to London's. Madrid's was fair, as was Moscow's. The London presentation, however, was brilliant. The smart money says that these presentations do not win votes, but a bidder can lose votes with an inferior presentation. I feel that this vote was an exception. I am sure that a few IOC members solidified their votes for London after the presentation.

At 7:00 p.m., we all went into the ballroom of Raffles Hotel for the announcement. The EC members, along with other VIPs, were seated in the centre section, with London on one side and Paris on the other. There were about 20 television cameras in front of the 100-strong Paris delegation and only two in front of the London group, who were deflated because they believed the name of the winner had been leaked to the press and it must be Paris. The truth is that not even President Jacques Rogge knew the identity of the winner. Rogge stepped to the podium, opened the sealed envelope and, in a clear voice, announced, *"London."* The Brits were in orbit and the French in a deep depression.

The IOC voters place their votes secretly using voting machines. The city with the lowest number of votes is dropped. Then another vote is taken until one city receives 50 per cent of the votes cast plus one, excluding abstentions and spoiled ballots. The votes in each round are not announced to the voting members. Paris was in the lead after the first round, with Moscow being dropped from the ballot. Paris retained its lead in the second round and New York was dropped. Voting in the third round was very close, as London took the lead with 39 votes. Paris beat Madrid by only two votes, 33 to 31. In the final round, London won by four votes, beating Paris 54 to 50.

It was a great honour to sit on the Evaluation Commission. It was two months of exciting but intense and exhausting work. The EC team was an outstanding and competent group of people who were great ambassadors for the Olympic movement. All bidding cities deserved to win, but of course that is not possible. I feel London will do a great job in hosting the athletes of the Olympic Games in 2012. I wish Sebastian Coe and Keith Mills all the luck with the enormous job they have undertaken. London's citizens will be the winners, because the legacies of the Games will endow the city for generations to come.

Chapter 18:
Coming Home

During Canada's 2003 federal election, the CBC sent a young journalist across the country in a recreational vehicle to interview Canadians. When he arrived in British Columbia's Okanagan Valley, he interviewed the Okanagan First Nation's Chief on national television.

"Chief, these are your ancestral lands and you have planted vineyards and developed golf courses for the white man to play. Do you think this is respectful of your heritage?"

"Better than poverty!" the Chief snapped back.

The journalist continued this line of questioning. *"What do you think of the leaders of the political parties in the federal election?"*

In the tradition of our First Nations' elders, the Chief answered wisely, *"Canada does not have leaders. We have politicians. Politicians do what they have to do to get re-elected. Leaders do what they believe in."*

Returning to Toronto after a decade as ISAF president and retiring from the IOC at age 70, I have become a keen and critical observer of the lack of support for our youth who are achievers and wish to carry Canada's flag proudly through international sport. I have openly and bluntly stated my concerns, challenging the National Sport Governing Bodies (NSGB) to stand up and champion proper funding of our athletes. Now that my daughter Martha made the 2008 Canadian Olympic Sailing Team, I feel this even more keenly as I now see how the non-professional athletes are left with an very large financial hole which, after carrying Canada's Flag so proudly, they must dig themselves out of.

The total federal sport budget is less than 10 per cent of what it is in the UK or France for elite athletes, and less than 40 per cent of the allocation in Australia, a country with only three-fifths of Canada's population. There are also sports colleges in Australia geared to the needs of athletes, but in Canada there are none. Our athletes must go to the USA on sport scholarships and some never return. Canada loses what should be role models for our youth.

One recent minister of sport said that Canada's population was less than the UK and France, and that on a per capita basis, Canada's funding of athletes is acceptable. My response to that politician was, *"At the starting line of the 100-metre dash, they do not give the Canadians a five-metre head start because we have fewer people, or the Sri Lankan a 10-metre advantage because their GNP is much lower."*

There has been little support for Summer Olympic sports. Politicians defend this by saying Canada is a Winter Sport country. Immigrants to Canada over the last few decades, however, are from warm countries, where the focus is on summer sports. I wonder if any politicians have walked through the streets of Toronto lately and seen for themselves the scarcity of Northern European faces. I asked a senior Sport Canada bureaucrat whom I had known for years why he did not stand up and champion the needs of athletes. His response was devastating: *"Sport Canada's first responsibility is to make the politicians look good."*

Toronto 2015 Pan American Games

Led by Olympic medallists, rower Doug Hamilton and track athlete Bill Crothers from Markham, several of us worked to have a Canadian Sports Institute Ontario (CSIO). The CSIO would employ some 1,000 people. Vancouver, Calgary, Winnipeg, Montreal all have their training centres funded substantially by the federal government. During the 2000 Federal election campaign the Liberal Government promised the CSIO for Toronto's Downsview Airport but it was never delivered.

Early in 2007 I was appointed to the Sport Advisory Committee to the Ministry of Health Promotion with many other distinguished Ontarian athletes. The Minister, Hon Jim Watson, asked the very prying question: *"Why has Ontario athletes participation in the Olympic Games receded from 50% in 1980 to under 25% in this decade?"*

Many of the academics present condemned the youth of today and their fixation on computer games. I responded *"No Focus on sport! No Facilities for training!"*.

I then gave the solution which was to Bid for the 2015 Pan American Games which Toronto would have had a good chance to win and would provide the same legacy for sport as the Olympic Games without the intense hype required. There was little support for the idea in the Advisory Committee and when the Canadian Olympic Committee, City of Toronto and Federal Government were ambivalent it appeared that the idea was dead.

I met Jim Watson in June 2007 at a patio party and pitched him one on one. He asked me to send him a briefing paper that I did and thought I would hear nothing more. Much to my surprise there was a small group assembled in September 2007 by the Ministry to explore the concept and the decision was made to explore the chances.

In January 2008 I went to Mexico City with Mike Chambers, COC President who was now supportive, to ask Mario Vasquez Rana, Pan Am Games President, if Toronto should bid. He was more than supportive and Premier McGuinty was informed that Toronto's chances were excellent and he jumped on the bandwagon without reservation.

As usually happens in government projects the politicians, bureaucrats and consultants took over and I was marginalized as my focus was totally on sport facilities. As Mario had indicated Toronto finally won the right to host a multi-sport international games and I was proud I had started the initiative. Those charged with delivering the 2015 Pan American Games will realize the enormity of the project and hopefully the result will be to deliver "A Sustainable Legacy to High-Performance Sport" which was the original raison d'etre as initiated by Jim Watson. Hopefully the Canadian Sport Institute Ontario will finally be a reality.

Sailing Downwind

> *"Do not ask where I came from. Do not dwell on where I am. Think about where I am going back to after being President of the USA."*
>
> – Harry S. Truman

I am now, in 2010, 75 years old, having made a challenging and enjoyable over 50-year journey through the world of international sport, but never ignoring my roots in Canada and Toronto. Mary and I still live in the house we bought in 1972 where we raised our family. In fact, we are the longest residing family on our dead-end street. Although the players have changed, the street hockey games are still intense; basketball nets are prevalent as well. Girls and boys all play together, a welcome change from yesteryear.

I still think I am that kid from Toronto Island who dreamed of seeing the world in my little sailboat, facing all challenges head on and enjoying whatever happens to present itself. I may see things occasionally from an unusual perspective, but I hope my views meet with understanding if not complete acceptance. In any case, I have personally derived no financial benefit from their expression. Through my eyes I am still 18.

Richard Pound wrote me, after one of my recent, rather blunt directives to him, "Time for you to stop and smell the roses." As I look ahead, I reflect on this and wonder whether I could ever stop standing up for what I believe in. How could I do that?

I am not well suited to the delaying tactics that are now prevalent throughout the political process, through which a small minority can stop almost anything—and usually does. H.M. King Juan Carlos was certainly right when he pointed out that it is a disease of our society to argue about the 10 per cent that is wrong with a proposal instead of focusing on the 90 per cent that is right. I trust that reading this, you will dwell on the 90 per cent that is unassailable. Life is never as simple as I perceive it to be, which I guess is a sign of optimism.

Sailors are always looking for the next shift in the wind, learning from what has gone before, but still positively trying to find solutions to difficult conditions. Sailors trust that the "Good Lord" will send only fair weather and favourable winds as they set sail in their fragile boats out to the open sea; they are, nevertheless, confident of their individual abilities to survive if challenged, no matter how difficult the sea may become. If a storm hits at sea, a sailor cannot get out and walk to a clubhouse for protection. We batten down the hatches and use our skills to deal with the challenges we face. Sailors never worry about how deep the water is, only how shallow.

It has become fashionable these days to use the euphemism that politicians are spending our taxpayers money like "drunken sailors". This is very demeaning and in fact totally wrong. Drunken sailors spend their own money to get themselves into embarrassing situations and politicians spend ours for the same result.

I would like to thank all those who have stuck with me during what has been an incredible voyage. After being focused on the international scene for so many years, it is so rewarding to find that my friends from the RCYC Junior Club, whom I met over 60 years ago, are still there to reminisce about the old days, and retell the stories that have become well embellished over time.

I gave up playing squash for 10 years but have joyfully returned to the Toronto Racquet Club to play. The Club has never strayed from its objectives as the world has become more complicated, especially as other clubs try to become all things to all people. By simply remaining a men's squash club with no other distractions, it is healthier than it has ever been. I hope they will never ask some consultant to analyze whether they might be able to lower fees by expanding the simple food and beverage facilities.

Yes, I did live through the "Golden Age of Sport" and was a keen first-hand participant. I have met so many people from all walks of life and have found even the highest and mightiest to be quite simple folk when they are alone and out of the limelight.

I cannot believe that Mary has stuck with me for over 40 years. She has always been my best friend, ignoring my tirades and always supporting me no matter what new windmill I was tilting at. She has the great ability to attend all functions appearing to be actively involved, yet astutely, leaving all the political issues to me. She would never allow herself to be enticed into editorializing on political issues. I trust she has enjoyed accompanying me through the exciting times and the challenges, both good and bad, that we have faced together.

Whenever possible, Martha and John have come along for the ride, and again Mary has been the glue holding everything together when I was not there. My sister Sandra has remained so very close and always supportive, if not perplexed by her brother's expeditions. I am sure that the next years will be just as exciting, as something always seems to come up to fill our time. *"Mary, let's get on with the next chapter of our life."*

My father, a rather practical man, long on common sense, always supplied unusual homilies to explain where one stood in life. I hope I have lived—and will continue to live—by the one he always reminded me of when I was feeling self-important:

"Hey, kid! Want to know how much you are going to be missed in this world? Put your hand in a bucket of water and see the hole you leave when you pull it out!"

Respectfully,
Paul Henderson
An Olympian from Toronto Island

Acronyms and Abbreviations

ACOG	Atlanta Organizing Committee
NSI	National Sport Institute
AC	America's Cup
NDP	New Democratic Party
BYC	Bayview Yacht Club
NFL	National Football League
AGO	Art Gallery of Ontario
NHL	National Hockey League
AIPS	Assoc. of International Presse Sportive
NYYC	New York Yacht Club
ASOIF	Assoc. of Summer Olympic International Federations
NZYA	New Zealand Yachting Association
ACOG	Atlanta Committee for the Olympic Games
NAYRU	North American Yacht Racing Union
BC	British Columbia
ORC	Offshore Racing Council
CBC	Canadian Broadcast Commission
SOCOG	Sydney Organizing Committee 2000
CNE	Canadian National Exhibition
QCYC	Queen City Yacht Club, Toronto
COA	Canadian Olympic Association
RCYC	Royal Canadian Yacht Club, Toronto
COC	Canadian Olympic Committee
SLC	Salt Lake City
CORK	Canadian Olympic Regatta Kingston
JAS	Juan Antonio Samaranch, President IOC
CYA	Canadian Yachting Association
RYC	Rochester Yacht Club, New York, USA
BnC	Bread not Circuses
SYC	Savannah Yacht Club, Georgia, USA
CAL	Carol Anne Letheren
RBYC	Royal Bermuda Yacht Club

CRYC	Coral Reef Yacht Club, Miami
RHYC	Royal Hamilton Yacht Club, Ontario
CAS	Court for Arbitration for Sport
RNZYS	Royal New Zealand Yacht Squadron
FD	Flying Dutchman
RORC	Royal Ocean Racing Club, London
GAISF	General Assembly of Int. Sport Federations
RStLYC	Royal St. Lawrence Yacht Club, Montreal
GM	General Motors
RVYC	Royal Vancouver Yacht Club
G+M	Gooderham and Worts Distillery
RYS	Royal Yacht Squadron, Cowes, England
RGH	R.G. Henderson and Son Ltd.
RYA	Royal Yachting Association
IDBF	International Dragon Boating Federation
VANOC	Vancouver Organizing Committee 2010
IPYC	Imperial Poona Yacht Club
TRC	Toronto Racquet Club
ICF	International Canoe Federation
WADA	World Anti-Doping Agency
IMS	International Measurement System
TWRC	Toronto Waterfront Revitalization Corp
IOC	International Olympic Committee
TOOC	Toronto/Ontario Olympic Committee
ISAF	International Sailing Federation
SLC	Salt Lake City
IYRU	International Yacht Racing Union
USOC	United States Olympic Committee
EC	IOC Evaluation Commission
USYRU	United States Yacht Racing Union
IYC	Island Yacht Club, Toronto
UofT	University of Toronto
LYRU	Lake Yacht Racing Union

Index